The Harriet Beecher Stowe Reader

ALSO BY CYNTHIA REIK

On Common Ground: A Selection of Hartford Writers (coeditor)

The

Harriet Beecher Stowe

Reader

Cynthia Reik

EDITOR

THE STOWE-DAY FOUNDATION

77 Forest Street

HARTFORD, CONNECTICUT

Unless otherwise noted, all selections—prose and poetry, fact and fiction—are from *The Writings of Harriet Beecher Stowe*, vols. 1–16, Boston: Houghton, Mifflin & Co., 1896, commonly referred to as the Riverside edition.

All letters, unless otherwise credited, are in the collections of the Stowe-Day Library and have been minimally edited—for spelling, punctuation, omissions, etc.—to increase clarity and to enhance reading facility and comprehension.

All images are from the photograph collection of the Stowe-Day Library.

The paper in this book meets the guidelines for permanence and durability of the *Committee on Production Guidelines of the Council on Library Resources.*

Designed and manufactured for the publisher,
in *THE UNITED STATES OF AMERICA,*
by *RAY FREIMAN & COMPANY,*
Stamford, Connecticut 06903

To those who come after:

MARGOT, JULIA, ELEANOR,

EMILY, AMANDA, LINDSEY,

DANIEL, AND SAMUEL

Acknowledgments

The Harriet Beecher Stowe Reader had its beginning when I was teaching a course, Women in Literature, in the Hartford Public High School, next door to the Harriet Beecher Stowe House and two doors from the Stowe-Day Foundation. One student wanted to read and do a paper on some of Harriet Beecher Stowe's short stories and articles. There was no easily accessible collection of these available, so the idea for this book was born.

The Hartford Public School System granted me a sabbatical, allowing me time to do the reading for the selections. Also, with the sabbatical I traveled to Professor E. Bruce Kirkham at Ball State University to review Stowe's letters, which he is editing; to the Huntington Library in San Marino, California; to the Sophia Smith Collection at Smith College; and to the Schlesinger Library at Radcliffe College and the Houghton Library at Harvard University to look at manuscripts.

The Stowe-Day Foundation was most helpful: Joseph S. Van Why, its director; Diana Royce, its librarian; Roberta Bradford, former research librarian; Beverly J. Zell, photography librarian; Ellice Schofield, former curator; and Earl French.

My husband lived with this book through its long gestation, always ready to read and discuss selections and to help tame the word processor. I do thank him.

East Hartford, Connecticut
1993

(vi)

Table of Contents

LETTERS

POETRY

(ix)

Introduction

The Harriet Beecher Stowe Reader is an opportunity to gain firsthand knowledge of the most read 19th-century American writer. In it are Harriet Beecher Stowe's responses to issues that concerned America in the 1800s: the values of small-town life, racism, the inequity in the roles of the sexes, and the anguish and rewards of parenting. This reader follows a suggestion of the American critic, Edmund Wilson, given in his book, *Patriotic Gore* (1962). "The best way to read Mrs. Stowe—except, of course, *Uncle Tom's Cabin*—would be probably in a volume of extracts which gave specimens of her social criticism, her intimate historical insights and the scattered reminiscences of her own life which she wrote down in various connections."

What kind of life produced such a writer as Harriet Beecher Stowe? In many ways it was an unusual one for a 19th-century American woman. She lived in seven locations in this country: Litchfield, Connecticut; Hartford, Connecticut; Boston, Massachusetts; Cincinnati, Ohio; Brunswick, Maine; Andover, Massachusetts; and Mandarin, Florida. Stowe also made three lengthy trips to Europe. Of the American locations, five involved serious participation in academic communities. Besides this involvement, she was part of the renowned Beecher family. Lyman Beecher, a famous Calvinist preacher, fathered by two wives seven sons who followed him into the ministry; a daughter, Catharine, remarkable for her work in the education of women; Mary; Harriet; and Isabella, a leader in the women's suffragist movement.

Unusual as Stowe's life was, it was firmly rooted in the practical. She supported herself for the 10 years between school and marriage by teaching. Her marriage to Calvin Ellis Stowe lasted for 50 years, during which she provided the major part of the family's financial support. She bore seven children and raised six to adulthood. She and her husband had twin daughters during the first year of their marriage. Four of her children predeceased her: an infant son of cholera; a college-age son by drowning; a young adult son as the result of alcoholism; and a married daughter after years of morphine addiction.

Harriet Beecher was born on June 14, 1811, the sixth child and fourth daughter of Lyman Beecher and Roxana Foote Beecher. Her mother died when Harriet was four. She was raised by her elder sister, Catharine; her mother's family, the Footes; and her father and his second wife, Harriet Porter Beecher. Because of the profession of her father and brothers, Harriet was brought up on biblical and Calvinistic rhetoric. But Lyman Beecher also shared with his daughter his love for Sir Walter Scott's novels, particularly *Ivanhoe*, which Harriet read 11 times. In addition, he introduced her to *The Pilgrim's Progress* and to Cotton Mather's *Magnalia*. He forbade her reading Lord Byron's poetry but she read *The Corsair* secretly. Later, on her own, she discovered Madame de Staël's *Corinne*, a novel that gave Harriet, as it gave to other women of that time, the idea and hope for an independent life. She went on to read the early Charles Dickens's novels, *Oliver Twist* (1838), *Nicholas Nickleby* (1839), and *David Copperfield* (1850). Harriet studied at Miss Sarah Pierce's School in Litchfield for five years and at her sister Catharine's female academy in Hartford for three years. By the age of 16 she was herself a teacher.

When the Beecher tribe, led by Lyman, who was to head the Lane Theological Seminary, moved to Cincinnati in 1831, Harriet and Catharine gave up leadership of the

Hartford school and moved west with the family. There they founded another school for girls and Harriet met and, in 1836, married Calvin Stowe, a widower and biblical scholar.

While living in Cincinnati, two years prior to her marriage, Harriet first wrote for publication. She originally shared "Uncle Lot," or "A New England Sketch," included in this reader, with the men and women of the Semi-Colon Club, a literary group to which she belonged. They encouraged her to enter the story in a regional writing contest; it won a fifty-dollar prize and publication in the *Western Monthly Magazine*. Stowe followed this success in 1843 with a collection of regional tales called *The Mayflower*.

Uncle Tom's Cabin, based, in part, on the Cincinnati experience of living in a border state, was written in Brunswick, Maine, to which Calvin Stowe had moved his family in 1850 in order to fill a teaching post at Bowdoin College, and in Andover, Massachusetts. This book, first published in an abolitionist newspaper, *The National Era*, sold 300,000 copies in its first year of publication and established Stowe as a writer of international reputation. Stowe went on to write more than 30 books of fiction, nonfiction, poetry, and drama.

The financial and literary success of *Uncle Tom's Cabin* allowed and encouraged her and her husband to travel three times to Europe, in 1853, in 1856, and in 1860. There she received the adulation of the crowds and broadened her outlook once again by observing Europe's reaction to slavery and seeing the Continent's own problems with rapid industrialization and urbanization. She published twice more on slavery, *A Key to Uncle Tom's Cabin* (1853) and *Dred* (1856).

In 1852 the family moved to Andover, Massachusetts, where they lived for 11 years as part of the Andover-Newton Theological Seminary community. After 1860, almost in horror at what had happened with the outbreak of the Civil War, Stowe's writing turned toward the portrayal of either earlier rural life or of high society life in the city. At home she was still raising her youngest son, Charley, and providing a home for her twin daughters.

The last years of their lives, after Calvin's retirement, the Stowes divided their time between Hartford, Connecticut, and Mandarin, Florida. In Hartford they joined two of the Beecher clan, Mary and Isabella, at Nook Farm, a literary colony where Harriet became its most famous member. Samuel Clemens (Mark Twain) was a newcomer. The Stowes had two houses in Hartford, first a dream house, *Oakholm,* and later a more practical home on Forest Street. In addition, they traveled widely to visit friends and family. This life continued until Calvin's last illness and death in 1886. After that Harriet suffered from the same hardening of the arteries and accompanying intermittent senility that her father, Lyman Beecher, had. She died in Hartford in July of 1896.

From the experience of this rich life, the first social issue Stowe addresses, the values of small-town life, is a topic to which she returned in later life. This collection, illustrates these values in most of her short stories and in the chapters from *The Minister's Wooing, The Pearl of Orr's Island,* and *Poganuc People.* In these she reaffirms the values of community: the recognition of an individual's contribution; the easy communication; the caring for the strays of society; and the supportive life for children growing up. People fill multiple roles: a farmer reads and discusses theology; his wife studies optics; their rebellious son goes to sea. Holidays, such as the Fourth of July, are celebrated in integrated groups.

Many American writers of the second half of the 19th century, of whom the vast percentage was women, have been labeled local colorists or regional writers in a somewhat deprecating manner. When a 20th-century writer, such as William Faulkner, centers the major part of his opus on a fictional southern county, Yoknapatawpha, he is not called a regionalist. Yet Stowe, in her New England novels and stories, and Faulkner are affirming the values of small-town life with their creations, Dolly and Snopes. As America becomes increasingly urbanized, it is important to recall these values and to try to incorporate their richness into the diverse communities that make up a city.

The second 19th-century American concern, racism and slavery, Harriet Beecher Stowe addresses in *Uncle Tom's Cabin, A Key to Uncle Tom's Cabin, Dred, The Minister's Wooing,* and in letters to Frederick Douglass, Lord Denman, and William Lloyd Garrison. Racism is shown to be both a southern and a northern problem. The responses Stowe gives prior to the Civil War on the part of the blacks allow of five possibilities. Uncle Tom preaches spiritual removal in the form of godliness and forbearance. George and Eliza, in *Uncle Tom,* physically escape to Canada to start a new, free life. Lucy, in the same novel, chooses suicide rather than go on without her child; Cassy goes mad to escape sexual bondage. In *Dred* the hero's father attempts armed rebellion.

The perpetrators of this racism, the whites in *Uncle Tom's Cabin,* are motivated by a variety of needs. The Shelbys display paternalistic feelings and economic needs. Legree is a mixture of masochism and lasciviousness and Sam and Haley of simple avarice. On the riverboat a nameless lady attributes the practice of slavery to blacks being lesser people, needing the guardianship of whites; while an unidentified man considers blacks fulfilling a biblical promise. The Rev. Dr. Joel Parker of Philadelphia is quoted as saying that slavery produces "no evils but such as are inseparable from any other relations in social and domestic life." In "The Edmundsons," from *A Key to Uncle Tom's Cabin,* Stowe models the character on her brother, Henry Ward Beecher, who appealed to northern whites to produce money to buy freedom for slaves.

In a transition piece, "Sojourner Truth, The Libyan Sibyl," Stowe discusses both slavery and the woman question. In response to a query about her views of woman's rights Sojourner Truth answers, "Ef women want any rights more'n dey's got, why don't dey jes' *take 'em,* an' not be talkin, about it?" In spite of this aggressive reply, Stowe's discussion of the third problem, the inequities between the roles of men and women, reveals a publicly cautious position and privately a more adventuresome one. Of course, some of this duplicity might well be due to the fact that Harriet's older sister, Catharine, already established herself as a public advocate of women's education and the professionalization of the whole field of domestic science. Harriet's younger half sister, Isabella, was a strong advocate of women's rights. Successful families have a way of allowing each member space in which to operate. *The Chimney-Corner,* Harriet's book on "the woman question," airs the problems of women but does not come down strongly on one side or the other.

In her letters to family and friends Stowe is more assertive. "[A] woman's own native name never ought to die out and be merged in the name of any man whatever" (1868). "You and Mr. Parton *both* must without delay get and read John Stuart Mill's book just published by the Appletons. It has wholly converted me" (1869). Stowe felt more confident in private in her answers to these questions.

The last topic, parenting, is addressed in the New England novels and in Stowe's letters to Mr. Gunn, head of the school of her youngest child, Charley. These writings provide insights into what Stowe feels are important in this human relationship. Such words as these to Mr. Gunn, "since he *will* walk the precipice I try to steady his hand" (1862), and from *Poganuc People,* "On this morning he [the father] longed to have his way as to their vote; but the boys had enough of his own nature in them to have a purpose and will of their own, and how they were to vote was an impenetrable secret locked up in the rocky fastnesses of their own bosoms," show a mind that took the precariousness of parenting seriously. The balance between holding on and letting go was and is ever a difficult one. Stowe also includes extrafamilial parents, such as Aunts Ruey and Roxy in *The Pearl of Orr's Island,* who are "gifted with an infinite diversity of practical 'faculty,' which made them an essential requisite in every family for miles and miles around." When parental duties are ignored, as in *Pink and White Tyranny,* Stowe's displeasure is obvious and an early death of the negligent mother is the only possible result.

Harriet Beecher Stowe is a sophisticated, sensitive, 19th-century novelist, essayist, and poet. She addressed herself to the major issues of America. As the late critic, Ellen Moers, reminds in her book, *Harriet Beecher Stowe and American Literature,* Stowe, as a writer, was recognized by her contemporaries, Tolstoy, Dickens, Sand, Eliot, Turgenev, Hugo, Heine, and Macauley. America rewarded her by making her the most read writer of that century.

The hymn, the excerpt of the book written for children, the illustrations of people, places, and things important to her life, the sample of Stowe's letters along with some of her short stories, articles, and chapters from her novels are all included to illustrate her power, her connectedness, and her diversity. Americans are ready to face the past honestly and accept women as authentic interpreters of the past. They are ready once again to read the writings of Harriet Beecher Stowe.

Novels

THE MOTHER'S STRUGGLE

from *Uncle Tom's Cabin*

Uncle Tom, a trusted, religious-minded slave, has the well-intentioned but fiscally irresponsible Mr. Shelby as his master. Shelby sells Tom and Harry, the young son of Eliza, whose husband is in the process of fleeing to Canada. Eliza, unable to bear separation from Harry as well, escapes with him to the free state of Ohio. Haley, the slave trader, follows in pursuit. Aunt Chloe, the Shelbys's cook and wife of Tom, and other members of the household with the connivance of Mrs. Shelby attempt to delay Haley's pursuit. Eliza, however, successfully crosses the Ohio River.

Uncle Tom's Cabin originally appeared as a serial novel in *The National Era* (1851–1852), an abolitionist newspaper. In 1852 John P. Jewett and Company of Boston published the novel in book form as a two-volume set. "The Mother's Struggle" is Chapter VII.

It is impossible to conceive of a human creature more wholly desolate and forlorn than Eliza, when she turned her footsteps from Uncle Tom's cabin.

Her husband's suffering and dangers, and the danger of her child, all blended in her mind with a confused and stunning sense of the risk she was running in leaving the only home she had ever known, and cutting loose from the protection of a friend whom she loved and revered. Then there was the parting from every familiar object,—the place where she had grown up, the trees under which she had played, the groves where she had walked many an

(3)

evening in happier days by the side of her young husband,—everything, as it lay in the clear, frosty starlight, seemed to speak reproachfully to her, and ask her whither she could go from a home like that?

But stronger than all was maternal love, wrought into a paroxysm of frenzy by the near approach of a fearful danger. Her boy was old enough to have walked by her side, and, in an indifferent case, she would only have led him by the hand; but now the bare thought of putting him out of her arms made her shudder, and she strained him to her bosom with a convulsive grasp as she went rapidly forward.

The frosty ground creaked beneath her feet, and she trembled at the sound; every quaking leaf and fluttering shadow sent the blood backward to her heart, and quickened her footsteps. She wondered within herself at the strength that seemed to be come upon her; for she felt the weight of her boy as if it had been a feather, and every flutter of fear seemed to increase the supernatural power that bore her on, while from her pale lips burst forth, in frequent ejaculations, the prayer to a Friend above,— "Lord, help! Lord, save me!"

If it were *your* Harry, mother, or your Willie, that were going to be torn from you by a brutal trader, to-morrow morning,—if you had seen the man, and heard that the papers were signed and delivered, and you had only from twelve o'clock till morning to make good your escape,— how fast could *you* walk? How many miles could you make in those few brief hours, with the darling at your bosom,— the little sleepy head on your shoulder,—the small, soft arms trustingly holding on to your neck?

For the child slept. At first, the novelty and alarm kept him waking; but his mother so hurriedly repressed every breath or sound, and so assured him that if he were only still she would certainly save him, that he clung quietly round her neck, only asking, as he found himself sinking to sleep,—

(*4*)

"Mother, I don't need to keep awake, do I?"

"No, my darling; sleep, if you want to."

"But, mother, if I do get asleep, you won't let him get me?"

"No! so may God help me!" said his mother, with a paler cheek and a brighter light in her large, dark eyes.

"You're *sure*, ain't you, mother?"

"Yes, *sure!*" said the mother, in a voice that startled herself; for it seemed to her to come from a spirit within, that was no part of her; and the boy dropped his little weary head on her shoulder and was soon asleep. How the touch of those warm arms, and gentle breathings that came in her neck, seemed to add fire and spirit to her movements. It seemed to her as if strength poured into her in electric streams from every gentle touch and movement of the sleeping, confiding child. Sublime is the dominion of the mind over the body, that, for a time, can make flesh and nerve impregnable, and string the sinews like steel, so that the weak become so mighty.

The boundaries of the farm, the grove, the wood-lot, passed by her dizzily as she walked on; and still she went, leaving one familiar object after another, slacking not, pausing not, till reddening daylight found her many a long mile from all traces of any familiar objects upon the open highway.

She had often been, with her mistress, to visit some connections in the little village of T——, not far from the Ohio River, and knew the road well. To go thither, to escape across the Ohio River, were the first hurried outlines of her plan of escape; beyond that, she could only hope in God.

When horses and vehicles began to move along the highway, with that alert perception peculiar to a state of excitement, and which seems to be a sort of inspiration, she became aware that her headlong pace and distracted air might bring on her remark and suspicion. She therefore put the boy on the ground, and, adjusting her dress and bonnet, she walked on at as rapid a pace as she thought consistent with the preservation of appearances. In her little bundle she had provided a store of cakes and apples, which she used as expedients for quickening the speed of the child, rolling the apple some yards before them, when the boy would run with all his might after it; and this ruse, often repeated, carried them over many a half-mile.

After a while, they came to a thick patch of woodland, through which murmured a clear brook. As the child complained of hunger and thirst, she climbed over the fence with him; and, sitting down behind a large rock which concealed them from the road, she gave him a breakfast out of her little package. The boy wondered and grieved that she could not eat; and when, putting his arms round her neck, he tried to wedge some of his cake into her mouth, it seemed to her that the rising in her throat would choke her.

"No, no, Harry darling! mother can't eat till you are safe! We must go on,—on,—till we come to the river!" And she hurried again into the road, and again constrained herself to walk regularly and composedly forward.

She was many miles past any neighborhood where she was personally known. If she should chance to meet any who knew her, she reflected that the well-known kindness of the family would be of itself a blind to suspicion, as making it an unlikely supposition that she could be a fugitive. As she was also so white as not to be known as of colored lineage without a critical survey, and her child was white also, it was much easier for her to pass on unsuspected.

On this presumption, she stopped at noon at a neat farmhouse to rest herself, and buy some dinner for her child and self; for, as the danger decreased with the distance, the supernatural tension of the nervous system lessened, and she found herself both weary and hungry.

(6)

The good woman, kindly and gossiping, seemed rather pleased than otherwise with having somebody come in to talk with; and accepted without examination Eliza's statement that she "was going on a little piece to spend a week with her friends,"—all which she hoped in her heart might prove strictly true.

An hour before sunset, she entered the village of T——, by the Ohio River, weary and footsore, but still strong in heart. Her first glance was at the river, which lay, like Jordan, between her and the Canaan of liberty on the other side.[1]

It was now early spring, and the river was swollen and turbulent; great cakes of floating ice were swinging heavily to and fro in the turbid waters. Owing to the peculiar form of the shore on the Kentucky side, the land bending far out into the water, the ice had been lodged and detained in great quantities, and the narrow channel which swept round the bend was full of ice, piled one cake over another, thus forming a temporary barrier to the descending ice, which lodged, and formed a great, undulating raft, filling up the whole river, and extending almost to the Kentucky shore.

Eliza stood, for a moment, contemplating this unfavorable aspect of things, which she saw at once must prevent the usual ferry-boat from running, and then turned into a small public house on the bank to make a few inquiries.

The hostess, who was busy in various fizzing and stewing operations over the fire, preparatory to the evening meal, stopped, with a fork in her hand, as Eliza's sweet and plaintive voice arrested her.

"What is it?" she said.

"Isn't there any ferry or boat that takes people over to B——now?" she said.

"No, indeed!" said the woman; "the boats has stopped running."

Eliza's look of dismay and disappointment struck the woman, and she said inquiringly,—

"Maybe you're wanting to get over?—anybody sick? Ye seem mighty anxious."

"I've got a child that's very dangerous," said Eliza. "I never heard of it till last night, and I've walked quite a piece to-day in hopes to get to the ferry."

"Well, now, that's onlucky," said the woman, whose motherly sympathies were much aroused; "I'm re'lly consarned for ye. Solomon!" she called, from the window, towards a small back building. A man, in leather apron and very dirty hands, appeared at the door.

"I say, Sol," said the woman, "is that ar man going to tote them bar'ls over to-night?"

"He said he should try, if't was anyway prudent," said the man.

"There's a man a piece down here, that's going over with some truck this evening, if he durs' to; he'll be in here to supper to-night, so you'd better set down and wait. That's a sweet little fellow," added the woman, offering him a cake.

But the child, wholly exhausted, cried with weariness. "Poor fellow! he isn't used to walking, and I've hurried him on so, said Eliza."

"Well, take him into this room," said the woman, opening into a small bedroom, where stood a comfortable bed. Eliza laid the weary boy upon it, and held his hand in hers till he was fast asleep. For her there was no rest. As a fire in her bones, the thought of the pursuer urged her on; and she gazed with longing eyes on the sullen, surging waters that lay between her and liberty.

Here we must take our leave of her for the present, to follow the course of her pursuers.

Though Mrs. Shelby had promised that the dinner should be hurried on table, yet it was soon seen, as the thing has often been seen before, that it required more than one to make a bargain. So, although the order was fairly given out in Haley's hearing, and carried to Aunt Chloe by at least half a dozen juvenile messengers, that dignitary only gave certain very gruff snorts and tosses of her head, and went on with every operation in an unusually leisurely and circumstantial manner.

For some singular reason, an impression seemed to reign among the servants generally that Missis would not be particularly disobliged by delay; and it was wonderful what a number of counter accidents occurred constantly to retard the course of things. One luckless wight contrived to upset the gravy; and then gravy had to be got up *de novo*, with due care and formality, Aunt Chloe watching and stirring with dogged precision, answering shortly, to all suggestions of haste, that she "warn't a-going to have raw gravy on the table to help nobody's catchings." One tumbled down with the water, and had to go to the spring for more; and another precipitated the butter into the path of events; and there was from time to time giggling news brought into the kitchen that "Mas'r Haley was mighty oneasy, and that he couldn't sit in his cheer noways, but was walkin' and stalkin' to the winders and through the porch."

"Sarves him right!" said Aunt Chloe indignantly. "He'll get wus nor oneasy, one of these days, if he don't mend his ways. *His* master'll be sending for him, and then see how he'll look!"

"He'll go to torment, and no mistake," said little Jake.

"He desarves it!" said Aunt Chloe grimly; "he's broke a many, many, many hearts,—I tell ye all!" she said, stopping with a fork uplifted in her hands; "it's like what Mas'r George reads in Ravelations,[2]—souls a-callin' under the altar! and a-callin' on the Lord for vengeance on sich!— and by and by the Lord he'll hear 'em,—so he will!"

Aunt Chloe, who was much revered in the kitchen, was listened to with open mouth; and, the dinner being now fairly sent in, the whole kitchen was at leisure to gossip with her and to listen to her remarks.

"Sich'll be burnt up forever, and no mistake; won't ther?" said Andy.

"I'd be glad to see it, I'll be boun'," said little Jake.

"Chil'en!" said a voice that made them all start. It was Uncle Tom, who had come in, and stood listening to the conversation at the door.

"Chil'en!" he said, "I'm afeard you don't know what ye're sayin'. Forever is a *dre'ful* word, chil'en; it's awful to think on't. You oughtenter wish that ar to any human crittur."

"We wouldn't to anybody but the soul-drivers," said Andy; "nobody can help wishing it to them, they's so awful wicked."

"Don't natur herself kinder cry out on 'em?" said Aunt Chloe. "Don't dey tear der suckin' baby right off his mother's breast and sell him, and der little children as is crying and holding on by her clothes,—don't dey pull 'em off and sells 'em? Don't dey tear wife and husband apart?" said Aunt Chloe, beginning to cry, "when it's jest takin' the very life on 'em?—and all the while does they feel one bit,—don't dey drink and smoke, and take it oncommon easy? Lor, if the devil don't get them, what's he good for?" And Aunt Chloe covered her face with her checked apron, and began to sob in good earnest.

"Pray for them that 'spitefully use you, the good book says," says Tom.[3]

"Pray for 'em!" said Aunt Chloe; "Lor, it's too tough! I can't pray for 'em."

"It's natur, Chloe, and natur's strong," said Tom, "but the Lord's grace is stronger; besides, you oughter think what an awful state a poor crittur's soul's in that'll do them ar things,—you oughter thank God that you ain't *like* him, Chloe. I'm sure I'd rather be sold, ten thousand times over, than to have all that ar poor crittur's got to answer for."

"So'd I, a heap," said Jake. "Lor, *should*n't we cotch it, Andy?"

Andy shrugged his shoulders, and gave an acquiescent whistle.

"I'm glad Mas'r didn't go off this morning, as he looked to," said Tom; "that ar hurt me more than sellin', it did. Mebbe it might have been natural for him, but 't would have come desp't hard on me, as has known him from a baby; but I've seen Mas'r, and I begin ter feel sort o' reconciled to the Lord's will now. Mas'r couldn't help hisself; he did right, but I'm feared things will be kinder goin' to rack when I'm gone. Mas'r can't be spected to be a-pryin' round everywhar, as I've done, a-keepin' up all the ends. The boys all means well, but they's powerful car'less. That ar troubles me."

The bell here rang, and Tom was summoned to the parlor.

"Tom," said his master kindly, "I want you to notice that I give this gentleman bonds to forfeit a thousand dollars if you are not on the spot when he wants you; he's going to-day to look after his other business, and you can have the day to yourself. Go anywhere you like, boy."

"Thank you, Mas'r," said Tom.

"And mind ycrself," said the trader, "and don't come it over your master with any o' ycr nigger tricks; for I'll take every cent out of him if you ain't thar. If he'd hear to me he wouldn't trust any on ye,—slippery as eels!"

"Mas'r," said Tom,—and he stood very straight,—"I was jist eight years old when ole Missis put you into my arms, and you wasn't a year old. 'Thar,' says she, 'Tom, that's to be *your* young Mas'r; take good care on him,' says she. And now I jist ask you, Mas'r, have I ever broke word to you, or gone contrary to you, 'specially since I was a Christian?"

Mr. Shelby was fairly overcome, and the tears rose to his eyes.

"My good boy," said he, "the Lord knows you say but the truth; and if I was able to help it, all the world shouldn't buy you."

"And sure as I am a Christian woman," said Mrs. Shelby, "you shall be redeemed as soon as I can anyway bring together means. Sir," she said to Haley, "take good account of whom you sell him to, and let me know."

"Lor, yes; for that matter," said the trader, "I may bring him up in a year, not much the wuss for wear, and trade him back."

"I'll trade with you then, and make it for your advantage," said Mrs. Shelby.

"Of course," said the trader, "all's equal with me; li'ves trade 'em up as down, so I does a good business. All I want is a livin', you know, ma'am; that's all any on us wants, I s'pose."

Mr. and Mrs. Shelby both felt annoyed and degraded by the familiar impudence of the trader, and yet both saw the absolute necessity of putting a constraint on their feelings. The more hopelessly sordid and insensible he appeared, the greater became Mrs. Shelby's dread of his succeeding in recapturing Eliza and her child, and of course the greater her motive for detaining him by every female artifice. She therefore graciously smiled, assented, chatted familiarly, and did all she could to make time pass imperceptibly.

At two o'clock Sam and Andy brought the horses up to the posts, apparently greatly refreshed and invigorated by the scamper of the morning.

Sam was there, new oiled from dinner, with an abundance of zealous and ready officiousness. As Haley approached, he was boasting, in flourishing style, to Andy, of the evident and eminent success of the operation, now that he had "fa'rly come to it."

"Your master, I s'pose, don't keep no dogs?" said Haley thoughtfully, as he prepared to mount.

"Heaps on 'em," said Sam triumphantly; "thar's Bruno,—he's a roarer! and, besides that, 'bout every nigger of us keeps a pup of some natur or uther."

"Poh!" said Haley,—and he said something else, too, with regard to the said dogs, at which Sam muttered,—

"I don't see no use cussin' on 'em, noway."

"But your master don't keep no dogs (I pretty much know he don't) for trackin' out niggers."

Sam knew exactly what he meant, but he kept on a look of earnest and desperate simplicity.

"Our dogs all smells round consid'able sharp. I spect they's the kind, though they hain't never had no practice. They's *fa'r* dogs, though, at most anything, if you'd get 'em started, Here, Bruno," he called, whistling to the lumbering Newfoundland, who came pitching tumultuously toward them.

"You go hang!" said Haley, getting up. "Come, tumble up now."

Sam tumbled up accordingly, dexterously contriving to tickle Andy as he did so, which occasioned Andy to split out into a laugh, greatly to Haley's indignation, who made a cut at him with his riding-whip.

"I's 'stonished at yer, Andy," said Sam, with awful gravity. "This yer's a seris bisness, Andy. Yer mustn't be a-makin' game. This yer ain't noway to help Mas'r."

"I shall take the straight road to the river," said Haley decidedly, after they had come to the boundaries of the estate. "I know the way of all of 'em,—they makes tracks for the underground."[4]

"Sartin," said Sam, "dat's de idee. Mas'r Haley hits de thing right in de middle. Now, der's two roads to de river,—de dirt road and der pike,—which Mas'r mean to take?"

Andy looked up innocently at Sam, surprised at hearing this new geographical fact, but instantly confirmed what he said by a vehement reiteration.

(*13*)

" 'Cause," said Sam, "I'd rather be 'clined to 'magine that Lizy'd take the dirt road, bein' it's the least traveled."

Haley, notwithstanding that he was a very old bird, and naturally inclined to be suspicious of chaff, was rather brought up by this view of the case.

"If yer warn't both on yer such cussed liars, now!" he said contemplatively, as he pondered a moment.

The pensive, reflective tone in which this was spoken appeared to amuse Andy prodigiously, and he drew a little behind, and shook so as apparently to run a great risk of falling off his horse, while Sam's face was immovably composed into the most doleful gravity.

"Course," said Sam, "Mas'r can do as he'd ruther; go de straight road, if Mas'r thinks best,—it's all one to us. Now, when I study 'pon it, I think de straight road de best, *deridedly.*"

"She would naturally go a lonesome way," said Haley, thinking aloud, and not minding Sam's remark.

"Dar ain't no sayin'," said Sam; "gals is pecular; they never does nothin' ye thinks they will; mose gen'lly the contrar. Gals is nat'lly made contrary; and so, if you thinks they've gone one road, it is sartin you'd better go t' other, and then you'll be sure to find 'em. Now, my private 'pinion is, Lizy took der dirt road; so I think we'd better take de straight one."

This profound generic view of the female sex did not seem to dispose Haley particularly to the straight road; and he announced decidedly that he should go the other, and asked Sam when they should come to it.

"A little piece ahead," said Sam, giving a wink to Andy with the eye which was on Andy's side of the head; and he added gravely, "but I've studded on de matter, and I'm quite clar we ought not to go dat ar way. I nebber been over it noway. It's despit lonesome, and we might lose our way,—whar we'd come to, de Lord only knows."

"Nevertheless," said Haley, "I shall go that way."

(14)

"Now I think on 't, I think I hearn 'em tell that dat ar road was all fenced up and down by der creek and thar, ain't it, Andy?"

Andy wasn't certain; he'd only "hearn tell" about that road, but never been over it. In short, he was strictly noncommittal.

Haley, accustomed to strike the balance of probabilities between lies of greater or lesser magnitude, thought that it lay in favor of the dirt road aforesaid. The mention of the thing he thought he perceived was involuntary on Sam's part at first, and his confused attempts to dissuade him he set down to a desperate lying on second thoughts, as being unwilling to implicate Eliza.

When, therefore, Sam indicated the road, Haley plunged briskly into it, followed by Sam and Andy.

Now, the road, in fact, was an old one, that had formerly been a thoroughfare to the river, but abandoned for many years after the laying of the new pike. It was open for about an hour's ride, and after that it was cut across by various farms and fences. Sam knew this fact perfectly well,—indeed, the road had been so long closed up that Andy had never heard of it. He therefore rode along with an air of dutiful submission, only groaning and vociferating occasionally that 't was "despit rough, and bad for Jerry's foot."

"Now, I jest give yer warning," said Haley; "I know yer; yer won't get me to turn off this yer road, with all yer fussin',—so you shet up!"

"Mas'r will go his own way!" said Sam, with rueful submission, at the same time winking most portentously to Andy, whose delight was now very near the explosive point.

Sam was in wonderful spirits,—professed to keep a very brisk lookout,—at one time exclaiming that he saw "a gal's bonnet" on the top of some distant eminence, or calling to Andy "if that thar wasn't 'Lizy' down in the hollow;" always making these exclamations in some rough or craggy part of the road, where the sudden quickening of speed was a special inconvenience to all parties concerned, and thus keeping Haley in a state of constant commotion.

After riding about an hour in this way, the whole party made a precipitate and tumultuous descent into a barnyard belonging to a large farming establishment. Not a soul was in sight, all the hands being employed in the fields; but, as the barn stood conspicuously and plainly square across the road, it was evident that their journey in that direction had reached a decided finale.

"Warn't dat ar what I telled Mas'r?" said Sam, with an air of injured innocence. "How does strange gentleman spect to know more about a country dan de natives born and raised?"

"You rascal!" said Haley, "you knew all about this."

"Didn't I tell yer I *know'd*, and yer wouldn't believe me? I telled Mas'r 't was all shet up, and fenced up, and I didn't spect we could get through,—Andy heard me."

It was all too true to be disputed, and the unlucky man had to pocket his wrath with the best grace he was able, and all three faced to the right about, and took up their line of march for the highway.

In consequence of all the various delays, it was about three quarters of an hour after Eliza had laid her child to sleep in the village tavern that the party came riding into the same place. Eliza was standing by the window, looking out in another direction, when Sam's quick eye caught a glimpse of her. Haley and Andy were two yards behind. At this crisis, Sam contrived to have his hat blown off, and uttered a loud and characteristic ejaculation, which startled her at once; she drew suddenly back; the whole train swept by the window, round to the front door.

A thousand lives seemed to be concentrated in that one moment to Eliza. Her room opened by a side door to the river. She caught her child, and sprang down the steps toward it. The trader caught a full glimpse of her, just as she was disappearing down the bank; and throwing himself from his horse, and calling loudly on Sam and Andy, he was after her like a hound after a deer. In that dizzy moment her feet to her scarce seemed to touch the ground, and a moment brought her to the water's edge. Right on behind they came; and, nerved with strength such as God gives only to the desperate, with one wild cry and flying leap, she vaulted sheer over the turbid current by the shore, on to the raft of ice beyond. It was a desperate leap,—impossible to anything but madness and despair; and Haley, Sam, and Andy instinctively cried out, and lifted up their hands, as she did it.

The huge green fragment of ice on which she alighted pitched and creaked as her weight came on it, but she stayed there not a moment. With wild cries and desperate energy she leaped to another and still another cake;— stumbling, — leaping, — slipping, — springing upwards again! Her shoes are gone,—her stockings cut from her feet,—while blood marked every step; but she saw nothing, felt nothing, till dimly, as in a dream, she saw the Ohio side, and a man helping her up the bank.

"Yer a brave gal, now, whoever ye ar!" said the man, with an oath.

Eliza recognized the voice and face of a man who owned a farm not far from her old home.

"Oh, Mr. Symmes!—save me,—do save me,—do hide me!" said Eliza.

"Why, what's this?" said the man. "Why, if 't ain't Shelby's gal!"

"My child!—this boy!—he'd sold him! There is his Mas'r," said she, pointing to the Kentucky shore. "Oh, Mr. Symmes, you've got a little boy!"

"So I have," said the man, as he roughly, but kindly, drew her up the steep bank. "Besides, you're a right brave gal. I like grit, wherever I see it."

When they had gained the top of the bank, the man paused. "I'd be glad to do something for ye," said he; "but then there's nowhar I could take ye. The best I can do is to

(*17*)

tell ye to go *thar*," said he, pointing to a large white house which stood by itself, off the main street of the village. "Go thar; they're kind folks. Thar's no kind o' danger but they'll help you,—they're up to all that sort o' thing."

"The Lord bless you!" said Eliza earnestly.

"No 'casion, no 'casion in the world," said the man. "What I've done's of no 'count."

"And oh, surely, sir, you won't tell any one!"

"Go to thunder, gal! What do you take a feller for? In course not," said the man. "Come, now, go along like a likely, sensible gal, as you are. You've arnt your liberty, and you shall have it, for all me."

The woman folded her child to her bosom, and walked firmly and swiftly away. The man stood and looked after her.

"Shelby, now, mebbe won't think this yer the most neighborly thing in the world; but what's a feller to do? If he catches one of my gals in the same fix, he's welcome to pay back. Somehow I never could see no kind o' crittur a strivin' and pantin' and trying to clar theirselves, with the dogs arter 'em, and go agin 'em. Besides, I don't see no kind of 'casion for me to be hunter and catcher for other folks, neither."

So spoke this poor heathenish Kentuckian, who had not been instructed in his constitutional relations,[5] and consequently was betrayed into acting in a sort of Christianized manner, which, if he had been better situated and more enlightened, he would not have been left to do.

Haley had stood a perfectly amazed spectator of the scene, till Eliza had disappeared up the bank, when he turned a blank, inquiring look on Sam and Andy.

"That ar was a tol'able fa'r stroke of business," said Sam.

"The gal's got seven devils in her, I believe!" said Haley. "How like a wildcat she jumped!"

"Wal, now," said Sam, scratching his head, "I hope Mas'r'll scuse us tryin' dat ar road. Don't think I feel spry enough for dat ar, noway!" and Sam gave a hoarse chuckle.

"*You* laugh!" said the trader, with a growl.

"Lord bless you, Mas'r, I couldn't help it now," said Sam, giving way to the long pent-up delight of his soul. "She looked so curis a leapin' and springin'—ice a-crackin'—and only to hear her,—plump! ker chunk! ker splash! Spring! Lord! how she goes it!" and Sam and Andy laughed till the tears rolled down their cheeks.

"I'll make yer laugh t' other side yer mouths!" said the trader, laying about their heads with his riding-whip.

Both ducked, and ran shouting up the bank, and were on their horses before he was up.

"Good-evening, Mas'r!" said Sam, with much gravity. "I bery much spect Missis be anxious 'bout Jerry. Mas'r Haley won't want us no longer. Missis wouldn't hear of our ridin' the critters over Lizy's bridge to-night;" and with a facetious poke into Andy's ribs, he started off, followed by the latter, at full speed,—their shouts of laughter coming faintly on the wind.

Notes

1. The Jordan, the principal river of Palestine, flows into the Dead Sea, 19 miles east of Canaan, an Old Testament country west of the Jordan and the Dead Sea. Symbolically, Eliza now stands between bondage (in Kentucky) and freedom (in Ohio).

2. The Book of Revelation is the last book of the New Testament.

3. "Love your enemies, bless them that curse you, do good to them that hate you, and pray for them which despitefully use you, and persecute you." *Matthew.* V, 44.

(*19*)

4. Prior to 1863 a network of antislavery people, the Underground Railroad, helped fugitive slaves to reach the northern states or Canada.

5. The Fugitive-Slave Law of 1850 directed all citizens to assist slaveholders in the recovery of runaway slaves.

IN WHICH IT APPEARS
THAT A SENATOR IS BUT A MAN

from *Uncle Tom's Cabin*

Eliza and Harry stop first at Senator Bird's house, interrupting a conversation that he and his wife are having on
the subject of a recently passed fugitive-slave law by the
Ohio legislature. The senator later that evening spirits Eliza
and her son to safety at the home of John Von Trompe, a
onetime slaveholder and now ardent abolitionist.
"In Which It Appears That a Senator Is but a Man"
appears as Chapter IX in *Uncle Tom's Cabin.*

The light of the cheerful fire shone on the rug and
carpet of a cosy parlor, and glittered on the sides of the
teacups and well-brightened teapot, as Senator Bird was
drawing off his boots, preparatory to inserting his feet in a
pair of new, handsome slippers, which his wife had been
working for him while away on his senatorial tour. Mrs.
Bird, looking the very picture of delight, was superintending the arrangements of the table, ever and anon mingling
admonitory remarks to a number of frolicsome juveniles
who were effervescing in all those modes of untold gambol
and mischief that have astonished mothers ever since the
flood.
"Tom, let the door-knob alone,—there's a man! Mary!
Mary! don't pull the cat's tail,—poor pussy! Jim, you
mustn't climb on that table,—no, no!—You don't know,

my dear, what a surprise it is to us all to see you here to-night!" said she at last, when she found a space to say something to her husband.

"Yes, yes, I thought I'd just make a run down, spend the night, and have a little comfort at home. I'm tired to death, and my head aches!"

Mrs. Bird cast a glance at a camphor-bottle which stood in the half-open closet, and appeared to meditate an approach to it, but her husband interposed.

"No, no, Mary, no doctoring! a cup of your good, hot tea, and some of our good, home living, is what I want. It's a tiresome business, this legislating!"

And the Senator smiled, as if he rather liked the idea of considering himself a sacrifice to his country.

"Well," said his wife, after the business of the tea-table was getting rather slack, "and what have they been doing in the Senate?"

Now, it was a very unusual thing for gentle little Mrs. Bird ever to trouble her head with what was going on in the House of the State, very wisely considering that she had enough to do to mind her own. Mr. Bird, therefore, opened his eyes in surprise, and said,—

"Not very much of importance."

"Well; but is it true that they have been passing a law forbidding people to give meat and drink to those poor colored folks that come along? I heard they were talking of some such law, but I didn't think any Christian legislature would pass it!"

"Why, Mary, you are getting to be a politician all at once."

"No, nonsense! I wouldn't give a fig for all your politics, generally, but I think this is something downright cruel and unchristian. I hope, my dear, no such law has been passed!"

"There has been a law passed forbidding people to help off the slaves that come over from Kentucky, my dear.

(22)

So much of that thing has been done by these reckless Abolitionists, that our brethren in Kentucky are very strongly excited, and it seems necessary, and no more than Christian and kind, that something should be done by our State to quiet the excitement."

"And what is the law? It don't forbid us to shelter these poor creatures a night, does it, and to give 'em something comfortable to eat, and a few old clothes, and to send them quietly about their business?"

"Why, yes, my dear; that would be aiding and abetting, you know."

Mrs. Bird was a timid, blushing little woman, about four feet in height, and with mild blue eyes and a peach-blow complexion, and the gentlest, sweetest voice in the world; as for courage, a moderate-sized cock turkey had been known to put her to rout at the very first gobble, and a stout housedog of moderate capacity, would bring her into subjection merely by a show of his teeth. Her husband and children were her entire world, and in these she ruled more by entreaty and persuasion than by command or argument. There was only one thing that was capable of arousing her, and that provocation came in on the side of her unusually gentle and sympathetic nature: anything in the shape of cruelty would throw her into a passion, which was the more alarming and inexplicable in proportion to the general softness of her nature. Generally the most indulgent and easy to be entreated of all mothers, still her boys had a very reverent remembrance of a most vehement chastisement she once bestowed on them, because she found them leagued with several graceless boys of the neighborhood stoning a defenseless kitten.

"I'll tell you what," Master Bill used to say, "I was scared that time. Mother came at me so that I thought she was crazy, and I was whipped and tumbled off to bed without any supper, before I could get over wondering what had come about; and after that I heard mother crying

(23)

outside the door, which made me feel worse than all the rest. I'll tell you what," he would say, "we boys never stoned another kitten!"

On the present occasion Mrs. Bird rose quickly, with very red cheeks, which quite improved her general appearance, and walked up to her husband, with quite a resolute air, and said, in a determined tone,—

"Now, John, I want to know if you think such a law as that is right and Christian?"

"You won't shoot me, now, Mary, if I say I do!"

"I never could have thought it of you, John; you didn't vote for it?"

"Even so, my fair politician."

"You ought to be ashamed, John! Poor, homeless, houseless creatures! It's a shameful, wicked, abominable law, and I'll break it, for one, the first time I get a chance; and I hope I *shall* have a chance, I do! Things have got to a pretty pass if a woman can't give a warm supper and a bed to poor, starving creatures, just because they are slaves, and have been abused and oppressed all their lives, poor things!"

"But, Mary, just listen to me. Your feelings are all quite right, dear, and interesting, and I love you for them; but then, dear, we mustn't suffer our feelings to run away with our judgment; you must consider it's not a matter of private feeling,—there are great public interests involved,—there is such a state of public agitation rising that we must put aside our private feelings."

"Now, John, I don't know anything about politics, but I can read my Bible; and there I see that I must feed the hungry, clothe the naked, and comfort the desolate;[1] and that Bible I mean to follow."

"But in cases where your doing so would involve a great public evil"—

"Obeying God never brings on public evils. I know it can't. It's always safest, all round, to *do as he* bids us."

"Now, listen to me, Mary, and I can state to you a very clear argument to show"—

"Oh, nonsense, John! you can talk all night, but you wouldn't do it. I put it to you, John,—would *you*, now, turn away a poor, shivering hungry creature from your door because he was a runaway? *Would* you, now?"

Now, if the truth must be told, our Senator had the misfortune to be a man who had a particularly humane and accessible nature, and turning away anybody that was in trouble never had been his forte; and what was worse for him in this particular pinch of the argument was, that his wife knew it, and of course was making an assault on rather an indefensible point. So he had recourse to the usual means of gaining time for such cases made and provided; he said "Ahem," and coughed several times, took out his pocket-handkerchief, and began to wipe his glasses. Mrs. Bird, seeing the defenseless condition of the enemy's territory, had no more conscience than to push her advantage.

"I should like to see you doing that, John,—I really should! Turning a woman out of doors in a snowstorm, for instance; or maybe you'd take her up and put her in jail, wouldn't you? You would make a great hand at that!"

"Of course, it would be a very painful duty," began Mr. Bird, in a moderate tone.

"Duty, John! don't use that word! You know it isn't a duty,—it can't be a duty! If folks want to keep their slaves from running away, let 'em treat 'em well,—that's my doctrine. If I had slaves (as I hope I never shall have), I'd risk their wanting to run away from me, or you either, John. I tell you folks don't run away when they are happy; and when they do run, poor creatures! they suffer enough with cold and hunger and fear, without everybody's turning against them; and, law or no law, I never will, so help me God!"

"Mary! Mary! my dear, let me reason with you."

"I hate reasoning, John,—especially reasoning on

such subjects. There's a way you political folks have of coming round and round a plain right thing; and you don't believe in it yourselves, when it comes to practice. I know *you* well enough, John. You don't believe it's right any more than I do; and you wouldn't do it any sooner than I."

At this critical juncture, old Cudjoe, the black man-of-all-work, put his head in at the door, and wished "Missis would come into the kitchen;" and our Senator, tolerably relieved, looked after his little wife with a whimsical mixture of amusement and vexation, and, seating himself in the armchair, began to read the papers.

After a moment, his wife's voice was heard at the door, in a quick, earnest tone,—"John! John! I do wish you'd come here a moment."

He laid down his paper and went into the kitchen, and started, quite amazed at the sight that presented itself: A young and slender woman, with garments torn and frozen, with one shoe gone, and the stocking torn away from the cut and bleeding foot, was laid back in a deadly swoon upon two chairs. There was the impress of the despised race on her face, yet none could help feeling its mournful and pathetic beauty, while its stony sharpness, its cold, fixed, deathly aspect, struck a solemn chill over him. He drew his breath short, and stood in silence. His wife, and their only colored domestic, old Aunt Dinah, were busily engaged in restorative measures; while old Cudjoe had got the boy on his knee, and was busy pulling off his shoes and stockings, and chafing his little cold feet.

"Sure, now, if she ain't a sight to behold!" said old Dinah compassionately; "'pears like 't was the heat that made her faint. She was tol'able peart when she cum in, and asked if she couldn't warm herself here a spell; and I was just a-askin' her where she cum from, and she fainted right down. Never done much hard work, guess, by the looks of her hands."

"Poor creature!" said Mrs. Bird compassionately, as

the woman slowly unclosed her large, dark eyes and looked vacantly at her. Suddenly an expression of agony crossed her face, and she sprang up, saying, "Oh, my Harry! Have they got him?"

The boy, at this, jumped from Cudjoe's knee, and, running to her side, put up his arms. "Oh, he's here! he's here!" she exclaimed.

"Oh, ma'am!" said she wildly to Mrs. Bird, "do protect us! don't let them get him!"

"Nobody shall hurt you here, poor woman," said Mrs. Bird encouragingly. "You are safe; don't be afraid."

"God bless you!" said the woman, covering her face and sobbing; while the little boy, seeing her crying, tried to get into her lap.

With many gentle and womanly offices which none knew better how to render than Mrs. Bird, the poor woman was, in time, rendered more calm. A temporary bed was provided for her on the settle, near the fire; and, after a short time, she fell into a heavy slumber, with the child, who seemed no less weary, soundly sleeping on her arm; for the mother resisted, with nervous anxiety, the kindest attempts to take him from her; and, even in sleep, her arm encircled him with an unrelaxing clasp, as if she could not even then be beguiled of her vigilant hold.

Mr. and Mrs. Bird had gone back to the parlor, where, strange as it may appear, no reference was made, on either side, to the preceding conversation; but Mrs. Bird busied herself with her knitting work, and Mr. Bird pretended to be reading the paper.

"I wonder who and what she is!" said Mr. Bird, at last, as he laid it down.

"When she wakes up and feels a little rested we will see," said Mrs. Bird.

"I say, wife!" said Mr. Bird, after musing in silence over his newspaper.

"Well, dear?"

"She couldn't wear one of your gowns, could she, by any letting down, or such matter? She seems to be rather larger than you are."

A quite perceptible smile glimmered on Mrs. Bird's face as she answered, "We'll see."

Another pause, and Mr. Bird again broke out,—

"I say, wife!"

"Well! what now?"

"Why, there's that old bombazine cloak, that you keep on purpose to put over me when I take my afternoon's nap; you might as well give her that,—she needs clothes."

At this instant, Dinah looked in to say that the woman was awake, and wanted to see Missis.

Mr. and Mrs. Bird went into the kitchen, followed by the two eldest boys, the smaller fry having, by this time, been safely disposed of in bed.

The woman was now sitting up on the settle by the fire. She was looking steadily into the blaze, with a calm, heart-broken expression, very different from her former agitated wildness.

"Did you want me?" said Mrs. Bird, in gentle tones. "I hope you feel better now, poor woman!"

A long-drawn, shivering sigh was the only answer; but she lifted her dark eyes, and fixed them on her with such a forlorn and imploring expression that the tears came into the little woman's eyes.

"You needn't be afraid of anything; we are friends here, poor woman! Tell me where you came from, and what you want," said she.

"I came from Kentucky," said the woman.

"When?" said Mr. Bird, taking up the interrogatory.

"To-night."

"How did you come?"

"I crossed on the ice."

"Crossed on the ice!" said every one present.

"Yes," said the woman slowly, "I did. God helping me,

I crossed on the ice; for they were behind me,—right behind,—and there was no other way!"

"Law, Missis," said Cudjoe, "the ice is all in broken-up
blocks, a-swinging and a-teetering up and down in the
water."

"I know it was,—I know it!" said she wildly; "but I did
it! I wouldn't have thought I could,—I didn't think I
should get over, but I didn't care! I could but die if I didn't.
The Lord helped me; nobody knows how much the Lord
can help 'em, till they try," said the woman, with a flashing eye.

"Were you a slave?" said Mr. Bird.

"Yes, sir; I belonged to a man in Kentucky."

"Was he unkind to you?"

"No, sir; he was a good master."

"And was your mistress unkind to you?"

"No, sir,—no! my mistress was always good to me."

"What could induce you to leave a good home, then,
and run away, and go through such dangers?"

The woman looked up at Mrs. Bird with a keen, scruti-
nizing glance, and it did not escape her that she was dressed
in deep mourning.

"Ma'am," she said suddenly, "have you ever lost a
child?"

The question was unexpected, and it was a thrust on a
new wound; for it was only a month since a darling child of
the family had been laid in the grave.

Mr. Bird turned around and walked to the window,
and Mrs. Bird burst into tears; but, recovering her voice,
she said,—

"Why do you ask that? I have lost a little one."

"Then you will feel for me. I have lost two, one after
another,—left 'em buried there when I came away; and I
had only this one left. I never slept a night without him; he
was all I had. He was my comfort and pride, day and night;
and, ma'am, they were going to take him away from me,—

(29)

to *sell* him,—sell him down south, ma'am, to go all alone,—
a baby that had never been away from his mother in his life!
I couldn't stand it, ma'am. I knew I never should be good
for anything if they did; and when I knew the papers were
signed, and he was sold, I took him and came off in the
night; and they chased me,—the man that bought him, and
some of Mas'r's folks,—and they were coming down right
behind me, and I heard 'em. I jumped right on to the ice;
and how I got across I don't know, but, first I knew, a man
was helping me up the bank."

The woman did not sob nor weep. She had gone to a
place where tears are dry; but every one around her was, in
some way characteristic of themselves, showing signs of
hearty sympathy.

The two little boys, after a desperate rummaging in
their pockets in search of those pocket-handkerchiefs
which mothers know are never to be found there, had
thrown themselves disconsolately into the skirts of their
mother's gown, where they were sobbing, and wiping their
eyes and noses, to their hearts' content. Mrs. Bird had her
face fairly hidden in her pocket-handerchief; and old Dinah, with tears streaming down her black, honest face, was
ejaculating, "Lord, have mercy on us!" with all the fervor of
a camp-meeting; while old Cudjoe, rubbing his eyes very
hard with his cuffs, and making a most uncommon variety
of wry faces, occasionally responded in the same key with
great fervor. Our Senator was a statesman, and of course
could not be expected to cry like other mortals; and so he
turned his back to the company and looked out of the
window, and seemed particularly busy in clearing his
throat and wiping his spectacle-glasses, occasionally blowing his nose in a manner that was calculated to excite suspicion, had any one been in a state to observe critically.

"How came you to tell me you had a kind master?" he
suddenly exclaimed, gulping down very resolutely some
kind of rising in his throat, and turning suddenly round
upon the woman.

"Because he *was* a kind master; I'll say that of him, anyway;—and my mistress was kind; but they couldn't help themselves. They were owing money; and there was some way, I can't tell how, that a man had a hold on them, and they were obliged to give him his will. I listened, and heard him telling mistress that, and she begging and pleading for me,—and he told her he couldn't help himself, and that the papers were all drawn,—and then it was I took him and left my home, and came away. I knew 't was no use of my trying to live if they did it; for 't 'pears like this child is all I have."

"Have you no husband?"

"Yes, but he belongs to another man. His master is real hard to him, and won't let him come to see me, hardly ever; and he's grown harder and harder upon us, and he threatens to sell him down south;—it's like I'll never see *him* again!"

The quiet tone in which the woman pronounced these words might have led a superficial observer to think that she was entirely apathetic; but there was a calm, settled depth of anguish in her large, dark eye that spoke of something far otherwise.

"And where do you mean to go, my poor woman?" said Mrs. Bird.

"To Canada, if I only knew where that was. Is it very far off, is Canada?" said she, looking up, with a simple, confiding air, to Mrs. Bird's face.

"Poor thing!" said Mrs. Bird involuntarily.

"Is 't a very great way off, think?" said the woman earnestly.

"Much farther than you think, poor child!" said Mrs. Bird; "but we will try to think what can be done for you. Here, Dinah, make her up a bed in your own room, close by the kitchen, and I'll think what to do for her in the morning. Meanwhile, never fear, poor woman; put your trust in God; he will protect you."

Mrs. Bird and her husband reëntered the parlor. She sat down in her little rocking-chair before the fire, swaying thoughtfully to and fro. Mr. Bird strode up and down the room, grumbling to himself, "Pish! pshaw! confounded awkward business!" At length, striding up to his wife, he said,—

"I say, wife, she'll have to get away from here this very night. That fellow will be down on the scent bright and early to-morrow morning: if 't was only the woman, she could lie quiet till it was over; but that little chap can't be kept still by a troop of horse and foot, I'll warrant me; he'll bring it all out, popping his head out of some window or door. A pretty kettle of fish it would be for me, too, to be caught with them both here just now! No; they'll have to be got off to-night."

"To-night! How is it possible?—where to?"

"Well, I know pretty well where to," said the Senator, beginning to put on his boots, with a reflective air; and, stopping when his leg was half in, he embraced his knee with both hands, and seemed to go off in deep meditation.

"It's a confounded awkward, ugly business," said he at last, beginning to tug at his boot-straps again, "and that's a fact!" After one boot was fairly on, the Senator sat with the other in his hand, profoundly studying the figure of the carpet. "It will have to be done, though, for aught I see,— hang it all!" and he drew the other boot anxiously on, and looked out of the window.

Now little Mrs. Bird was a discreet woman,—a woman who never in her life said, "I told you so!" and, on the present occasion, though pretty well aware of the shape her husband's meditations were taking, she very prudently forbore to meddle with them, only sat very quietly in her chair, and looked quite ready to hear her liege lord's intentions, when he should think proper to utter them.

"You see," he said, there's my old client, Van Trompe, has come over from Kentucky and set all his slaves free; and he has bought a place seven miles up the creek here, back in the woods, where nobody goes, unless they go on purpose; and it's a place that isn't found in a hurry. There she'd be safe enough; but the plague of the thing is, nobody could drive a carriage there to-night but *me*."

"Why not? Cudjoe is an excellent driver."

"Ay, ay, but here it is. The creek has to be crossed twice; and the second crossing is quite dangerous, unless one knows it as I do. I have crossed it a hundred times on horseback, and know exactly the turns to take. And so, you see, there's no help for it. Cudjoe must put in the horses, as quietly as may be, about twelve o'clock, and I'll take her over; and then, to give color to the matter, he must carry me on to the next tavern, to take the stage for Columbus, that comes by about three or four, and so it will look as if I had had the carriage only for that. I shall get into business bright and early in the morning. But I'm thinking I shall feel rather cheap there, after all that's been said and done; but, hang it, I can't help it!"

"Your heart is better than your head in this case, John," said the wife, laying her little white hand on his. "Could I ever have loved you, had I not known you better than you know yourself?" And the little woman looked so handsome, with the tears sparkling in her eyes, that the Senator thought he must be a decidedly clever fellow to get such a pretty creature into such a passionate admiration of him; and so what could he do but walk off soberly to see about the carriage? At the door, however, he stopped a moment, and then, coming back, he said, with some hesitation,—

"Mary, I don't know how you'd feel about it, but there's that drawer full of things—of—of—poor little Henry's." So saying, he turned quickly on his heel, and shut the door after him.

His wife opened the little bedroom door adjoining her room, and, taking the candle, set it down on the top of a bureau there; then from a small recess she took a key, and put it thoughtfully in the lock of a drawer, and made a

(*33*)

sudden pause, while two boys, who, boy-like, had followed close on her heels, stood looking, with silent, significant glances, at their mother. And, oh, mother that reads this, has there never been in your house a drawer, or a closet, the opening of which has been to you like the opening again of a little grave? Ah, happy mother that you are, if it has not been so!

Mrs. Bird slowly opened the drawer. There were little coats of many a form and pattern, piles of aprons, and rows of small stockings; and even a pair of little shoes, worn and rubbed at the toes, were peeping from the folds of a paper. There was a toy horse and wagon, a top, a ball,—memorials gathered with many a tear and many a heart-break! She sat down by the drawer, and, leaning her head on her hands over it, wept till the tears fell through her fingers into the drawer; then, suddenly raising her head, she began, with nervous haste, selecting the plainest and most substantial articles, and gathering them into a bundle.

"Mamma," said one of the boys, gently touching her arm, "are you going to give away *those* things?"

"My dear boys," she said softly and earnestly, "if our dear, loving little Henry looks down from heaven, he would be glad to have us do this. I could not find it in my heart to give them away to any common person,—to any-body that was happy; but I give them to a mother more heartbroken and sorrowful than I am; and I hope God will send his blessings with them!"

There are in this world blessed souls, whose sorrows all spring up into joys for others; whose earthly hopes, laid in the grave with many tears, are the seed from which spring healing flowers and balm for the desolate and the dis-tressed. Among such is the delicate woman who sits there by the lamp, dropping slow tears, while she prepares the memorials of her own lost one for the outcast wanderer.

After a while, Mrs. Bird opened a wardrobe, and, taking from thence a plain, serviceable dress or two, she sat

(*34*)

down busily to her work-table, and, with needle, scissors, and thimble at hand, quietly commenced the "letting-down" process which her husband had recommended, and continued busily at it till the old clock in the corner struck twelve, and she heard the low rattling of wheels at the door.

"Mary," said her husband, coming in with his overcoat in his hand, "you must wake her up now; we must be off."

Mrs. Bird hastily deposited the various articles she had collected in a small plain trunk, and, locking it, desired her husband to see it in the carriage, and then proceeded to call the woman. Soon, arrayed in a cloak, bonnet, and shawl that had belonged to her benefactress, she appeared at the door with her child in her arms. Mr. Bird hurried her into the carriage, and Mrs. Bird pressed on after her to the carriage steps. Eliza leaned out of the carriage and put out her hand,—a hand as soft and beautiful as was given in return. She fixed her large, dark eyes, full of earnest meaning, on Mrs. Bird's face, and seemed going to speak. Her lips moved,—she tried once or twice, but there was no sound,—and pointing upward, with a look never to be forgotten, she fell back in the seat, and covered her face. The door was shut, and the carriage drove on.

What a situation, now, for a patriotic Senator, that had been all the week before spurring up the legislature of his native State to pass more stringent resolutions against escaping fugitives, their harborers and abettors!

Our good Senator in his native State had not been exceeded by any of his brethren at Washington in the sort of eloquence which has won for them immortal renown! How sublimely he had sat with his hands in his pockets, and scouted all sentimental weakness of those who would put the welfare of a few miserable fugitives before great state interests!

He was as bold as a lion about it, and "mightily convinced" not only himself, but everybody that heard him;

(35)

but then his idea of a fugitive was only an idea of the letters that spell the word,—or, at the most, the image of a little newspaper picture of a man with a stick and bundle, with "Ran away from the subscriber" under it. The magic of the real presence of distress,—the imploring human eye, the frail, trembling human hand, the despairing appeal of helpless agony,—these he had never tried. He had never thought that a fugitive might be a hapless mother, a defenseless child,—like that one which was now wearing his lost boy's little well-known cap; and so, as our poor Senator was not stone or steel,—as he was a man, and a downright noble-hearted one, too,—he was, as everybody must see, in a sad case for his patriotism. And you need not exult over him, good brother of the Southern States; for we have some inklings that many of you, under similar circumstances, would not do much better. We have reason to know, in Kentucky as in Mississippi, are noble and generous hearts, to whom never was tale of suffering told in vain. Ah, good brother! is it fair for you to expect of us services which your own brave, honorable heart would not allow you to render, were you in our place?

Be that as it may, if our good Senator was a political sinner, he was in a fair way to expiate it by his night's penance. There had been a long continuous period of rainy weather, and the soft, rich earth of Ohio, as every one knows, is admirably suited to the manufacture of mud,— and the road was an Ohio railroad of the good old times.

"And, pray, what sort of a road may that be?" says some Eastern traveler, who has been accustomed to connect no ideas with a railroad but those of smoothness or speed.

Know, then, innocent Eastern friend, that in benighted regions of the West, where the mud is of unfathomable and sublime depth, roads are made of round rough logs, arranged transversely side by side, and coated over in their pristine freshness with earth, turf, and whatsoever may come to hand, and then the rejoicing native calleth it a road, and straightway essayeth to ride thereupon. In process of time, the rains wash off all the turf and grass aforesaid, move the logs hither and thither in picturesque positions, up, down, and crosswise, with divers chasms and ruts of black mud intervening.

Over such a road as this our Senator went stumbling along, making moral reflections as continuously as under the circumstances could be expected,—the carriage proceeding along much as follows,—bump! bump! bump! slush! down in the mud!—the Senator, woman, and child reversing their positions so suddenly as to come, without any very accurate adjustment, against the windows of the down-hill side. Carriage sticks fast, while Cudjoe on the outside is heard making a great muster among the horses. After various ineffectual pullings and twitchings, just as the Senator is losing all patience, the carriage suddenly rights itself with a bounce,—two front wheels go down into another abyss, and Senator, woman, and child all tumble promiscuously on to the front seat,—Senator's hat is jammed over his eyes and nose quite unceremoniously, and he considers himself fairly extinguished;—child cries, and Cudjoe on the outside delivers animated addresses to the horses, who are kicking, and floundering, and straining, under repeated cracks of the whip. Carriage springs up, with another bounce,—down go the hind wheels,—Senator, woman, and child fly over on to the back seat, his elbows encountering her bonnet, and both her feet being jammed into his hat, which flies off in the concussion. After a few moments the "slough" is passed, and the horses stop, panting; the Senator finds his hat, the woman straightens her bonnet and hushes her child, and they brace themselves firmly for what is yet to come.

For a while only the continuous bump! bump! intermingled, just by way of variety, with divers side plunges and compound shakes; and they begin to flatter themselves that they are not so badly off, after all. At last, with a square plunge, which puts all on to their feet and then down into their seats with incredible quickness, the carriage stops,—and, after much outside commotion, Cudjoe appears at the door.

"Please, sir, it's powerful bad spot, this yer. I don't know how we's to get clar out. I'm a-thinkin' we'll have to be a-gettin' rails."

The Senator despairingly steps out, picking gingerly for some firm foothold; down goes one foot an immeasurable depth,—he tries to pull it up, loses his balance, and tumbles over into the mud, and is fished out, in a very despairing condition, by Cudjoe.

But we forbear, out of sympathy to our readers' bones. Western travelers, who have beguiled the midnight hour in the interesting process of pulling down rail fences to pry their carriages out of mud-holes, will have a respectful and mournful sympathy with our unfortunate hero. We beg them to drop a silent tear, and pass on.

It was full late in the night when the carriage emerged, dripping and bespattered, out of the creek, and stood at the door of a large farmhouse.

It took no inconsiderable perseverance to arouse the inmates; but at last the respectable proprietor appeared, and undid the door. He was a great, tall, bristling Orson[2] of a fellow, full six feet and some inches in his stockings, and arrayed in a red flannel hunting-shirt. A very heavy *mat* of sandy hair, in a decidedly tousled condition, and a beard of some days' growth, gave the worthy man an appearance, to say the least, not particularly prepossessing. He stood for a few minutes holding the candle aloft, and blinking on our travelers with a dismal and mystified expression that was truly ludicrous. It cost some effort of our Senator to induce him to comprehend the case fully; and while he is doing his best at that, we shall give him a little introduction to our readers.

Honest old John Van Trompe was once quite a considerable land-holder and slave-owner in the State of Kentucky. Having "nothing of the bear about him but the skin," and being gifted by nature with a great, honest, just heart, quite equal to his gigantic frame, he had been for some years witnessing with repressed uneasiness the workings of a system equally bad for oppressor and oppressed. At last, one day, John's great heart had swelled altogether too big to wear his bonds any longer; so he just took his pocketbook out of his desk, and went over into Ohio and bought a quarter of a township of good, rich land, made out free papers for all his people,—men, women, and children,— packed them up in wagons, and sent them off to settle down; and then honest John turned his face up the creek, and sat quietly down on a snug, retired farm, to enjoy his conscience and his reflections.

"Are you the man that will shelter a poor woman and child from slave-catchers?" said the Senator explicitly.

"I rather think I am," said honest John, with some considerable emphasis.

"I thought so," said the Senator.

"If there's anybody comes," said the good man, stretching his tall muscular form upward, "why here I'm ready for him; and I've got seven sons, each six foot high, and they'll be ready for 'em. Give our respects to 'em," said John; "tell 'em it's no matter how soon they call,—makes no kinder difference to us," said John, running his fingers through the shock of hair that thatched his head, and bursting out into a great laugh.

Weary, jaded, and spiritless, Eliza dragged herself up to the door, with her child lying in a heavy sleep on her arm. The rough man held the candle to her face, and, uttering a kind of compassionate grunt, opened the door of a small bedroom adjoining to the large kitchen where they were standing, and motioned her to go in. He took down a candle, and, lighting it, set it upon the table, and then addressed himself to Eliza.

"Now, I say, gal, you needn't be a bit afeard, let who

will come here. I'm up to all that sort o' thing," said he, pointing to two or three goodly rifles over the mantel-piece; "and most people that know me know that 't wouldn't be healthy to try to get anybody out o' my house when I'm agin it. So *now* you jist go to sleep now, as quiet as if yer mother was a-rockin' ye," said he, as he shut the door.

"Why, this is an uncommon handsome un," he said to the Senator. "Ah, well; handsome uns has the greatest cause to run, sometimes, if they has any kind o' feelin', such as decent women should. I know all about that."

The Senator, in a few words, briefly explained Eliza's history.

"Oh! ou! aw! now, I want to know?" said the good man pitifully; "sho! now sho! That's natur now, poor crittur! hunted down now like a deer,—hunted down, jest for havin' natural feelin's, and doin' what no kind o' mother could help a-doin'! I tell ye what, these yer things make me come the nighest to swearin', now, o' most anything," said honest John, as he wiped his eyes with the back of a great, freckled, yellow hand. "I tell yer what, stranger, it was years and years before I'd jine the church, 'cause the ministers round in our parts used to preach that the Bible went in for these ere cuttings-up,—and I couldn't be up to 'em with their Greek and Hebrew, and so I took up agin 'em, Bible and all. I never jined the church till I found a minister that was up to 'em all in Greek and all that, and he said right the contrary; and then I took right hold, and jined the church,—I did now, fact," said John, who had been all this time uncorking some very frisky bottled cider, which at this juncture he presented.

"Ye'd better jest put up here, now, till daylight," said he heartily, "and I'll call up the old woman, and have a bed got ready for you in no time."

"Thank you, my good friend," said the Senator. "I must be along, to take the night stage for Columbus."

"Ah! well, then, if you must, I'll go a piece with you,

and show you a cross-road that will take you there better than the road you came on. That road's mighty bad."

John equipped himself, and, with a lantern in hand, was soon seen guiding the Senator's carriage towards a road that ran down in a hollow, back of his dwelling. When they parted, the Senator put into his hand a ten-dollar bill.

"It's for her," he said briefly.

"Ay, ay," said John with equal conciseness.

They shook hands, and parted.

Notes

1. "For I was an hungred, and ye gave me meat: I was thirsty, and ye gave me drink: I was a stranger, and ye took me in: Naked, and ye clothed me: I was sick, and ye visited me: I was in prison, and ye came unto me." *Matthew*. XXV, 35, 36.

2. The tale of Orson and Valentine, twin brothers born in a forest, is from the Charlemagne cycle of romances, a series of medieval ballads about Charlemagne and his peers. Orson, carried off by a bear, grew up rough, uncouth, uncivilized; Valentine, raised by a regal uncle, became a member of the king's court.

SELECT INCIDENT OF LAWFUL TRADE

from *Uncle Tom's Cabin*

Having suffered the loss of Harry, Haley, the slave trader, returns to the Shelbys to collect Uncle Tom. Together the two start on the long journey that will eventually lead to Tom's being sold "down the river."

"Select Incident of Lawful Trade" is Chapter XII in *Uncle Tom's Cabin.*

"In Ramah there was a voice heard,—weeping, and lamentation, and great mourning; Rachel weeping for her children, and would not be comforted."[1]

Mr. Haley and Tom jogged onward in their wagon, each, for a time, absorbed in his own reflections. Now, the reflections of two men sitting side by side are a curious thing,—seated on the same seat, having the same eyes, ears, hands, and organs of all sorts, and having pass before their eyes the same objects,—it is wonderful what a variety we shall find in these same reflections!

As, for example, Mr. Haley: he thought first of Tom's length, and breadth, and height and what he would sell for, if he was kept fat and in good case till he got him into market. He thought of how he should make out his gang; he thought of the respective market value of certain supposititious men and women and children who were to compose it, and other kindred topics of the business; then he thought of himself, and how humane he was: that, whereas other men chained their "niggers" hand and foot both, he only put fetters on the feet, and left Tom the use of his hands, as long as he behaved well; and he sighed to think how ungrateful human nature was, so that there was even room to doubt whether Tom appreciated his mercies. He had been taken in so by "niggers" whom he had favored; but still he was astonished to consider how good-natured he yet remained!

As to Tom, he was thinking over some words of an unfashionable old book, which kept running through his head again and again, as follows: "We have here no continuing city, but we seek one to come; wherefore God himself is not ashamed to be called our God; for he hath prepared for us a city."[2] These words of an ancient volume, got up principally by "ignorant and unlearned men," have, through all time, kept up, somehow, a strange sort of power over the minds of poor, simple fellows like Tom. They stir up the soul from its depths, and rouse, as with trumpet call, courage, energy, and enthusiasm, where before was only the blackness of despair.

Mr. Haley pulled out of his pocket sundry newspapers, and began looking over their advertisements, with absorbed interest. He was not a remarkably fluent reader, and was in the habit of reading in a sort of recitative half-aloud, by way of calling in his ears to verify the deductions of his eyes. In this tone he slowly recited the following paragraph:—

EXECUTOR'S SALE,—NEGROES!—Agreeably to order of court, will be sold, on Tuesday, February 20, before the Court-house door, in the town of Washington, Kentucky, the following negroes: Hagar, aged 60; John, aged 30; Ben, aged 21; Saul, aged 25; Albert, aged 14. Sold for the benefit of the creditors and heirs of the estate of Jesse Blutchford, Esq.

SAMUEL MORRIS, *Executors.*
THOMAS FLINT,

"This yer I must look at," said he to Tom, for want of somebody else to talk to. "Ye see, I'm going to get up a prime gang to take down with ye, Tom; it'll make it sociable and pleasant-like,—good company will, ye know. We must drive right to Washington first and foremost, and then I'll clap you into jail while I does the business."

Tom received this agreeable intelligence quite meekly; simply wondering, in his own heart, how many of these doomed men had wives and children, and whether they would feel as he did about leaving them. It is to be confessed, too, that the naïve, off-hand information that he was to be thrown into jail by no means produced an agreeable impression on a poor fellow who had always prided himself on a strictly honest and upright course of life. Yes, Tom, we must confess it, was rather proud of his honesty, poor fellow,—not having very much else to be proud of; if he had belonged to some of the higher walks of society, he, perhaps, would never have been reduced to such straits. However, the day wore on, and the evening saw Haley and Tom comfortably accommodated in Washington,—the one in a tavern, and the other in a jail.

About eleven o'clock the next day, a mixed throng was gathered around the court-house steps,—smoking, chewing, spitting, swearing, and conversing, according to their respective tastes and turns,—waiting for the auction to commence. The men and women to be sold sat in a group apart, talking in a low tone to each other. The woman who had been advertised by the name of Hagar was a regular African in feature and figure. She might have been sixty, but was older than that by hard work and disease, was partially blind, and somewhat crippled with rheumatism. By her side stood her only remaining son, Albert, a bright-looking little fellow of fourteen years. The boy was the only survivor of a large family, who had been successively sold away from her to a southern market. The mother held on to him with both her shaking hands, and eyed with intense trepidation every one who walked up to examine him.

(44)

"Don't be 'feard, Aunt Hagar," said the oldest of the men. "I spoke to Mas'r Thomas 'bout it, and he thought he might manage to sell you in a lot both together."

"Dey needn't call me worn out yet," said she, lifting her shaking hands. "I can cook yet, and scrub, and scour,—I'm wuth a-buying, if I do come cheap; tell 'em dat ar,—you *tell* 'em," she added earnestly.

Haley here forced his way into the group, walked up to the old man, pulled his mouth open and looked in, felt of his teeth, made him stand and straighten himself, bend his back, and perform various evolutions to show his muscles; and then passed on to the next, and put him through the same trial. Walking up last to the boy, he felt of his arms, straightened his hands, and looked at his fingers, and made him jump, to show his agility.

"He ain't gwine to be sold widout me!" said the old woman, with passionate eagerness; "he and I goes in a lot together; I's rail strong yet, Mas'r, and can do heaps o' work,—heaps on it, Mas'r."

"On plantation?" said Haley, with a contemptuous glance. "Likely story!" and, as if satisfied with his examination, he walked out and looked, and stood with his hands in his pockets, his cigar in his mouth, and his hat cocked on one side, ready for action.

"What think of 'em?" said a man who had been following Haley's examination, as if to make up his own mind from it.

"Wal," said Haley, spitting, "I shall put in, I think, for the youngerly ones and the boy."

"They want to sell the boy and the old woman together," said the man.

"Find it a tight pull; why, she's an old rackabones,— not worth her salt."

"You wouldn't, then?" said the man.

"Anybody'd be a fool 't would. She's half blind, crooked with rheumatis, and foolish to boot."

"Some buys up these yer old critturs, and ses there's a

sight more wear in 'em than a body'd think," said the man reflectively.

"No go, 't all," said Haley; "wouldn't take her for a present,—fact,—I've *seen*, now."

"Wal, 't is kinder pity, now, not to buy her with her son,—her heart seems so sot on him,—s'pose they fling her in cheap."

"Them that's got money to spend that ar way, it's all well enough. I shall bid off on that ar boy for a plantation hand; wouldn't be bothered with her, noway,—not if they'd give her to me," said Haley.

"She'll take on despit," said the man.

"Nat'lly, she will," said the trader coolly.

The conversation was here interrupted by a busy hum in the audience; and the auctioneer, a short, bustling, important fellow, elbowed his way into the crowd. The old woman drew in her breath, and caught instinctively at her son.

"Keep close to yer mammy, Albert,—close,—dey'll put us up togedder," she said.

"Oh, mammy, I'm 'feard they won't," said the boy.

"Dey must, child; I can't live, noways, if they don't!" said the old creature vehemently.

The stentorian tones of the auctioneer, calling out to clear the way, now announced that the sale was about to commence. A place was cleared, and the bidding began. The different men on the list were soon knocked off at prices which showed a pretty brisk demand in the market: two of them fell to Haley.

"Come now, young un," said the auctioneer, giving the boy a touch with his hammer, "be up and show your springs, now."

"Put us two up togedder—togedder,—do please, Mas'r," said the old woman, holding fast to her boy.

"Be off," said the man gruffly, pushing her hands away; "you come last. Now darkey, spring;" and, with the

(46)

word, he pushed the boy toward the block, while a deep, heavy groan rose behind him. The boy paused and looked back; but there was no time to stay, and, dashing the tears from his large, bright eyes, he was up in a moment.

His fine figure, alert limbs, and bright face raised an instant competition, and half a dozen bids simultaneously met the ear of the auctioneer. Anxious, half frightened, he looked from side to side, as he heard the clatter of contending bids,—now here, now there,—till the hammer fell. Haley had got him. He was pushed from the block toward his new master, but stopped one moment and looked back, when his poor old mother, trembling in every limb, held out her shaking hands toward him.

"Buy me too, Mas'r, for de dear Lord's sake!—buy me,—I shall die if you don't!"

"You'll die if I do, that's the kink of it," said Haley,— "no!" And he turned on his heel.

The bidding for the poor old creature was summary. The man who had addressed Haley, and who seemed not destitute of compassion, bought her for a trifle, and the spectators began to disperse.

The poor victims of the sale, who had been brought up in one place together for years, gathered round the despairing old mother, whose agony was pitiful to see.

"Couldn't dey leave me one? Mas'r allers said I should have one,—he did," she repeated over and over, in heartbroken tones.

"Trust in the Lord, Aunt Hagar," said the oldest of the men sorrowfully.

"What good will it do?" said she, sobbing passionately.

"Mother, mother,—don't! don't!" said the boy. "They say you's got a good master."

"I don't care,—I don't care. Oh, Albert! Oh, my boy, you's my last baby. Lord, how ken I?"

"Come, take her off, can't some of ye?" said Haley dryly; "don't do no good for her to go on that ar way."

The old men of the company, partly by persuasion and partly by force, loosed the poor creature's last despairing hold, and, as they led her off to her new master's wagon, strove to comfort her.

"Now!" said Haley, pushing his three purchases together and producing a bundle of handcuffs, which he proceeded to put on their wrists; and fastening each handcuff to a long chain, he drove them before him to the jail.

A few days saw Haley, with his possessions, safely deposited on one of the Ohio boats. It was the commencement of his gang, to be augmented, as the boat moved on, by various other merchandise of the same kind, which he or his agent had stored for him in various points alongshore.

The La Belle Rivière, as brave and beautiful a boat as ever walked the waters of her namesake river, was floating gayly down the stream, under a brilliant sky, the Stripes and Stars of free America waving and fluttering overhead; the guards crowded with well-dressed ladies and gentlemen walking and enjoying the delightful day. All was full of life, buoyant and rejoicing,—all but Haley's gang, who were stored, with other freight, on the lower deck, and who, somehow, did not seem to appreciate their various privileges, as they sat in a knot, talking to each other in low tones.

"Boys," said Haley, coming up briskly, "I hope you keep up good heart and are cheerful. Now, no sulks, ye see; keep stiff upper lip, boys; do well by me, and I'll do well by you."

The boys addressed responded the invariable "Yes, Mas'r," for ages the watchword of poor Africa; but it's to be owned they did not look particularly cheerful: they had their various little prejudices in favor of wives, mothers, sisters, and children seen for the last time, and, though "they that wasted them required of them mirth,"[3] it was not instantly forthcoming.

"I've got a wife," spoke out the article enumerated as "John, aged thirty,"—and he laid his chained hand on Tom's knee,—"and she don't know a word about this, poor girl!"

"Where does she live?" said Tom.

"In a tavern a piece down here," said John; "I wish, now, I *could* see her once more in this world," he added.

Poor John! It *was* rather natural; and the tears that fell, as he spoke, came as naturally as if he had been a white man. Tom drew a long breath from a sore heart, and tried, in his poor way, to comfort him.

And overhead, in the cabin, sat fathers and mothers, husbands and wives; and merry, dancing children moved round among them, like so many little butterflies, and everything was going on quite easy and comfortable.

"Oh, mamma," said a boy, who had just come up from below, "there's a negro-trader on board, and he's brought four or five slaves down there."

"Poor creatures!" said the mother, in a tone between grief and indignation.

"What's that?" said another lady.

"Some poor slaves below," said the mother.

"And they've got chains on," said the boy.

"What a shame to our country that such sights are to be seen!" said another lady.

"Oh, there's a great deal to be said on both sides of the subject," said a genteel woman, who sat at her state-room door sewing, while her little boy and girl were playing round her. "I've been south, and I must say I think the negroes are better off than they would be to be free."

"In some respects, some of them are well off, I grant," said the lady to whose remark she had answered. "The most dreadful part of slavery, to my mind, is its outrages on the feelings and affections,—the separating of families, for example."

"That *is* a bad thing, certainly," said the other lady,

(*49*)

holding up a baby's dress she had just completed, and looking intently on its trimmings; "but then, I fancy, it don't occur often."

"Oh, it does," said the first lady eagerly; "I've lived many years in Kentucky and Virginia both, and I've seen enough to make any one's heart sick. Suppose, ma'am, your two children, there, should be taken from you and sold?"

"We can't reason from our feelings to those of this class of persons," said the other lady, sorting out some worsteds on her lap.

"Indeed, ma'am, you can know nothing of them, if you say so," answered the first lady warmly. "I was born and brought up among them. I know they *do* feel just as keenly—even more so, perhaps—as we do."

The lady said "Indeed!" yawned, and looked out the cabin window, and finally repeated, for a finale, the remark with which she had begun,—"After all, I think they are better off than they would be to be free."

"It's undoubtedly the intention of Providence that the African race should be servants,—kept in a low condition," said a grave-looking gentleman in black, a clergyman, seated by the cabin door. " 'Cursed be Canaan; a servant of servants shall he be,' the Scripture says."[4]

"I say, stranger, is that ar what that text means?" said a tall man, standing by.

"Undoubtedly. It pleased Providence, for some inscrutable reason, to doom the race to bondage, ages ago; and we must not set up our opinion against that."

"Well, then, we'll all go ahead and buy up niggers," said the man, "if that's the way of Providence,—won't we, Squire?" said he, turning to Haley, who had been standing, with his hands in his pockets, by the stove, and intently listening to the conversation.

"Yes," continued the tall man, "we must all be resigned to the decrees of Providence. Niggers must be sold, and

(*50*)

trucked round, and kept under; it's what they's made for. 'Pears like this yer view's quite refreshing, ain't it, stranger?" said he to Haley.

"I never thought on 't," said Haley. "I couldn't have said as much myself; I hain't no larning. I took up the trade just to make a living; if 't ain't right, I calculated to 'pent on 't in time, *ye* know."

"And now you'll save yourself the trouble, won't ye?" said the tall man. "See what 't is, now, to know Scripture. If ye'd only studied yer Bible, like this yer good man, ye might have know'd it before, and saved ye a heap o' trouble. Ye could jist have said, 'Cussed be'—what's his name?—and 't would all have come right." And the stranger, who was no other than the honest drover whom we introduced to our readers in the Kentucky tavern,[5] sat down and began smoking, with a curious smile on his long, dry face.

A tall, slender young man, with a face expressive of great feeling and intelligence, here broke in, and repeated the words, " 'All things whatsoever ye would that men should do unto you, do ye even so unto them.'[6] I suppose," he added, "*that* is Scripture as much as 'Cursed be Canaan.' "

"Wal, it seems quite *as* plain a text, stranger," said John the drover, "to poor fellows like us, now;" and John smoked on like a volcano.

The young man paused, looked as if he was going to say more, when suddenly the boat stopped, and the company made the usual steamboat rush to see where they were landing.

"Both them ar chaps parsons?" said John to one of the men, as they were going out.

The man nodded.

As the boat stopped, a black woman came running wildly up the plank, darted into the crowd, flew up to where the slave gang sat, and threw her arms round that

(51)

unfortunate piece of merchandise before enumerated, "John, aged thirty," and with sobs and tears bemoaned him as her husband.

But what needs tell the story, told too oft,—every day told,—of heart-strings rent and broken,—the weak broken and torn for the profit and convenience of the strong! It needs not be told; every day is telling it,—telling it, too, in the ear of One who is not deaf, though he be long silent.

The young man, who had spoken for the cause of humanity and God before, stood with folded arms, looking on this scene. He turned, and Haley was standing at his side.

"My friend," he said, speaking with thick utterance, "how can you, how dare you, carry on a trade like this? Look at those poor creatures! Here I am, rejoicing in my heart that I am going home to my wife and child; and the same bell which is a signal to carry me onward towards them will part this poor man and his wife forever. Depend upon it, God will bring you into judgment for this."

The trader turned away in silence.

"I say, now," said the drover, touching his elbow, "there's differences in parsons, ain't there? 'Cussed be Canaan' don't seem to go down with this un, does it?"

Haley gave an uneasy growl.

"And that ar ain't the worst on 't," said John; "mabbe it won't go down with the Lord, neither, when ye come to settle with him, one o' these days, as all on us must, I reckon."

Haley walked reflectively to the other end of the boat.

"If I make pretty handsomely on one or two next gangs," he thought, "I reckon I'll stop off this yer; it's really getting dangerous." And he took out his pocketbook, and began adding over his accounts,—a process which many gentlemen besides Mr. Haley have found a specific for an uneasy conscience.

The boat swept proudly away from the shore, and all

went on merrily, as before. Men talked, and loafed, and read, and smoked. Women sewed, and children played, and the boat passed on her way.

One day, when she lay to for a while at a small town in Kentucky, Haley went up into the place on a little matter of business.

Tom, whose fetters did not prevent his taking a moderate circuit, had drawn near the side of the boat, and stood listlessly gazing over the railings. After a time, he saw the trader returning, with an alert step, in company with a colored woman, bearing in her arms a young child. She was dressed quite respectably, and a colored man followed her bringing along a small trunk. The woman came cheerfully onward, talking, as she came, with the man who bore her trunk, and so passed up the plank into the boat. The bell rung, the steamer whizzed, the engine groaned and coughed, and away swept the boat down the river.

The woman walked forward among the boxes and bales of the lower deck, and, sitting down, busied herself with chirruping to her baby.

Haley made a turn or two about the boat, and then, coming up, seated himself near her, and began saying something to her in an indifferent undertone.

Tom soon noticed a heavy cloud passing over the woman's brow, and that she answered rapidly, and with great vehemence.

"I don't believe it,—I won't believe it!" he heard her say. "You're jist a-foolin' with me."

"If you won't believe it, look here!" said the man, drawing out a paper; "this yer's the bill of sale, and there's your master's name to it; and I paid down good solid cash for it, too, I can tell you,—so, now!"

"I don't believe Mas'r would cheat me so; it can't be true!" said the woman, with increasing agitation.

"You can ask any of these men here that can read writing. Here!" he said to a man that was passing by, "jist read this yer, won't you? This yer gal won't believe me when I tell her what 't is."

"Why, it's a bill of sale, signed by John Fosdick," said the man, "making over to you the girl Lucy and her child. It's all straight enough, for aught I see."

The woman's passionate exclamations collected a crowd around her, and the trader briefly explained to them the cause of the agitation.

"He told me that I was going down to Louisville, to hire out as cook to the same tavern where my husband works,— that's what Mas'r told me, his own self; and I can't believe he'd lie to me," said the woman.

"But he has sold you, my poor woman, there's no doubt about it," said a good-natured-looking man, who had been examining the papers; "he has done it, and no mistake."

"Then it's no account talking," said the woman, suddenly growing quite calm; and, clasping her child tighter in her arms, she sat down on her box, turned her back round, and gazed listlessly into the river.

"Going to take it easy, after all!" said the trader. "Gal's got grit, I see."

The woman looked calm as the boat went on; and a beautiful soft summer breeze passed like a compassionate spirit over her head,—the gentle breeze, that never inquires whether the brow is dusky or fair that it fans. And she saw sunshine sparkling on the water in golden ripples, and heard gay voices, full of ease and pleasure, talking around her everywhere; but her heart lay as if a great stone had fallen on it. Her baby raised himself up against her, and stroked her cheeks with his little hands; and, springing up and down, crowing and chatting, seemed determined to arouse her. She strained him suddenly and tightly in her arms, and slowly one tear after another fell on his wondering, unconscious face; and gradually she seemed, and little by little, to grow calmer, and busied herself with tending and nursing him.

The child, a boy of ten months, was uncommonly large and strong of his age, and very vigorous in his limbs. Never for a moment still, he kept his mother constantly busy in holding him, and guarding his springing activity.

"That's a fine chap!" said a man, suddenly stopping opposite to him, with his hands in his pockets. "How old is he?"

"Ten months and a half," said the mother.

The man whistled to the boy, and offered him part of a stick of candy, which he eagerly grabbed at, and very soon had it in a baby's general depository, to wit, his mouth.

"Rum fellow!" said the man. "Knows what's what!" and he whistled and walked on. When he had got to the other side of the boat, he came across Halcy, who was smoking on top of a pile of boxes.

The stranger produced a match and lighted a cigar, saying as he did so,—

"Decentish kind o' wench you've got round there, stranger."

"Why, I reckon she *is* tol'able fair," said Haley, blowing the smoke out of his mouth.

"Taking her down south?" said the man.

Haley nodded, and smoked on.

"Plantation hand?" said the man.

"Wal," said Haley, "I'm fillin' out an order for a plantation, and I think I shall put her in. They told me she was a good cook; and they can use her for that, or set her at the cotton-picking. She's got the right fingers for that; I looked at 'em. Sell well either way;" and Haley resumed his cigar.

"They won't want the young un on a plantation," said the man.

"I shall sell him, first chance I find," said Haley, lighting another cigar.

(55)

"S'pose you'd be selling him tol'able cheap," said the stranger, mounting the pile of boxes and sitting down comfortably.

"Don't know 'bout that," said Haley; "he's a pretty smart young un,—straight, fat, strong; flesh as hard as a brick!"

"Very true, but then there's all the bother and expense of raisin'."

"Nonsense!" said Haley; "they is raised as easy as any kind of crittur there is going; they ain't a bit more trouble than pups. This yer chap will be running all round in a month."

"I've got a good place for raisin', and I thought of takin' in a little more stock," said the man. "Our cook lost a young un last week,—got drownded in a washtub while she was a-hangin' out clothes,—and I reckon it would be well enough to set her to raisin' this yer."

Haley and the stranger smoked awhile in silence, neither seeming willing to broach the test question of the interview. At last the man resumed:—

"You wouldn't think of wantin' more than ten dollars for that ar chap, seeing you *must* get him off yer hand anyhow?"

Haley shook his head and spit impressively.

"That won't do, noways," he said, and began his smoking again.

"Well, stranger, what will you take?"

"Well, now," said Haley, "I *could* raise that ar chap myself, or get him raised; he's oncommon likely and healthy, and he'd fetch a hundred dollars six months hence; and in a year or two he'd bring two hundred, if I had him in the right spot; so I sha'n't take a cent less nor fifty for him now."

"Oh, stranger! that's rediculous, altogether," said the man.

"Fact!" said Haley, with a decisive nod of his head.

"I'll give thirty for him," said the stranger, "but not a cent more."

"Now, I'll tell ye what I will do," said Haley, spitting again, with renewed decision. "I'll split the difference, and say forty-five; and that's the most I will do."

"Well, agreed!" said the man, after an interval.

"Done!" said Haley. "Where do you land?"

"At Louisville," said the man.

"Louisville," said Haley. "Very fair, we get there about dusk. Chap will be asleep,—all fair,—get him off quietly, and no screaming,—happens beautiful,—I like to do everything quietly,—I hates all kind of agitation and fluster." And so, after a transfer of certain bills had passed from the man's pocketbook to the trader's, he resumed his cigar.

It was a bright, tranquil evening when the boat stopped at the wharf at Louisville. The woman had been sitting with her baby in her arms, now wrapped in a heavy sleep. When she heard the name of the place called out, she hastily laid the child down in a little cradle formed by the hollow among the boxes, first carefully spreading under it her cloak; and then she sprung to the side of the boat, in hopes that, among the various hotel-waiters who thronged the wharf, she might see her husband. In this hope, she pressed forward to the front rails, and, stretching far over them, strained her eyes intently on the moving heads on the shore, and the crowd pressed in between her and the child.

"Now's your time," said Haley, taking the sleeping child up, and handing him to the stranger. "Don't wake him up, and set him to crying, now; it would make a devil of a fuss with the gal." The man took the bundle carefully, and was soon lost in the crowd that went up the wharf.

When the boat, creaking, and groaning, and puffing, had loosed from the wharf, and was beginning slowly to strain herself along, the woman returned to her old seat. The trader was sitting there,—the child was gone!

(57)

"Why, why,—where?" she began in bewildered surprise.

"Lucy," said the trader, "your child's gone; you may as well know it first as last. You see, I know'd you couldn't take him down south; and I got a chance to sell him to a firstrate family, that'll raise him better than you can."

The trader had arrived at that stage of Christian and political perfection, which has been recommended by some preachers and politicians of the North lately, in which he had completely overcome every humane weakness and prejudice. His heart was exactly where yours, sir, and mine could be brought with proper effort and cultivation. The wild look of anguish and utter despair that the woman cast on him might have disturbed one less practiced, but he was used to it. He had seen that same look hundreds of times. You can get used to such things, too, my friend; and it is the great object of recent efforts to make our whole Northern community used to them, for the glory of the Union. So the trader only regarded the mortal anguish which he saw working in those dark features, those clenched hands, and suffocating breathings, as necessary incidents of the trade, and merely calculated whether she was going to scream, and get up a commotion on the boat; for, like other supporters of our peculiar institution, he decidedly disliked agitation.

But the woman did not scream. The shot had passed too straight and direct through the heart for cry or tear.

Dizzily she sat down. Her slack hands fell lifeless by her side. Her eyes looked straight forward, but she saw nothing. All the noise and hum of the boat, the groaning of the machinery, mingled dreamily to her bewildered ear; and the poor dumb-stricken heart had neither cry nor tear to show for its utter misery. She was quite calm.

The trader, who, considering his advantages, was almost as humane as some of our politicians, seemed to feel called on to administer such consolation as the case admitted of.

"I know this yer comes kinder hard at first, Lucy," said he; "but such a smart, sensible gal as you are won't give way to it. You see it's *necessary* and can't be helped!"

"Oh, don't, Mas'r, don't!" said the woman, with a voice like one that is smothering.

"You're a smart wench, Lucy," he persisted; "I mean to do well by ye, and get ye a nice place down river; and you'll soon get another husband,—such a likely gal as you"—

"Oh, Mas'r, if you *only* won't talk to me now," said the woman, in a voice of such quick and living anguish that the trader felt that there was something at present in the case beyond his style of operation. He got up, and the woman turned away, and buried her head in her cloak.

The trader walked up and down for a time, and occasionally stopped and looked at her.

"Takes it hard, rather," he soliloquized, "but quiet, tho',—let her sweat awhile; she'll come right by and by!"

Tom had watched the whole transaction from first to last, and had a perfect understanding of its results. To him, it looked like something unutterably horrible and cruel, because, poor, ignorant black soul! he had not learned to generalize, and to take enlarged views. If he had only been instructed by certain ministers of Christianity, he might have thought better of it, and seen in it an every-day incident of a lawful trade; a trade which is the vital support of an institution which some American divines tell us has no evils but such as are inseparable from any other relations in social and domestic life. But Tom, as we see, being a poor, ignorant fellow, whose reading had been confined entirely to the New Testament, could not comfort and solace himself with views like these. His very soul bled within him for what seemed to him the *wrongs* of the poor suffering thing that lay like a crushed reed on the boxes; the feeling, living, bleeding, yet immortal *thing* which American state law coolly classes with the bundles, and bales, and boxes, among which she is lying.

Tom drew near, and tried to say something; but she only groaned. Honestly, and with tears running down his own cheeks, he spoke of a heart of love in the skies, of a pitying Jesus, and an eternal home; but the ear was deaf with anguish, and the palsied heart could not feel.

Night came on,—night calm, unmoved, and glorious, shining down with her innumerable and solemn angel eyes, twinkling, beautiful, but silent. There was no speech nor language, no pitying voice nor helping hand, from that distant sky. One after another the voices of business or pleasure died away; all on the boat were sleeping, and the ripples at the prow were plainly heard. Tom stretched himself out on a box, and there, as he lay, he heard, ever and anon, a smothered sob or cry from the prostrate creature.—"Oh! what shall I do? O Lord! O good Lord, do help me!" and so, ever and anon, until the murmur died away in silence.

At midnight Tom waked with a sudden start. Something black passed quickly by him to the side of the boat, and he heard a splash in the water. No one else saw or heard anything. He raised his head,—the woman's place was vacant! He got up, and sought about him in vain. The poor bleeding heart was still at last, and the river rippled and dimpled just as brightly as if it had not closed above it.

Patience! patience! ye whose hearts swell indignant at wrongs like these. Not one throb of anguish, not one tear of the oppressed, is forgotten by the Man of Sorrows, the Lord of Glory. In his patient, generous bosom he bears the anguish of a world. Bear thou, like him, in patience, and labor in love; for, sure as he is God, "the year of his redeemed *shall* come."[7]

The trader waked up bright and early, and came out to

see to his live-stock. It was now his turn to look about in perplexity.

"Where alive is that gal?" he said to Tom.

Tom, who had learned the wisdom of keeping counsel, did not feel called on to state his observations and suspicions, but said he did not know.

"She surely couldn't have got off in the night at any of the landings, for I was awake, and on the lookout, whenever the boat stopped. I never trust these yer things to other folks."

This speech was addressed to Tom quite confidentially, as if it was something that would be specially interesting to him. Tom made no answer.

The trader searched the boat from stem to stern, among boxes, bales, and barrels, around the machinery, by the chimneys, in vain.

"Now, I say, Tom, be fair about this yer," he said, when, after a fruitless search, he came where Tom was standing. "You know something about it, now. Don't tell me,—I know you do. I saw the gal stretched out here about ten o'clock, and ag'in at twelve, and ag'in between one and two; and then at four she was gone, and you was a-sleeping right there all the time. Now, you know something,—you can't help it."

"Well, Mas'r," said Tom, "towards morning something brushed by me, and I kinder half woke; and then I hearn a great splash, and then I clare woke up, and the gal was gone. That's all I know on 't."

The trader was not shocked nor amazed; because, as we said before, he was used to a great many things that you are not used to. Even the awful presence of Death struck no solemn chill upon him. He had seen Death many times,— met him in the way of trade, and got acquainted with him,—and he only thought of him as a hard customer that embarrassed his property operations very unfairly; and so he only swore that the gal was a baggage, and that he was devilish unlucky, and that, if things went on in this way, he should not make a cent on the trip. In short, he seemed to consider himself an ill-used man decidedly; but there was no help for it, as the woman had escaped into a state which *never will* give up a fugitive,—not even at the demand of the whole glorious Union. The trader, therefore, sat discontentedly down, with his little account-book, and put down the missing body and soul under the head of *losses!*

"He's a shocking creature, isn't he,—this trader? so unfeeling! It's dreadful, really!"

"Oh, but nobody thinks anything of these traders! They are universally despised,—never received into any decent society."

But who, sir, makes the trader? Who is most to blame? The enlightened, cultivated, intelligent man who supports the system of which the trader is the inevitable result, or the poor trader himself? You make the public sentiment that calls for his trade, that debauches and depraves him till he feels no shame in it; and in what are you better than he?

Are you educated and he ignorant, you high and he low, you refined and he coarse, you talented and he simple?

In the day of a future Judgment, these very considerations may make it more tolerable for him than for you.

In concluding these little incidents of lawful trade, we must beg the world not to think that American legislators are entirely destitute of humanity, as might, perhaps, be unfairly inferred from the great efforts made in our national body to protect and perpetuate this species of traffic.

Who does not know how our great men are outdoing themselves in declaiming against the *foreign* slave-trade? There are a perfect host of Clarksons and Wilberforces[8] risen up among us on that subject, most edifying to hear and behold. Trading negroes from Africa, dear reader, is so horrid. It is not to be thought of! But trading them from Kentucky,—that's quite another thing!

Notes

1. "In Rama was there a voice heard, lamentations, and weeping, and great mourning; Rachel weeping *for* her children, and would not be comforted, because they are not." *Matthew.* II, 18.

2. "For here we have no continuing city, but we seek one to come." *Hebrews.* XIII, 14. "But now they desire a better *country*, that is, an heavenly: wherefore God is not ashamed to be called their God: for he hath prepared for them a city." *Hebrews.* XI, 16.

3. "For there they that carried us away captive required of us a song; and they that wasted us *required of us* mirth, saying, Sing us *one* of the songs of Zion." *Psalms.* CXXXVII, 3.

4. "And he said, Cursed *be* Canaan: a servant of servants shall he be unto his brethren." *Genesis.* IX, 25.

5. Chapter XI, "In Which Property Gets into an Improper State of Mind."

6. "Therefore all things whatsoever ye would that men should to do you, do ye even so to them: for this is the law and the prophets." *Matthew.* VII, 12.

7. "For the day of vengeance *is* in mine heart, and the year of my redeemed is come." *Isaiah.* LXIII, 4.

8. Thomas Clarkson, 1760–1846, English abolitionist; William Wilberforce, 1750–1833, English opponent of the slave trade.

THE CONSPIRATORS
from *Dred*

Dred is a story about a wealthy, white, southern family, the Gordons. The novel is concerned with the four Gordon children—Nina and Tom, full biological offspring of the now dead parents, and Harry and Sue, the mulatto offspring of Mr. Gordon—and their relationships.

Dred: A Tale of the Great Dismal Swamp, first published in 1856, is based on the Southampton Insurrection in Virginia, 1831, led by Nat Turner, 1800–1831, a black minister. Among the insurrectionists was one named Dred. In this novel Harriet Beecher Stowe makes this historical figure a son of an earlier insurrectionist, Denmark Vesey, c.1767–1822. Télémaque (later corrupted to Denmark), after winning a lottery in 1800, bought his freedom for $600.00 and became a carpenter in Charleston, South Carolina. Saddened, perhaps, by the fact that his own children were being born and raised in slavery, he conspired with a small group from 1818 to 1822 to foment an uprising to rectify the situation. Upon discovery of the plot, Vesey was tried, convicted, and executed.

"The Conspirators" constitutes Chapter XIX of *Dred.*

We owe our readers now some words of explanation respecting the new personage who has been introduced into our history; therefore we must go back somewhat, and allude to certain historical events of painful significance.

It has been a problem to many, how the system of slavery in America should unite the two apparent inconsis-

(64)

tencies of a code of slave-laws more severe than that of any other civilized nation with an average practice at least as indulgent as any other; for bad as slavery is at the best, it may yet be admitted that the practice, as a whole, has been less cruel in this country than in many. An examination into history will show us that the cruelty of the laws resulted from the effects of indulgent practice. During the first years of importation of slaves into South Carolina, they enjoyed many privileges. Those who lived in intelligent families, and had any desire to learn, were instructed in reading and writing. Liberty was given them to meet in assemblies of worship, in class-meetings, and otherwise, without the presence of white witnesses; and many were raised to situations of trust and consequence. The result of this was the development of a good degree of intelligence and manliness among the slaves. There arose among them grave, thoughtful, energetic men, with their ears and eyes open, and their minds constantly awake to compare and reason.

When minds come into this state, in a government professing to be founded on principles of universal equality, it follows that almost every public speech, document, or newspaper becomes an incendiary publication.

Of this fact the southern slave states have ever exhibited the most singular unconsciousness. Documents containing sentiments most dangerous for slaves to hear have been publicly read and applauded among them. The slave has heard, amid shouts, on the Fourth of July, that his masters held the truth to be self-evident that all men were born equal, and had an *inalienable right* to life, liberty, and the pursuit of happiness; and that all governments derive their just power from the consent of the governed.[1] Even the mottoes of newspapers have embodied sentiments of the most insurrectionary character.

Such inscriptions as "Resistance to tyrants is obedience to God"[2] stand, to this day, in large letters, at the head of

(65)

southern newspapers; while speeches of senators and public men, in which the principles of universal democracy are asserted, are constant matters of discussion. Under such circumstances, it is difficult to induce the servant, who feels that he is a man, to draw those lines which seem so obvious to masters, by whom this fact has been forgotten. Accordingly we find that when the discussions for the admission of Missouri as a slave state[3] produced a wave whose waters undulated in every part of the Union, there were found among the slaves men of unusual thought and vigor, who were no inattentive witnesses and listeners. The discussions were printed in the newspapers; and what was printed in the newspapers was further discussed at the post-office door, in the tavern, in the bar-room, at the dinner-party, where black servants were listening behind the chairs. A free colored man in the city of Charleston, named Denmark Vesey, was the one who had the hardihood to seek to use the electric fluid in the cloud thus accumulated. He conceived the hopeless project of imitating the example set by the American race, and achieving independence for the blacks.

Our knowledge of this man is derived entirely from the printed reports of the magistrates who gave an account of the insurrection of which he was the instigator, and who will not, of course, be supposed to be unduly prejudiced in his favor. They state that he was first brought to the country by one Captain Vesey, a young lad, distinguished for personal beauty and great intelligence, and that he proved, for twenty years, a most faithful slave; but on drawing a prize of fifteen hundred dollars in the lottery, he purchased his freedom of his master, and worked as a carpenter in the city of Charleston. He was distinguished for strength and activity, and, as the accounts state, maintained such an irreproachable character, and enjoyed so much the confidence of the whites, that when he was accused, the charge was not only discredited, but he was not even arrested for several days after, and not till the proof of his guilt had become too strong to be doubted. His historians go on, with considerable *naïveté*, to remark:—

"It is difficult to conceive what motive he had to enter into such a plot, unless it was the one mentioned by one of the witnesses, who said that Vesey had several children who were slaves, and that he said, on one occasion, he wished he could see them free, as he himself artfully remarked in his defense on his trial."[4]

It appears that the project of rousing and animating the blacks to this enterprise occupied the mind of Vesey for more than four years, during which time he was continually taking opportunities to animate and inspire the spirits of his countrymen. The account states that the speeches in Congress of those opposed to the admission of Missouri into the Union, perhaps garbled and misrepresented, furnished him with ample means for inflaming the minds of the colored population.

"Even while walking in the street," the account goes on to say, "he was not idle; for if his companion bowed to a white person, as slaves universally do, he would rebuke him, and observe, 'that all men were born equal, and that he was surprised that any one would degrade himself by such conduct; that he would never cringe to the whites nor ought any one to who had the feelings of a man.'* When answered, 'We are slaves,' he would say sarcastically and indignantly, 'You deserve to remain slaves!' And if he were further asked, 'What can we do?' he would remark, 'Go and buy a spelling-book, and read the fable of "Hercules and the Wagoner." '[5] He also sought every opportunity of entering into conversation with white persons, during which conversation he would artfully introduce some bold remark on slavery; and sometimes, when, from the character he was conversing with, he found he might be still bolder,

---

* These extracts are taken from the official report.

he would go so far that, had not his declarations been clearly proved, they would scarcely have been credited."

But his great instrument of influence was a book that has always been prolific of insurrectionary movements, under all systems of despotism.

"He rendered himself perfectly familiar with all those parts of Scripture which he thought he could pervert to his purpose, and would readily quote them to prove that slavery was contrary to the laws of God, and that slaves were bound to attempt their emancipation, however shocking and bloody might be the consequences; that such efforts would not only be pleasing to the Almighty, but were absolutely enjoined."

Vesey, in the course of time, associated with himself five slave men of marked character—Rolla, Ned, Peter, Monday, and Gullah Jack. Of these, the account goes on to say:—

"In the selection of his leaders, Vesey showed great penetration and sound judgment. Rolla was plausible, and possessed uncommon self-possession; bold and ardent, he was not to be deterred from his purpose by danger. Ned's appearance indicated that he was a man of firm nerves and desperate courage. Peter was intrepid and resolute, true to his engagements, and cautious in observing secrecy where it was necessary; he was not to be daunted nor impeded by difficulties, and though confident of success, was careful in providing against any obstacles or casualties which might arise, and intent upon discovering every means which might be in their power, if thought of beforehand. Gullah Jack was regarded as a sorcerer, and, as such, feared by the natives of Africa, who believed in witchcraft. He was not only considered invulnerable, but that he could make others so by his charms, and that he could, and certainly would, provide all his followers with arms. He was artful, cruel, bloody; his disposition, in short, was diabolical. His influence among the Africans was inconceivable. Monday was firm, resolute, discreet, and intelligent.

"It is a melancholy truth that the general good conduct of all the leaders, except Gullah Jack, was such as rendered them objects least liable to suspicion. Their conduct had secured them, not only the unlimited confidence of their owners, but they had been indulged in every comfort, and allowed every privilege compatible with their situation in the community; and though Gullah Jack was not remarkable for the correctness of his deportment, he by no means sustained a bad character. But," adds the report, "not only were the leaders of good character, and very much indulged by their owners, but this was very generally the case with all who were convicted, many of them possessing the highest confidence of their owners, and not one a bad character.

"The conduct and behavior of Vesey and his five leaders during their trial and imprisonment may be interesting to many. When Vesey was tried, he folded his arms, and seemed to pay great attention to the testimony given against him, but with his eyes fixed on the floor. In this situation he remained immovable until the witnesses had been examined by the court, and cross-examined by his counsel, when he requested to be allowed to examine the witnesses himself, which he did. The evidence being closed, he addressed the court at considerable length. When he received his sentence, tears trickled down his cheeks.

"Rolla, when arraigned, affected not to understand the charge against him, and when, at his request, it was explained to him, assumed, with wonderful adroitness, astonishment and surprise. He was remarkable throughout his trial for composure and great presence of mind. When he was informed that he was convicted, and was advised to prepare for death, he appeared perfectly confounded, but exhibited no signs of fear.

"In Ned's behavior there was nothing remarkable. His countenance was stern and immovable, even while he was receiving sentence of death. From his looks it was impossible to discover or conjecture what were his feelings. Not so with Peter Poyes. In his countenance were strongly marked disappointed ambition, revenge, indignation, and an anxiety to know how far the discoveries had extended. He did not appear to fear personal consequences, for his whole behavior indicated the reverse, but exhibited an evident anxiety for the success of their plan, in which his whole soul was embarked. His countenance and behavior were the same when he received his sentence, and his only words were, on retiring, 'I suppose you'll let me see my wife and family before I die,' and that in no supplicating tone. When he was asked, a day or two after, 'If it was possible that he could see his master and family murdered, who had treated him so kindly?' he replied to the question only by a smile. In their prison, the convicts resolutely refused to make any confessions or communications which might implicate others; and Peter Poyes sternly enjoined it upon them to maintain this silence,—'Do not open your lips; die silent, as you will see me do!' and in this resolute silence they met their fate. Twenty-two of the conspirators were executed upon one gallows."

The account says that "Peter Poyes was one of the most active of the recruiting agents. All the principal conspirators kept a list of those who had consented to join them, and Peter was said, by one of the witnesses, to have had six hundred names on his list; but so resolutely to the last did he observe his pledge of secrecy to his associates, that, of the whole number arrested and tried, not one of them belonged to his company. In fact, in an insurrection in which thousands of persons were supposed to have been implicated, only thirty-six were convicted."

Among the children of Denmark Vesey was a boy by a Mandingo slave woman, who was his father's particular favorite. The Mandingos are one of the finest of African tribes, distinguished for intelligence, beauty of form, and an indomitable pride and energy of nature. As slaves, they are considered particularly valuable by those who have tact enough to govern them, because of their great capability and their proud faithfulness; but they resent a government of brute force, and under such are always fractious and dangerous.

This boy received from his mother the name of Dred; a name not unusual among the slaves, and generally given to those of great physical force.

The development of this child's mind was so uncommon as to excite astonishment among the negroes. He early acquired the power of reading, by an apparent instinctive faculty, and would often astonish those around him with things which he had discovered in books. Like other children of a deep and fervent nature, he developed great religious ardor, and often surprised the older negroes by his questions and replies on this subject. A son so endowed could not but be an object of great pride and interest to a father like Denmark Vesey. The impression seemed to prevail universally among the negroes that this child was born for extraordinary things; and perhaps it was the yearning to acquire liberty for the development of such a mind which first led Denmark Vesey to reflect on the nature of slavery, and the terrible weights which it lays on the human intellect, and to conceive the project of liberating a race.

The Bible, of which Vesey was an incessant reader, stimulated this desire. He likened his own position of comparative education, competence, and general esteem among the whites to that of Moses among the Egyptians; and nourished the idea that, like Moses, he was sent as a deliverer.[6] During the process of the conspiracy, this son, though but ten years of age, was his father's confidant; and he often charged him, though he should fail in the attempt, never to be discouraged. He impressed it upon his mind that he should never submit tamely to the yoke of slavery; and nourished the idea already impressed, that some more than ordinary destiny was reserved for him. After the discovery of the plot, and the execution of its leaders, those more immediately connected with them were sold from the state, even though not proved to have participated. With the most guarded caution, Vesey had exempted this son from suspicion. It had been an agreed policy with them both, that in the presence of others they should counterfeit alienation and dislike. Their confidential meetings with each other had been stolen and secret. At the time of his father's execution, Dred was a lad of fourteen. He could not be admitted to his father's prison, but he was a witness of the undaunted aspect with which he and the other conspirators met their doom. The memory dropped into the depths of his soul, as a stone drops into the desolate depths of a dark mountain lake.

Sold to a distant plantation, he became noted for his desperate, unsubduable disposition. He joined in none of the social recreations and amusements of the slaves, labored with proud and silent assiduity, but on the slightest rebuke or threat, flashed up with a savage fierceness which, supported by his immense bodily strength, made him an object of dread among overseers. He was one of those of whom they gladly rid themselves, and like a fractious horse, was sold from master to master. Finally, an overseer, hardier than the rest, determined on the task of subduing him. In the scuffle that ensued Dred struck him to the earth, a dead man, made his escape to the swamps, and was never afterwards heard of in civilized life.

The reader who consults the map will discover that the whole eastern shore of the southern states, with slight interruptions, is belted by an immense chain of swamps, regions of hopeless disorder, where the abundant growth and vegetation of nature, sucking up its forces from the humid soil, seem to rejoice in a savage exuberance, and bid defiance to all human efforts either to penetrate or subdue. These wild regions are the homes of the alligator, the moccasin, and the rattlesnake. Evergreen trees, mingling freely with the deciduous children of the forest, form here dense jungles, verdant all the year round, and which afford shelter to numberless birds, with whose warbling the leafy desolation perpetually resounds. Climbing vines and parasitic plants, of untold splendor and boundless exuberance of growth, twine and interlace, and hang from the heights of the highest trees pennons of gold and purple,—triumphal banners, which attest the solitary majesty of nature. A species of parasitic moss wreathes its abundant draperies from tree to tree, and hangs in pearly festoons through which shine the scarlet berry and green leaves of the American holly.

What the mountains of Switzerland were to the persecuted Vaudois,[7] this swampy belt has been to the American slave. The constant effort to recover from thence fugitives has led to the adoption, in these states, of a separate profession, unknown at this time in any other Christian land—hunters, who train and keep dogs for the hunting of men, women, and children. And yet, with all the convenience of this profession, the reclaiming of the fugitives from these fastnesses of nature has been a work of such expense and difficulty that the near proximity of the swamp has always been a considerable check on the otherwise absolute power of the overseer. Dred carried with him to the swamp but one solitary companion—the Bible of his father. To him it was not the messenger of peace and good will, but the herald of woe and wrath!

As the mind, looking on the great volume of nature, sees there a reflection of its own internal passions, and seizes on that in it which sympathizes with itself,—as the fierce and savage soul delights in the roar of torrents, the thunder of avalanches, and the whirl of ocean storms,—so

(73)

is it in the great answering volume of revelation. There is something there for every phase of man's nature; and hence its endless vitality and stimulating force. Dred had heard read in the secret meetings of conspirators the wrathful denunciations of ancient prophets against oppression and injustice. He had read of kingdoms convulsed by plagues; of tempest, and pestilence, and locusts; of the sea cleft in twain, that an army of slaves might pass through and of their pursuers whelmed in the returning waters. He had heard of prophets and deliverers, armed with supernatural powers, raised up for oppressed people; had pondered on the nail of Jael, the goad of Shamgar, the pitcher and lamp of Gideon; and thrilled with fierce joy as he read how Samson, with his two strong arms, pulled down the pillars of the festive temple, and whelmed his triumphant persecutors in one grave with himself.[8]

In the vast solitudes which he daily traversed, these things entered deep into his soul. Cut off from all human companionship, often going weeks without seeing a human face, there was no recurrence of every-day and prosaic ideas to check the current of the enthusiasm thus kindled. Even in the soil of the cool Saxon heart the Bible has thrown out its roots with an all-pervading energy, so that the whole framework of society may be said to rest on soil held together by its fibres. Even in cold and misty England, armies have been made defiant and invincible by the incomparable force and deliberate valor which it breathes into men. But when this Oriental seed,[9] an exotic among us, is planted back in the fiery soil of a tropical heart, it bursts forth with an incalculable ardor of growth.

A stranger cannot fail to remark the fact that, though the slaves of the South are unable to read the Bible for themselves, yet most completely have its language and sentiment penetrated among them, giving a Hebraistic coloring to their habitual mode of expression. How much greater, then, must have been the force of the solitary perusal of this volume on so impassioned a nature!—a nature, too, kindled by memories of the self-sacrificing ardor with which a father and his associates had met death at the call of freedom; for none of us may deny that, wild and hopeless as this scheme was, it was still the same in kind with the more successful one which purchased for our fathers a national existence.

A mind of the most passionate energy and vehemence, thus awakened, for years made the wild solitudes of the swamp its home. That book, so full of startling symbols and vague images, had for him no interpreter but the silent courses of nature. His life passed in a kind of dream. Sometimes, traversing for weeks these desolate regions, he would compare himself to Elijah traversing for forty days and nights the solitudes of Horeb; or to John the Baptist in the wilderness, girding himself with camel's hair, and eating locusts and wild honey.[10] Sometimes he would fast and pray for days; and then voices would seem to speak to him, and strange hieroglyphics would be written upon the leaves. In less elevated moods of mind, he would pursue, with great judgment and vigor, those enterprises necessary to preserve existence. The negroes lying out in the swamps are not so wholly cut off from society as might at first be imagined. The slaves of all the adjoining plantations, whatever they may pretend, to secure the good will of their owners, are at heart secretly disposed, from motives both of compassion and policy, to favor the fugitives. They very readily perceive that, in the event of any difficulty occurring to themselves, it might be quite necessary to have a friend and protector in the swamp; and therefore they do not hesitate to supply these fugitives, so far as they are able, with anything which they may desire. The poor whites, also, who keep small shops in the neighborhood of plantations, are never particularly scrupulous, provided they can turn a penny to their own advantage, and willingly supply necessary wares in exchange for game, with which the swamp abounds.

Dred, therefore, came in possession of an excellent rifle, and never wanted for ammunition, which supplied him with an abundance of food. Besides this, there are here and there elevated spots in the swampy land, which, by judicious culture, are capable of great productiveness. And many such spots Dred had brought under cultivation, either with his own hands, or from those of other fugitives, whom he had received and protected. From the restlessness of his nature, he had not confined himself to any particular region, but had traversed the whole swampy belt of both the Carolinas, as well as that of Southern Virginia; residing a few months in one place, and a few months in another. Wherever he stopped, he formed a sort of retreat, where he received and harbored fugitives. On one occasion, he rescued a trembling and bleeding mulatto woman from the dogs of the hunters, who had pursued her into the swamp. This woman he made his wife, and appeared to entertain a very deep affection for her. He made a retreat for her, with more than common ingenuity, in the swamp adjoining the Gordon plantation; and after that, he was more especially known in that locality. He had fixed his eye upon Harry, as a person whose ability, address, and strength of character might make him at some day a leader in a conspiracy against the whites. Harry, in common with many of the slaves on the Gordon plantation, knew perfectly well of the presence of Dred in the neighborhood, and had often seen and conversed with him. But neither he nor any of the rest of them ever betrayed before any white person the slightest knowledge of the fact.

This ability of profound secrecy is one of the invariable attendants of a life of slavery. Harry was acute enough to know that his position was by no means so secure that he could afford to dispense with anything which might prove an assistance in some future emergency. The low white traders in the neighborhood also knew Dred well; but as long as they could drive an advantageous trade with him he was secure from their intervention. So secure had he been, that he had been even known to mingle in the motley throng of a camp-meeting unmolested. Thus much with regard to one who is to appear often on the stage before our history is done.

Notes

1. Patriotic oratory at Independence Day celebrations frequently included the recitation of or quotations from the Declaration of Independence, first issued on July 4, 1776.

2. "Rebellion to tyrants is obedience to God" (anonymous) was the motto inscribed on the seal of Thomas Jefferson, 1743–1826, the principal writer of the Declaration of Independence and later the third president of the United States, 1801–1809.

3. The Missouri Compromise, 1820, led to the admission of Missouri into the Union in 1821 as a slave state; whereas in all remaining territory, slavery thereafter should be forever prohibited.

4. *An Account of the Late Intended Insurrection among a Portion of the Blacks of This City. Published by the Authority of the Corporation of Charleston* (South Carolina, 1822) and repeated in *An Official Report of the Trials of Sundry Negroes Charged with an Attempt to Raise an Insurrection in the State of South Carolina* (1822) by L.H. Kennedy and Thomas Parker. Stowe quotes extensively from this account, as she acknowledges in a footnote.

5. One of Aesop's fables, the moral of which is that Heaven helps those who first help themselves. Traditionally, Aesop is credited with being a 6th-century fabulist.

6. In the Old Testament, Moses led the Hebrews, enslaved in Egypt, to freedom and founded the Israelite nation.

7. The inhabitants of Vaud, a canton in Switzerland, were historically persecuted because of their allegiance to the Protestant Reformation.

8. All references are to episodes in the Old Testament and tell of defeating an oppressor. Jael killed the king of Canaan, who had sought refuge in her tent, by hammering a tent nail through his temples while he slept. Shamgar slew 600 of his foes with an oxgoad, or cattle prod. Gideon, in facing his enemies, furnished 300 of his men with trumpets, earthen pitchers, and lamps. After dividing them into three groups that surrounded the hostile forces, he instructed them to respond to his signal by simultaneously blowing the instruments, smashing the vessels, and holding aloft the torches. The resulting din caught the enemies unawares, scattering their troops in alarm. Samson, chained by his oppressors to the two main pillars of a house in which they were assembled to feast and make fun of the helpless prisoner, prayed to God for the strength to pull down the pillars with his own hands. Crouching, he exerted all his might, and the building collapsed, killing thousands of his foes.

9. Symbolically, the Bible.

10. In the Old Testament, Elijah the Prophet, sentenced to death for his beliefs, fled from his enemies and traveled in the wilderness until he received divine instructions. John the Baptist, the last Hebrew prophet in the New Testament, foretold the coming of Jesus Christ.

THE FRIENDS AND RELATIONS OF JAMES

from *The Minister's Wooing*

Set in 18th-century Newport, Rhode Island, *The Minister's Wooing* tells the story of the romance between Mary Scudder and James Marvyn, her wayward cousin. Mary's mother, the housekeeper for Dr. Samuel Hopkins, a prominent clergyman and theologian, wants her daughter to marry the eminent minister. Mary, secretly in love with James, who is presumed lost at sea, agrees to the engagement. Complications arise, however, when James returns home—very much alive.

From December 1858 through December 1859 the *Atlantic Monthly* ran installments of *The Minister's Wooing*. In 1859 the novel was offered in a two-volume set. "The Friends and Relations of James" is Chapter VII of *The Minister's Wooing*.

Mr. Zebedee Marvyn, the father of James, was the sample of an individuality so purely the result of New England society and education, that he must be embodied in our story as a representative man of the times.

He owned a large farm in the immediate vicinity of Newport, which he worked with his own hands and kept under the most careful cultivation. He was a man past the middle of life, with a white head, a keen blue eye, and a face graven deeply with the lines of energy and thought. His was one of those clearly cut minds which New England forms among her farmers, as she forms quartz crystals in her mountains, by a sort of gradual influence flowing through every pore of her soil and system.

His education, properly so called, had been merely that of those common schools and academies with which the States are thickly sown, and which are the springs of so much intellectual activity. Here he had learned to think and to inquire,—a process which had not ceased with his school-days. Though toiling daily with his sons and hired man in all the minutiæ of a farmer's life, he kept an observant eye on the field of literature, and there was not a new publication heard of which he did not immediately find means to add to his yearly increasing stock of books. In particular was he a well-read and careful theologian, and all the controversial tracts, sermons, and books, with which then (as ever since) New England abounded, not only lay on his shelves, but had his penciled annotations, queries, and comments thickly scattered along their margins. There was scarce an office of public trust which had not at one time or another been filled by him. He was deacon of the church, chairman of the school-committee, justice of the peace, had been twice representative in the State legislature, and was in permanence a sort of adviser-general in all cases between neighbor and neighbor. Among other acquisitions, he had gained some knowledge of the general forms of law, and his advice was often asked in preference to that of the regular practitioners.

His dwelling was one of those large, square, white, green-blinded mansions, cool, clean, and roomy, wherein the respectability of New England in those days rejoiced. The windows were shaded by clumps of lilacs; the deep yard with its white fence inclosed a sweep of clean, short grass, and a few fruit trees. Opposite the house was a small blacksmith's-shed, which, of a wet day, was sparkling and lively with bellows and ringing forge, while Mr. Zebedee and his sons were hammering and pounding and putting in order anything that was out of the way in farming-tools or establishments. Not unfrequently the latest scientific work or the last tractate of theology lay open by his side, the contents of which would be discussed with a neighbor or two as they entered; for, to say the truth, many a neighbor, less forehanded and thrifty, felt the benefit of this arrangement of Mr. Zebedee, and would drop in to see if he "wouldn't just tighten that rivet," or "kind o' ease out that 'ere brace," or "let a feller have a turn with his bellows, or a stroke or two on his anvil,"—to all which the good man consented with a grave obligingness. The fact was, that, as nothing in the establishment of Mr. Marvyn was often broken or lost or out of place, he had frequent applications to lend to those less fortunate persons, always to be found, who supply their own lack of considerateness from the abundance of their neighbors.

He who is known always to be in hand, and always obliging, in a neighborhood, stands the chance sometimes of having nothing for himself. Mr. Zebedee reflected quietly on this subject, taking it, as he did all others, into grave and orderly consideration, and finally provided a complete set of tools, which he kept for the purpose of lending; and when any of these were lent, he told the next applicant quietly, that the axe or the hoe was already out, and thus he reconciled the Scripture which commanded him "to do good and lend"[1] with that law of order which was written in his nature.

Early in life Mr. Marvyn had married one of the handsomest girls of his acquaintance, who had brought him a thriving and healthy family of children, of whom James was the youngest. Mrs. Marvyn was, at this time, a tall, sad-eyed, gentle-mannered woman, thoughtful, earnest, deep-natured, though sparing in the matter of words. In all her household arrangements, she had the same thrift and order which characterized her husband; but hers was a mind of a finer and higher stamp than his.

In her bedroom, near by her work-basket, stood a table covered with books; and so systematic were her household arrangements, that she never any day missed her regular hours for reading. One who should have looked over this table would have seen there how eager and hungry a mind was hid behind the silent eyes of this quiet woman. History, biography, mathematics, volumes of the encyclopædia, poetry, novels, all alike found their time and place there; and while she pursued her household labors, the busy, active soul within traveled cycles and cycles of thought, few of which ever found expression in words. What might be that marvelous music of the Miserere,[2] of which she read, that it convulsed crowds and drew groans and tears from the most obdurate? What might be those wondrous pictures of Raphael and Leonardo da Vinci?[3] What would it be to see the Apollo, the Venus?[4] What was the charm that enchanted the old marbles,—charm untold and inconceivable to one who had never seen even the slightest approach to a work of art? Then those glaciers of Switzerland, that grand, unapproachable mixture of beauty and sublimity in her mountains!—what would it be to one who could see it? Then what were all those harmonies of which she read,— masses, fugues, symphonies? Oh, could she once hear the Miserere of Mozart,[5] just to know what music was like! And the cathedrals, what were they? How wonderful they must be, with their forests of arches, many-colored as autumn woods with painted glass, and the chants and anthems rolling down their long aisles! On all these things she pondered quietly, as she sat often on Sundays in the old staring, rattle-windowed meeting-house, and looked at the uncouth old pulpit, and heard the choir faw-sol-la-ing or singing fuguing tunes; but of all this she said nothing.

Sometimes, for days, her thoughts would turn from these subjects and be absorbed in mathematical or metaphysical studies. "I have been following that treatise on Optics for a week, and never understood it till to-day," she once said to her husband. "I have found now that there has been a mistake in drawing the diagrams. I have corrected

(82)

it, and now the demonstration is complete. Dinah, take care, that wood is hickory, and it takes only seven sticks of that size to heat the oven."

It is not to be supposed that a woman of this sort was an inattentive listener to preaching so stimulating to the intellect as that of Dr. Hopkins. No pair of eyes followed the web of his reasonings with a keener and more anxious watchfulness than those sad, deep-set, hazel ones; and as she was drawn along the train of its inevitable logic, a close observer might have seen how the shadows deepened over them. For, while others listened for the clearness of the thought, for the acuteness of the argument, she listened as a soul wide, fine-strung, acute, repressed, whose every fibre is a nerve, listens to the problem of its own destiny,— listened as the mother of a family listens, to know what were the possibilities, the probabilities, of this mysterious existence of ours to herself and those dearer to her than herself.

The consequence of all her listening was a history of deep inward sadness. That exultant joy or that entire submission, with which others seemed to view the scheme of the universe, as thus unfolded, did not visit her mind. Everything to her seemed shrouded in gloom and mystery; and that darkness she received as a token of unregeneracy, as a sign that she was one of those who are destined, by a mysterious decree, never to receive the light of the glorious gospel of Christ. Hence, while her husband was a deacon of the church, she, for years, had sat in her pew while the sacramental elements were distributed, a mournful spectator. Punctilious in every duty, exact, reverential, she still regarded herself as a child of wrath, an enemy to God, and an heir of perdition; nor could she see any hope of remedy, except in the sovereign, mysterious decree of an Infinite and Unknown Power, a mercy for which she waited with the sickness of hope deferred.

Her children had grown up successively around her, intelligent and exemplary. Her eldest son was mathematical professor in one of the leading colleges of New England. Her second son, who jointly with his father superintended the farm, was a man of wide literary culture and of fine mathematical genius; and not unfrequently, on winter evenings, the son, father, and mother worked together, by their kitchen fireside, over the calculations for the almanac for the ensuing year, which the son had been appointed to edit.

Everything in the family arrangements was marked by a sober precision, a grave and quiet self-possession. There was little demonstrativeness of affection between parents and children, brothers and sisters, though great mutual love and confidence. It was not pride, nor sternness, but a sort of habitual shamefacedness, that kept far back in each soul those feelings which are the most beautiful in their outcome; but after a while, the habit became so fixed a nature, that a caressing or affectionate expression could not have passed the lips of one to another without a painful awkwardness. Love was understood, once for all, to be the basis on which their life was built. Once for all, they loved each other, and after that, the less said, the better. It had cost the woman's heart of Mrs. Marvyn some pangs, in the earlier part of her wedlock, to accept of this once for all in place of those daily outgushings which every woman desires should be like God's loving-kindnesses, "new every morning;"[6] but hers, too, was a nature strongly inclining inward, and, after a few tremulous movements, the needle of her soul settled, and her life-lot was accepted,—not as what she would like or could conceive, but as a reasonable and good one. Life was a picture painted in low, cool tones, but in perfect keeping; and though another and brighter style might have pleased better, she did not quarrel with this.

Into this steady, decorous, highly respectable circle the youngest child, James, made a formidable irruption. One sometimes sees launched into a family circle a child of so different a nature from all the rest, that it might seem as if, like an aerolite, he had fallen out of another sphere. All the other babies of the Marvyn family had been of that orderly, contented sort, who sleep till it is convenient to take them up, and while awake suck their thumbs contentedly and look up with large, round eyes at the ceiling when it is not convenient for their elders and betters that they should do anything else. In farther advanced childhood, they had been quiet and decorous children, who could be all dressed and set up in chairs, like so many dolls, of a Sunday morning, patiently awaiting the stroke of the church-bell to be carried out and put into the wagon which took them over the two-miles' road to church. Possessed of such tranquil, orderly, and exemplary young offshoots, Mrs. Marvyn had been considered eminent for her "faculty" in bringing up children.

But James was destined to put "faculty," and every other talent which his mother possessed, to rout. He was an infant of moods and tenses, and those not of any regular verb. He would cry of nights, and he would be taken up of mornings, and he would not suck his thumb, nor a bundle of caraway-seed tied in a rag and dipped in sweet milk, with which the good gossips in vain endeavored to pacify him. He fought manfully with his two great fat fists the battle of babyhood, utterly reversed all nursery maxims, and reigned as baby over the whole prostrate household. When old enough to run alone, his splendid black eyes and glossy rings of hair were seen flashing and bobbing in every forbidden place and occupation. Now trailing on his mother's gown, he assisted her in salting her butter by throwing in small contributions of snuff or sugar, as the case might be; and again, after one of those mysterious periods of silence which are of most ominous significance in nursery experience, he would rise from the demolition of her indigo-bag, showing a face ghastly with blue streaks, and looking more like a gnome than the son of a respectable mother. There

(85)

was not a pitcher of any description of contents left within reach of his little tiptoes and busy fingers that was not pulled over upon his giddy head without in the least seeming to improve its steadiness. In short, his mother remarked that she was thankful every night when she had fairly gotten him into bed and asleep; James had really got through one more day and killed neither himself nor any one else.

As a boy, the case was little better. He did not take to study,—yawned over books, and cut out moulds for running anchors when he should have been thinking of his columns of words in four syllables. No mortal knew how he learned to read, for he never seemed to stop running long enough to learn anything; and yet he did learn, and used the talent in conning over travels, sea-voyages, and lives of heroes and naval commanders. Spite of father, mother, and brother, he seemed to possess the most extraordinary faculty of running up unsavory acquaintances. He was hale-fellow well-met with every Tom and Jack and Jim and Ben and Dick that strolled on the wharves, and astonished his father with minutest particulars of every ship, schooner, and brig in the harbor, together with biographical notes of the different Toms, Dicks, and Harrys by whom they were worked.

There was but one member of the family that seemed to know at all what to make of James, and that was their negro servant, Candace.

In those days, when domestic slavery prevailed in New England, it was quite a different thing in its aspects from the same institution in more southern latitudes. The hard soil, unyielding to any but the most considerate culture, the thrifty, close, shrewd habits of the people, and their untiring activity and industry, prevented, among the mass of the people, any great reliance on slave labor.

Added to this, there were from the very first, in New England, serious doubts in the minds of thoughtful and conscientious people in reference to the lawfulness of slavery; this scruple prevented many from availing themselves of it, and proved a restraint on all, so that nothing like plantation-life existed, and what servants were owned were scattered among different families, of which they came to be regarded and to regard themselves as a legitimate part and portion. Slavery was something foreign, grotesque, and picturesque in a life of the most matter-of-fact sameness; it was even as if one should see clusters of palm-trees scattered here and there among Yankee wooden meeting-houses, or open one's eyes on clumps of yellow-striped aloes growing among hardhack and huckleberry bushes in the pastures.

Mr. Marvyn, as a man of substance, numbered two or three in his establishment, among whom Candace reigned chief. The presence of these tropical specimens of humanity, with their wide, joyous, rich, physical abundance of nature, and their hearty *abandon* of outward expression, was a relief to the still, clear-cut lines in which the picture of New England life was drawn, that an artist must appreciate.

No race has ever shown such infinite and rich capabilities of adaptation to varying soil and circumstances as the negro. Alike to them the snows of Canada, the hard, rocky land of New England, with its set lines and orderly ways, or the gorgeous profusion and loose abundance of the Southern States. Sambo and Cuffy expand under them all. New England yet preserves among her hills and valleys the lingering echoes of the jokes and jollities of various sable worthies, who saw alike in orthodoxy and heterodoxy, in Dr. This-side and Dr. That-side, only food for more abundant merriment; in fact, the minister of those days not unfrequently had his black shadow, a sort of African Boswell,[7] who powdered his wig, brushed his boots, defended and patronized his sermons, and strutted complacently about as if through virtue of his blackness he had absorbed every ray of his master's dignity and wisdom. In

(87)

families, the presence of these exotics was a godsend to the children, supplying from the abundant outwardness and demonstrativeness of their nature that aliment of sympathy so dear to childhood, which the repressed and quiet habits of New England education denied. Many and many a New Englander counts among his pleasantest early recollections the memory of some of these genial creatures, who by their warmth of nature were the first and most potent mesmerizers of his childish mind.

Candace was a powerfully built, majestic black woman, corpulent, heavy, with a swinging majesty of motion like that of a ship in a ground-swell. Her shining black skin and glistening white teeth were indications of perfect physical vigor which had never known a day's sickness; her turban, of broad red and yellow bandanna stripes, had even a warm tropical glow; and her ample skirts were always ready to be spread over every childish transgression of her youngest pet and favorite, James.

She used to hold him entranced long winter evenings, while she sat knitting in the chimney-corner, and crooned to him strange, wild African legends of the things that she had seen in her childhood and early days, for she had been stolen when about fifteen years of age; and these weird, dreamy talks increased the fervor of his roving imagination, and his desire to explore the wonders of the wide and unknown world. When rebuked or chastised, it was she who had secret bowels of mercy for him, and hid doughnuts in her ample bosom to be secretly administered to him in mitigation of the sentence that sent him supperless to bed; and many a triangle of pie, many a wedge of cake, had conveyed to him surreptitious consolations which his more conscientious mother longed, but dared not, to impart. In fact, these ministrations, if suspected, were winked at by Mrs. Marvyn, for two reasons: first, that mothers are generally glad of any loving-kindness to an erring boy, which they are not responsible for; and second, that Candace was so set in her ways and opinions that one might as well come in front of a ship under full sail as endeavor to stop her on a matter where her heart was engaged.

To be sure, she had her own private and special quarrels with "Massa James" when he disputed any of her sovereign orders in the kitchen, and would sometimes pursue him with uplifted rolling-pin and floury hands when he had snatched a gingernut or cookey without suitable deference or supplication, and would declare, roundly, that there "never was sich an aggravatin' young un." But if, on the strength of this, any one else ventured a reproof, Candace was immediately round on the other side: "Dat ar' chile gwin' to be spiled, 'cause dey's allers a-pickin' at him; he's well enough, on'y let him alone."

Well, under this miscellaneous assortment of influences,—through the order and gravity and solemn monotone of life at home, with the unceasing tick-tack of the clock forever resounding through clean, empty-seeming rooms,—through the sea, ever shining, ever smiling, dimpling, soliciting, like a magical charger who comes saddled and bridled and offers to take you to fairyland,—through acquaintance with all sorts of foreign, outlandish ragamuffins among the ships in the harbor,—from disgust of slow-moving oxen, and long-drawn, endless furrows round the fifteen-acre lot,—from misunderstandings with grave elder brothers, and feeling somehow as if, he knew not why, he grieved his mother all the time just by being what he was and couldn't help being,—and finally, by a bitter break with his father, in which came that last wrench for an individual existence which some time or other the young growing mind will give to old authority,—by all these united, was the lot at length cast; for one evening James was missing at supper, missing by the fireside, gone all night, not at home to breakfast,—till, finally, a strange, weird, most heathenish-looking cabin-boy, who had often been forbidden the premises by Mr. Marvyn, brought in a letter, half-defiant, half-penitent, which announced that James had sailed in the Ariel the evening before.

Mr. Zebedee Marvyn set his face as a flint, and said, "He went out from us because he was not of us;"[8] whereat old Candace lifted her great floury fist from the kneading-trough, and, shaking it like a large snowball, said, "Oh, you go 'long, Massa Marvyn; ye'll live to count dat ar' boy for de staff o' your old age yet, now I tell ye; got de makin' o' ten or'nary men in him; kittles dat's full allers will bile over; good yeast will blow out de cork,—lucky ef it don't bust de bottle. Tell ye, der's angels has der hooks in sich, and when de Lord wants him dey'll haul him in safe and sound." And Candace concluded her speech by giving a lift to her whole batch of dough and flinging it down in the trough with an emphasis that made the pewter on the dresser rattle.

This apparently irreverent way of expressing her mind, so contrary to the deferential habits studiously incul-cated in family discipline, had grown to be so much a matter of course to all the family that nobody ever thought of rebuking it. There was a sort of savage freedom about her which they excused in right of her having been born and bred a heathen, and of course not to be expected to come at once under the yoke of civilization. In fact, you must all have noticed, my dear readers, that there are some sorts of people for whom everybody turns out as they would for a railroad-car, without stopping to ask why; and Candace was one of them.

Moreover, Mr. Marvyn was not displeased with this defense of James, as might be inferred from his mention-ing it four or five times in the course of the morning, to say how foolish it was,—wondering why it was that Candace and everybody else got so infatuated with that boy, and ending, at last, after a long period of thought, with the remark that these poor African creatures often seemed to have a great deal of shrewdness in them, and that he was often astonished at the penetration that Candace showed.

At the end of the year James came home, more quiet and manly than he had ever been before,—so handsome with his sunburnt face, and his keen, dark eyes and glossy curls, that half the girls in the front gallery lost their hearts the first Sunday he appeared in church. He was tender as a woman to his mother, and followed her with his eyes, like a lover, wherever she went; he made due and manly acknowledgments to his father, but declared his fixed and settled intention to abide by the profession he had chosen; and he brought home all sorts of strange foreign gifts for every member of the household. Candace was glorified with a flaming red and yellow turban of Moorish stuff, from Mogadore, together with a pair of gorgeous yellow morocco slippers with peaked toes, which, though there appeared no call to wear them in her common course of life, she would put on her fat feet and contemplate with daily satisfaction. She became increasingly strengthened thereby in the conviction that the angels who had their hooks in Massa James's jacket were already beginning to shorten the line.

Notes

1. "But love ye your enemies, and do good, and lend, hoping for nothing again; and your reward shall be great, and ye shall be the children of the Highest: for he is kind unto the unthankful and *to* the evil." *Luke.* VI, 35.

2. Any of several musical renditions of the 50th Psalm of the Vulgate, an edition of the Latin Bible used by the Roman Catholic Church.

3. Raphael Sanzio, 1483–1520, and Leonardo da Vinci, 1452–1510, renowned Italian artists.

4. Any of a number of sculptures representing the Roman deities of the sun (Apollo) and love (Venus).

5. Wolfgang Amadeus Mozart, 1756–1791, Austrian composer and musician.

6. *Lamentations.* III, 23.

7. James Boswell, 1740–1795, Scottish biographer of Samuel Johnson, 1709–1784, English author and lexicographer. For two decades Boswell followed after Johnson, recording his every word and deed; in 1791 he published his *Life of Johnson,* considered by many critics the finest biography ever written.

8. "They went out from us, but they were not of us; for if they had been of us, they would *no doubt* have continued with us: but *they went out,* that they might be made manifest that they were not all of us." *I John.* II, 19.

THE TEST OF THEOLOGY
from *The Minister's Wooing*

For years the Rev. Dr. Samuel Hopkins has been working on his System of Theology, a work he hopes to publish that will set forth clearly man's relationship to God. Hopkins solicits the support of Simeon Brown, a wealthy Newport slave trader and leading contributor in Hopkins's congregation, to stop immediately the traffic in human beings.
"The Test of Theology" is Chapter X of *The Minister's Wooing*.

The Doctor went immediately to his study and put on his best coat and his wig, and, surmounting them by his cocked hat, walked manfully out of the house, with his gold-headed cane in his hand.

"There he goes!" said Mrs. Scudder, looking regretfully after him. "He is *such* a good man! but he has not the least idea how to get along in the world. He never thinks of anything but what is true; he hasn't a particle of management about him."

"Seems to me," said Mary, "that is like an Apostle. You know, mother, St. Paul says, 'In simplicity and godly sincerity, not with fleshly wisdom, but by the grace of God, we have had our conversation in the world.' "[1]

"To be sure,—that is just the Doctor," said Mrs. Scudder; "that's as like him as if it had been written for him. But that kind of way, somehow, don't seem to do in our times; it won't answer with Simeon Brown,—I know the man. I know just as well, now, how it will all seem to him, and what will be the upshot of this talk, if the Doctor goes there! It won't do any good; if it would, I would be willing. I feel as much desire to have this horrid trade in slaves stopped as anybody; your father, I'm sure, said enough about it in his time; but then I know it's no use trying. Just as if Simeon Brown, when he is making his hundreds of thousands in it, is going to be persuaded to give it up! He won't; he'll only turn against the Doctor, and won't pay his part of the salary, and will use his influence to get up a party against him, and our church will be broken up and the Doctor driven away,—that's all that will come of it; and all the good that he is doing now to these poor negroes will be overthrown, and they never will have so good a friend. If he would stay here and work gradually, and get his System of Theology printed,—and Simeon Brown would help at that,—and only drop words in season here and there, till people are brought along with him, why, by and by something might be done; but now, it's just the most imprudent thing a man could undertake."

"But, mother, if it really is a sin to trade in slaves and hold them, I don't see how he can help himself. I quite agree with him. I don't see how he came to let it go so long as he has."

"Well," said Mrs. Scudder, "if worst comes to worst, and he will do it, I, for one, shall stand by him to the last."

"And I, for another," said Mary.

"I would like him to talk with Cousin Zebedee about it," said Mrs. Scudder. "When we are up there this afternoon, we will introduce the conversation. He is a good, sound man, and the Doctor thinks much of him, and perhaps he may shed some light upon this matter."

Meanwhile the Doctor was making the best of his way, in the strength of his purpose to test the orthodoxy of Simeon Brown.

Honest old granite boulder that he was, no sooner did he perceive a truth than he rolled after it with all the massive gravitation of his being, inconsiderate as to what might lie in his way; from which it is to be inferred, that, with all his intellect and goodness, he would have been a very clumsy and troublesome inmate of the modern American Church. How many societies, boards, colleges, and other good institutions have reason to congratulate themselves that he has long been among the saints!

With him logic was everything, and to perceive a truth and not act in logical sequence from it a thing so incredible, that he had not yet enlarged his capacity to take it in as a possibility. That a man should refuse to hear truth, he could understand. In fact, he had good reason to think the majority of his townsmen had no leisure to give to that purpose. That men hearing truth should dispute it and argue stoutly against it, he could also understand; but that a man could admit a truth and not admit the plain practice resulting from it was to him a thing incomprehensible. Therefore, spite of Mrs. Katy Scudder's discouraging observations, our good Doctor walked stoutly and with a trusting heart.

At the moment when the Doctor, with a silent uplifting of his soul to his invisible Sovereign, passed out of his study, on this errand, where was the disciple whom he went to seek?

In a small, dirty room, down by the wharf, the windows veiled by cobwebs and dingy with the accumulated dust of ages, he sat in a greasy leathern chair by a rickety office table, on which were a great pewter inkstand, an account book, and divers papers tied with red tape.

Opposite to him was seated a square-built individual, a man of about forty, whose round head, shaggy eyebrows, small, keen eyes, broad chest, and heavy muscles showed a preponderance of the animal and brutal over the intellectual and spiritual. This was Mr. Scroggs, the agent of a rice plantation, who had come on, bringing an order for a new relay of negroes to supply the deficit occasioned by fever, dysentery, and other causes, in their last year's stock.

"The fact is," said Simeon, "this last shipload wasn't as

good a one as usual; we lost more than a third of it, so we can't afford to put them a penny lower."

"Ay," said the other, "but then there are so many women!"

"Well," said Simeon, "women ain't so strong, perhaps, to start with, but then they stan' it out, perhaps, in the long run, better. They're more patient; some of these men, the Mandingoes, particularly, are pretty troublesome to manage. We lost a splendid fellow, coming over, on this very voyage. Let 'em on deck for air, and this fellow managed to get himself loose and fought like a dragon. He settled one of our men with his fist, and another with a marlinspike that he caught,—and, in fact, they had to shoot him down. You'll have his wife; there's his son, too,—fine fellow, fifteen year old by his teeth."

"What! that lame one?"

"Oh, he ain't lame! it's nothing but the cramps from stowing. You know, of course, they are more or less stiff. He's as sound as a nut."

"Don't much like to buy relations, on account of their hatching up mischief together," said Mr. Scroggs.

"Oh, that's all humbug! You must keep 'em from coming together, anyway. It's about as broad as 't is long. There'll be wives and husbands and children among 'em before long, start 'em as you will. And then this woman will work better for having the boy; she's kinder set on him; she jabbers lots of lingo to him, day and night."

"Too much, I doubt," said the overseer, with a shrug.

"Well, well, I'll tell you," said Simeon, rising. "I've got a few errands up town, and you just step over with Matlock and look over the stock; just set aside any that you want, and when I see 'em all together, I'll tell you just what you shall have 'em for. I'll be back in an hour or two."

And so saying, Simeon Brown called an underling from an adjoining room, and, committing his customer to his care, took his way up town, in a serene frame of mind, like a man who comes from the calm performance of duty.

Just as he came upon the street where was situated his own large and somewhat pretentious mansion, the tall figure of the Doctor loomed in sight, sailing majestically down upon him, making a signal to attract his attention.

"Good morning, Doctor," said Simeon.

"Good morning, Mr. Brown," said the Doctor. "I was looking for you. I did not quite finish the subject we were talking about at Mrs. Scudder's table last night. I thought I should like to go on with it a little."

"With all my heart, Doctor," said Simeon, not a little flattered. "Turn right in. Mrs. Brown will be about her house business, and we will have the keeping-room all to ourselves. Come right in."

The "keeping-room" of Mr. Simeon Brown's house was an intermediate apartment between the ineffable glories of the front parlor and that court of the gentiles, the kitchen; for the presence of a large train of negro servants made the latter apartment an altogether different institution from the throne-room of Mrs. Katy Scudder.

This keeping-room was a low-studded apartment, finished with the heavy oaken beams of the wall left full in sight, boarded over and painted. Two windows looked out on the street, and another into a sort of courtyard, where three black wenches, each with a broom, pretended to be sweeping, but were in fact chattering and laughing, like so many crows.

On one side of the room stood a heavy mahogany sideboard, covered with decanters, labeled Gin, Brandy, Rum, etc.; for Simeon was held to be a provider of none but the best, in his housekeeping. Heavy mahogany chairs, with crewel coverings, stood sentry about the room; and the fireplace was flanked by two broad armchairs, covered with stamped leather.

(97)

On ushering the Doctor into this apartment, Simeon courteously led him to the sideboard.

"We mustn't make our discussions too dry, Doctor," he said. "What will you take?"

"Thank you, sir," said the Doctor, with a wave of his hand, "nothing this morning."

And depositing his cocked hat in a chair, he settled himself into one of the leathern easy chairs, and, dropping his hands upon his knees, looked fixedly before him, like a man who is studying how to enter upon an inwardly absorbing subject.

"Well, Doctor," said Simeon, seating himself opposite, sipping comfortably at a glass of rum and water, "our views appear to be making a noise in the world. Everything is preparing for your volumes; and when they appear, the battle of New Divinity,[2] I think, may fairly be considered as won."

Let us consider that though a woman may forget her firstborn, yet a man cannot forget his own system of theology,—because therein, if he be a true man, is the very elixir and essence of all that is valuable and hopeful to the universe; and considering this, let us appreciate the settled purpose of our friend, whom even this tempting bait did not swerve from the end which he had in view.

"Mr. Brown," he said, "all our theology is as a drop in the ocean of God's majesty, to whose glory we must be ready to make any and every sacrifice."

"Certainly," said Mr. Brown, not exactly comprehending the turn the Doctor's thoughts were taking.

"And the glory of God consisteth in the happiness of all his rational universe, each in his proportion, according to his separate amount of being, so that when we devote ourselves to God's glory, it is the same as saying that we devote ourselves to the highest happiness of his created universe."

"That's clear, sir," said Simeon, rubbing his hands, and taking out his watch to see the time.

The Doctor hitherto had spoken in a laborious manner, like a man who is slowly lifting a heavy bucket of thought out of an internal well.

"I am glad to find your mind so clear on this all-important point, Mr. Brown,—the more so as I feel that we must immediately proceed to apply our principles, at whatever sacrifice of worldly goods; and I trust, sir, that you are one who at the call of your Master would not hesitate even to lay down all your worldly possessions for the greater good of the universe."

"I trust so, sir," said Simeon, rather uneasily, and without the most distant idea what could be coming next in the mind of his reverend friend.

"Did it never occur to you, my friend," said the Doctor, "that the enslaving of the African race is a clear violation of the great law which commands us to love our neighbor as ourselves, and a dishonor upon the Christian religion, more particularly in us Americans, whom the Lord hath so marvelously protected in our recent struggle for our own liberty?"[3]

Simeon started at the first words of this address, much as if some one had dashed a bucket of water on his head, and after that rose uneasily, walking the room and playing with the seals of his watch.

"I—I never regarded it in this light," he said.

"Possibly not, my friend," said the Doctor, "so much doth established custom blind the minds of the best of men. But since I have given more particular attention to the case of the poor negroes here in Newport, the thought has more and more labored in my mind,—more especially as our own struggles for liberty have turned my attention to the rights which every human creature hath before God,— so that I find much in my former blindness and the comparative dumbness I have heretofore maintained on this subject wherewith to reproach myself; for, though I have borne somewhat of a testimony, I have not given it that force which so important a subject required. I am humbled before God for my neglect, and resolved now by His grace to leave no stone unturned till this iniquity be purged away from our Zion."[4]

"Well, Doctor," said Simeon, "you are certainly touching on a very dark and difficult subject, and one in which it is hard to find out the path of duty. Perhaps it will be well to bear it in mind, and by looking at it prayerfully some light may arise. There are such great obstacles in the way, that I do not see at present what can be done; do you, Doctor?"

"I intend to preach on the subject next Sunday, and hereafter devote my best energies in the most public way to this great work," said the Doctor.

"You, Doctor?—and now, immediately? Why, it appears to me you cannot do it. You are the most unfit man possible. Whosoever duty it may be, it does not seem to me to be yours. You already have more on your shoulders than you can carry; you are hardly able to keep your ground now, with all the odium of this new theology upon you. Such an effort would break up your church,—destroy the chance you have to do good here,—prevent the publication of your system."

"If it's nobody's system but mine, the world won't lose much, if it never be published; but if it be God's system, nothing can hinder its appearing. Besides, Mr. Brown, I ought not to be one man alone. I count on your help. I hold it as a special providence, Mr. Brown, that in our own church an opportunity will be given to testify to the reality of disinterested benevolence. How glorious the opportunity for a man to come out and testify by sacrificing his worldly living and business! If you, Mr. Brown, will at once, at whatever sacrifice, quit all connection with this detestable and diabolical slave trade, you will exhibit a spectacle over which angels will rejoice, and which will strengthen and encourage me to preach and write and testify."

Mr. Simeon Brown's usual demeanor was that of the

most leathery imperturbability. In calm theological reasoning, he could demonstrate in the dryest tone that if the eternal torment of six bodies and souls were absolutely the necessary means for preserving the eternal blessedness of thirty-six, benevolence would require us to rejoice in it, not in itself considered, but in view of greater good. And when he spoke, not a nerve quivered; the great mysterious sorrow with which the creation groaneth and travaileth, the sorrow from which angels veil their faces, never had touched one vibrating chord either of body or soul; and he laid down the obligations of man to unconditional submission in a style which would have affected a person of delicate sensibility much like being mentally sawn in sunder. Benevolence, when Simeon Brown spoke of it, seemed the grimmest and unloveliest of Gorgons;[5] for his mind seemed to resemble those fountains which petrify everything that falls into them. But the hardest-shelled animals have a vital and sensitive part, though only so large as the point of a needle; and the Doctor's innocent proposition to Simeon, to abandon his whole worldly estate for his principles, touched this spot.

When benevolence required but the acquiescence in certain possible things which might be supposed to happen to his soul, which, after all, he was comfortably certain never would happen, or the acquiescence in certain supposititious sacrifices for the good of that most intangible of all abstractions, Being in general, it was a dry, calm subject. But when it concerned the immediate giving up of his slave ships and a transfer of business, attended with all that confusion and loss which he foresaw at a glance, then he felt, and felt too much to see clearly. His swarthy face flushed, his little blue eye kindled, he walked up to the Doctor, and began speaking in the short, energetic sentences of a man thoroughly awake to what he is talking about.

"Doctor, you're too fast. You are not a practical man, Doctor. You are good in your pulpit—nobody better. Your theology is clear; nobody can argue better. But come to practical matters, why, business has its laws, Doctor. Ministers are the most unfit men in the world to talk on such subjects; it's departing from their sphere; they talk about what they don't understand. Besides, you take too much for granted. I'm not sure that this trade is an evil. I want to be convinced of it. I'm sure it's a favor to these poor creatures to bring them to a Christian land. They are a thousand times better off. Here they can hear the gospel and have some chance of salvation."

"If we want to get the gospel to the Africans," said the Doctor, "why not send whole shiploads of missionaries to them, and carry civilization and the arts and Christianity to Africa, instead of stirring up wars, tempting them to ravage each other's territories, that we may get the booty? Think of the numbers killed in the wars,—of all that die on the passage? Is there any need of killing ninety-nine men to give the hundredth one the gospel, when we could give the gospel to them all? Ah, Mr. Brown, what if all the money spent in fitting out ships to bring the poor negroes here, so prejudiced against Christianity that they regard it with fear and aversion, had been spent in sending it to them? Africa would have been covered with towns and villages, rejoicing in civilization and Christianity!"

"Doctor, you are a dreamer," replied Simeon, "an unpractical man. Your situation prevents your knowing anything of real life."

"Amen! the Lord be praised therefor!" said the Doctor, with a slowly increasing flush mounting to his cheek, showing the burning brand of a smouldering fire of indignation.

"Now let me just talk common sense, Doctor,—which has its time and place, just as much as theology; and if you have the most theology, I flatter myself I have the most common sense; a business man must have it. Now just look at your situation,—how you stand. You've got a most important work to do. In order to do it, you must keep your pulpit, you must keep our church together. We are few and weak. We are a minority. Now there's not an influential man in your society that don't either hold slaves or engage in the trade; and if you open upon this subject as you are going to do, you'll just divide and destroy the church. All men are not like you; men are men, and will be, till they are thoroughly sanctified, which never happens in this life, and there will be an instant and most unfavorable agitation. Minds will be turned off from the discussion of the great saving doctrines of the gospel to a side issue. You will be turned out,—and you know, Doctor, you are not appreciated as you ought to be, and it won't be easy for you to get a new settlement; and then subscriptions will all drop off from your book, and you won't be able to get that out; and all this good will be lost to the world just for want of common sense."

"There is a kind of wisdom in what you say, Mr. Brown," replied the Doctor, naïvely; "but I fear much that it is the wisdom spoken of in James iii. 15, which 'descendeth not from above, but is earthly, sensual, devilish.' You avoid the very point of the argument, which is, Is this a sin against God? That it is, I am solemnly convinced; and shall I 'use lightness? or the things that I purpose do I purpose according to the flesh, that with me there should be yea, yea, and nay, nay?'⁶ No, Mr. Brown, immediate repentance, unconditional submission, these are what I must preach as long as God gives me a pulpit to stand in, whether men will hear or whether they will forbear."

"Well, Doctor," said Simeon, shortly, "you can do as you like; but I give you fair warning that I, for one, shall stop my subscription, and go to Dr. Stiles's church."

"Mr. Brown," said the Doctor solemnly, rising and drawing his tall figure to its full height, while a vivid light gleamed from his blue eye, "as to that, you can do as you like; but I think it my duty, as your pastor, to warn you that I have perceived, in my conversation with you this morning, such a want of true spiritual illumination and discernment as leads me to believe that you are yet in the flesh, blinded by that 'carnal mind' which 'is not subject to the law of God, neither indeed can be.'[7] I much fear you have no part nor lot in this matter, and that you have need seriously to set yourself to search into the foundations of your hope; for you may be like him of whom it is written (Isaiah xliv. 20), 'He feedeth on ashes: a deceived heart hath turned him aside, that he cannot deliver his soul, nor say, Is there not a lie in my right hand?' "

The Doctor delivered this address to his man of influence with the calmness of an ambassador charged with a message from a sovereign, for which he is no otherwise responsible than to speak it in the most intelligible manner; and then, taking up his hat and cane, he bade him good-morning, leaving Simeon Brown in a tumult of excitement which no previous theological discussion had ever raised in him.

Notes

1. *II Corinthians.* I, 12.

2. Also called New School or New Light, this group of Calvinists held that, among other beliefs, God gave man a free will that allowed him to make moral decisions. The Old School or Old Light Calvinists maintained that man, born of original sin, was unable to make choices, thereby placing his fate entirely in the hands of God.

3. The American Revolutionary War.

4. Biblically, the city of Jerusalem; symbolically, America.

5. In Greek mythology, three ocean-dwelling sisters, hideous in appearance, whose mere looks were capable of turning into stone any who gazed upon them.

6. *II Corinthians.* I, 17.

7. *Romans.* VIII, 7.

AUNT ROXY AND AUNT RUEY

from *The Pearl of Orr's Island*

The Pearl of Orr's Island takes place on an island off Bath,
Maine. The novel opens with a double tragedy—the killing
of James Lincoln in a shipwreck and the death of his wife,
Naomi, in childbirth after delivering their daughter, Mara.
Captain and Mrs. Zephaniah Pennel, the maternal grand-
parents, are left to raise the orphaned girl.

Published in book form in 1862, *The Pearl of Orr's Is-
land: A Story of the Coast of Maine* was first serialized in the
Independent from January 1861 through April 1862. "Aunt
Roxy and Aunt Ruey" is Chapter IV of the novel.

The sea lay like an unbroken mirror all around the
pine-girt, lonely shores of Orr's Island. Tall, kingly spruces
wore their regal crowns of cones high in air, sparkling with
diamonds of clear exuded gum; vast old hemlocks of pri-
meval growth stood darkling in their forest shadows, their
branches hung with long hoary moss; while feathery
larches, turned to brilliant gold by autumn frosts, lighted
up the darker shadows of the evergreens. It was one of
those hazy, calm, dissolving days of Indian summer, when
everything is so quiet that the faintest kiss of the wave on
the beach can be heard, and white clouds seem to faint into
the blue of the sky, and soft swathing bands of violet vapor
make all earth look dreamy, and give to the sharp, clearcut
outlines of the northern landscape all those mysteries of

light and shade which impart such tenderness to Italian scenery.

The funeral was over; the tread of many feet, bearing the heavy burden of two broken lives, had been to the lonely graveyard, and had come back again,—each footstep lighter and more unconstrained as each one went his way from the great old tragedy of Death to the common cheerful walks of Life.

The solemn black clock stood swaying with its eternal "tick-tock, tick-tock," in the kitchen of the brown house on Orr's Island. There was there that sense of a stillness that can be felt,—such as settles down on a dwelling when any of its inmates have passed through its doors for the last time, to go whence they shall not return. The best room was shut up and darkened, with only so much light as could fall through a little heart-shaped hole in the window-shutter,— for except on solemn visits, or prayer meetings, or weddings, or funerals, that room formed no part of the daily family scenery.

The kitchen was clean and ample, with a great open fireplace and wide stone hearth, and oven on one side, and rows of old-fashioned splint-bottomed chairs against the wall. A table scoured to snowy whiteness, and a little workstand whereon lay the Bible, the "Missionary Herald" and the "Weekly Christian Mirror," before named, formed the principal furniture. One feature, however, must not be forgotten,—a great sea-chest, which had been the companion of Zephaniah through all the countries of the earth. Old, and battered, and unsightly it looked, yet report said that there was good store within of that which men for the most part respect more than anything else; and, indeed, it proved often when a deed of grace was to be done,—when a woman was suddenly made a widow in a coast gale, or a fishing-smack was run down in the fogs off the banks, leaving in some neighboring cottage a family of orphans,—

in all such cases, the opening of this sea-chest was an event of good omen to the bereaved; for Zephaniah had a large heart and a large hand, and was apt to take it out full of silver dollars when once it went in. So the ark of the covenant could not have been looked on with more reverence than the neighbors usually showed to Captain Pennel's sea-chest.

The afternoon sun is shining in a square of light through the open kitchen-door, whence one dreamily disposed might look far out to sea, and behold ships coming and going in every variety of shape and size.

But Aunt Roxy and Aunt Ruey, who for the present were sole occupants of the premises, were not people of the dreamy kind, and consequently were not gazing off to sea, but attending to very terrestrial matters that in all cases somebody must attend to. The afternoon was warm and balmy, but a few smouldering sticks were kept in the great chimney, and thrust deep into the embers was a mongrel species of snub-nosed tea-pot, which fumed strongly of catnip-tea, a little of which gracious beverage Miss Roxy was preparing in an old-fashioned cracked India china tea-cup, tasting it as she did so with the air of a connoisseur.

Apparently this was for the benefit of a small something in long white clothes, that lay face downward under a little blanket of very blue new flannel, and which something Aunt Roxy, when not otherwise engaged, constantly patted with a gentle tattoo, in tune to the steady trot of her knee. All babies knew Miss Roxy's tattoo on their backs, and never thought of taking it in ill part. On the contrary, it had a vital and mesmeric effect of sovereign force against colic, and all other disturbers of the nursery; and never was infant known so pressed with those internal troubles which infants cry about, as not speedily to give over and sink to slumber at this soothing appliance.

At a little distance sat Aunt Ruey, with a quantity of black crape strewed on two chairs about her, very busily employed in getting up a mourning-bonnet, at which she snipped, and clipped, and worked, zealously singing, in a high cracked voice, from time to time, certain verses of a funeral psalm.

Miss Roxy and Miss Ruey Toothacre were two brisk old bodies of the feminine gender and singular number, well known in all the region of Harpswell Neck and Middle Bay, and such was their fame that it had even reached the town of Brunswick, eighteen miles away.

They were of that class of females who might be denominated, in the Old Testament language, "cunning women,"[1]—that is, gifted with an infinite diversity of practical "faculty," which made them an essential requisite in every family for miles and miles around. It was impossible to say what they could not do: they could make dresses, and make shirts and vests and pantaloons, and cut out boys' jackets, and braid straw, and bleach and trim bonnets, and cook and wash, and iron and mend, could upholster and quilt, could nurse all kinds of sicknesses, and in default of a doctor, who was often miles away, were supposed to be infallible medical oracles. Many a human being had been ushered into life under their auspices,—trotted, chirruped in babyhood on their knees, clothed by their handiwork in garments gradually enlarging from year to year, watched by them in the last sickness, and finally arrayed for the long repose by their hands.

These universally useful persons receive among us the title of "aunt" by a sort of general consent, showing the strong ties of relationship which bind them to the whole human family. They are nobody's aunts in particular, but aunts to human nature generally. The idea of restricting their usefulness to any one family, would strike dismay through a whole community. Nobody would be so unprincipled as to think of such a thing as having their services more than a week or two at most. Your country factotum knows better than anybody else how absurd it would be

"To give to a part what was meant for mankind."[2]

Nobody knew very well the ages of these useful sisters. In that cold, clear, severe climate of the North, the roots of human existence are hard to strike; but, if once people do take to living, they come in time to a place where they seem never to grow any older, but can always be found, like last year's mullein stalks, upright, dry, and seedy, warranted to last for any length of time.

Miss Roxy Toothacre, who sits trotting the baby, is a tall, thin, angular woman, with sharp black eyes, and hair once black, but now well streaked with gray. These ravages of time, however, were concealed by an ample mohair frisette of glossy blackness woven on each side into a heap of stiff little curls, which pushed up her cap border in rather a bristling and decisive way. In all her movements and personal habits, even to her tone of voice and manner of speaking, Miss Roxy was vigorous, spicy, and decided. Her mind on all subjects was made up, and she spoke generally as one having authority; and who should, if she should not? Was she not a sort of priestess and sibyl in all the most awful straits and mysteries of life? How many births, and weddings, and deaths had come and gone under her jurisdiction! And amid weeping or rejoicing, was not Miss Roxy still the master-spirit,—consulted, referred to by all?—was not her word law and precedent? Her younger sister, Miss Ruey, a pliant, cozy, easy-to-be-entreated personage, plump and cushiony, revolved around her as a humble satellite. Miss Roxy looked on Miss Ruey as quite a frisky young thing, though under her ample frisette of carroty hair her head might be seen white with the same snow that had powdered that of her sister. Aunt Ruey had a face much resembling the kind of one you may see, reader, by looking at yourself in the convex side of a silver milk-pitcher. If you try the experiment, this description will need no further amplification.

The two almost always went together, for the variety of talent comprised in their stock could always find employment in the varying wants of a family. While one nursed the sick, the other made clothes for the well; and thus they were always chippering and chatting to each other, like a pair of antiquated house-sparrows, retailing over harmless gossips, and moralizing in that gentle jog-trot which befits serious old women. In fact, they had talked over everything in Nature, and said everything they could think of to each other so often, that the opinions of one were as like those of the other as two sides of a peapod. But as often happens in cases of the sort, this was not because the two were in all respects exactly alike, but because the stronger one had mesmerized the weaker into consent.

Miss Roxy was the master-spirit of the two, and, like the great coining machine of a mint, came down with her own sharp, heavy stamp on every opinion her sister put out. She was matter-of-fact, positive, and declarative to the highest degree, while her sister was naturally inclined to the elegiac and the pathetic, indulging herself in sentimental poetry, and keeping a store thereof in her threadcase, which she had cut from the "Christian Mirror." Miss Roxy sometimes, in her brusque way, popped out observations on life and things, with a droll, hard quaintness that took one's breath a little, yet never failed to have a sharp crystallization of truth,—frosty though it were. She was one of those sensible, practical creatures who tear every veil, and lay their fingers on every spot in pure businesslike goodwill; and if we shiver at them at times, as at the first plunge of a cold bath, we confess to an invigorating power in them after all.

"Well, now," said Miss Roxy, giving a decisive push to the tea-pot, which buried it yet deeper in the embers, "ain't it all a strange kind o' providence that this 'ere little thing is left behind so; and then their callin' on her by such a strange, mournful kind of name,—Mara. I thought sure as could be 'twas Mary, till the minister read the passage from Scriptur'.[3] Seems to me it's kind o' odd. I'd call it Maria, or I'd put an Ann on to it. Mara-ann, now, wouldn't sound so strange."

"It's a Scriptur' name, sister," said Aunt Ruey, "and that ought to be enough for us."

"Well, I don't know," said Aunt Roxy. "Now there was Miss Jones down on Mure P'int called her twins Tiglath-Pileser and Shalmaneser,[4]—Scriptur' names both, but I never liked 'em. The boys used to call 'em, Tiggy and Shally, so no mortal could guess they was Scriptur'."

"Well," said Aunt Ruey, drawing a sigh which caused her plump proportions to be agitated in gentle waves, " 'tain't much matter, after all, *what* they call the little thing, for 't ain't 't all likely it's goin' to live,—cried and worried all night, and kep' a-suckin' my cheek and my night-gown, poor little thing! This 'ere 's a baby that won't get along without its mother. What Mis' Pennel 's a-goin' to do with it when we is gone, I'm sure I don't know. It comes kind o' hard on old people to be broke o' their rest. If it's goin' to be called home, it's a pity, as I said, it didn't go with its mother"—

"And save the expense of another funeral," said Aunt Roxy. "Now when Mis' Pennel's sister asked her what she was going to do with Naomi's clothes, I couldn't help wonderin' when she said she should keep 'em for the child."

"She had a sight of things, Naomi did," said Aunt Ruey. "Nothin' was never too much for her. I don't believe that Cap'n Pennel ever went to Bath or Portland without havin' it in his mind to bring Naomi somethin'."

"Yes, and she had a faculty of puttin' of 'em on," said Miss Roxy, with a decisive shake of the head. "Naomi was a still girl, but her faculty was uncommon; and I tell you, Ruey, 't ain't everybody hes faculty as hes things."

"The poor Cap'n," said Miss Ruey, "he seemed greatly supported at the funeral, but he's dreadful broke down since. I went into Naomi's room this morning, and there the old man was a-sittin' by her bed, and he had a pair of her shoes in his hand,—you know what a leetle bit of a foot she had. I never saw nothin' look so kind o' solitary as that poor old man did!"

"Well," said Miss Roxy, "she was a master-hand for keepin' things, Naomi was; her drawers is just a sight; she's got all the little presents and things they ever give her since she was a baby, in one drawer. There's a little pair of red shoes there that she had when she wa'n't more 'n five year old. You 'member, Ruey, the Cap'n brought 'em over from Portland when we was to the house a-makin' Mis' Pennel's figured black silk that he brought from Calcutty. You 'member they cost just five and sixpence; but, law! the Cap'n he never grudged the money when 't was for Naomi. And so she's got all her husband's keepsakes and things just as nice as when he giv' 'em to her."

"It's real affectin'," said Miss Ruey, "I can't all the while help a-thinkin' of the Psalm,—

 " 'So fades the lovely blooming flower,—
 Frail, smiling solace of an hour;
 So quick our transient comforts fly,
 And pleasure only blooms to die.' "[5]

"Yes," said Miss Roxy; "and, Ruey, I was a-thinkin' whether or no it wa'n't best to pack away them things, 'cause Naomi hadn't fixed no baby drawers, and we seem to want some."

"I was kind o' hintin' that to Mis' Pennel this morning," said Ruey, "but she can't seem to want to have 'em touched."

"Well, we may just as well come to such things first as last," said Aunt Roxy; "'cause if the Lord takes our friends, he does take 'em; and we can't lose 'em and have 'em too, and we may as well give right up at first, and done with it, that they are gone, and we've got to do without 'em, and not to be hangin' on to keep things just as they was."

"So I was a-tellin' Mis' Pennel," said Miss Ruey, "but she'll come to it by and by. I wish the baby might live, and kind o' grow up into her mother's place."

"Well," said Miss Roxy, "I wish it might, but there 'd be a sight o' trouble fetchin' on it up. Folks can do pretty well with children when they're young and spry, if they do get 'em up nights; but come to grandchildren, it's pretty tough."

"I'm a-thinkin', sister," said Miss Ruey, taking off her spectacles and rubbing her nose thoughtfully, "whether or no cow's milk ain't goin' to be too hearty for it, it's such a pindlin' little thing. Now, Mis' Badger she brought up a seven-months' child, and she told me she gave it nothin' but these 'ere little seed cookies, wet in water, and it throve nicely,—and the seed is good for wind."

"Oh, don't tell me none of Mis' Badger's stories," said Miss Roxy, "I don't believe in 'em. Cows is the Lord's ordinances for bringing up babies that's lost their mothers; it stands to reason they should be,—and babies that can't eat milk, why they can't be fetched up; but babies can eat milk, and this un will if it lives, and if it can't it won't live." So saying, Miss Roxy drummed away on the little back of the party in question, authoritatively, as if to pound in a wholesome conviction at the outset.

"I hope," said Miss Ruey, holding up a strip of black crape, and looking through it from end to end so as to test its capabilities, "I hope the Cap'n and Mis' Pennel'll get some support at the prayer-meetin' this afternoon."

"It's the right place to go to," said Miss Roxy, with decision.

"Mis' Pennel said this mornin' that she was just beat out tryin' to submit; and the more she said, 'Thy will be done,'[6] the more she didn't seem to feel it."

"Them's common feelin's among mourners, Ruey. These 'ere forty years that I've been round nussin', and layin'-out, and tendin' funerals, I've watched people's exercises. People's sometimes supported wonderfully just at the time, and maybe at the funeral; but the three or four weeks after, most everybody, if they's to say what they feel, is unreconciled."

"The Cap'n, he don't say nothin'," said Miss Ruey.

"No, he don't, but he looks it in his eyes," said Miss Roxy; "he's one of the kind o' mourners as takes it deep; that kind don't cry; it's a kind o' dry, deep pain; them's the worst to get over it,—sometimes they just says nothin', and in about six months they send for you to nuss 'em in consumption or somethin'. Now, Mis' Pennel, she can cry and she can talk,—well, she'll get over it; but *he* won't get no support unless the Lord reaches right down and lifts him up over the world. I've seen that happen sometimes, and I tell you, Ruey, that sort makes powerful Christians."

At that moment the old pair entered the door. Zephaniah Pennel came and stood quietly by the pillow where the little form was laid, and lifted a corner of the blanket. The tiny head was turned to one side, showing the soft, warm cheek, and the little hand was holding tightly a morsel of the flannel blanket. He stood swallowing hard for a few moments. At last he said, with deep humility, to the wise and mighty woman who held her, "I'll tell you what it is, Miss Roxy, I'll give all there is in my old chest yonder if you'll only make her—live."

Notes

1. "Thus saith the Lord of hosts, Consider ye, and call for the mourning women, that they may come; and send for *cunning women*, that they may come." *Jeremiah*. IX, 17.

2.   Written of Edmund Burke, 1729–1797, British statesman, in *Retaliation*, 1774, a poem by Oliver Goldsmith, 1728–1774, English writer: "Who born for the universe, narrow'd his mind,/And to party gave up what was meant for mankind."

3.   "And when they came to Marah, they could not drink of the waters of Marah; for they *were* bitter: therefore the name of it was called Marah." *Exodus.* XV, 23.

4.   Both are mentioned in the Old Testament as kings of Assyria.

5.   Anna Steele ("Theodosia"), 1706–1778, English writer of hymns.

6.   *Matthew.* VI, 10.

NEWPORT; OR, THE PARADISE
OF NOTHING TO DO

from *Pink and White Tyranny*

The flirtatious Lillie Ellis, newly married to the staid John Seymour, tires of her small-town, married life and persuades her husband to let her vacation—while their house is being redecorated—at fashionable Newport, Rhode Island. Her high style of living causes "talk" among the society folk and eventually reaches the ears of John.

Pink and White Tyranny, published in 1871, first ran as a serial from August 1870 through August 1871 in *Old and New*, a magazine. "Newport; or, The Paradise of Nothing To Do" is Chapter XI of the novel.

Behold, now, our Lillie at the height of her heart's desire, installed in fashionable apartments at Newport, under the placid chaperonship of dear mamma, who never saw the least harm in any earthly thing her Lillie chose to do. All the dash and flash and furbelow of uppertendom were there; and Lillie now felt the full power and glory of being a rich, pretty, young married woman, with oceans of money to spend, and nothing on earth to do but follow the fancies of the passing hour.

This was Lillie's highest ideal of happiness; and didn't she enjoy it? Wasn't it something to flame forth in wondrous toilets in the eyes of Belle Trevors and Margy Silloway and Lottie Cavers, who were *not* married; and before the Simpkinses and the Tomkinses and the

Jenkinses, who, last year, had said hateful things about her, and intimated that she had gone off in her looks, and was on the way to be an old maid?

And wasn't it a triumph when all her old beaux came flocking round her, and her parlors became a daily resort and lounging-place for all the idle swains, both of her former acquaintance and of the newcomers, who drifted with the tide of fashion? Never had she been so much the rage; never had she been declared so "stunning." The effect of all this good fortune on her health was immediate. We all know how the spirits affect the bodily welfare; and hence, my dear gentlemen, we desire it to be solemnly impressed on you that there is nothing so good for a woman's health as to give her her own way.

Lillie now, from this simple cause, received enormous accessions of vigor. While at home with plain, sober John, trying to walk in the quiet paths of domesticity, how did her spirits droop! If you only could have had a vision of her brain and spinal system, you would have seen how there was no nervous fluid there, and how all the fine little cords and fibres that string the muscles were wilting like flowers out of water; but now she could bathe the longest and the strongest of any one, could ride on the beach half the day, and dance the german into the small hours of the night, with a degree of vigor which showed conclusively what a fine thing for her the Newport air was. Her dancing-list was always overcrowded with applicants; bouquets were showered on her; and the most superb "turn-outs," with their masters for charioteers, were at her daily disposal.

All this made talk. The world doesn't forgive success; and the ancients informed us that even the gods were envious of happy people. It is astonishing to see the quantity of very proper and rational moral reflection that is excited in the breast of society by any sort of success in life. How it shows them the vanity of earthly enjoyments, the impropriety of setting one's heart on it! How does a successful married flirt impress all her friends with the gross impropriety of having one's head set on gentlemen's attentions!

"I must say," said Belle Trevors, "that dear Lillie does astonish me. Now, I shouldn't want to have that dissipated Danforth lounging in my rooms every day, as he does in Lillie's; and then taking her out driving day after day; for my part, I don't think it's respectable."

"Why don't you speak to her?" said Lottie Cavers.

"Oh, my dear! she wouldn't mind me. Lillie always was the most imprudent creature; and if she goes on so, she'll certainly get awfully talked about. That Danforth is a horrid creature; I know all about him."

As Miss Belle had herself been driving with the "horrid creature" only the week before Lillie came, it must be confessed that her opportunities for observation were of an authentic kind.

Lillie, as queen in her own parlor, was all grace and indulgence. Hers was now to be the sisterly rôle, or, as she laughingly styled it, the maternal. With a ravishing morning-dress, and with a killing little cap of about three inches in extent on her head, she enacted the young matron, and gave full permission to Tom, Dick, and Harry to make themselves at home in her room, and smoke their cigars there in peace. She "adored the smell;" in fact, she accepted the present of a fancy box of cigarettes from Danforth with graciousness, and would sometimes smoke one purely for good company. She also encouraged her followers to unveil the tender secrets of their souls confidentially to her, and offered gracious mediations on their behalf with any of the flitting Newport fair ones. When they, as in duty bound, said that they saw nobody whom they cared about now she was married, that she was the only woman on earth for them,—she rapped their knuckles briskly with her fan, and bid them mind their manners. All this mode of proceeding gave her an immense success.

But, as we said before, all this was talked about; and ladies in their letters, chronicling the events of the passing hour, sent the tidings up and down the country; and so Miss Letitia Ferguson got a letter from Mrs. Wilcox with full pictures and comments; and she brought the same to Grace Seymour.

"I dare say," said Letitia, "these things have been exaggerated; they always are: still, it does seem desirable that your brother should go there, and be with her."

"He can't go and be with her," said Grace, "without neglecting his business, already too much neglected. Then the house is all in confusion under the hands of painters; and there is that young artist up there,—a very elegant gentleman,—giving orders to right and left, every one of which involves further confusion and deeper expense; for my part, I see no end to it. Poor John has got 'the Old Man of the Sea'[1] on his back in the shape of this woman; and I expect she'll be the ruin of him yet. I can't want to break up his illusion about her; because, what good will it do? He has married her, and must live with her; and, for Heaven's sake, let the illusion last while it can! I'm going to draw off, and leave them to each other; there's no other way."

"You are, Gracie?"

"Yes; you see John came to me, all stammering and embarrassment, about this making over of the old place; but I put him at ease at once. 'The most natural thing in the world, John,' said I. 'Of course Lillie has her taste; and it's her right to have the house arranged to suit it.' And then I proposed to take all the old family things, and furnish the house that I own on Elm Street, and live there, and let John and Lillie keep house by themselves. You see, there is no helping the thing. Married people must be left to themselves; nobody can help them. They must make their own discoveries, fight their own battles, sink or swim, together; and I have determined that not by the winking of an eye will I interfere between them."

"Well, but do you think John wants you to go?"

"He feels badly about it; and yet I have convinced him that it's best. Poor fellow! all these changes are not a bit to his taste. He liked the old place as it was, and the old ways; but John is so unselfish. He has got it in his head that Lillie is very sensitive and peculiar, and that her spirits require all these changes, as well as Newport air."

"Well," said Letitia, "if a man begins to say A in that line, he must say B."

"Of course," said Grace; "and also C and D, and so on, down to X, Y, Z. A woman, armed with sick headaches, nervousness, debility, presentiments, fears, horrors, and all sorts of imaginary and real diseases, has an eternal armory of weapons of subjugation. What can a man do? Can he tell her that she is lying and shamming? Half the time she isn't; she can actually work herself into about any physical state she chooses. The fortnight before Lillie went to Newport she really looked pale, and ate next to nothing; and she managed admirably to seem to be trying to keep up, and not to complain,—yet you see how she can go on at Newport."

"It seems a pity John couldn't understand her."

"My dear, I wouldn't have him for the world. Whenever he does, he will despise her; and then he will be wretched. For John is no hypocrite, any more than I am. No, I earnestly pray that his soap-bubble may not break."

"Well, then," said Letitia, "at least, he might go down to Newport for a day or two; and his presence there might set some things right: it might at least check reports. You might just suggest to him that unfriendly things were being said."

"Well, I'll see what I can do," said Grace.

So, by a little feminine tact in suggestion, Grace dispatched her brother to spend a day or two in Newport.

His coming and presence interrupted the lounging hours in Lillie's rooms; the introduction to "my husband" shortened the interviews. John was courteous and affable;

but he neither smoked nor drank, and there was a mutual repulsion between him and many of Lillie's *habitués*.

"I say, Dan," said Bill Sanders to Danforth, as they were smoking on one end of the veranda, "you are driven out of your lodgings since Seymour came."

"No more than the rest of you," said Danforth.

"I don't know about that, Dan. I think *you* might have been taken for master of those premises. Look here now, Dan, why didn't you *take* little Lil yourself? Everybody thought you were going to last year."

"Didn't want her; knew too much," said Danforth. "Didn't want to keep her; she's too cursedly extravagant. It's jolly to have this sort of concern on hand; but I'd rather Seymour'd pay her bills than I."

"Who thought you were so practical, Dan?"

"Practical! that I am; I'm an old bird. Take my advice, boys, now: keep shy of the girls, and flirt with the married ones,—then you don't get roped in."

"I say, boys," said Tom Nichols, "isn't she a case, now? What a head she has! I bet she can smoke equal to any of us."

"Yes; I keep her in cigarettes," said Danforth; "she's got a box of them somewhere under her ruffles now."

"What if Seymour should find them?" said Tom.

"Seymour? pooh! he's a muff and a prig. I bet you he won't find her out; she's the jolliest little humbugger there is going. She'd cheat a fellow out of the sight of his eyes. It's perfectly wonderful."

"How came Seymour to marry her?"

"He? Why, he's a pious youth, green as grass itself; and I suppose she talked religion to him. Did you ever hear her talk religion?"

A roar of laughter followed this, out of which Danforth went on. "By George, boys, she gave me a Prayer-Book once! I've got it yet."

"Well, if that isn't the best thing I ever heard!" said Nichols.

"It was at the time she was laying siege to me, you see. She undertook the part of guardian angel, and used to talk lots of sentiment. The girls get lots of that out of George Sand's[2] novels about the *holiness* of doing just as you've a mind to, and all that," said Danforth.

"By George, Dan, you oughtn't to laugh. She may have more good in her than you think."

"Oh, humbug! don't I know her?"

"Well, at any rate she's a wonderful creature to hold her looks. By George, how she does hold out! You'd say, now, she wasn't more than twenty."

"Yes; she understands getting herself up," said Danforth, "and touches up her cheeks a bit now and then."

"She don't paint, though?"

"Don't paint! *Don't* she? I'd like to know if she don't; but she does it like an artist, like an old master, in fact."

"Or like a young mistress," said Tom, and then laughed at his own wit.

Now, it so happened that John was sitting at an open window above, and heard occasional snatches of this conversation quite sufficient to impress him disagreeably. He had not heard enough to know exactly what had been said, but enough to feel that a set of coarse, low-minded men were making quite free with the name and reputation of his Lillie, and he was indignant.

"She is so pretty, so frank, and so impulsive," he said. "Such women are always misconstrued. I'm resolved to caution her."

"Lillie," he said, "who is this Danforth?"

"Charlie Danforth—oh! he's a millionaire that I refused. He was wild about me,—is now, for that matter. He perfectly haunts my rooms, and is always teasing me to ride with him."

(*123*)

"Well, Lillie, if I were you, I wouldn't have anything to do with him."

"John, I don't mean to, any more than I can help. I try to keep him off all I can; but one doesn't want to be rude, you know."

"My darling," said John, "you little know the wickedness of the world, and the cruel things that men will allow themselves to say of women who are meaning no harm. You can't be too careful, Lillie."

"Oh! I am careful. Mamma is here, you know, all the while; and I never receive except she is present."

John sat abstractedly fingering the various objects on the table; then he opened a drawer in the same mechanical manner.

"Why, Lillie! what's this? what in the world are these?"

"Oh, John! sure enough! well, there is something I was going to ask you about. Danforth used always to be sending me things, you know, before we were married,—flowers and confectionery, and one thing or other; and since I have been here now, he has done the same, and I really didn't know what to do about it. You know I didn't want to quarrel with him, or get his ill will; he's a high-spirited fellow, and a man one doesn't want for an enemy; so I have just passed it over easy as I could."

"But, Lillie, a box of cigarettes!—of course, they can be of no use to you."

"Of course: they are only a sort of curiosity that he imports from Spain with his cigars."

"I've a great mind to send them back to him myself," said John.

"Oh, don't, John! why, how it would look! as if you were angry, or thought he meant something wrong. No; I'll contrive a way to give 'em back without offending him. I am up to all such little ways."

"Come, now," she added, "don't let's be cross just the little time you have to stay with me. I do wish our house were not all torn up, so that I could go home with you, and leave Newport and all its bothers behind."

"Well, Lillie, you could go, and stay with me at Gracie's," said John, brightening at this proposition.

"Dear Gracie,—so she has got a house all to herself; how I shall miss her! but, really, John, I think she will be happier. Since you would insist on revolutionizing our house, you know"—

"But, Lillie, it was to please you."

"Oh, I know it! but you know I begged you not to. Well, John, I don't think I should like to go in and settle down on Grace; perhaps, as I am here, and the sea air and bathing strengthen me so, we may as well put it through. I will come home as soon as the house is done."

"But perhaps you would want to go with me to New York to select the furniture?"

"Oh, the artist does all that! Charlie Ferrola will give his orders to Simon & Sauls, and they will do everything up complete. It's the way they all do—saves lots of trouble."

John went home, after three days spent in Newport, feeling that Lillie was somehow an injured fair one, and that the envious world bore down always on beauty and prosperity. But incidentally he heard and overheard much that made him uneasy. He heard her admired as a "bully" girl, a "fast one;" he heard of her smoking, he overheard something about "painting."

The time was that John thought Lillie an embryo angel,—an angel a little bewildered and gone astray, and with wings a trifle the worse for the world's wear,—but essentially an angel of the same nature with his own revered mother. Gradually the mercury had been falling in the tube of his estimation. He had given up the angel; and now to himself he called her "a silly little pussy," but he did it with a smile. It was such a neat, white, graceful pussy; and all his own pussy too, and purred and rubbed its little head on no coat-sleeve but his,—of that he was certain. Only a bit silly.

She would still fib a little, John feared, especially when he looked back to the chapter about her age,—and then, perhaps, about the cigarettes. Well, she might, perhaps, in a wild, excited hour, have smoked one or two, just for fun, and the thing had been exaggerated. She had promised fairly to return those cigarettes,—he dared not say to himself that he feared she would not. He kept saying to himself that she would. It was necessary to say this often to make himself believe it.

As to painting—well, John didn't like to ask her, because, what if she shouldn't tell him the truth? And if she did paint, was it so great a sin, poor little thing? He would watch, and bring her out of it. After all, when the house was all finished and arranged, and he got her back from Newport, there would be a long, quiet, domestic winter at Springdale; and they would get up their reading-circles, and he would set her to improving her mind, and gradually the vision of this empty, fashionable life would die out of her horizon, and she would come into his ways of thinking and doing.

But, after all, John managed to be proud of her. When he read in the columns of "The Herald"[3] the account of the Splandangerous ball in Newport, and of the entrancingly beautiful Mrs. J. S., who appeared in a radiant dress of silvery gauze made *à la nuage,* etc., etc., John was rather pleased than otherwise. Lillie danced till daylight,—it showed that she must be getting back her strength,—and she was voted the belle of the scene. Who wouldn't take the comfort that is to be got in anything? John owned this fashionable meteor,—why shouldn't he rejoice in it?

Two years ago, had anybody told him that one day he should have a wife that told fibs, and painted, and smoked cigarettes, and danced all night at Newport, and yet that he should love her, and be proud of her, he would have said, Is thy servant a dog?[4] He was then a considerate, thoughtful John, serious and careful in his life-plans; and the wife that was to be his companion was something celestial. But so it is. By degrees we accommodate ourselves to the actual and existing. To all intents and purposes, for us it is the inevitable.

Notes

1. From *Arabian Nights' Entertainment (A Thousand and One Nights)*, a collection of ancient Oriental tales, a monster who jumped on the back of Sinbad the Sailor and refused to dismount.

2. Pen name of Armandine Lucile Aurore Dupin, 1804–1876, French novelist.

3. Newspaper published in New York City from 1834–1924.

4. *II Kings*. VIII, 13.

ELECTION DAY IN POGANUC

from *Poganuc People*

Poganuc People, Harriet Beecher Stowe's last novel, is a fictionalized account of her childhood in Litchfield, Connecticut. Poganuc is the Indian name for this area of the state. In the state election of 1818 the town is split over the issue of the established state church (Congregational), with the Federalists favoring the arrangement and the Democrats (aided by the Episcopalians) opposing. Dolly Cushing (Harriet Beecher Stowe) comforts her father, the Rev. Dr. Cushing (Lyman Beecher) when the election goes against his side.

From November 1877 through June 1878 the *Christian Union* published Harriet Beecher Stowe's autobiographical novel of her childhood, *Our Folks at Poganuc.* Later in 1878 the work was retitled and printed in book form as *Poganuc People: Their Loves and Lives.* "Election Day in Poganuc" is Chapter IX.

The month of March had dawned over the slippery, snow-clad hills of Poganuc. The custom that enumerates this as among the spring months was in that region the most bitter irony. Other winter months were simple winter—cold, sharp, and hard enough—but March was winter with a practical application, driven in by winds that pierced through joints and marrow. Not an icicle of all the stalactites which adorned the fronts of houses had so much as thought of thawing; the snowbanks still lay in white billows above the tops of the fences; the roads, through which the ox-sleds of the farmers crunched and squeaked their way, were cut deep down through heavy drifts, and there was still the best prospect in the world for future snowstorms; but yet it was called "spring." And the voting day had come; and Zeph Higgins, full of the energy of a sovereign and voter, was up at four o'clock in the morning, bestirring himself with a tempestuous clatter to rouse his household and be by daylight on the way to town to exercise his rights.

The feeble light of a tallow dip seemed to cut but a small circle into the darkness of the great kitchen. The frost sparkled white on the back of the big fireplace, where the last night's coals lay raked up under banks of ashes. An earthquake of tramping cowhide boots shook the rafters and stairs, and the four boys appeared on the scene of action. Backlog and forestick were soon piled and kindlings laid, and the fire roared and snapped and crackled up the ample chimney. Meek, shadowy Mrs. Higgins, with a step like a snowflake, and resignation and submission in every line of her face, was proceeding to cut off frozen sausages from the strings of the same that garnished the kitchen walls. The teakettle was hung over the blaze, and Zeph and the boys, with hats crowded down to their eyes, and tippets tied over their ears, ploughed their way to the barn to milk and feed the stock.

When they returned, while the teakettle was puffing and the sausages frying and sizzling, there was an interval in which Zeph called to family prayers, and began reading the Bible with a voice as loud and harsh as the winds that were blowing out of doors.

Zeph always read the Bible straight along in course, without a moment's thought or inquiry as to the sense of what he was reading, which this morning was from Zechariah xi.,[1] as follows: "Open thy doors, O Lebanon, that the fire may devour thy cedars. Howl, fir tree; for the cedar is fallen; because all the mighty are spoiled: howl, O ye oaks of Bashan; for the forest of the vintage is come down. There is a voice of the howling of the shepherds; for their glory is spoiled: a voice of the roaring of young lions; for the pride of Jordan is spoiled." Zeph rendered the whole chapter with his harshest tones, and then, all standing, he enunciated in stentorian voice the morning prayer, whose phrases were an heirloom that had descended from father to son for generations.

The custom of family worship was one of the most rigid inculcations of the Puritan order of society, and came down from parent to child with the big family Bible, where the births, deaths, and marriages of the household stood recorded. In Zeph's case the custom seemed to be merely an inherited tradition, which had dwindled into a habit purely mechanical. Yet, who shall say?

Of a rugged race, educated in hardness, wringing his substance out of the very teeth and claws of reluctant nature, on a rocky and barren soil, and under a harsh, forbidding sky, who but the All-Seeing could judge him? In that hard soul there may have been thus uncouthly expressed a loyalty for Something Higher, however dimly perceived. It was acknowledging that even he had his master. One thing is certain, the custom of family prayers, such as it was, was a great comfort to the meek saint by his side, to whom any form of prayer, any pause from earthly care and looking up to a heavenly Power, was a blessed rest. In that daily toil, often beyond her strength, when she never received a word of sympathy or praise, it was a comfort all day to her to have had a chapter in the Bible and a prayer in the morning. Even though the chapter were one that she could not by possibility understand a word of, yet it put her in mind of things in that same dear book that she did understand; things that gave her strength to live and hope to die by, and it was enough! Her faith in the Invisible Friend was so strong that she needed but to touch the hem of his garment. Even a table of genealogies out of *his* book was a sacred charm, an amulet of peace.

Four sons—tall, stout, and ruddy, in different stages of progression—surrounded the table and caused sausages, rye and Indian bread, and pork and beans rapidly to disappear. Of these sons two only were of the age to vote. Zeph rigorously exacted of his boys the full amount of labor which the law allowed till their majority; but at twenty-one he recognized their legal status, and began giving them the wages of hired men. On this morning he longed to have his way as to their vote; but the boys had enough of his own nature in them to have a purpose and will of their own, and how they were to vote was an impenetrable secret locked up in the rocky fastnesses of their own bosoms.

As soon as there were faint red streaks in the wintry sky, Zeph's sled was on the road, well loaded up with cordwood to be delivered at Colonel Davenport's door; for Zeph never forgot business nor the opportunity of earning an honest penny. The oxen that drew his sled were sleek, well-fed beasts, the pride of Zeph's heart; and as the red sunlight darted across the snowy hills their breath steamed up, a very luminous cloud of vapor, which in a few moments congealed in sparkling frost lines on their patient eye-winkers and every little projecting hair around their great noses. The sled-runners creaked and grated as Zeph, with loud "Whoa," "Haw," or "Gee," directed the plodding course of his beasts. The cutting March wind was blowing right into his face; his shaggy, grizzled eyebrows and bushy beard were whitening apace; but he was in good spirits—he was going to vote against the Federalists;[2] and as the largest part of the aristocracy of Town Hill[3] were Federalists, he rejoiced all the more. Zeph was a creature born to oppose, as much as white bears are made to walk on ice. And how, we ask, would New England's rocky soil and icy hills have been made mines of wealth unless there had been human beings born to oppose, delighting to combat and wrestle, and with an unconquerable power of will?

Zeph had taken a thirteen-acre lot so rocky that a sheep could scarce find a nibble there, had dug out and blasted and carted the rocks, wrought them into a circumambient stone fence, ploughed and planted, and raised crop after crop of good rye thereon. He did it with heat, with zeal, with dogged determination; he did it all the more because neighbors said he was a fool for trying, and that he could never raise anything on that lot. There was a stern joy in this hand-to-hand fight with nature. He got his bread as Samson did his honeycomb, out of the carcass of the slain lion. "Out of the eater came forth meat, and out of the strong came forth sweetness."[4] Even the sharp March wind did not annoy him. It was a controversial wind, and that suited him; it was fighting him all the way, and he enjoyed beating it. Such a human being has his place in the Creator's scheme.

Poganuc was, for a still town, pretty well alive on that day. Farmers in their blue linsey frocks, with their long cart-whips, and their sleds hitched here and there at different doors, formed frequent objects in the picture. It was the day when they felt themselves as good as anybody. The court house was surrounded by groups earnestly discussing the political questions; many of them loafers who made a sort of holiday, and interspersed their observations and remarks with visits to the bar-room of Glazier's Tavern, which was doing a thriving business that morning.

Standing by the side of the distributer of the Federal votes might be seen a tall, thin man, with a white head and an air of great activity and keenness. In his twinkling eye and in every line and wrinkle of his face might be read the observer and the humorist; the man who finds something to amuse him in all the quips and turns and oddities of human nature. This was Israel Dennie, high sheriff of the county, one of the liveliest and shrewdest of the Federal leaders, who was, so to speak, crackling with activity, and entering into the full spirit of the day in all its phases.

"Here comes one of your party, Adams," he said, with a malicious side twinkle, to the distributer of the Democratic[5] votes, as Abe Bowles, a noted *mauvais sujet* of the village, appeared out of Glazier's bar-room, coming forward with a rather uncertain step and flushed face.

"Walk up, friend; here you are."

"I'm a-goin' for toleration," said Abe, with thick utterance. "We've ben tied up too tight by these 'ere ministers, we have. I don't want no priestcraft, I don't. I believe every man's got to do as he darn pleases, I do."

"And go straight to the devil if he wants to," said Squire Dennie smoothly. "Go ahead, my boy, and put in your vote."

"There comes old Zeph Higgins," he added, with alertness; "let us have a bit of fun with him."

"Hulloa, Higgins; step this way; here's Mr. Adams to give you your vote. You're going to vote the Democratic ticket, you know."

"No, I ain't, nuther," said Zeph, from the sheer mechanical instinct of contradiction.

"Not going to vote with the Democrats, Higgins? All right, then you're going to vote the Federal ticket; here 't is."

"No, I ain't, nuther. You let me alone. I ain't a-goin' to be dictated to. I'm a-goin' to vote jest as I'm a mind ter. I won't vote for nuther, ef I ain't a mind ter, and I'll vote for jest which one I want ter, and no other."

"So you shall, Higgins,—so you shall," said Squire Dennie sympathetically, laying his hand on Zeph's shoulder.

"I sha'n't, nuther; you let me alone," said Zeph, shaking off the sheriff's hand; and clutching at the Democratic ticket, he pushed up towards the polls.

"There's a fellow, now," said Sheriff Dennie, looking after him with a laugh. "That fellow's so contrary that he hates to do the very thing he wants to, if anybody else wants him to do it. If there was any way of voting that would spite both parties and please nobody, he'd take that. The only way to get that fellow to heaven would be to set out to drive him to hell; then he'd turn and run up the narrow way, full chisel."

It was some comfort to Zeph, however, to work his way up to the polls with Judge Belcher right in front and with Colonel Davenport's aristocratic, powdered head and stately form pushing him along behind, their broadcloth crowded against his homespun carter's frock, and he, Zephaniah, that day just as good as either. He would not have been so well pleased if he knew that his second son, Abner,—following not long after him,—dropped in the box the Federalist ticket. It was his right as a freeman; but he had no better reason for his preference than the wish to please his mother. He knew that Dr. Cushing was a Federalist, and that his mother was heart and soul for everything that Dr. Cushing was for, and therefore he dropped this vote for his mother; and thus, as many times before and since, a woman voted through her son. In fact, the political canvas just at this epoch had many features that might shock the pious sensibilities of a good housemother. The union of all the minor religious denominations to upset the dominant rule of the Congregationalists had been reinforced and supplemented by all that Jacobin and irreligious element which the French Revolution had introduced into America.[6]

The Poganuc "Banner," a little weekly paper published in the village, expended its energies in coarse and scurrilous attacks upon ministers in general, and Dr. Cushing in particular. It ridiculed church members, churches, Sunday-keeping, preaching, and prayers; in short, every custom, preference, and prejudice which it had been the work of years to establish in New England was assailed with vulgar wit and ribaldry.

Of course, the respectable part of the Democratic party did not exactly patronize these views; yet they felt for them that tolerance which even respectable people often feel in a rude push of society in a direction where they wish to go. They wanted the control of the state; and if rabid, drinking, irreligious men would give it to them, why not use them after their kind? When the brutes had won the battle for them, they would take care of the brutes, and get them back into their stalls.

The bar-room of Glazier's Tavern was the scene of the feats and boasts of this class of voters. Long before this time the clergy of Connecticut, alarmed at the progress of intemperance, had begun to use influence in getting stringent laws and restraints upon drinking, and the cry, of course, was, "Down with the laws."

"Tell ye what," said Mark Merrill, "we've ben tied up so tight we couldn't wink mor' 'n six times a week, and the parsons want to git it so we can't wink at all; and we won't have it so no longer; we're goin' to have liberty."

"Down with the tithing-man, say I," said Tim Sykes. "Whose business is it what I do Sundays? I ain't goin' to have no tithing-man spying on my liberty. I'll do jest what I'm a mind ter, Sundays. Ef I wan' ter go a-fishin' Sundays, I'll go a-fishin'."

"Tell ye what," said Liph Kingsley, as he stirred his third glass of grog, "this 'ere priestcraft's got to go down. Reason's got on her throne, and chains is fallin'. I'm a freeman—I be."

"You look like it," said Hiel, who stood with his hands in his pockets contemptuously surveying Liph, while with leering eye and unsteady hand he stirred his drink.

"That 'ere's what you call Reason, is 't?" added Hiel. "Wal, she's got on a pretty topplish throne, seems to me. I bet you Reason can't walk a crack now," he said, as Liph, having taken off his glass, fell with a helpless dump upon the settle.

"Sot down like a spoonful of apple saas," said Hiel, looking him over sarcastically. The laugh now turned against the poor brute, and Hiel added, "Wal, boys, s'pose you like this 'ere sort of thing. Folks is different; for my part, I like to kinder keep up a sort o' difference 'tween me and a hog. That 'ere's my taste; but you're welcome to yourn," and Hiel went out to carry his observations elsewhere.

Hiel felt his own importance to the community of Poganuc Centre too much to have been out of town on this day, when its affairs needed so much seeing to; therefore he had deputed Ned Bissel, a youth yet wanting some two years of the voting age, to drive his team for him while he gave his undivided attention to public interests; and indeed, as nearly as mortal man can be omnipresent, Hiel had been everywhere and heard everything, and, as the French say, "assisted" generally at the political struggle. Hiel considered himself as the provisional owner and caretaker of the town of Poganuc. It was *our* town, and Dr. Cushing was *our* minister, and the great meeting-house on the green was *our* meeting-house, and the singers' seat therein was *our* singers' seat, and he was ready to bet on any sermon, or action, or opinion of *our* minister. Hiel had not yet, as he phrased it, experienced religion, nor joined the church; but he "calculated he should some of these days." It wasn't Dr. Cushing's fault if he wasn't converted, he was free to affirm. Hiel had been excessively scandalized with the scurrilous attacks of the Poganuc "Banner," and felt specially called to show his colors on that day. He had assured his mother on going out that morning that she needn't be a mite afeard, for he was a-goin' to stand up for the minister through thick and thin, and if any of them Democrats "saassed" him he'd give 'em as good as they sent.

In virtue of his ardent political zeal, he felt himself to-day on equal and speaking terms with all the Federal magnates; he clapped Colonel Davenport on the shoulder assuringly, and talked about "our side," and was familiar with Judge Belcher and Sheriff Dennie—darting hither and thither, observing and reporting with untiring zeal.

But, after all, that day the Democrats beat, and got the State of Connecticut. Sheriff Dennie was the first to carry the news of defeat into the parsonage at eventide.

"Well, doctor, we're smashed. Democrats beat us all to flinders."

A general groan arose.

"Yes, yes," said the sheriff. "Everything has voted that could stand on its hind legs, and the hogs are too many for us. It's a bad beat—bad beat."

That night when little Dolly came in to family prayers, she looked around wondering. Her father and mother looked stricken and overcome. There was the sort of heaviness in the air that even a child can feel when deep emotions are aroused. The boys, who knew only in a general way that their father's side had been beaten, looked a little scared at his dejected face.

"Father, what makes you feel so bad?" said Will, with that surprised wonder with which children approach emotions they cannot understand.

"I feel for the Church of God, my child," he said, and then he sung for the evening psalm:—

> "I love thy kingdom, Lord,
> The house of thine abode;
> The Church our dear Redeemer saved
> With his own precious blood.
>
> "For her my tears shall fall,
> For her my prayers ascend;
> To her my cares and toils be given
> Till toils and cares shall end."[7]

In the prayer that followed he pleaded for New England with all the Hebraistic imagery by which she was identified with God's ancient people:—

"Give ear, O Shepherd of Israel; thou that leadest

Joseph like a flock; thou that dwellest between the cherubims, shine forth. . . . Thou hast brought a vine out of Egypt; thou didst cast forth the heathen, and plant it; thou preparedst room for it and didst cause it to take deep root, and it filled the land. The hills were covered with the shadow of it, and the boughs thereof were like the goodly cedars. Why hast thou then broken down her hedges so that all that pass by the way do pluck her? The boar out of the wood doth waste it; the wild beast of the field doth devour it. Return, we beseech thee, O Lord, and visit this vine and vineyard that thou hast planted and the branch that thou madest strong for thyself."[8]

It was with a voice tremulous and choking with emotion that Dr. Cushing thus poured forth the fears and the sorrows of his heart for the New England of the Puritans;[9] the ideal church and state which they came hither to found.

Little Dolly cried from a strange childish fear, because of the trouble in her father's voice. The pleading tones affected her, she knew not why. The boys felt a martial determination to stand by their father and a longing to fight for him. All felt as if something deep and dreadful must have happened, and after prayers Dolly climbed into her father's lap, and put both arms around his neck, and said, "Papa, there sha'n't anything hurt you. I'll defend you." She was somewhat abashed by the cheerful laugh which followed, but the doctor kissed her and said, "So you shall, dear; be sure and not let anything catch me," and then he tossed her up in his arms gleefully, and she felt as if the trouble, whatever it was, could not be quite hopeless.

But Dolly marveled in her own soul as she went to bed. She heard the boys without stint reviling the Democrats as the authors of all mischief; and yet Bessie Lewis's father was a Democrat, and he seemed a nice, cheery, good-natured man, who now and then gave her sticks of candy, and there was his mother, dear old Madam Lewis, who gave her the Christmas cooky. How could it be that such good people were Democrats? Poor Dolly hopelessly sighed over the mystery, but dared not ask questions.

But the Rev. Mr. Coan rejoiced in the result of the election. Not that he was by any means friendly to the ideas of the Jacobinical party by whose help it had been carried; but because, as he said, it opened a future for the church— for he, too, had his idea of "The Church." Meanwhile the true church, invisible to human eyes,—one in spirit, though separated by creeds,—was praying and looking upward, in the heart of Puritan and Ritualist,[10] in the heart of old Madam Lewis, of the new church, and of old Mrs. Higgins, whose soul was with the old meeting-house; of all everywhere who with humble purpose and divine aspiration were praying, "Thy kingdom come; Thy will be done."[11]

That kingdom was coming even then,—for its coming is in safer hands than those on either side,—and there came a time, years after, when Parson Cushing, looking back on that election and its consequences, could say with another distinguished Connecticut clergyman:—

"I suffered more than tongue can tell for the best thing that ever happened to old Connecticut."[12]

Notes

1. Verses, 1–3.

2. A political party formed in 1787 in support of a federal constitution and a strong centralized government. It elected the first two presidents of the United States. The Federalists were especially powerful in local New England politics.

3. The wealthy section of Poganuc.

4.   In the Old Testament Samson found a swarm of bees and honey in a slain lion. *Judges*. XIV, 5–8; 14.

5.   The Democratic Party, formed in 1792, opposed a strong central government. Founded by Thomas Jefferson, 1743–1826, third president of the United States, it was originally called the Republican Party, later the Democratic-Republican Party.

6.   Until 1818 the Congregational Church was the established church in Connecticut. The Democrats were often disparagingly compared to the Jacobins, political extremists during the French Revolution, 1789.

7.   Timothy Dwight, 1752–1817, American clergyman. Stanzas 1 and 3.

8.   *Psalms*. LXXX, 1; 8–10; 12–15.

9.   English Protestants, opposed to the established church, who emigrated to New England in the 17th century.

10.   Refers to Episcopalianism.

11.   *Matthew*. VI, 10.

12.   Lyman Beecher, 1775–1863, Congregational clergyman and father of Harriet Beecher Stowe.

DOLLY'S "FOURTH"

from *Poganuc People*

In the character of Dolly Cushing, Harriet Beecher Stowe recalls fictionally her introduction to the celebration of Independence Day, the Fourth of July. Accompanied by Nabby Higgins, the Cushings's house servant, Dolly enjoys the events of the day—the oratory, parades, military reenactments.

"Dolly's 'Fourth' " is Chapter XVIII of *Poganuc People*.

Bang! went the cannon on the green, just as the first red streak appeared over Poganuc hills, and open flew Dolly's great blue eyes. Every boy in town was out of bed as if he had been fired out of a pop-gun, and into his clothes and out on the green with a celerity scarcely short of the miraculous. Dolly's little toilet took more time; but she, too, was soon out upon the scene with her curls in a wild, unbrushed tangle, her little breast swelling and beating with a great enthusiasm for General Washington[1] and liberty and her country, all of which were somehow to be illustrated and honored that day in Poganuc. As the first rays of the rising sun struck the stars and stripes floating over the court house, and the sound of distant drum and fife announced the coming in of the Poganuc Rangers, Dolly was so excited that she burst into tears.

"What in the world are you crying for, Dolly?" said Bill, rather impatiently. "I don't see anything to cry about."

"I can't help it, Will," said Dolly, wiping her eyes; "it's so glorious!"

"If that isn't just like a girl!" said Bill. Contempt could go no farther, and Dolly retreated abashed. She was a girl—there was no help for that; but for this one day she envied the boys—the happy boys who might some day grow up and fight for their country, and do something glorious like General Washington. Meanwhile, from mouth to mouth, every one was giving in advance an idea of what the splendors of the day were to be.

"I tell ye," said Abe Bowles, "this 'ere's goin' to be a reel slam-bang, this 'ere is. Colonel Davenport is a-goin' to review the troops, and wear the very same uniform he wore at Long Island."[2]

"Yes," said Liph Kingsley, "and old Cæsar's goin' to wear his uniform and wait on the colonel. Tell ye what, the old snowball is on his high heels this morning—got a suit of the colonel's old uniform. Won't he strut and show his ivories!"

"Hulloa, boys, there's going to be a sham fight; Hiel told me so," said Bob Cushing. "Some are going to be British and some Americans, and the Americans are going to whip the British and make 'em run."

"Tell ye what," said Jake Freeman, "there'll be a bangin' and poppin'! won't there, boys!"

"Oh," said Dolly, who irrepressibly was following her brothers into the throng, "they won't *really* shoot anybody, will they?"

"Oh no, they'll only fire powder, of course," said Bill majestically; "don't you know that?"

Dolly was rebuked and relieved at once.

"I say, boys," said Nabby, appearing suddenly among the throng, "your ma says you must come right home to breakfast this minit; and you, Dolly Cushing, what are you out here for, round among the fellers like a tomboy? Come right home."

"Why, Nabby, I wanted to see!" pleaded Dolly.

"Oh yes, you're allers up to everything and into every-thing, and your hair not brushed nor nothin'. You'll see it all in good time—come right away. Don't be a-lookin' at them trainers, now," she added, giving herself, however, a good observing glance to where across the green a knot of the Poganuc Rangers were collecting, and where Hiel, in full glory of his uniform, with his gold epaulets and cocked hat, was as busy and impressive as became the situation.

"Oh, Nabby, do look; there's Hiel," cried Dolly.

"Yes; yes; I see plain enough there's Hiel," said Nabby; "he thinks he's mighty grand, I suppose. He'll be conceit-eder'n ever, I expect."

Just at that moment, Hiel, recognizing Nabby, took off his gold-laced hat and bowed with a graceful flourish. Nabby returned a patronizing little nod, and either the morning dawn, or the recent heat of the kitchen fire, or *something*, flushed her cheeks. It was to be remarked in evidence of the presence of mind that distinguishes the female sex that, though she had been sent out on a hurried errand to call the children, yet she had on her best bonnet, and every curl of her hair had evidently been carefully and properly attended to that morning.

"Of course, I wasn't going to look like a fright," she soliloquized. "Not that I care for any of 'em; but looks is looks any time o' day."

At the minister's breakfast-table the approaching so-lemnities were discussed. The procession was to form at the court house at nine o'clock. Democrats and Federalists had united to distribute impartially as possible the honors of the day.[3] As Colonel Davenport, the only real live Revolution-ary officer the county boasted, was an essential element of the show, and as he was a stanch Federalist, it was necessary to be conciliatory. Then there was the Federal ex-governor to sit on the platform with the newly elected Democratic governor. The services were in the meeting-house, as the largest building in town; and Dr. Cushing was appointed to make the opening prayer. As a compliment to the Episcopal church the Federal members of the committee allotted a closing prayer to the Rev. Simeon Coan.[4] That young man, however, faithful to the logic of his creed, politely declined joining in public services where his assisting might be held to recognize the ordination of an unauthorized sectarian preacher;[5] and so the Rev. Dr. Goodman, of Skantic, was appointed in his place. Squire Lewis was observed slightly to elevate his eyebrows and shrug his shoulders as he communicated to the committee the grounds of his rector's refusal. He was, in fact, annoyed, and a little embarrassed, by the dry, amused expression of Sheriff Dennie's countenance.

"Oh, speak it all out; never fear, Lewis," he said. "I like to see a man face the music. Your minister is a logical fellow, and keeps straight up to what he teaches. You old Episcopalians were getting loose in your ideas; you needed cording up."

"There's such a thing as cording too tight and breaking a string sometimes," muttered the squire, who was not well pleased at the scruple that kept his church unrepresented in the exercise.

The domestic arrangements for the parson's family were announced at the breakfast-table. The boys were endowed with the magnificent sum of six cents each and turned loose for the day, with the parting admonition to keep clear of powder—a most hopeless and unnecessary charge, since powder was the very heart and essence of all the glory of the day.

At an early hour the bell of the meeting-house rung out over all the neighboring hills and valleys; the summons was replied to by streams of wagons on the roads leading to Poganuc for a square of ten miles round. Not merely Poganuc—North, South, East, West, and Centre—was in motion, but several adjacent towns and villages sent forth their trainers—bands of militia, who rose about midnight and marched till morning to be on time.

By nine o'clock nominally (but far nearer to ten really) the procession started from the court house with drum and fife and banners. Dolly had been committed for the day to the charge of Nabby, who should see that she took no harm, and engineer for her the best chances of seeing all that went on; while Mrs. Cushing, relieved of this care, took her seat quietly among the matronage of Poganuc and waited for the entrance of the procession. But Dolly saw them start from the court house, with beat of drum and peal of fife; and Dolly saw the banners, and saw Colonel Davenport with his white hair and splendid physique, now more splendid in the blue and gold of his military dress; and they all marched with majestic tread towards the meeting-house. Then Nabby hurried with her charge and got for her a seat by herself in the front singers' seat in the gallery, where she could see them all file in and take their seats on the platform. Nabby had been one of the flowers of this singers' seat before her father's change of base had transferred her to the Episcopal church, and her presence to-day was welcomed by many old friends—for Nabby had a good, strong, clear voice of her own, and was no small addition to the choral force.

The services opened by the national Puritan[6] psalm:—

"Let children hear the mighty deeds
Which God performed of old,
Which in our younger years we saw
And which our fathers told.

"Our lips shall teach them to our sons,
And they again to theirs,
That generations yet unborn
May teach them to their heirs.

"That they may learn, in God alone
Their hope securely stands;
That they may ne'er his laws forget,
But practice his commands."[7]

The wild warble of "St. Martin's,"[8] the appointed tune whose wings bore these words, swelled and billowed and reverberated through the house, carrying with it that indefinable thrill which always fills a house when deep emotions are touched—deepest among people habitually reserved and reticent of outward demonstration. It was this solemn undertone, this mysterious, throbbing sub-bass of repressed emotion, which gave the power and effect to the Puritan music. After the singing came Dr. Cushing's prayer—which was a recounting of God's mercies to New England from the beginning, and of his deliverances from her enemies, and of petitions for the glorious future of the United States of America—that they might be chosen vessels, commissioned to bear the light of liberty and religion through all the earth and to bring in the great millennial day, when wars should cease and the whole world, released from the thralldom of evil, should rejoice in the light of the Lord.

The millennium was ever the star of hope in the eyes of the New England clergy; their faces were set eastward, towards the dawn of that day, and the cheerfulness of those anticipations illuminated the hard tenets of their theology with a rosy glow. They were children of the morning. The doctor, however, did not fail to make use of his privilege to give some very decided political hits, and some petitions arose which caused sensation between the different parties. The New England clergyman on these occasions had his political antagonists at decided advantage. If he could not speak at them he could pray at them, and of course there was no reply to an impeachment in the court of heaven. So

when the doctor's prayer was over, glances were inter-
changed, showing the satisfaction or dissatisfaction, as
might be, of the listeners.

And now rose Colonel Davenport to read the Declaration of Independence.[9] Standing square and erect, his
head thrown back, he read in a resonant and emphatic
voice that great enunciation upon which American national existence was founded. Dolly had never heard it
before, and even now had but a vague idea of what was
meant by some parts of it; but she gathered enough from
the recital of the abuses and injuries which had driven her
nation to this course to feel herself swelling with indignation, and ready with all her little mind and strength to
applaud that concluding Declaration of Independence
which the colonel rendered with resounding majesty. She
was as ready as any of them to pledge her "life, fortune, and
sacred honor" for such a cause. The heroic element was
strong in Dolly; it had come down by "ordinary generation"
from a line of Puritan ancestry, and just now it swelled her
little frame and brightened her cheeks and made her long
to do something, she scarce knew what; to fight for her
country or to make some declaration on her own account.

But now came the oration of the day, pronounced by a
lively young Virginia law student in the office of Judge
Gridley. It was as ornate and flowery, as full of patriotism
and promise, as has been the always approved style of such
productions. The bird of our nation received the usual
appropriate flourishes, flew upward and sunward, waved
his pinions, gazed with undaunted eye on the brightness,
and did all other things appointed for the American Ea-
gle[10] to do on the Fourth of July. It was a nicely written
classical composition, and eminently satisfactory to the audience; and Dolly, without any very direct conception of its
exact meaning, was delighted with it, and so were all the
Poganuc people.

Then came the singing of an elaborate anthem, on which the choir had been practicing for a month beforehand, and in which the various parts ran, and skipped, and hopped, and chased each other round and round, and performed all sorts of unheard-of trills and quavers and musical evolutions, with a heartiness of self-satisfaction that was charming to witness.

Then, when all was over, the procession marched out—the magnates on the stage to a dinner, and the Poganuc military to refresh themselves at Glazier's, preparatory to the grand review in the afternoon. Dolly spent her six cents for gingerbread, and walked unwearyingly the rounds of sight-seeing with Nabby, her soul inly uplifted with the grandeur of the occasion.

In the afternoon came the military display; and Colonel Davenport on his white horse reviewed the troops; and just behind him, also mounted, was old Cato, with his gold-laced hat and plume, his buff breeches and long-tailed blue coat. On the whole, this solemn black attendant formed a striking and picturesque addition to the scene. And so there were marching and countermarching and military evolutions of all kinds, and Hiel, with his Poganuc Rangers, figured conspicuously in the eyes of all. It was a dangerous sight for Nabby. She really could not help feeling a secret awe for Hiel, as if he had been wafted away from her into some higher sphere; he looked so very determined and martial that she began to admit that he might carry any fortress that he set himself seriously to attack. After the regular review came the sham fight, which was, in fact, but an organized military frolic. Some of the West Poganuc youth had dressed themselves as Indians, and other companies, drawn by lot, were to personate the British, and there was skirmishing and fighting and running, to the wild and crazy delight of the boys. A fort, which had been previously constructed of bushes and trees, was furiously attacked by British and Indians, and set on fire; and then the Americans bursting out scattered both the fire and the forces, and performed prodigies of valor. In short, it was a day of days to Dolly and the children, and when sober twilight drew on they came home intoxicated with patriotism and sight-seeing.

On her way home Dolly was spied out by her old friend Judge Gridley, who always delighted to have a gossip with her.

"Ha, my little Dolly, are you out to-day?"

"To be sure, sir," said Dolly; "indeed I'm out. Oh, hasn't it been glorious! I've never been so happy in my life. I never heard the Declaration of Independence before."

"Well, and what do you think of it?" asked the judge.

"I never heard anything like it," said Dolly. "I didn't know before how they did abuse us, and wasn't it grand that we wouldn't bear it! I never heard anything so splendid as that last part."

"You would have made a good soldier."

"If I were a man I would. Only think of it, Colonel Davenport fought in the war! I'm so glad we can see one man that did. If we had lived then, I know my papa and all my brothers would have fought; we would have had 'liberty or death.' "[11]

Dolly pronounced these words, which she had heard in the oration, with a quivering eagerness. The old judge gave her cheek a friendly pinch.

"You'll do," he said; "but now you must let Nabby here get you home and quiet you down, or you won't sleep all night. Good-by, Pussy."

And so went off Dolly's Fourth of July. But Hiel made an evening call at the parsonage in his full regimentals, and stayed to a late hour unreproved. There were occasions when even the nine o'clock bell did not send a young fellow home. This appeared to be one of them.

Notes

1. George Washington, 1732–1799, commander-in-chief of the American forces during the American Revolution, 1775–1783, and first president of the United States, 1789–1797.

2. Battle of Long Island, August 27, 1776, a defeat for the American forces in New York.

3. Members of the two opposing political parties in New England. See notes 2 and 5 in preceding selection, "Election Day in Poganuc."

4. The newly elected Democrats were closely identified with the Episcopalians.

5. The Episcopalians maintained the ordination of their clergy was in direct succession from the Apostles and that Protestant, hence Congregational, clergy lacked the "authority" of Christ's laying on of hands.

6. See note 9, "Election Day in Poganuc."

7. Isaac Watts, 1674–1748, English writer of hymns and paraphraser of psalms. Stanzas 1, 3, and 4.

8. A melody commonly used for the setting of several hymns.

9. Issued on July 4, 1776, this document listed the grievances of the American colonies against Great Britain and declared them to be free and independent of the mother country.

10. Emblem of the United States of America.

11. "I know not what course others may take, but as for me, give me liberty, or give me death." Spoken by Patrick Henry, 1736–1799, patriot of the American Revolution, in a speech before the Virginia Convention, 1775.

CHAPTER IX.

IN WHICH IT APPEARS THAT A SENATOR IS BUT A MAN.

Scene from *Uncle Tom's Cabin*, Illustrated Edition, 1853

Eliza gaar over Floden.

Illustration of Eliza's crossing the ice, *Onkel Tomc Hytte*,
Norwegian edition, 1895

« Nelle ultime ore di vita, una bianca figura inesorabile... »

Ghost visiting Simon Legree in *La Capanna Dello Zio Tom*,
Italian edition, 1950

Sojourner Truth, c. 1863–1864

The Libyan Sibyl, sculpture in marble by William Wetmore Story
Credit: National Museum of American Art, Smithsonian Institution, Gift of the Estate of Henry Cabot Lodge

Harriet Beecher Stowe writes from her winter home in Mandarin, Florida, January 13, 1876, to a Mrs. Strong, who rents her Hartford home in the absence of the Stowes. This letter illustrates Stowe's habit of crosshatching, a practice that makes reading her correspondence difficult.

Casco Bay, Maine, painted by Harriet Beecher Stowe

Short Fiction

UNCLE LOT

In November, 1833, Harriet Beecher read a story about her granduncle, Lot Benton, to the members of the Semi-Colon Club, a literary group to which she belonged in Cincinnati, Ohio. James Hall, a fellow member and editor of a regional magazine, invited her to submit her piece to a fiction contest being sponsored by his publication. On April 3, 1834, *Western Monthly Magazine* published "A New England Sketch" and awarded Miss Beecher the $50.00 prize. Her first signed story carried the label, "Prize Tale." Frequently reprinted in newspapers and magazines in the succeeding years, the tale was included in *The Mayflower; or, Sketches of Scenes and Characters among the Descendants of the Pilgrims,* Harriet Beecher Stowe's first collection of her shorter works in 1843. The story appeared here as "Uncle Tim" because the author felt the sketch was "too personal for presentation upon a national stage." Stowe herself always referred to the tale as "Uncle Lot."

And so I am to write a story—but of what, and where? Shall it be radiant with the sky of Italy? or eloquent with the beau ideal of Greece? Shall it breathe odor and languor from the orient, or chivalry from the occident? or gayety from France? or vigor from England? No, no; these are all too old—too romance-like—too obviously picturesque for me. No; let me turn to my own land—my own New England; the land of bright fires and strong hearts; the land of deeds, and not of words; the land of fruits, and not of flowers; the land often spoken against, yet always respected; "the latchet of whose shoes the nations of the earth are not worthy to unloose."[1]

Now, from this very heroic apostrophe, you may suppose that I have something very heroic to tell. By no means. It is merely a little introductory breeze of patriotism, such as occasionally brushes over every mind, bearing on its wings the remembrance of all we ever loved or cherished in the land of our early years; and if it should seem to be rodomontade to any people in other parts of the earth, let them only imagine it to be said about "Old Kentuck," old England, or any other corner of the world in which they happened to be born and they will find it quite rational.

But, as touching our story, it is time to begin. Did you ever see the little village of Newbury,[2] in New England? I dare say you never did; for it was just one of those out-of-the-way places where nobody ever came unless they came on purpose: a green little hollow, wedged like a bird's nest between half a dozen high hills, that kept off the wind and kept out foreigners; so that the little place was as straitly *sui generis* as if there were not another in the world. The inhabitants were all of that respectable old standfast family who make it a point to be born, bred, married, to die, and be buried all in the selfsame spot. There were just so many houses, and just so many people lived in them; and nobody ever seemed to be sick, or to die either, at least while I was there. The natives grew old till they could not grow any older, and then they stood still, and *lasted* from generation to generation. There was, too, an unchangeability about all the externals of Newbury. Here was a red house, and there was a brown house, and across the way was a yellow house; and there was a straggling rail fence or a tribe of mullein stalks between. The minister lived here, and Squire Moses lived there, and Deacon Hart lived under the hill, and Messrs. Nadab and Abihu Peters lived by the crossroad, and the old "widder" Smith lived by the meeting-house, and Ebenezer Camp kept a shoemaker's shop on one side, and Patience Mosely kept a milliner's shop in front; and there was old Comfort Scran, who kept store for the whole town, and sold axeheads, brass thimbles, licorice balls, fancy handkerchiefs, and everything else you can think of. Here, too, was the general post-office, where you might see letters marvelously folded, directed wrong side upward, stamped with a thimble, and superscribed to some of the Dollys, or Pollys, or Peters, or Moseses aforenamed or not named.

For the rest, as to manners, morals, arts, and sciences, the people in Newbury always went to their parties at three o'clock in the afternoon, and came home before dark; always stopped all work the minute the sun was down on Saturday night; always went to meeting on Sunday; had a schoolhouse with all the ordinary inconveniences; were in neighborly charity with each other; read their Bibles, feared their God, and were content with such things as they had—the best philosophy, after all. Such was the place into which Master James Benton made an irruption in the year eighteen hundred and no matter what. Now, this James is to be our hero, and he is just the hero for a sensation—at least, so you would have thought, if you had been in Newbury the week after his arrival. Master James was one of those whole-hearted, energetic Yankees, who rise in the world as naturally as cork does in water. He possessed a great share of that characteristic national trait so happily denominated "cuteness," which signifies an ability to do everything without trying, and to know everything without learning, and to make more use of one's ignorance than other people do of their knowledge. This quality in James was mingled with an elasticity of animal spirits, a buoyant cheerfulness of mind, which, though found in the New England character, perhaps, as often as anywhere else, is not ordinarily regarded as one of its distinguishing traits.

As to the personal appearance of our hero, we have not much to say of it—not half so much as the girls in

Newbury found it necessary to remark, the first Sabbath that he shone out in the meeting-house. There was a saucy frankness of countenance, a knowing roguery of eye, a joviality and prankishness of demeanor, that was wonderfully captivating, especially to the ladies.

It is true that Master James had an uncommonly comfortable opinion of himself, a full faith that there was nothing in creation that he could not learn and could not do; and this faith was maintained with an abounding and triumphant joyfulness, that fairly carried your sympathies along with him, and made you feel quite as much delighted with his qualifications and prospects as he felt himself. There are two kinds of self-sufficiency: one is amusing, and the other is provoking. His was the amusing kind. It seemed, in truth, to be only the buoyancy and overflow of a vivacious mind, delighted with everything delightful, in himself or others. He was always ready to magnify his own praise, but quite as ready to exalt his neighbor, if the channel of discourse ran that way: his own perfections being more completely within his knowledge, he rejoiced in them more constantly; but, if those of any one else came within the same range, he was quite as much astonished and edified as if they had been his own.

Master James, at the time of his transit to the town of Newbury, was only eighteen years of age; so that it was difficult to say which predominated in him most, the boy or the man. The belief that he could, and the determination that he would, be something in the world had caused him to abandon his home, and, with all his worldly effects tied in a blue cotton pocket-handkerchief, to proceed to seek his fortune in Newbury. And never did stranger in Yankee village rise to promotion with more unparalleled rapidity, or boast a greater plurality of employment. He figured as schoolmaster all the week, and as chorister on Sundays, and taught singing and reading in the evenings, besides studying Latin and Greek with the minister, nobody knew when;

thus fitting for college, while he seemed to be doing everything else in the world besides.

James understood every art and craft of popularity, and made himself mightily at home in all the chimney-corners of the region round about; knew the geography of everybody's cider barrel and apple bin, helping himself and every one else therefrom with all bountifulness; rejoicing in the good things of this life, devouring the old ladies' doughnuts and pumpkin pies with most flattering appetite, and appearing equally to relish every body and thing that came in his way.

The degree and versatility of his acquirements were truly wonderful. He knew all about arithmetic and history, and all about catching squirrels and planting corn; made poetry and hoe-handles with equal celerity; wound yarn and took out grease spots for old ladies, and made nosegays and knick-knacks for young ones; caught trout Saturday afternoons, and discussed doctrines on Sundays, with equal adroitness and effect. In short, Mr. James moved on through the place

"Victorious,
Happy and glorious,"[3]

welcomed and privileged by everybody in every place; and when he had told his last ghost story, and fairly flourished himself out of doors at the close of a long winter's evening, you might see the hard face of the good man of the house still phosphorescent with his departing radiance, and hear him exclaim, in a paroxysm of admiration, that "Jemeses talk re'ly did beat all; that he was sartainly most a miraculous cre'tur!"

It was wonderfully contrary to the buoyant activity of Master James's mind to keep a school. He had, moreover, so much of the boy and the rogue in his composition, that he could not be strict with the iniquities of the curly pates

(*157*)

under his charge; and when he saw how determinately every little heart was boiling over with mischief and motion, he felt in his soul more disposed to join in and help them to a frolic than to lay justice to the line, as was meet. This would have made a sad case, had it not been that the activity of the master's mind communicated itself to his charge, just as the reaction of one brisk little spring will fill a manufactory with motion; so that there was more of an impulse towards study in the golden, good-natured day of James Benton than in the time of all that went before or came after him.

But when "school was out," James's spirits foamed over as naturally as a tumbler of soda water, and he could jump over benches and burst out of doors with as much rapture as the veriest little elf in his company. Then you might have seen him stepping homeward with a most felicitous expression of countenance, occasionally reaching his hand through the fence for a bunch of currants, or over it after a flower, or bursting into some back yard to help an old lady empty her washtub, or stopping to pay his devoirs to Aunt This or Mistress That, for James well knew the importance of the "powers that be,"[4] and always kept the sunny side of the old ladies.

We shall not answer for James's general flirtations, which were sundry and manifold; for he had just the kindly heart that fell in love with everything in feminine shape that came in his way, and if he had not been blessed with an equal facility in falling out again, we do not know what ever would have become of him. But at length he came into an abiding captivity, and it is quite time that he should; for having devoted thus much space to the illustration of our hero, it is fit we should do something in behalf of our heroine; and, therefore, we must beg the reader's attention while we draw a diagram or two that will assist him in gaining a right idea of her.

Do you see yonder brown house, with its broad roof sloping almost to the ground on one side, and a great, unsupported sunbonnet of a piazza shooting out over the front door? You must often have noticed it; you have seen its tall wellsweep, relieved against the clear evening sky, or observed the feather beds and bolsters lounging out of its chamber windows on a still summer morning; you recollect its gate, that swung with a chain and a great stone; its pantry window, latticed with little brown slabs, and looking out upon a forest of beanpoles. You remember the zephyrs that used to play among its pea brush, and shake the long tassels of its corn patch, and how vainly any zephyr might essay to perform similar flirtations with the considerate cabbages that were solemnly vegetating near by. Then there was the whole neighborhood of purple-leaved beets and feathery parsnips; there were the billows of gooseberry bushes rolled up by the fence, interspersed with rows of quince-trees; and far off in one corner was one little patch, penuriously devoted to ornament, which flamed with mari-golds, poppies, snappers, and four-o'clocks. Then there was a little box by itself with one rose geranium in it, which seemed to look around the garden as much like a stranger as a French dancing-master in a Yankee meeting-house.

That is the dwelling of Uncle Lot Griswold. Uncle Lot, as he was commonly called, had a character that a painter would sketch for its lights and contrasts rather than its symmetry. He was a chestnut burr, abounding with briers without and with substantial goodness within. He had the strong-grained practical sense, the calculating worldly wis-dom of his class of people in New England; he had, too, a kindly heart; but all the strata of his character were crossed by a vein of surly petulance, that, halfway between joke and earnest, colored everything that he said and did.

If you asked a favor of Uncle Lot, he generally kept you arguing half an hour, to prove that you really needed it, and to tell you that he could not all the while be troubled with helping one body or another, all which time you might observe him regularly making his preparations to grant your request, and see, by an odd glimmer of his eye, that he was preparing to let you hear the "conclusion of the whole matter,"[5] which was, "Well, well—I guess—I'll go, on the *hull*—I s'pose I must, at least;" so off he would go and work while the day lasted, and then wind up with a farewell exhortation "not to be a-callin' on your neighbors when you could get along without." If any of Uncle Lot's neighbors were in any trouble, he was always at hand to tell them that "they shouldn't 'a' done so;" that "it was strange they couldn't had more sense;" and then to close his exhortations by laboring more diligently than any to bring them out of their difficulties, groaning in spirit, meanwhile, that folks would make people so much trouble.

"Uncle Lot, father wants to know if you will lend him your hoe to-day," says a little boy, making his way across a cornfield.

"Why don't your father use his own hoe?"

"Ours is broke."

"Broke! How came it broke?"

"I broke it yesterday, trying to hit a squirrel."

"What business had you to be hittin' squirrels with a hoe?—say!"

"But father wants to borrow yours."

"Why don't you have that mended? It's a great pester to have everybody usin' a body's things."

"Well, I can borrow one somewhere else, I suppose," says the suppliant. After the boy has stumbled across the ploughed ground, and is fairly over the fence, Uncle Lot calls,—

"Hallo, there, you little rascal! what are you goin' off without the hoe for?"

"I didn't know as you meant to lend it."

"I didn't say I wouldn't, did I? Here, come and take it—stay, I'll bring it; and do tell your father not to be a-lettin' you hunt squirrels with his hoes next time."

Uncle Lot's household consisted of Aunt Sally, his wife, and an only son and daughter; the son, at the time our story begins, was at a neighboring literary institution. Aunt

Sally was precisely as clever, as easy to be entreated, and kindly in externals, as her helpmate was the reverse. She was one of those respectable, pleasant old ladies whom you might often have met on the way to church on a Sunday, equipped with a great fan and a psalm-book, and carrying some dried orange peel or a stalk of fennel, to give to the children if they were sleepy in meeting. She was as cheerful and domestic as the teakettle that sung by her kitchen fire, and slipped along among Uncle Lot's angles and peculiarities as if there never was anything the matter in the world; and the same mantle of sunshine seemed to have fallen on Miss Grace, her only daughter.

Pretty in her person and pleasant in her ways, endowed with native self-possession and address, lively and chatty, having a mind and a will of her own, yet good-humored withal, Miss Grace was a universal favorite. It would have puzzled a city lady to understand how Grace, who never was out of Newbury in her life, knew the way to speak, and act, and behave, on all occasions, exactly as if she had been taught how. She was just one of those wild flowers which you may sometimes see waving its little head in the woods, and looking so civilized and garden-like, that you wonder if it really did come up and grow there by nature. She was an adept in all household concerns, and there was something amazingly pretty in her energetic way of bustling about, and "putting things to rights." Like most Yankee damsels, she had a longing after the tree of knowledge, and, having exhausted the literary fountains of a district school, she fell to reading whatsoever came in her way. True, she had but little to read; but what she perused she had her own thoughts upon, so that a person of information, in talking with her, would feel a constant wondering pleasure to find that she had so much more to say of this, that, and the other thing than he expected.

Uncle Lot, like every one else, felt the magical brightness of his daughter, and was delighted with her praises, as might be discerned by his often finding occasion to remark that "he didn't see why the boys need to be all the time a-comin' to see Grace, for she was nothing so extraor'nary, after all." About all matters and things at home she generally had her own way, while Uncle Lot would scold and give up with a regular good grace that was quite creditable.

"Father," says Grace, "I want to have a party next week."

"You sha'n't go to havin' your parties, Grace. I always have to eat bits and ends a fortnight after you have one, and I won't have it so." And so Uncle Lot walked out, and Aunt Sally and Miss Grace proceeded to make the cake and pies for the party.

When Uncle Lot came home, he saw a long array of pies and rows of cakes on the kitchen table.

"Grace—Grace—Grace, I say! What is all this here flummery for?"

"Why, it is to eat, father," said Grace, with a good-natured look of consciousness.

Uncle Lot tried his best to look sour; but his visage began to wax comical as he looked at his merry daughter; so he said nothing, but quietly sat down to his dinner.

"Father," said Grace, after dinner, "we shall want two more candlesticks next week."

"Why, can't you have your party with what you've got?"

"No, father, we want two more."

"I can't afford it, Grace—there's no sort of use on't— and you sha'n't have any."

"Oh, father, now do," said Grace.

"I won't, neither," said Uncle Lot, as he sallied out of the house, and took the road to Comfort Scran's store.

In half an hour he returned again; and fumbling in his pocket, and drawing forth a candlestick, leveled it at Grace.

"There's your candlestick."

"But, father, I said I wanted two."

"Why, can't you make one do?"

"No, I can't; I must have two."

"Well, then, there's t'other; and here's a fol-de-rol for you to tie round your neck." So saying, he bolted for the door, and took himself off with all speed. It was much after this fashion that matters commonly went on in the brown house.

But having tarried long on the way, we must proceed with the main story.

James thought Miss Grace was a glorious girl; and as to what Miss Grace thought of Master James, perhaps it would not have been developed had she not been called to stand on the defensive for him with Uncle Lot. For, from the time that the whole village of Newbury began to be wholly given unto the praise of Master James, Uncle Lot set his face as a flint against him—from the laudable fear of following the multitude. He therefore made conscience of stoutly gainsaying everything that was said in his behalf, which, as James was in high favor with Aunt Sally, he had frequent opportunities to do.

So when Miss Grace perceived that Uncle Lot did not like our hero as much as he ought to do, she, of course, was bound to like him well enough to make up for it. Certain it is that they were remarkably happy in finding opportunities of being acquainted; that James waited on her, as a matter of course, from singing-school; that he volunteered making a new box for her geranium on an improved plan; and above all, that he was remarkably particular in his attentions to Aunt Sally—a stroke of policy which showed that James had a natural genius for this sort of matters. Even when emerging from the meeting-house in full glory, with flute and psalm-book under his arm, he would stop to ask her how she did; and if 't was cold weather, he would carry her foot-stove all the way home from meeting, discoursing upon the sermon and other serious matters, as Aunt Sally observed, "in the pleasantest, prettiest way that ever ye see." This flute was one of the crying sins of James in the eyes of Uncle Lot. James was particularly fond of it, because he had learned to play on it by intuition; and on the decease of the old pitchpipe, which was slain by a fall from the gallery, he took the liberty to introduce the flute in its place. For this and other sins, and for the good reasons above named, Uncle Lot's countenance was not towards James, neither could he be moved to him-ward by any manner of means.

To all Aunt Sally's good words and kind speeches, he had only to say that "he didn't like him; that he hated to see him a-manifesting and glorifying there in the front gallery Sundays, and a-acting everywhere as if he was master of all: he didn't like it and he wouldn't." But our hero was no whit cast down or discomfited by the malcontent aspect of Uncle Lot. On the contrary, when report was made to him of divers of his hard speeches, he only shrugged his shoulders, with a very satisfied air, and remarked that "he knew a thing or two for all that."

"Why, James," said his companion and chief counselor, "do you think Grace likes you?"

"I don't know," said our hero, with a comfortable appearance of certainty.

"But you can't get her, James, if Uncle Lot is cross about it."

"Fudge! I can make Uncle Lot like me if I have a mind to try."

""Well then, Jim, you'll have to give up that flute of yours, I tell you now."

"Fa, sol, la—I can make him like me and my flute too."

"Why, how will you do it?"

"Oh, I'll work it," said our hero.

"Well, Jim, I tell you now, you don't know Uncle Lot if you say so: for he is just the *settest* crittur in his way that ever you saw."

"I do know Uncle Lot, though, better than most folks; he is no more cross than I am; and as to his being set, you have nothing to do but make him think he is in his own way when he is in yours—that is all."

"Well," said the other, "but you see I don't believe it."

"And I'll bet you a gray squirrel that I'll go there this very evening, and get him to like me and my flute both," said James.

Accordingly the late sunshine of that afternoon shone full on the yellow buttons of James as he proceeded to the place of conflict. It was a bright, beautiful evening. A thunder-storm had just cleared away, and the silver clouds lay rolled up in masses around the setting sun; the rain-drops were sparkling and winking to each other over the ends of the leaves, and all the bluebirds and robins, breaking forth into song, made the little green valley as merry as a musical box.

James's soul was always overflowing with that kind of poetry which consists in feeling unspeakably happy; and it is not to be wondered at, considering where he was going, that he should feel in a double ecstasy on the present occasion. He stepped gayly along, occasionally springing over a fence to the right to see whether the rain had swollen the trout brook, or to the left to notice the ripening of Mr. Somebody's watermelons—for James always had an eye on all his neighbors' matters as well as his own.

In this way he proceeded till he arrived at the picket fence that marked the commencement of Uncle Lot's ground. Here he stopped to consider. Just then four or five sheep walked up, and began also to consider a loose picket, which was hanging just ready to drop off; and James began to look at the sheep. "Well, mister," said he, as he observed the leader judiciously drawing himself through the gap, "in with you—just what I wanted;" and having waited a moment to ascertain that all the company were likely to follow, he ran with all haste towards the house, and swinging open the gate, pressed all breathless to the door.

"Uncle Lot, there are four or five sheep in your garden!" Uncle Lot dropped his whetstone and scythe.

"I'll drive them out," said our hero; and with that, he ran down the garden alley, and made a furious descent on the enemy; bestirring himself, as Bunyan says, "lustily and with good courage,"[6] till every sheep had skipped out much quicker than it skipped in; and then, springing over the fence, he seized a great stone, and nailed on the picket so effectually that no sheep could possibly encourage the hope of getting in again. This was all the work of a minute, and he was back again; but so exceedingly out of breath that it was necessary for him to stop a moment and rest himself. Uncle Lot looked ungraciously satisfied.

"What under the canopy set you to scampering so?" said he; "I could 'a' driv out them critturs myself."

"If you are at all particular about driving them out yourself, I can let them in again," said James.

Uncle Lot looked at him with an odd sort of twinkle in the corner of his eye.

"'Spose I must ask you to walk in," said he.

"Much obliged," said James; "but I am in a great hurry." So saying, he started in very business-like fashion towards the gate.

"You'd better jest stop a minute."

"Can't stay a minute."

"I don't see what possesses you to be all the while in sich in hurry; a body would think you had all creation on your shoulders."

"Just my situation, Uncle Lot," said James, swinging open the gate.

"Well, at any rate, have a drink of cider, can't ye?" said Uncle Lot, who was now quite engaged to have his own way in the case.

James found it convenient to accept this invitation, and Uncle Lot was twice as good-natured as if he had stayed in the first of the matter.

Once fairly forced into the premises, James thought fit to forget his long walk and excess of business, especially as about that moment Aunt Sally and Miss Grace returned from an afternoon call. You may be sure that the last thing these respectable ladies looked for was to find Uncle Lot and Master James tête-à-tête, over a pitcher of cider; and when, as they entered, our hero looked up with something of a mischievous air, Miss Grace in particular was so puzzled that it took her at least a quarter of an hour to untie her bonnet strings. But James stayed, and acted the agreeable to perfection. First, he must needs go down into the garden to look at Uncle Lot's wonderful cabbages, and then he promenaded all around the corn patch, stopping every few moments and looking up with an appearance of great gratification, as if he had never seen such corn in his life; and then he examined Uncle Lot's favorite apple-tree with an expression of wonderful interest.

"I never!" he broke forth, having stationed himself against the fence opposite to it; "what kind of an apple-tree is that?"

"It's a bellflower, or somethin' another," said Uncle Lot.

"Why, where did you get it? I never saw such apples!" said our hero, with his eyes still fixed on the tree.

Uncle Lot pulled up a stalk or two of weeds, and threw them over the fence, just to show that he did not care anything about the matter; and then he came up and stood by James.

"Nothin' so remarkable, as I know on," said he.

Just then Grace came to say that supper was ready. Once seated at table, it was astonishing to see the perfect and smiling assurance with which our hero continued his addresses to Uncle Lot. It sometimes goes a great way towards making people like us to take it for granted that they do already; and upon this principle James proceeded. He talked, laughed, told stories, and joked with the most fearless assurance, occasionally seconding his words by looking Uncle Lot in the face, with a countenance so full of good will as would have melted any snowdrift of prejudices in the world.

James also had one natural accomplishment, more

courtier-like than all the diplomacy in Europe, and that was the gift of feeling a *real* interest for anybody in five minutes; so that, if he began to please in jest, he generally ended in earnest. With great simplicity of mind, he had a natural tact for seeing into others, and watched their motions with the same delight with which a child gazes at the wheels and springs of a watch, to "see what it will do."

The rough exterior and latent kindness of Uncle Lot were quite a spirit-stirring study; and when tea was over, as he and Grace happened to be standing together in the front door, he broke forth,—

"I do really like your father, Grace!"

"Do you?" said Grace.

"Yes, I do. He has something in him, and I like him all the better for having to fish it out."

"Well, I hope you will make him like you," said Grace unconsciously; and then she stopped, and looked a little ashamed.

James was too well bred to see this, or look as if Grace meant any more than she said,—a kind of breeding not always attendant on more fashionable polish,—so he only answered,—

"I think I shall, Grace, though I doubt whether I can get him to own it."

"He is the kindest man that ever was," said Grace; "and he always acts as if he was ashamed of it."

James turned a little away, and looked at the bright evening sky, which was glowing like a calm, golden sea; and over it was the silver new moon, with one little star to hold the candle for her. He shook some bright drops off from a rosebush near by, and watched to see them shine as they fell, while Grace stood very quietly waiting for him to speak again.

"Grace," said he at last, "I am going to college this fall."

"So you told me yesterday," said Grace.

James stooped down over Grace's geranium, and began to busy himself with pulling off all the dead leaves, remarking in the mean while,—

"And if I do get him to like me, Grace, will you like me too?"

"I like you now very well," said Grace.

"Come, Grace, you know what I mean," said James, looking steadfastly at the top of the apple-tree.

"Well, I wish, then, you would understand what I mean without my saying any more about it," said Grace.

"Oh, to be sure I will!" said our hero, looking up with a very intelligent air; and so, as Aunt Sally would say, the matter was settled, with "no words about it."

Now shall we narrate how our hero, as he saw Uncle Lot approaching the door, had the impudence to take out his flute, and put the parts together, arranging and adjusting the stops with great composure?

"Uncle Lot," said he, looking up, "this is the best flute that ever I saw."

"I hate them tooting critturs," said Uncle Lot snappishly.

"I declare! I wonder how you can," said James; "for I do think they exceed"—

So saying, he put the flute to his mouth, and ran up and down a long flourish.

"There! what do you think of that?" said he, looking in Uncle Lot's face with much delight.

Uncle Lot turned and marched into the house, but soon faced to the right-about, and came out again, for James was fingering "Yankee Doodle"—that appropriate national air for the descendants of the Puritans.

Uncle Lot's patriotism began to bestir itself; and now, if it had been anything, as he said, but "that 'ere flute"—As it was, he looked more than once at James's fingers.

"How under the sun could you learn to do that?" said he.

"Oh, it's easy enough," said James, proceeding with

another tune; and, having played it through, he stopped a moment to examine the joints of his flute, and in the mean time addressed Uncle Lot: "You can't think how grand this is for pitching tunes—I always pitch the tunes on Sunday with it."

"Yes; but I don't think it's a right and fit instrument for the Lord's house," said Uncle Lot.

"Why not? It is only a kind of a long pitchpipe, you see," said James; "and, seeing the old one is broken, and this will answer, I don't see why it is not better than nothing."

"Why, yes, it may be better than nothing," said Uncle Lot; "but, as I always tell Grace and my wife, it ain't the right kind of instrument, after all; it ain't solemn."

"Solemn!" said James; "that is according as you work it: see here, now."

So saying, he struck up Old Hundred,[7] and proceeded through it with great perseverance.

"There, now!" said he.

"Well, well, I don't know but it is," said Uncle Lot; "but as I said at first, I don't like the look of it in meetin'."

"But yet you really think it is better than nothing," said James, "for you see I couldn't pitch my tunes without it."

"Maybe 't is," said Uncle Lot; "but that isn't sayin' much."

This, however, was enough for Master James, who soon after departed, with his flute in his pocket, and Grace's last words in his heart; soliloquizing as he shut the gate, "There, now, I hope Aunt Sally won't go to praising me; for, just so sure as she does, I shall have it all to do over again."

James was right in his apprehension. Uncle Lot could be privately converted, but not brought to open confession; and when, the next morning, Aunt Sally remarked, in the kindness of her heart,—

"Well, I always knew you would come to like James," Uncle Lot only responded, "Who said I did like him?"

"But I'm sure you seemed to like him last night."

"Why, I couldn't turn him out o' doors, could I? I don't think nothin' of him but what I always did."

But it was to be remarked that Uncle Lot contented himself at this time with the mere general avowal, without running it into particulars, as was formerly his wont. It was evident that the ice had begun to melt, but it might have been a long time in dissolving, had not collateral incidents assisted.

It so happened that about this time George Griswold, the only son before referred to, returned to his native village, after having completed his theological studies at a neighboring institution. It is interesting to mark the gradual development of mind and heart, from the time that the white-headed, bashful boy quits the country village for college, to the period when he returns, a formed and matured man; to notice how gradually the rust of early prejudices begins to cleave from him—how his opinions, like his handwriting, pass from the cramped and limited forms of a country school into that confirmed and characteristic style which is to mark the man for life. In George this change was remarkably striking. He was endowed by nature with uncommon acuteness of feeling and fondness for reflection—qualities as likely as any to render a child backward and uninteresting in early life.

When he left Newbury for college, he was a taciturn and apparently phlegmatic boy, only evincing sensibility by blushing and looking particularly stupefied whenever anybody spoke to him. Vacation after vacation passed, and he returned more and more an altered being; and he who once shrank from the eye of the deacon, and was ready to sink if he met the minister, now moved about among the dignitaries of the place with all the composure of a superior being.

It was only to be regretted that, while the mind improved, the physical energies declined, and that every visit to his home found him paler, thinner, and less prepared in

(*171*)

body for the sacred profession to which he had devoted himself. But now he was returned, a minister—a real minister, with a right to stand in the pulpit and preach; and what a joy and glory to Aunt Sally—and to Uncle Lot, if he were not ashamed to own it!

The first Sunday after he came, it was known far and near that George Griswold was to preach; and never was a more ready and expectant audience.

As the time for reading the first psalm approached, you might see the white-headed men turning their faces attentively towards the pulpit; the anxious and expectant old women, with their little black bonnets, bent forward to see him rise. There were the children looking, because everybody else looked; there was Uncle Lot in the front pew, his face considerately adjusted; there was Aunt Sally, seeming as pleased as a mother could seem; and Miss Grace, lifting her sweet face to her brother, like a flower to the sun; there was our friend James in the front gallery, his joyous countenance a little touched with sobriety and expectation; in short, a more embarrassingly attentive audience never greeted the first effort of a young minister. Under these circumstances there was something touching in the fervent self-forgetfulness which characterized the first exercises of the morning—something which moved every one in the house.

The devout poetry of his prayer, rich with the Orientalism of Scripture, and eloquent with the expression of strong yet chastened emotion, breathed over his audience like music, hushing every one to silence, and beguiling every one to feeling. In the sermon, there was the strong intellectual nerve, the constant occurrence of argument and statement, which distinguishes a New England discourse; but it was touched with life by the intense, yet half-subdued, feeling with which he seemed to utter it. Like the rays of the sun, it enlightened and melted at the same moment.

(*172*)

The strong peculiarities of New England doctrine, involving, as they do, all the hidden machinery of mind, all the mystery of its divine relations and future progression, and all the tremendous uncertainties of its eternal good or ill, seemed to have dwelt in his mind, to have burned in his thoughts, to have wrestled with his powers, and they gave to his manner the fervency almost of another world; while the exceeding paleness of his countenance, and a tremulousness of voice that seemed to spring from bodily weakness, touched the strong workings of his mind with a pathetic interest, as if the being so early absorbed in another world could not be long for this.

When the services were over, the congregation dispersed with the air of people who had felt rather than heard; and all the criticism that followed was similar to that of old Deacon Hart,—an upright, shrewd man,—who, as he lingered a moment at the church door, turned and gazed with unwonted feeling at the young preacher.

"He's a blessed cre'tur!" said he, the tears actually making their way to his eyes; "I hain't been so near heaven this many a day. He's a blessed cre'tur of the Lord; that's my mind about him!"

As for our friend James, he was at first sobered, then deeply moved, and at last wholly absorbed by the discourse; and it was only when meeting was over that he began to think where he really was.

With all his versatile activity, James had a greater depth of mental capacity than he was himself aware of, and he began to feel a sort of electric affinity for the mind that had touched him in a way so new; and when he saw the mild minister standing at the foot of the pulpit stairs, he made directly towards him.

"I do want to hear more from you," said he, with a face full of earnestness; "may I walk home with you?"

"It is a long and warm walk," said George, smiling.

"Oh, I don't care for that, if it does not trouble *you*,"

said James; and leave being gained, you might have seen them slowly passing along under the trees, James pouring forth all the floods of inquiry which the sudden impulse of his mind had brought out, and supplying his guide with more questions and problems for solution than he could have gone through with in a month.

"I cannot answer all your questions now," said he, as they stopped at Uncle Lot's gate.

"Well, then, when will you?" said James eagerly. "Let me come home with you to-night?"

The minister smiled assent, and James departed, so full of new thoughts that he passed Grace without even seeing her. From that time a friendship commenced between the two which was a beautiful illustration of the affinities of opposites. It was like a friendship between morning and evening—all freshness and sunshine on one side, and all gentleness and peace on the other.

The young minister, worn by long-continued ill health, by the fervency of his own feelings, and the gravity of his own reasonings, found pleasure in the healthful buoyancy of a youthful, unexhausted mind, while James felt himself sobered and made better by the moonlight tranquillity of his friend. It is one mark of a superior mind to understand and be influenced by the superiority of others; and this was the case with James. The ascendancy which his new friend acquired over him was unlimited, and did more in a month towards consolidating and developing his character than all the four years' course of a college. Our religious habits are likely always to retain the impression of the first seal which stamped them, and in this case it was a peculiarly happy one. The calmness, the settled purpose, the mild devotion of his friend, formed a just alloy to the energetic and reckless buoyancy of James's character, and awakened in him a set of feelings without which the most vigorous mind must be incomplete.

The effect of the ministrations of the young pastor, in awakening attention to the subjects of his calling in the village, was marked, and of a kind which brought pleasure to his own heart. But, like all other excitement, it tends to exhaustion, and it was not long before he sensibly felt the decline of the powers of life. To the best regulated mind there is something bitter in the relinquishment of projects for which we have been long and laboriously preparing, and there is something far more bitter in crossing the long-cherished expectations of friends. All this George felt. He could not bear to look on his mother, hanging on his words and following his steps with eyes of almost childish delight—on his singular father, whose whole earthly ambition was bound up in his success, and think how soon the "candle of their old age" must be put out. When he returned from a successful effort, it was painful to see the old man, so evidently delighted, and so anxious to conceal his triumph, as he would seat himself in his chair, and begin with, "George, that 'ere doctrine is rather of a puzzler; but you seem to think you've got the run on't. I should re'ly like to know what business you have to think you know better than other folks about it;" and, though he would cavil most courageously at all George's explanations, yet you might perceive, through all, that he was inly uplifted to hear how his boy could talk.

If George was engaged in argument with any one else, he would sit by, with his head bowed down, looking out from under his shaggy eyebrows with a shamefaced satisfaction very unusual with him. Expressions of affection from the naturally gentle are not half so touching as those which are forced out from the hard-favored and severe; and George was affected, even to pain, by the evident pride and regard of his father.

"He never said so much to anybody before," thought he, "and what will he do if I die?"

In such thoughts as these Grace found her brother engaged one still autumn morning, as he stood leaning against the garden fence.

"What are you solemnizing here for, this bright day, brother George?" said she, as she bounded down the alley.

The young man turned, and looked on her happy face with a sort of twilight smile.

"How happy you are, Grace!" said he.

"To be sure I am; and you ought to be too, because you are better."

"I am happy, Grace—that is, I hope I shall be."

"You are sick, I know you are," said Grace; "you look worn out. Oh, I wish your heart could *spring* once, as mine does."

"I am not well, dear Grace, and I fear I never shall be," said he, turning away, and fixing his eyes on the fading trees opposite.

"Oh George! dear George, don't, don't say *that,* you'll break all our hearts," said Grace, with tears in her own eyes.

"Yes, but it is *true,* sister: I do not feel it on my own account so much as— However," he added, "it will all be the same in heaven."

It was but a week after this that a violent cold hastened the progress of debility into a confirmed malady. He sunk very fast. Aunt Sally, with the self-deceit of a fond and cheerful heart, thought every day that "he *would* be better," and Uncle Lot resisted conviction with all the obstinate pertinacity of his character, while the sick man felt that he had not the heart to undeceive them.

James was now at the house every day, exhausting all his energy and invention in the case of his friend; and any one who had seen him in his hours of recklessness and glee, could scarcely recognize him as the being whose step was so careful, whose eye so watchful, whose voice and touch were so gentle, as he moved around the sick-bed. But the same quickness which makes a mind buoyant in gladness often makes it gentlest and most sympathetic in sorrow.

It was now nearly morning in the sick-room. George had been restless and feverish all night; but towards day he fell into a slight slumber, and James sat by his side, almost holding his breath lest he should waken him. It was yet dusk, but the sky was brightening with a solemn glow, and the stars were beginning to disappear; all, save the bright and morning one, which, standing alone in the east, looked tenderly through the casement, like the eye of our Heavenly Father, watching over us when all earthly friendships are fading.

George awoke with a placid expression of countenance, and fixing his eyes on the brightening sky, murmured faintly,—

> "The sweet, immortal morning sheds
> Its blushes round the spheres."[8]

A moment after, a shade passed over his face; he pressed his fingers over his eyes, and the tears dropped silently on his pillow.

"George! *dear* George!" said James, bending over him.

"It's my friends—it's my father—my mother," said he faintly.

"Jesus Christ will watch over them," said James soothingly.

"Oh, yes, I know He will; for *He* loved his own which were in the world; He loved them unto the end. But I am dying—and before I have done any good."

"Oh, do not say so," said James; "think, think what you have done, if only for *me*. God bless you for it! God *will* bless you for it; it will follow you to heaven; it will bring me there. Yes, I will do as you have taught me. I will give my life, my soul, my whole strength to it; and then you will not have lived in vain."

George smiled, and looked upward; "his face was as that of an angel;"[9] and James, in his warmth, continued,—

"It is not I alone who can say this; we all bless you;

(*177*)

every one in his place blesses you; you will be had in everlasting remembrance by some hearts here, I know."

"Bless God!" said George.

"We do," said James. "I bless him that I ever knew you; we all bless him, and we love you, and shall forever."

The glow that had kindled over the pale face of the invalid again faded as he said,—

"But, James, I must—I ought to—tell my father and mother; I ought to, and how can I?"

At that moment the door opened, and Uncle Lot made his appearance. He seemed struck with the paleness of George's face; and coming to the side of the bed, he felt his pulse, and laid his hand anxiously on his forehead, and, clearing his voice several times, inquired "if he didn't feel a little better."

"No, father," said George; then taking his hand, he looked anxiously in his face, and seemed to hesitate a moment. "Father," he began, "you know that we ought to submit to God."

There was something in his expression at this moment which flashed the truth into the old man's mind. He dropped his son's hand with an exclamation of agony, and, turning quickly, left the room.

"Father! father!" said Grace, trying to rouse him, as he stood with his arms folded by the kitchen window.

"Get away, child!" said he roughly.

"Father, mother says breakfast is ready."

"I don't want any breakfast," said he, turning short about. "Sally, what are you fixing in that 'ere porringer?"

"Oh, it's only a little tea for George; 't will comfort him up, and make him feel better, poor fellow."

"You won't make him feel better—he's gone," said Uncle Lot hoarsely.

"Oh, dear heart, no!" said Aunt Sally.

"Be still a-contradicting me; I won't be contradicted all the time by nobody. The short of the case is, that George is goin' to die just as we've got him ready to be a minister and all; and I wish to pity I was in my grave myself, and so"— said Uncle Lot, as he plunged out of the door, and shut it after him.

It is well for a man that there is one Being who sees the suffering heart as it is, and not as it manifests itself through the repellances of outward infirmity, and who, perhaps, feels more for the stern and wayward than for those whose gentler feelings win for them human sympathy. With all his singularities, there was in the heart of Uncle Lot a depth of religious sincerity; but there are few characters where religion does anything more than struggle with natural defect, and modify what would else be far worse.

In this hour of trial, all the native obstinacy and pertinacity of the old man's character rose, and while he felt the necessity of submission, it seemed impossible to submit; and thus reproaching himself, struggling in vain to repress the murmurs of nature, repulsing from him all external sympathy, his mind was "tempest-tossed, and not comforted."[10]

It was on the still afternoon of the following Sabbath that he was sent for, in haste, to the chamber of his son. He entered, and saw that the hour was come. The family were all there. Grace and James, side by side, bent over the dying one, and his mother sat afar off, with her face hid in her apron, "that she might not see the death of the child."[11] The aged minister was there, and the Bible lay open before him. The father walked to the side of the bed. He stood still, and gazed on the face now brightening with "life and immortality." The son lifted up his eyes; he saw his father, smiled, and put out his hand.

"I am glad you are come," said he.

"O George, to the pity, don't! don't smile on me so! I know what is coming; I have tried, and tried, and I can't, I can't have it so;" and his frame shook, and he sobbed audibly. The room was still as death; there was none that seemed able to comfort him. At last the son repeated, in a sweet, but interrupted voice, those words of man's best Friend: "Let not your heart be troubled; in my Father's house are many mansions."[12]

"Yes; but I can't help being troubled; I suppose the Lord's will must be done, but it'll kill me."

"O father, don't, don't break my heart," said the son, much agitated. "I shall see you again in heaven, and you shall see me again; and then 'your heart shall rejoice, and your joy no man taketh from you.' "[13]

"I never shall get to heaven if I feel as I do now," said the old man. "I cannot have it so."

The mild face of the sufferer was overcast. "I wish he saw all that I do," said he, in a low voice. Then looking towards the minister, he articulated, "Pray for us."

They knelt in prayer. It was soothing, as real prayer always must be; and when they rose, every one seemed more calm. But the sufferer was exhausted; his countenance changed; he looked on his friends; there was a faint whisper, "Peace I leave with you"[14]—and he was in heaven.

We need not dwell on what followed. The seed sown by the righteous often blossoms over their grave; and so was it with this good man. The words of peace which he spoke unto his friends while he was yet with them came into remembrance after he was gone; and though he was laid in the grave with many tears, yet it was with softened and submissive hearts.

"The Lord bless him," said Uncle Lot, as he and James were standing, last of all, over the grave. "I believe my heart is gone to heaven with him; and I think the Lord really did know what was best after all."

Our friend James seemed now to become the support of the family; and the bereaved old man unconsciously began to transfer to him the affections that had been left vacant.

"James," said he to him one day, "I suppose you know that you are about the same to me as a son."

"I hope so," said James kindly.

"Well, well, you'll go to college next week, and none o' y'r keepin' school to get along. I've got enough to bring you safe out—that is, if you'll be car'ful and stiddy."

James knew the heart too well to refuse a favor in which the poor old man's mind was comforting itself. He had the self-command to abstain from any extraordinary expressions of gratitude, but took it kindly, as a matter of course.

"Dear Grace," said he to her, the last evening before he left home, "I am changed; we both are altered since we first knew each other; and now I am going to be gone a long time, but I am sure"—

He stopped to arrange his thoughts.

"Yes, you may be sure of all those things that you wish to say, and cannot," said Grace.

"Thank you," said James; then, looking thoughtfully, he added, "God help me. I believe I have mind enough to be what I mean to; but whatever I am or have shall be given to God and my fellow men; and then, Grace, your brother in heaven will rejoice over me."

"I believe he does now," said Grace. "God bless you, James; I don't know what would have become of us if you had not been here.

"Yes, you will live to be like him, and to do even more good," she added, her face brightening as she spoke, till James thought she really must be right.

It was five years after this that James was spoken of as an eloquent and successful minister in the state of C.,[15] and was settled in one of its most thriving villages. Late one autumn evening, a tall, bony, hard-favored man was observed making his way into the outskirts of the place.

"Hallo, there!" he called to a man over the other side of a fence; "what town is these 'ere?"

"It's Farmington, sir."

"Well, I want to know if you know anything of a boy of mine that lives here?"

"A boy of yours? Who?"

"Why, I've got a boy here, that's livin' on the town, and I thought I'd jest look him up."

"I don't know any boy that is living on the town. What's his name?"

"Why," said the old man, pushing his hat off from his forehead, "I believe they call him James Benton."

"James Benton! Why, that is our minister's name!"

"Oh, wal, I believe he is the minister, come to think on't. He's a boy o' mine, though. Where does he live?"

"In that white house that you see set back from the road there, with all those trees round it."

At this instant a tall, manly-looking person approached from behind. Have we not seen that face before? It is a touch graver than of old, and its lines have a more thoughtful significance; but all the vivacity of James Benton sparkles in that quick smile as his eye falls on the old man.

"I thought you could not keep away from us long," said he with the prompt cheerfulness of his boyhood, and laying hold of both of Uncle Lot's hard hands.

They approached the gate; a bright face glances past the window, and in a moment Grace is at the door.

"Father! dear father!"

"You'd better make believe be so glad," said Uncle Lot, his eyes glistening as he spoke.

"Come, come, father, I have authority in these days," said Grace, drawing him towards the house; "so no disrespectful speeches; away with your hat and coat, and sit down in this great chair."

(*182*)

"So, ho! Miss Grace," said Uncle Lot, "you are at your old tricks, ordering round as usual. Well, if I must, I must;" so down he sat.

"Father," said Grace, as he was leaving them, after a few days' stay, "it's Thanksgiving Day next month, and you and mother must come and stay with us."

Accordingly, the following month found Aunt Sally and Uncle Lot by the minister's fireside, delighted witnesses of the Thanksgiving presents which a willing people were pouring in; and the next day they had once more the pleasure of seeing a son of theirs in the sacred desk, and hearing a sermon that everybody said was "the best that he ever preached;" and it is to be remarked, that this was the standing commentary on all James's discourses, so that it was evident he was going on unto perfection.

"There's a great deal that's worth having in this 'ere life after all," said Uncle Lot, as he sat by the coals of the bright evening fire of that day; "that is, if we'd only take it when the Lord lays it in our way."

"Yes," said James; "and let us only take it as we should and this life will be cheerfulness, and the next fullness of joy."

Notes

1. "The latchet of whose shoes I am not worthy to stoop down and unloose." *Mark.* I, 7.

2. Guilford, Connecticut.

3. From "God Save the King," the English national anthem, by Henry Carey, 1687?–1743, English poet.

4. "The powers that be are ordained of God." *Romans.* XIII, 1.

5. "Let us hear the conclusion of the whole matter: Fear God, and keep his commandments; for this is the whole duty of man." *Ecclesiastes.* XII, 13.

6. John Bunyan, 1628–1688, English writer, in *The Pilgrim's Progress.*

7. A popular hymn, "Morning and Evening Hymn," by Thomas Ken, 1637–1711, English hymn writer, commonly referred to as "Praise God, from whom all blessings flow."

8. Source unknown.

9. "And all that sat in the council, looking steadfastly on him, saw his face as it had been the face of an angel." *Acts.* VI, 15.

10. "O thou afflicted, tossed with tempest, and not comforted!" *Isaiah.* LIV, 11.

11. *Genesis.* XXI, 16.

12. "Let not your heart be troubled: ye believe in God, believe also in me. In my Father's house are many mansions." *John.* XIV, 1, 2.

13. *John.* XVI, 22.

14. *John.* XIV, 27.

15. Connecticut.

THE YANKEE GIRL.

Giftbooks, popular in the second quarter of the 19th cen-
tury, were illustrated literary anthologies of poetry, short
stories, tales, and sketches. They were published, in decora-
tive formats, annually and marketed for holiday gift giving.
"The Yankee Girl" first appeared in 1842 in such a volume.
As "Uncle Lot" defines the Yankee farmer, so "The Yankee
Girl" outlines the unique character of the practical-minded
New England woman.
Text: *The Token and Atlantic Souvenir: An Offering for
Christmas and the Year*, 1842 (Boston: David H. Williams)

Every land has its own "beau ideal" of woman, and its
own ladies have been bepraised in certain good set terms,
with which everybody the least read in polite literature is
perfectly acquainted. Who has not heard of the noble bearing, the beauty and domestic virtue of the dames of England? Of the sprightliness, grace and fascination of the
ladies of France? How have the light footstep of Spain, the
melting eye of Italy been said and sung. And to this florist's
feast of nations, may not the plain old farmer, New England, come, spade in hand, and bring the flower of his own
land? Let the English lady be enthroned as the lily,—the
French, the ever bright and varying tulip,—the Spanish
and Italian, the full moss rose: the richest and most volup-
tuous of flowers. The Yankee girl is the rose laurel, whose
blossoms no garden flower ever excelled in rosy delicacy
and gracefulness of form, but whose root asks neither gar-
den-bed nor gardener's care, but will take for itself strong

(185)

hold where there is a handful of earth in the cleft of a rock, whose polished leaf shakes green and cheerful over the snows of the keenest winter. In her you shall find the union of womanly delicacy and refinement with manly energy and decision, womanly ingenuity and versatility in contrivance, with manly promptness and efficiency in execution.

While some ladies found their claim to interest on a delicate ignorance and inability as to all the practical parts of life, the only fear of the New England girl is that there should be anything that woman ever did, which she cannot do, and has not done a little better than ever it was done before. Born of frugal parents, who, with any other habits would be poor, she learns early to make energy and ingenuity supply the place of wealth. Born in a land where all are equal, no princess could surpass her in the feeling of self-respect. Born where the universal impulse of all is to rise, there is nothing in the way of knowledge and accomplishment, which she does not hope some day to acquire, and even without any advantages of culture, womanly tact, quickness of mind, and lady-like self-possession, add the charm of grace to her beauty. Now if you wish to find this lady of our fancy you must not look for her in our cities, where all the young ladies speak French, play on the piano, and are taught to be as much like one another as their bonnets. If you wish to investigate the flowers of a country, you do not look for them under the shade of damask curtains, in the windows of drawing rooms, but seek them, as they grow free and individual at the roots of old mossy trees, and in the clefts of overhanging ledges of rocks, or forming eye-lashes to the thousand bright eyes of merry brooks. So if you would see this Yankee girl as she is, take a flight up with us,—up—up—not to the skies, but to the north of New Hampshire. Alight with us now in this cosy little nook, where the retiring mountains have left space for cultivation, and hard hands have been found to improve it. There, on the green breasted turf, have been dropped some dozen or so of dwellings, a meeting house, and a school house, all in very nondescript and unutterable styles of architecture. There, in that village which never was roused by the rattle and tramp of the mail coach, whose only road has a green ribband of turf in the middle, with a little turfy line on each side, you will perhaps find what I speak of. How still and sabbath-like seems the place to-day—does anybody live here? There is nobody to be seen in the streets—nothing stirring but the leaves of the dense heavy sugar maples, that shade the old brown houses, and the blue flies and humble bees which are buzzing about, with great pretension to business, in the clover fields. But stay! there are signs of life; else why the rows of shining milk pans,—and hark! by the loud drawl from the open windows of yonder school house, you perceive there is a rising generation in the land. Come with us, where a large, motherly, old-fashioned house seems to have sat down to cool itself on that velvet slope of turf, while the broad masses of the maples and the superb arches of the elms, form an array of foliage about it, truly regal. That house is the palace royal of one of the sovereign people of New Hampshire, to wit, Jonathan Parsons. Jonathan is a great man, and rich in the land, a wise man, and a man of valor, moreover. He is great, politically, for he keeps the post office. He is rich too, for he is the undisputed possessor of all that he wants. He is wise, for he knows a little more than anybody about him, and as to his valor, it is self-evident from the fact that he has been promoted with unparalleled rapidity to be Captain, Colonel, and finally General Parsons. Accordingly he is commonly recognized by his martial title, "the General." He is a hale, upright, cheerful man of fifty or thereabouts, with a bluff, ruddy face, and a voice as cheerful and ringing as a sleigh-bell. He turns his hand to more kinds of business than any one in the village, and, what is uncommon, thrives in all. He keeps the post office, and therewith also a small assortment of groceries, thread,

(*187*)

tape, darning needles, tin pans, and axe-heads, and the usual miscellaneous stock of a country store. He has a thriving farm,—possesses legal knowledge enough to draw deeds and contracts, and conduct all the simple law business of his neighbourhood, and besides this, he attends, in a general way, not only to the government of the United States, but of all the countries in the world; for Jonathan takes a weekly newspaper from Boston, and makes up his mind once as to all matters and things the world around, and his convictions, doubts and opinions on these points, are duly expounded to his townsmen, while he is weighing out sugar or tea, or delivering letters in the course of the week. It is a pity that the President of the United States or the crowned heads of Europe never send to Jonathan for his opinion,—for they would always find it snugly made up and ready for instant delivery. We have only to say in addition, that besides the patriarchal wealth of flocks and herds, Jonathan has a patriarchal complement of sons and daughters, among whom we shall only mention the eldest, whom we introduce by the ever verdant name of Mary. The village had called her mother a beauty before her, and Mary has borne that name ever since she shook the golden curls of careless childhood. Yet it is not the impression of mere physical beauty that she produces upon you: there is both intelligence and energy in the deep violet of her eye, and decision as well as sweetness in the outline of her beautiful mouth. Her form, naturally slender, is developed by constant and healthful exercise, and displays in every motion the elastic grace of her own mountain sweet-brier. And, more than all this, there is a certain cool, easy air, a freedom and nobility of manner, a good taste in speaking and acting, that give to her, though untaught in the ways of the world, that charm beyond beauty, which is woman's most graceful gift. For this instinctive sense of what really is due to one's self and others—this perception of times, places and proprieties, which forms the highest attraction of the lady, though it may be wrought out by laborious drilling, and the tutelage of etiquette, is often the free gift of nature, poured on the fair head of some one who has never trod a carpet, seen a piano, or taken one step in the labyrinth of artificial life.

Mary's amount of accomplishments, so called, was small,—including not a word of French, and no more music than was comprised in the sweetest of natural voices, taught in the common evening singing school of the village. But as a daughter and sister and housewife, her accomplishments were innumerable. Enter the cool, quiet house, not a room of which boasts a carpet, but whose snowy floors need no such concealment. The chief of all that is done in the house, in providing, making, mending, cleaning, and keeping in order, is by the single hands of Mary and her mother. We know this may lead the minds of some of our readers to very prosaic particulars. We have heard a deal of heroines playing on the harp and so forth, but who ever heard of a heroine washing or ironing? The most that has ever been accomplished in these respects, was by the lovely Charlotte of Goethe,[1] whom he introduces to us cutting bread and butter for her little brothers and sisters. We can assure all our fair readers who are inclined to be fastidious on the point, however, that had they lived under the roof of Jonathan Parsons, they could scarcely have been scandalized by any disagreeable particulars. Even at the wash bench, our heroine, in her neat, close fitting calico, never looked so little like a lady as some fair ones we have seen in curl papers and morning gowns, before they were made up for company; and moreover, much that seems so laborious would be over with and out of sight, long before they are in the habit of having their eyes open in the morning. Many days they would find our heroine in possession of leisure to draw, read, write, sew or work muslin, quite equal to their own. They would see that by ingenuity and that quick observation in which pretty women are seldom lacking, she could fashion her attire so as not to be far from the rules of good usage; and that, though her knowledge from books was limited, her mind was active and full of thought, and as ready to flash at the entrance of knowledge, as a diamond at the entrance of light.

You are not to suppose that a lady of such accomplishments, natural and acquired, a lady of rank and station, moreover, passed to her seventeenth year unwooed. So far from it, there was scarcely a personable article in the way of a beau, who had not first or last tried a hand in this matter. There were two dilapidated old bachelors, one disconsolate widower, half a dozen school masters, one doctor and one lawyer, already numbered among the killed and wounded, and still Miss Mary carried her head with that civil, modest, "what-do-I-care-for-you" air, that indicated that her heart remained entirely untouched—and all the wonder was, whom would she marry?

It came to pass, one bright summer afternoon, that as two young gentlemen, strangers in the village, were riding by the house of Jonathan Parsons, the sudden explosion of a gun caused the horse of one of them to start, and throw his rider, who, falling against a post in front of the door, was very seriously injured. The consequence of all this was, that the two very good looking young gentlemen were detained at the house for some two or three weeks. They were from Canada, and had come down into New Hampshire on a summer shooting and exploring expedition. The younger of them was the young Earl of Beresford, and the gentleman with him, a Mr. Vincent, his travelling companion, to whom happened the unlucky accident. He was so seriously hurt as to be confined entirely to his bed, and my young lord being thus suddenly thrown out of business, and into a dismally calm, roomy, clean, uninteresting old house, with no amusement but to tend a sick friend, and no reading but Scott's Family Bible[2] and the Almanac, thought himself in very deplorable circumstances, until he caught a glimpse of the elegant form and face of Mary, which suddenly roused him from his apathy. Now when one is treading carpeted floors, lounging on damask sofas, and smelling cologne water, a pretty girl is very much a matter of course, unless her beauty be of a peculiarly rare and striking character. But where there are no curtains, no pictures, no carpets, and nothing more luxurious than a very high backed, perpendicular rocking chair, a pretty girl becomes an angel forthwith, and such was the case at present. The young earl really thought, all things considered, that he would do our fair Yankee the honor to institute a flirtation with her—so at least said his manner, when he made his first advances. He was repulsed, however, with a cool and determined indifference, which seemed to him quite unaccountable. We could have told the young gentleman the reason. It was not that Mary had not a woman's love of admiration, when honestly and sincerely offered, but there was something in the gallantry of Beresford altogether too taking-for-granted and condescending. She could perceive from his travelling equipments, his general air and manner, that he had alighted among them from quite another orb of society than any of which she had ever conceived, and there was a something indefinite even in his politeness, that told her that he looked down both on her and her parents as beings of a vastly inferior order,—and the thought roused all the woman's pride within her. No princess of the blood could have been more stately, self-possessed and politely determined to keep one at a distance, than our village beauty.

The Earl of Beresford was a mere man of fashion, with no more than a barely comfortable degree of reflection and feeling. Entirely incapable of estimating the real worth of Mary's character, and valuing her merely by the rules of conventional life, he was still struck, by the quiet determination of her manner, into something like respect. Our gentleman, however, had been thoroughly accustomed to have his own way, and as is usual with such persons, the thing he could not attain assumed in his eyes a sovereign value. He, moreover, piqued himself particularly on his success with women, and was not disposed to yield his laurels in an obscure country village. Consequently, the more Mary receded, the more eagerly he advanced,—the less she seemed disposed to value his attentions, the more obsequious they became, till at length my young lord grew so excited, that he determined on the magnanimous expedient of declaring his name and rank and making love in regular form, rather than lose the game.

"Vincent!—" said Beresford to his friend, one evening, after walking up and down the room several times, adjusting his collar and brushing up his whiskers, like a man that is getting ready to say something.

"Well, Beresford, out with it," said Vincent.

"Vincent, I have come to a very serious determination."

"I should think you might have," said Vincent, laughing. "We have been in serious circumstances lately."

"Nay, but without joking—"

"Well, without joking, then."

"I have determined to be married."

"For the two hundred and fortieth time," replied Vincent.

"Vincent, do be serious."

"Serious! have I not been dolefully serious, ever since I came head first into this philosophic retreat?—However, Will, proceed to particulars, for any news is better than no news."

"Well, then, Vincent, I am determined to marry this lovely little hostess of ours."

"Not old Mrs. Parsons, I presume," said Vincent, laughing, "there would be little eclat in an elopement with her."

Beresford grew angry, but as Vincent still continued to

(*192*)

laugh, was at last obliged to join, though with a very poor grace.

"Now, Vincent," he resumed, "you may spare both your wit and your wisdom, for my determination is unalterable:—you know, of course, I mean the lovely Mary."

"Pshaw!" said Vincent, growing serious in his turn. "Now, Beresford, is not this just like you? Because you are here, in a stupid place, and in want of amusement, must you set yourself to ruin the peace of an honest, artless country girl:—it's too bad,—I'm ashamed of you."

"Ashamed! too bad! what do you mean? Did I not tell you that I am going to marry her?"

"And do I not know you will do no such thing!" replied Vincent,—"did you ever see a handsome woman, of honorable principles, that you have not had a six-weeks' vow of marrying?"

"But, Vincent—"

"But, Beresford," interrupted Vincent, "do you not know well enough, that all your vows and promises will wear only till you get to Quebec—and after the first ball then comes the old story,—unavoidable alteration—cruel necessity must prevent, and so forth,—and so the poor girl who has been the dupe of your good looks and fair speeches, is forgotten. Now, Beresford, you know all this as well as I do."

"But, Vincent, you do not understand the case."

"So you have told me regularly in every flirtation since you have been in the country. Come, now, Will, for once be advised, and let this affair alone. Besides, think of the absurdity of the thing,—introducing a wife whom you have picked up, like a partridge, on a shooting tour—nobody knows when or where."

"Oh, as to that," replied Beresford, "I can take her to Quebec and put her into a convent, to acquire accomplishments. She has an air and manner worthy of a countess, now—and then one can make up some little romance as to her parentage,—at all events, marriage is the only terms on which she can be gained, so marry her I will."

"And have you gained her consent, and that of her parents, to this wise scheme?"

"Her consent!" said Beresford,—"of course, she will consent, though I have not yet opened the subject with her."

"And pray how do you know that?"

"How do I know! why, I shall tell her who I am, and plead the cause officially, you see,—and, with all deference to the élite of this region, such offers do not occur every day,—she must see this, of course."

"Well," replied Vincent, "I have seen little of her, to be sure, but from the sobriety of mind and good sense that seem to characterize the family, I have some hopes that you will not succeed."

"That's past praying for, I fear," said Beresford, "if I may judge from certain little indications, and so forth,"—and Beresford turned on his heel and whistled himself out of the room, with a very contented and assured appearance.

His confident expectations had arisen simply from the fact that our heroine, from the joint influence of acquaintanceship and natural good humour, had grown, of late, much more approachable; besides which, for a few days past a more marked change of manner had supervened:— Mary had become absent, occasionally melancholy and more than usually excitable,—her color was varying, her eye restless, and there was a nervous tremor of manner, entirely different from any thing she had ever before exhibited. The truth was, that she was wholly engrossed by certain little perplexities and sorrows of her own; but, as Beresford knew nothing of the kind, he formed for himself a very natural and satisfactory theory, as to the cause of her altered manner.

Accordingly, at the close of a still afternoon, when Mary's mother and sisters were absent, Beresford stole suddenly upon her, as she was sitting by an open window curtained by green vines. He commenced his enterprise by a series of complimentary remarks, in just that assumed, comfortable way, that is inexpressibly vexatious to an inexperienced and sensitive woman—a manner that seems to say, "I understand all about you, and can manage you to admiration." Mary felt annoyed, yet conscious of her own inability to meet, on his own ground, the practised and ready man of the world, who addressed her.

"Mr. Beresford," she said at length, after some silence, "I presume that all this is very fine in its way, but I beg you will not waste it upon me,—I really have not the cultivation to appreciate it."

Beresford protested that he was entirely and devoutly serious in every word.

"I am very sorry for it, if you are," said Mary, smiling.

Beresford proceeded to reveal his name and title, and to make an offer in regular form.

With some surprise, but with great simplicity and decision, our heroine declined the proposal.

Beresford pleaded the advantages of station he had to offer, his own disinterestedness, and so forth.

"Indeed, Mr. Beresford," replied Mary, "I do not know enough about these things to feel in the least honored or tempted by them. It may, very possibly, seem to you that you do me a great honor by this proposal, but I have no such feeling. You are accustomed to such a different kind of society, such a different manner of estimating things, from any thing I have ever known, that I cannot very well understand your feelings. If I ever marry, it will be one who can fully appreciate the affection I give, for its own sake, and not one who will always look upon me as a sort of ornamental appendage to his station, and so forth."

"Some Yankee pedler or tinker, perhaps," replied Beresford, angrily.

"Very possibly," replied Mary, calmly, "and yet he may be more truly noble, than the only earl I ever had the honor of knowing,"—and our heroine left the room.

"Handsomely done, that!" said the earl, walking up and down the room—"'pon my word, a dutchess could not have executed the thing better. I was a fool for being angry with her, for, after all, it would have been awkward if she had consented,"—and the earl, who never in his life troubled himself five minutes about any thing, made up his mind to pass off the whole as a good joke; and in less than three weeks from this time, he was desperately in love with a captivating little opera dancer at Quebec.

And yet on the evening of that very day, you might have caught glimpses of the white dress of Mary, as she stood beneath the old vine arbour, in the garden, alone with one other, listening to the oft told tale again. But this time one might perhaps see that she listens with no unwilling ear, while a manly hand clasps hers, and words of passionate feeling are poured forth.

"I must go, Mary—brightest, dearest, loveliest,—with such a form and face, such a soul, what might you not demand in one that dared hope for you, and I have nothing to offer—nothing."

"And do you think that I count a heart and soul like yours for nothing?" said Mary.

"Yes, but there is so long an uncertainty before me—so much to be done single-handed, and not a soul thinks I shall succeed—not a soul—not even my own mother."

"Yes, George, you know I do," said Mary, "and you know what I say is worth more than all put together."

"Indeed I do—indeed I do,—or I should have given up in despair long ago, my life, my angel."

"To be sure I am an angel," said Mary, "and so I beg of you, believe every word I say,—that six or seven years from this time, you will come back here the great Mr. George Evarts, and everybody will be making bows and shaking hands."

"Ah, Mary!" said the young man, smiling,—and immediately after his face changed; an anxious and thoughtful cloud again seemed to settle upon it,—he took her hand and spoke with an expression of sorrow, such as she had never before seen.

"Mary, I fear I have done you wrong, to involve you in my uncertainties—to make your happiness in any respect dependent on my doubtful success in a long, hard struggle. I ought not to leave you bound to me by any promise. If, during these future years, you see one who makes you an immediate offer of heart and hand—one worthy of you—and you think that if it were not for me—"

"I am to take him, of course," said Mary. "Well, I will remember it. Oh, George, this is just like you,—always desponding, when you hope most. Come back to me five or ten years hence, and if you have any advice of the kind to give then—why, I'll think of it."

But what was said after this we will not stop to relate; we will only pause a little in our story, to explain the "who and what" of the last scene.

There dwelt in the village, a poor, pale, sickly, desponding widow, whose husband had been a carpenter, but being suddenly killed by a fall, had left to his wife no other treasure than a small house and garden, and as bright and vigorous a shoot of boyhood as ever grew up, fair and flourishing by an old, decaying stock. Little George was a manly, daring, resolute fellow, with a heart running over with affection and protecting zeal for his mother, and for a while he hoed in the garden, drove the cow, milked, and helped in various matters in-doors, with an energy and propriety that caused him to be held up as a pattern in the neighbourhood. But when the days drew on that he should be put to some effective way of making a living, the various wise advisers of his mother began to shake their heads,—for with a deal of general ability he seemed to have no elective affinity for any thing in particular.

There was a good natured shoemaker, who offered fully to teach him the mysteries of his craft, and his mother looked upon it as a providential opening, and George was persuaded to essay upon the lapstone; but it would not do. Then Jonathan Parsons, being a neighbourly, advising man, thought he knew what was best for the boy, and offered to take him on his farm and make something of him; and so George wielded spade and hoe and axe, and a very capable young farmer he promised to be; but after a while he declared off from this also. In short, he seemed in the eyes of many to be in danger of falling into that very melancholy class of instances of clever people, who, in common phrase, "don't seem to stick to any thing."

But the gossips of the place were for once mistaken, for there was that which George did stick to, after all. He had in his veins that instinctive something or other, which leads one to feel after and find what he is made for. George had come across various odd volumes of books—history, travels, biography,—and these had awakened in his mind a burning desire to do or be something in the world—something, he scarce knew what, and so he determined he would go to college. And what a sighing and wondering there was from his old mother, and what talking and amazement among the village worthies. Jonathan Parsons gave the young man a faithful and fatherly lecture, from the top of a codfish barrel, on the subject of tempting Providence, and other kindred topics, enforcing his remarks by alluding to the example of Jack Simpson, a poor nondescript, who was generally reported to have lost his wits in the attempt to study Latin, as a most forcible illustration of his argument. Poor George had but one friend to encourage him amid all this opposition, and that was our warm-hearted and trusting Mary. He had become acquainted with her during his stay at her father's, and she had entered warmly into all his plans, and encouraged his scheme with all a girl's confident, undoubting enthusiasm. They had never, until the evening interview we relate, settled any definite expectations for the future, for both knew that it was not a subject to be mentioned to Jonathan Parsons, who would set it down as a clear indication of lunacy on the part of Mary, and of something worse upon that of the gentleman.

We will not tell of the year-long efforts that had been made by our hero, up to the date of his last interview—of the ragged Latin Grammar studied by firelight at his mother's hearth—the Euclid[3] pored over during the long hours of the night, while he was tending a saw-mill for a neighbouring farmer. Suffice it to say, that alone and unassisted, he had now conquered the preparatory studies necessary to fit him for college, and had earned, beside, a small stock of money. This, his little all, he laid out in a pedler's box and the necessary outfit for it, and after bidding adieu to Mary, and promising his mother to send her a portion of all his earnings, he left his native village with the determination never to return, till he had fulfilled the destiny he appointed for himself.

Six years from this time, and Mary was a beautiful woman of three-and-twenty, and not only beautiful, but educated and accomplished; for her own efforts had procured for her advantages of culture superior to what it is the lot of many to attain. George returned to his native village, a newly admitted lawyer, with the offer of a partnership in a very extensive business in Boston. Of course, everybody in the village altered their minds about him directly. His old mother laughed and almost blushed when complimented on her son, and said that somehow George always did seem to have it in him, and his neighbours, one and all, remembered how they had prophesied that George would be a remarkable man. As to Jonathan Parsons, he shook hands with him in extra style, invited him to drop in and see him any time, and even inquired his opinion as to one or two measures of Congress, about which he professed he had not yet made up his mind; and Mary——ah, well! Mr. George and Miss Mary had a deal of business by themselves in the little front room, from which came in time as gay a wedding as ever made an old house ring with merriment; and then they took a house in Boston, and Mr. George Evarts began to make a figure in the papers, as a leading young man in the political world, which made Jonathan Parsons a more zealous reader of them than ever; for, as he often took occasion to remark, "he felt that he had some hand in forming that young man's mind."

Many years after this, the Earl of Beresford and our heroine again met at a court drawing room in his own land, and to her, as the wife of the American Minister, his Lordship was formally presented. He was now a regular married man, somewhat gouty, and exceedingly fastidious in the matter of women, as his long experience on these subjects had entitled him to be. He was struck, however, with the noble simplicity of Mary's manners, and with a beauty which, though altered in style, time had done little to efface; nor did he know, till the evening was over, that he had been in close attendance on the little village beauty of New Hampshire and the wife of a Yankee Pedler.

Notes

1. Charlotte is the object of the hero's affections in *The Sorrows of Werther*, 1774, a novel by Johann Wolfgang von Goethe, 1749–1832, German author: "Charlotte held a brown loaf in her hand, and was cutting slices for the little ones all round in proportion to their age and appetite."

2. Thomas Scott, 1747–1821, English clergyman, published the *Family Bible, with Notes* (also called the *Holy Bible, with Notes*) in several volumes, 1788–1792.

3. Euclid, c.300 B.C., Greek author of *Elements*, a textbook on geometry.

THE CANAL BOAT

"The Canal Boat," a comic sketch depicting the difficulties of travel in the early half of the 19th century, was originally published in Godey's Lady's Book and Ladies' American Magazine in October, 1841. Two years later Stowe included it in her first collection, The Mayflower; or, Sketches of Scenes and Characters among the Descendants of the Pilgrims.

Of all the ways of traveling which obtain among our locomotive nation, this said vehicle, the canal boat, is the most absolutely prosaic and inglorious. There is something picturesque, nay, almost sublime, in the lordly march of your well-built, high-bred steamboat. Go, take your stand on some overhanging bluff, where the blue Ohio winds its thread of silver, or the sturdy Mississippi tears its path through unbroken forests, and it will do your heart good to see the gallant boat walking the waters with unbroken and powerful tread; and, like some fabled monster of the wave, breathing fire, and making the shores resound with its deep respirations. Then there is something mysterious, even awful, in the power of steam. See it curling up against a blue sky, some rosy morning—graceful, floating, intangible, and to all appearance the softest and gentlest of all spiritual things; and then think that it is this fairy spirit that keeps all the world alive and hot with motion; think how excellent a servant it is, doing all sorts of gigantic works, like the genii of old; and yet, if you let slip the talisman only for a moment, what terrible advantage it will take of you! and you will confess that steam has some claims both to the beautiful and the terrible. For our own part, when we are down among the machinery of a steamboat in full play, we conduct ourselves very reverently, for we consider it as a very serious neighborhood; and every time the steam whizzes with such red-hot determination from the escape valve, we start as if some of the spirits were after us. But in a canal boat there is no power, no mystery, no danger; one cannot blow up, one cannot be drowned, unless by some special effort: one sees clearly all there is in the case—a horse, a rope, and a muddy strip of water—and that is all.

Did you ever try it, reader? If not, take an imaginary trip with us, just for experiment. "There's the boat!" exclaims a passenger in the omnibus, as we are rolling down from the Pittsburgh Mansion House to the canal. "Where?" exclaim a dozen of voices, and forthwith a dozen heads go out of the window. "Why, down there, under that bridge; don't you see those lights?" "What! that little thing?" exclaims an inexperienced traveler; "dear me! we can't half of us get into it!" "We! indeed," says some old hand in the business; "I think you'll find it will hold us and a dozen more loads like us." "Impossible!" say some. "You'll see," say the initiated; and, as soon as you get out, you *do* see, and hear too, what seems like a general breaking loose from the Tower of Babel,[1] amid a perfect hailstorm of trunks, boxes, valises, carpet-bags, and every describable and indescribable form of what a Westerner calls "plunder."

"That's my trunk!" barks out a big, round man. "That's my bandbox!" screams a heart-stricken old lady, in terror for her immaculate Sunday caps. "Where's my little red box? I had two carpet-bags and a—My trunk had a scarle— Hallo! where are you going with that portmanteau? Husband! husband! do see after the large basket and the little hair trunk—oh, and the baby's little chair!" "Go below—go below, for mercy's sake, my dear; I'll see to the baggage."

At last, the feminine part of creation, perceiving that, in this particular instance, they gain nothing by public speaking, are content to be led quietly under hatches; and amusing is the look of dismay which each newcomer gives to the confined quarters that present themselves. Those who were so ignorant of the power of compression as to suppose the boat scarce large enough to contain them and theirs, find, with dismay, a respectable colony of old ladies, babies, mothers, big baskets, and carpet-bags already established. "Mercy on us!" says one, after surveying the little room, about ten feet long and six high, "where are we all to sleep to-night?" "Oh, me! what a sight of children!" says a young lady, in a despairing tone. "Poh!" says an initiated traveler; "children! scarce any here; let's see,—one; the woman in the corner, two; that child with the bread and butter, three; and then there's that other woman with two. Really, it's quite moderate for a canal boat. However, we can't tell till they have all come."

"All! for mercy's sake, you don't say there are any more coming!" exclaim two or three in a breath; "they can't come; there is not room!"

Notwithstanding the impressive utterance of this sentence, the contrary is immediately demonstrated by the appearance of a very corpulent, elderly lady, with three well-grown daughters, who come down looking about them most complacently, entirely regardless of the unchristian looks of the company. What a mercy it is that fat people are always good-natured!

After this follows an indiscriminate raining down of all shapes, sizes, sexes, and ages—men, women, children, babies, and nurses. The state of feeling becomes perfectly desperate. Darkness gathers on all faces. "We shall be smothered! we shall be crowded to death! we can't stay here!" are heard faintly from one and another; and yet, though the boat grows no wider, the walls no higher, they do live, and do stay there, in spite of repeated protestations to the contrary. Truly, as Sam Slick[2] says, "there's a sight of wear in human natur'."

But, meanwhile, the children grow sleepy, and divers interesting little duets and trios arise from one part or another of the cabin.

"Hush, Johnny! be a good boy," says a pale, nursing mamma, to a great, bristling, white-headed phenomenon, who is kicking very much at large in her lap.

"I won't be a good boy, neither," responds Johnny, with interesting explicitness; "I want to go to bed, and so-o-o-o!" and Johnny makes up a mouth as big as a teacup, and roars with good courage, and his mamma asks him "if he ever saw pa do so," and tells him that "he is mamma's dear, good little boy, and must not make a noise," with various observations of the kind, which are so strikingly efficacious in such cases. Meanwhile, the domestic concert in other quarters proceeds with vigor. "Mamma, I'm tired!" bawls a child. "Where's the baby's nightgown?" calls a nurse. "Do take Peter upon your lap, and keep him still." "Pray get out some biscuits to stop their mouths." Meanwhile, sundry babies strike in "con spirito," as the music books have it, and execute various flourishes; the disconsolate mothers sigh, and look as if all was over with them; and the young ladies appear extremely disgusted, and wonder "what business women have to be traveling round with babies."

To these troubles succeeds the turning-out scene, when the whole caravan is ejected into the gentlemen's cabin, that the beds may be made. The red curtains are put down, and in solemn silence all the last mysterious preparations begin. At length it is announced that all is ready. Forthwith the whole company rush back, and find the walls embellished by a series of little shelves, about a foot wide, each furnished with a mattress and bedding, and hooked to the ceiling by a very suspiciously slender cord. Direful are the ruminations and exclamations of inexperienced travelers, particularly young ones, as they eye these very equivocal accommodations, "What, sleep up there! I won't sleep on one of those top shelves, I know. The cords will certainly break." The chambermaid here takes up the conversation, and solemnly assures them that such an accident is not to be thought of at all; that it is a natural impossibility—a thing that could not happen without an actual miracle; and since it becomes increasingly evident that thirty ladies cannot all sleep on the lowest shelf, there is some effort made to exercise faith in this doctrine; nevertheless, all look on their neighbors with fear and trembling; and when the stout lady talks of taking a shelf, she is most urgently pressed to change places with her alarmed neighbor below. Points of location being after a while adjusted, comes the last struggle. Everybody wants to take off a bonnet or look for a shawl, to find a cloak, or get a carpet-bag, and all set about it with such zeal that nothing can be done. "Ma'am, you're on my foot!" says one. "Will you please to move, ma'am?" says somebody, who is gasping and struggling behind you. "Move!" you echo. "Indeed, I should be very glad to, but I don't see much prospect of it." "Chambermaid!" calls a lady, who is struggling among a heap of carpet-bags and children at one end of the cabin. "Ma'am!" echoes the poor chambermaid, who is wedged fast, in a similar situation, at the other. "Where's my cloak, chambermaid?" "I'd find it, ma'am, if I could move." "Chambermaid, my basket!" "Chambermaid, my parasol!" "Chambermaid, my carpet-bag!" "Mamma, they push me so!" "Hush, child,—crawl under there, and lie still till I can undress you." At last, however, the various distresses are over, the babies sink to sleep, and even that much-enduring being, the chambermaid, seeks out some corner for repose. Tired and drowsy, you are just sinking into a doze, when bang! goes the boat against the sides of a lock; ropes scrape, men run and shout, and up fly the heads of all the top shelfites, who are generally the more juvenile and airy part of the company.

"What's that! what's that!" flies from mouth to mouth, and forthwith they proceed to awaken their respective relations. "Mother! Aunt Hannah! do wake up; what is this awful noise?" "Oh, only a lock!" "Pray be still," groan out the sleepy members from below.

"A lock!" exclaim the vivacious creatures, ever on the alert for information; "and what is a lock, pray?"

"Don't you know what a lock is, you silly creatures? Do lie down and go to sleep."

"But say, there ain't any danger in a lock, is there?" respond the querists. "Danger!" exclaims a deaf old lady, poking up her head; "what's the matter? There hain't nothin' burst, has there?" "No, no, no!" exclaim the provoked and despairing opposition party, who find that there is no such thing as going to sleep till they have made the old lady below and the young ladies above understand exactly the philosophy of a lock. After a while the conversation again subsides; again all is still; you hear only the trampling of horses and the rippling of the rope in the water, and sleep again is stealing over you. You doze, you dream, and all of a sudden you are startled by a cry, "Chambermaid! wake up the lady that wants to be set ashore." Up jumps chambermaid, and up jump the lady and two children, and forthwith form a committee of inquiry as to ways and means. "Where's my bonnet?" says the lady, half awake, and fumbling among the various articles of that name. "I thought I hung it up behind the door." "Can't you find it?" says poor chambermaid, yawning and rubbing her eyes. "Oh, yes, here it is," says the lady; and then the cloak, the shawl, the gloves, the shoes, receive each a separate discussion. At last all seems ready, and they begin to move off, when, lo! Peter's cap is missing. "Now, where can it be?" soliloquizes the lady. "I put it right here by the table leg; maybe it got into some of the berths." At this suggestion, the chambermaid takes the candle, and goes round deliberately to every berth, poking the light directly in the face of every sleeper. "Here it is," she exclaims, pulling at something black under one pillow. "No, indeed, those are my shoes," says the vexed sleeper. "Maybe it's here," she resumes, darting upon something dark in another berth. "No, that's my bag," responds the occupant. The chambermaid then proceeds to turn over all the children on the floor, to see if it is not under them, in the course of which process they are most agreeably waked up and enlivened; and when everybody is broad awake, and most uncharitably wishing the cap, and Peter too, at the bottom of the canal, the good lady exclaims, "Well, if this isn't lucky; here I had it safe in my basket all the time!" And she departs amid the—what shall I say, execrations?—of the whole company, ladies though they be.

Well, after this follows a hushing up and wiping up among the juvenile population, and a series of remarks commences from the various shelves, of a very edifying and instructive tendency. One says that the woman did not seem to know where anything was; another says that she has waked them all up; a third adds that she has waked up all the children, too; and the elderly ladies make moral reflections on the importance of putting your things where you can find them—being always ready; which observations, being delivered in an exceedingly doleful and drowsy tone, form a sort of sub-bass to the lively chattering of the upper shelfites, who declare that they feel quite wide awake,—that they don't think they shall go to sleep again to-night,—and discourse over everything in creation, until you heartily wish you were enough related to them to give them a scolding.

At last, however, voice after voice drops off; you fall into a most refreshing slumber; it seems to you that you sleep about a quarter of an hour, when the chambermaid pulls you by the sleeve. "Will you please to get up, ma'am? We want to make the beds." You start and stare. Sure enough, the night is gone. So much for sleeping on board canal boats.

Let us not enumerate the manifold perplexities of the morning toilet in a place where every lady realizes most forcibly the condition of the old woman who lived under a broom: "All she wanted was elbow room."[3] Let us not tell how one glass is made to answer for thirty fair faces, one ewer and vase for thirty lavations; and—tell it not in Gath![4]—one towel for a company! Let us not intimate how ladies' shoes have, in a night, clandestinely slid into the gentlemen's cabin, and gentlemen's boots elbowed, or rather, *toed* their way among ladies' gear, nor recite the exclamations after runaway property that are heard. "I can't find nothin' of Johnny's shoe!" "Here's a shoe in the water pitcher—is this it?" "My side-combs are gone!" exclaims a nymph with disheveled curls. "Massy! do look at my bonnet!" exclaims an old lady, elevating an article crushed into as many angles as there are pieces in a mince pie. "I never did sleep so much together in my life," echoes a poor little French lady, whom despair has driven into talking English.

But our shortening paper warns us not to prolong our catalogue of distresses beyond reasonable bounds, and therefore we will close with advising all our friends, who intend to try this way of traveling for pleasure, to take a good stock both of patience and clean towels with them, for we think that they will find abundant need for both.

Notes

1. *Genesis.* XI, 9. The Tower of Babel, in the Old Testament, was a structure designed to reach heaven. God, angered at such audacity, punished its builders by making their speech unintelligible to one another.

2. Sam Slick was the pseudonym of Thomas Chandler Haliburton, 1796–1865, British-American humorist.

3. Source unknown.

4. *2 Samuel.* I, 20.

THE CORAL RING

"The Coral Ring," a temperance tale, first appeared in 1843 in *The Christian Souvenir* (Boston: H. B. Williams), a giftbook annual. Its plot reflects the historical interest in the temperance movement, a cause closely linked to feminism and the broadening of voting rights in 19th-century America.

"There is no time of life in which young girls are so thoroughly selfish as from fifteen to twenty," said Edward Ashton deliberately, as he laid down a book he had been reading, and leaned over the centre table.

"You insulting fellow!" replied a tall, brilliant-looking creature, who was lounging on an ottoman hard by, over one of Dickens's last works.[1]

"Truth, coz, for all that," said the gentleman, with the air of one who means to provoke a discussion.

"Now, Edward, this is just one of your wholesale declarations, for nothing only to get me into a dispute with you, you know," replied the lady. "On your conscience, now (if you have one), is it not so?"

"My conscience feels quite easy, cousin, in subscribing to that sentiment as my confession of faith," replied the gentleman, with provoking *sang froid*.

"Pshaw! it's one of your fusty old bachelor notions. See what comes, now, of your living to your time of life without a wife,—disrespect for the sex, and all that. Really, cousin, your symptoms are getting alarming."

"Nay, now, Cousin Florence," said Edward, "you are a girl of moderately good sense, with all your nonsense. Now don't you (I know you do) think just so, too?"

"Think just so, too!—do you hear the creature?" replied Florence. "No, sir; you can speak for yourself in this matter, but I beg leave to enter my protest when you speak for me, too."

"Well, now, where is there, coz, among all our circle, a young girl that has any sort of purpose or object in life, to speak of, except to make herself as interesting and agreeable as possible? to be admired, and to pass her time in as amusing a way as she can? Where will you find one between fifteen and twenty that has any serious regard for the improvement and best welfare of those with whom she is connected at all, or that modifies her conduct in the least with reference to it? Now, cousin, in very serious earnest, you have about as much real character, as much earnestness and depth of feeling, and as much good sense, when one can get at it, as any young lady of them all; and yet, on your conscience, can you say that you live with any sort of reference to anybody's good, or to anything but your own amusement and gratification?"

"What a shocking adjuration!" replied the lady, "prefaced, too, by a three-story compliment. Well, being so adjured, I must think to the best of my ability. And now, seriously and soberly, I don't see as I am selfish. I do all that I have any occasion to do for anybody. You know that we have servants to do everything that is necessary about the house, so that there is no occasion for my making any display of housewifery excellence. And I wait on mamma if she has a headache, and hand papa his slippers and newspaper, and find Uncle John's spectacles for him twenty times a day (no small matter that), and then"—

"But, after all, what is the object and purpose of your life?"

"Why, I haven't any. I don't see how I can have any,—that is, as I am made. Now, you know, I've none of the fussing, baby-tending, herb-tea-making recommendations of Aunt Sally, and divers others of the class commonly called *useful.* Indeed, to tell the truth, I think useful persons are commonly rather fussy and stupid. They are just like the boneset, and hoarhound, and catnip,—very necessary to be raised in a garden, but not in the least ornamental."

"And you charming young ladies, who philosophize in kid slippers and French dresses, are the tulips and roses,—very charming, and delightful, and sweet, but fit for nothing on earth but parlor ornaments."

"Well, parlor ornaments are good in their way," said the young lady, coloring, and looking a little vexed.

"So you give up the point, then," said the gentleman, "that you girls are good for—just to amuse yourselves, amuse others, look pretty, and be agreeable?"

"Well, and if we behave well to our parents, and are amiable in the family—I don't know;—and yet," said Florence, sighing, "I have often had a sort of vague idea of something higher that we might become; yet, really, what more than this is expected of us? what else can we do?"

"I used to read in old-fashioned novels about ladies visiting the sick and the poor," replied Edward. "You remember 'Coelebs in Search of a Wife'?"[2]

"Yes, truly; that is to say, I remember the story part of it, and the love scenes; but as for all those everlasting conversations of Dr. Barlow, Mr. Stanley,[3] and nobody knows who else, I skipped those, of course. But really, this visiting and tending the poor, and all that, seems very well in a story, where the lady goes into a picturesque cottage, half overgrown with honeysuckle, and finds an emaciated but still beautiful woman propped up by pillows. But come to the downright matter of fact of poking about in all these

(213)

vile, dirty alleys, and entering little dark rooms, amid troops of grinning children, and smelling codfish and onions, and nobody knows what,—dear me, my benevolence always evaporates before I get through. I'd rather pay anybody five dollars a day to do it for me than do it myself. The fact is, that I have neither fancy nor nerves for this kind of thing."

"Well, granting, then, that you can do nothing for your fellow-creatures unless you are to do it in the most genteel, comfortable, and picturesque manner possible, is there not a great field for a woman like you, Florence, in your influence over your associates? With your talents for conversation, your tact and self-possession, and ladylike gift of saying anything you choose, are you not responsible, in some wise, for the influence you exert over those by whom you are surrounded?"

"I never thought of that," replied Florence.

"Now, you remember the remarks that Mr. Fortesque made the other evening on the religious services at church?"

"Yes, I do; and I thought then he was too bad."

"And I do not suppose there was one of you ladies in the room that did not think so, too; but yet the matter was all passed over with smiles, and with not a single insinuation that he had said anything unpleasing or disagreeable."

"Well, what could we do? One does not want to be rude, you know."

"Do! Could you not, Florence,—you who have always taken the lead in society, and who have been noted for always being able to say and do what you please,—could you not have shown him that those remarks were unpleasing to you, as decidedly as you certainly would have done if they had related to the character of your father or brother? To my mind, a woman of true moral feeling should consider herself as much insulted when her religion is treated with contempt as if the contempt were shown to herself. Do you not know the power which is given to you women to awe and restrain us in your presence, and to guard the sacredness of things which you treat as holy? Believe me, Florence, that Fortesque, infidel as he is, would reverence a woman with whom he dared not trifle on sacred subjects."

Florence rose from her seat with a heightened color, her dark eyes brightening through tears.

"I am sure what you say is just, cousin, and yet I have never thought of it before. I will—I am determined to begin, after this, to live with some better purpose than I have done."

"And let me tell you, Florence, in starting a new course, as in learning to walk, taking the first step is everything. Now, I have a first step to propose to you."

"Well, cousin"—

"Well, you know, I suppose, that among your train of adorers you number Colonel Elliot?"

Florence smiled.

"And perhaps you do not know, what is certainly true, that, among the most discerning and cool part of his friends, Elliot is considered as a lost man."

"Good heavens! Edward, what do you mean?"

"Simply this: that, with all his brilliant talents, his amiable and generous feelings, and his success in society, Elliot has not self-control enough to prevent his becoming confirmed in intemperate habits."

"I never dreamed of this," replied Florence. "I knew that he was spirited and free, fond of society, and excitable; but never suspected anything beyond."

"Elliot has tact enough never to appear in ladies' society when he is not in a fit state for it," replied Edward; "but yet it is so."

"But is he really so bad?"

"He stands just on the verge, Florence; just where a word fitly spoken might turn him. He is a noble creature, full of all sorts of fine impulses and feelings; the only son of a mother who dotes on him, the idolized brother of sisters who love him as you love your brother, Florence; and he stands where a word, a look,—so they be of the right kind,—might save him."

"And why, then, do you not speak to him?" said Florence.

"Because I am not the best person, Florence. There is another who can do it better; one whom he admires, who stands in a position which would forbid his feeling angry; a person, cousin, whom I have heard in gayer moments say that she knew how to say anything she pleased without offending anybody."

"Oh, Edward!" said Florence coloring; "do not bring up my foolish speeches against me, and do not speak as if I ought to interfere in this matter, for indeed I cannot do it. I never could in the world, I am certain I could not."

"And so," said Edward, "you, whom I have heard say so many things which no one else could say, or dared to say,—you, who have gone on with your laughing assurance in your own powers of pleasing,—shrink from trying that power when a noble and generous heart might be saved by it. You have been willing to venture a great deal for the sake of amusing yourself and winning admiration, but you dare not say a word for any high or noble purpose. Do you not see how you confirm what I said of the selfishness of you women?"

"But you must remember, Edward, this is a matter of great delicacy."

"That word 'delicacy' is a charming cover-all in all these cases, Florence. Now, here is a fine, noble-spirited young man, away from his mother and sisters, away from any family friend who might care for him, tempted, betrayed, almost to ruin, and a few words from you, said as a woman knows how to say them, might be his salvation. But you will coldly look on and see him go to destruction, because you have too much delicacy to make the effort,—

like the man that would not help his neighbor out of the water because he had never had the honor of an introduction."

"But, Edward, consider how peculiarly fastidious Elliot is,—how jealous of any attempt to restrain and guide him."

"And just for that reason it is that *men* of his acquaintance cannot do anything with him. But what are you women made with so much tact and power of charming for, if it is not to do these very things that we cannot do? It is a delicate matter—true; and has not Heaven given to you a fine touch and a fine eye for just such delicate matters? Have you not seen, a thousand times, that what might be resented as an impertinent interference on the part of a man, comes to us as a flattering expression of interest from the lips of a woman?"

"Well, but, cousin, what would you have me do? How would you have me do it?" said Florence earnestly.

"You know that Fashion, which makes so many wrong turns and so many absurd ones, has at last made one good one, and it is now a fashionable thing to sign the temperance pledge.[4] Elliot himself would be glad to do it, but he foolishly committed himself against it in the outset, and now feels bound to stand to his opinion. He has, too, been rather rudely assailed by some of the apostles of the new state of things, who did not understand the peculiar points of his character; in short, I am afraid that he will feel bound to go to destruction for the sake of supporting his own opinion. Now, if I should undertake with him, he might shoot me; but I hardly think there is anything of the sort to be apprehended in your case. Just try your enchantments: you have bewitched wise men into doing foolish things before now; try, now, if you can't bewitch a foolish man into doing a wise thing."

Florence smiled archly, but instantly grew more thoughtful.

"Well, cousin," she said, "I will try. Though you are liberal in your ascriptions of power, yet I can put the matter to the test of experiment."

Florence Elmore was, at the time we speak of, in her twentieth year. Born of one of the wealthiest families in ——, highly educated and accomplished, idolized by her parents and brothers, she had entered the world as one born to command. With much native nobleness and magnanimity of character, with warm and impulsive feelings, and a capability of everything high or great, she had hitherto lived solely for her own amusement, and looked on the whole brilliant circle by which she was surrounded, with all its various actors, as something got up for her special diversion. The idea of influencing any one, for better or worse, by anything she ever said or did, had never occurred to her. The crowd of admirers of the other sex who, as a matter of course, were always about her, she regarded as so many sources of diversion; but the idea of feeling any sympathy with them as human beings, or of making use of her power over them for their improvement, was one that had never entered her head.

Edward Ashton was an old bachelor cousin of Florence's, who, having earned the title of oddity in general society, availed himself of it to exercise a turn for telling the truth to the various young ladies of his acquaintance, especially to his fair cousin Florence. We remark, by the bye, that these privileged truth-tellers are quite a necessary of life to young ladies in the full tide of society, and we really think it would be worth while for every dozen of them to unite to keep a person of this kind on a salary for the benefit of the whole. However, that is nothing to our present purpose; we must return to our fair heroine, whom we left, at the close of the last conversation, standing in deep revery by the window.

"It's more than half true," she said to herself,—"more than half. Here am I, twenty years old, and never have thought of anything, never done anything, except to amuse and gratify myself; no purpose, no object; nothing high, nothing dignified, nothing worth living for! Only a parlor ornament—heigh-ho! Well, I really do believe I could do something with this Elliot; and yet how dare I try?"

Now, my good readers, if you are anticipating a love story, we must hasten to put in our disclaimer; you are quite mistaken in the case. Our fair, brilliant heroine was, at this time of speaking, as heart-whole as the diamond on her bosom, which reflected the light in too many sparkling rays ever to absorb it. She had, to be sure, half in earnest, half in jest, maintained a bantering, platonic sort of friendship with George Elliot. She had danced, ridden, sung, and sketched with him, but so had she with twenty other young men; and as to coming to anything tender with such a quick, brilliant, restless creature, Elliot would as soon have undertaken to sentimentalize over a glass of soda-water. No; there was decidedly no love in the case.

"What a curious ring that is!" said Elliot to her, a day or two after, as they were reading together.

"It is a knight's ring," said she playfully, as she drew it off and pointed to a coral cross set in the gold, "a ring of the red-cross knights.[5] Come, now, I've a great mind to bind you to my service with it."

"Do, lady fair," said Elliot, stretching out his hand for the ring.

"Know, then," said she, "if you take this pledge, that you must obey whatever commands I lay upon you in its name."

"I swear!" said Elliot, in the mock heroic, and placed the ring on his finger.

An evening or two after, Elliot attended Florence to a party at Mrs. B.'s. Everything was gay and brilliant, and there was no lack either of wit or wine. Elliot was standing in a little alcove, spread with refreshments, with a glass of wine in his hand. "I forbid it; the cup is poisoned!" said a voice in his ear. He turned quickly, and Florence was at his side. Every one was busy, with laughing and talking, around, and nobody saw the sudden start and flush that these words produced as Elliot looked earnestly in the lady's face. She smiled, and pointed playfully to the ring; but, after all, there was in her face an expression of agitation and interest which she could not repress, and Elliot felt, however playful the manner, that she was in earnest; and, as she glided away in the crowd, he stood with his arms folded, and his eyes fixed on the spot where she disappeared.

"Is it possible that I am suspected,—that there are things said of me as if I were in danger?" were the first thoughts that flashed through his mind. How strange that a man may appear doomed, given up, and lost, to the eye of every looker-on, before he begins to suspect himself! This was the first time that any defined apprehension of loss of character had occurred to Elliot, and he was startled as if from a dream.

"What the deuce is the matter with you, Elliot? You look as solemn as a hearse!" said a young man near by.

"Has Miss Elmore cut you?" said another.

"Come, man, have a glass," said a third.

"Let him alone,—he's bewitched," said a fourth. "I saw the spell laid on him. None of us can say but our turn may come next."

An hour later, that evening, Florence was talking with her usual spirit to a group who were collected around her, when, suddenly looking up, she saw Elliot, standing in an abstracted manner at one of the windows that looked out into the balcony.

"He is offended, I dare say," she thought; "but what do I care? For once in my life I have tried to do a right thing,—a good thing. I have risked giving offense for less than this, many a time." Still, Florence could not but feel tremulous, when, a few moments after, Elliot approached her and offered his arm for a promenade. They walked up and down the room, she talking volubly, and he answering yes and no, till at length, as if by accident, he drew her into the balcony which overhung the garden. The moon was shining brightly, and everything without, in its placid quietness, contrasted strangely with the busy, hurrying scene within.

"Miss Elmore," said Elliot abruptly, "may I ask you, sincerely, had you any design in a remark you made to me in the early part of the evening?"

Florence paused, and, though habitually the most practiced and self-possessed of women, the color actually receded from her cheek as she answered,—

"Yes, Mr. Elliot; I must confess that I had."

"And is it possible, then, that you have heard anything?"

"I have heard, Mr. Elliot, that which makes me tremble for you, and for those whose life, I know, is bound up in you; and, tell me, were it well or friendly in me to know that such things were said, that such danger existed, and not to warn you of it?"

Elliot stood for a few moments in silence.

"Have I offended? Have I taken too great a liberty?" said Florence gently.

Hitherto Elliot had only seen in Florence the self-possessed, assured, light-hearted woman of fashion; but there was a reality and depth of feeling in the few words she had spoken to him, in this interview, that opened to him entirely a new view in her character.

"No, Miss Elmore," replied he earnestly, after some pause; "I may be pained, offended I cannot be. To tell the truth, I have been thoughtless, excited, dazzled; my spirits, naturally buoyant, have carried me, often, too far; and lately I have painfully suspected my own powers of resistance. I have really felt that I needed help, but have been too proud to confess, even to myself, that I needed it. You, Miss Elmore, have done what, perhaps, no one else could have done. I am overwhelmed with gratitude, and I shall bless you for it to the latest day of my life. I am ready to pledge myself to anything you may ask on this subject."

"Then," said Florence, "do not shrink from doing what is safe, and necessary, and right for you to do, because you have once said you would not do it. You understand me?"

"Precisely," replied Elliot, "and you shall be obeyed."

It was not more than a week before the news was circulated that even George Elliot had signed the pledge of temperance. There was much wondering at this sudden turn among those who had known his utter repugnance to any measure of the kind, and the extent to which he had yielded to temptation; but few knew how fine and delicate had been the touch to which his pride had yielded.

Notes

1. Charles Dickens, 1812–1870, English novelist.

2. A novel by Hannah More, 1745–1833, English writer, published in 1809 about a bachelor eager to be married.

3. Characters in *Coelebs in Search of a Wife*.

4. An oath or promise to abstain entirely from using alcoholic liquors as beverages.

5. The Red Cross Knight, the hero of the first book of *The Faerie Queen*, 1590, by Edmund Spenser, 1552–1599, English poet, fought against error, temptation, and falsehood.

CAPTAIN KIDD'S[1] MONEY

Capitalizing upon the popularity of Sam Lawson, the comic character she created in *Oldtown Folks,* Harriet Beecher Stowe wrote several more stories about him, based on anecdotes from her husband's New England boyhood. "Captain Kidd's Money" was initially printed in the *Atlantic Monthly,* 1870, and later collected in *Oldtown Fireside Stories* (Boston: J. R. Osgood & Co., 1872).

One of our most favorite legendary resorts was the old barn.

Sam Lawson[2] preferred it on many accounts. It was quiet and retired, that is to say, at such a distance from his own house, that he could not hear if Hepsy called ever so loudly, and farther off than it would be convenient for that industrious and painstaking woman to follow him. Then there was the soft fragrant cushion of hay, on which his length of limb could be easily bestowed.

Our barn had an upper loft with a swinging outer door that commanded a view of the old mill, the waterfall, and the distant windings of the river, with its grassy green banks, its graceful elm draperies, and its white flocks of water-lilies; and then on this Saturday afternoon we had Sam all to ourselves. It was a drowsy, dreamy October day, when the hens were lazily "craw-crawing," in a soft, conversational undertone with each other, as they scratched and picked the hayseed under the barn windows. Below in the barn black Caesar sat quietly hatcheling flax, sometimes gurgling and giggling to himself with an overflow of that interior jollity with which he seemed to be always full. The African in New England was a curious contrast to everybody around him in the joy and satisfaction that he seemed to feel in the mere fact of being alive. Every white person was glad or sorry for some appreciable cause in the past, present, or future, which was capable of being definitely stated; but black Caesar was in an eternal giggle and frizzle and simmer of enjoyment for which he could give no earthly reason: he was an "embodied joy," like Shelley's skylark.[3]

"Jest hear him," said Sam Lawson, looking pensively over the haymow, and strewing hayseed down on his wool. "How that 'ere critter seems to tickle and laugh all the while 'bout nothin'. Lordy massy, he don't seem never to consider that 'this life's a dream, an empty show.' "[4]

"Look here, Sam," we broke in, anxious to cut short a threatened stream of morality, "you promised to tell us about Captain Kidd, and how you dug for his money."

"Did I, now? Wal, boys, that 'ere history o' Kidd's is a warnin' to fellers. Why, Kidd had pious parents and Bible and sanctuary privileges when he was a boy, and yet come to be hanged. It's all in this 'ere song I'm a-goin' to sing ye. Lordy massy! I wish I had my bass-viol now. Caesar," he said, calling down from his perch, "can't you strike the pitch o' 'Cap'n Kidd'[5] on your fiddle?"

Caesar's fiddle was never far from him. It was, in fact, tucked away in a nice little nook just over the manger; and he often caught an interval from his work to scrape a dancing-tune on it, keeping time with his heels, to our great delight.

A most wailing minor-keyed tune was doled forth, which seemed quite refreshing to Sam's pathetic vein, as he sang in his most lugubrious tones:—

" 'My name was Robert Kidd[6]
    As I sailed, as I sailed,
My name was Robert Kidd;
God's laws I did forbid,
And so wickedly I did,
    As I sailed, as I sailed.'

"Now ye see, boys, he's a-goin' to tell how he abused his
religious privileges; just hear now:—

'My father taught me well,
    As I sailed, as I sailed;
My father taught me well
To shun the gates of hell,
But yet I did rebel,
    As I sailed, as I sailed.

'He put a Bible in my hand,
    As I sailed, as I sailed;
He put a Bible in my hand,
And I sunk it in the sand
Before I left the strand,
    As I sailed, as I sailed.'

"Did ye ever hear o' such a hardened, contrary critter,
boys? It's awful to think on. Wal, ye see that 'ere's the way
fellers allers begin the ways o' sin, by turnin' their backs on
the Bible and the advice o' pious parents. Now hear what he
come to:—

'Then I murdered William More,[7]
    As I sailed, as I sailed;
I murdered William More,
And left him in his gore,
Not many leagues from shore,
    As I sailed, as I sailed.

(225)

'To execution dock
I must go, I must go.
To execution dock,
While thousands round me flock,
To see me on the block,
I must go, I must go.'

"There was a good deal more on 't," said Sam, pausing, "but I don't seem to remember it; but it's real solemn and affectin'."

"Who was Captain Kidd, Sam?" said I.

"Wal, he was an officer in the British navy, and he got to bein' a pirate: used to take ships and sink 'em, and murder the folks; and so they say he got no end o' money,—gold and silver and precious stones, as many as the Wise Men in the East. But ye see, what good did it all do him? He couldn't use it, and dar's n't keep it; so he used to bury it in spots round here and there in the awfullest heathen way ye ever heard of. Why, they say he allers used to kill one or two men or women or children of his prisoners, and bury with it, so that their sperits might keep watch on it ef anybody was to dig arter it. That 'ere thing has been tried and tried and tried, but no man nor mother's son on 'em ever got a cent that dug. 'Twas tried here'n Oldtown;[8] and they come pretty nigh gettin' on't, but it gin 'em the slip. Ye see, boys, *it's the Devil's money*, and he holds a pretty tight grip on 't."

"Well, how was it about digging for it? Tell us, did you do it? Were you there? Did you see it? And why couldn't they get it?" we both asked eagerly and in one breath.

"Why, Lordy massy! boys, your questions tumbles over each other thick as martins out o' a martin-box. Now, you jest be moderate and let alone, and I'll tell you all about it from the beginnin' to the end. I didn't railly have no hand in't, though I was knowin' to 't, as I be to most things that goes on round here; but my conscience wouldn't railly 'a' let me start on no sich undertakin'.

(226)

"Wal, the one that fust sot the thing a-goin' was old Mother Hokum, that used to live up in that little tumbledown shed by the cranberry-pond up beyond the spring pastur'. They had a putty bad name, them Hokums. How they got a livin' nobody knew; for they didn't seem to pay no attention to raisin' nothin' but childun, but the deuce knows, there was plenty o' them. Their old hut was like a rabbit-pen: there was a tow-head to every crack and cranny. 'Member what old Caesar said once when the word come to the store that old Hokum had got twins. 'S'pose de Lord knows best,' says Caesar, 'but *I* thought dere was Hokums enough afore.' Wal, even poor workin' industrious folks like me finds it's hard gettin' along when there's so many mouths to feed. Lordy massy! there don't never seem to be no end on 't, and so it ain't wonderful, come to think on 't, ef folks like them Hokums gets tempted to help along in ways that ain't quite right. Anyhow, folks did use to think that old Hokum was too sort o' familiar with their wood-piles 'long in the night, though they couldn't never prove it on him; and when Mother Hokum come to houses round to wash, folks use sometimes to miss pieces, here and there, though they never could find 'em on her; then they was allers a-gettin' in debt here and a-gettin' in debt there. Why, they got to owin' two dollars to Joe Gidger for butcher's meat. Joe was sort o' good-natured and let 'em have meat, 'cause Hokum he promised so fair to pay; but he couldn't never get it out o' him. 'Member once Joe walked clear up to the cranberry-pond arter that 'ere two dollars; but Mother Hokum she see him a-comin' jest as he come past the juniper-bush on the corner. She says to Hokum, 'Get into bed, old man, quick, and let me tell the story,' says she. So she covered him up; and when Gidger come in she come up to him, and says she, 'Why, Mr. Gidger, I'm jest ashamed to see ye: why, Mr. Hokum was jest a-comin' down to pay ye that 'ere money last week, but ye see he was took down with the small-pox'—Joe didn't hear no more; he just turned round, and he streaked it out

(227)

that 'ere door with his coat-tails flyin' out straight ahind him; and old Mother Hokum she jest stood at the window holdin' her sides and laughin' fit to split, to see him run. That 'ere's jest a sample o' the ways them Hokums cut up.

"Wal, you see, boys, there's a queer kind o' rock down on the bank o' the river, that looks sort o' like a gravestone. The biggest part on 't is sunk down under ground, and it's pretty well growed over with blackberry-vines; but, when you scratch the bushes away, they used to make out some queer marks on that 'ere rock. They was sort o' lines and crosses; and folks would have it that them was Kidd's private marks, and that there was one o' the places where he hid his money.

"Wal, there's no sayin' fairly how it come to be thought so; but fellers used to say so, and they used sometimes to talk it over to the tahvern, and kind o' wonder whether or no, if they should dig, they wouldn't come to suthin'.

"Wal, old Mother Hokum she heard on 't, and she was a sort o' enterprisin' old crittur: fact was, she had to be, 'cause the young Hokums was jest like bag-worms, the more they growed the more they eat, and I expect she found it pretty hard to fill their mouths; and so she said if there *was* anything under that 'ere rock, they'd as good's have it as the Devil; and so she didn't give old Hokum no peace o' his life, but he must see what there was there.

"Wal, I was with 'em the night they was a-talkin' on 't up. Ye see, Hokum he got thirty-seven cents' worth o' lemons and sperit. I see him goin' by as I was out a-splittin' kindlin's; and says he, 'Sam, you jest go 'long up to our house to-night,' says he: 'Toddy Whitney and Harry Wiggin's comin' up, and we're goin' to have a little suthin' hot,' says he; and he kind o' showed me the lemons and sperit. And I told him I guessed I would go 'long. Wal, I kind o' wanted to see what they'd be up to, ye know.

"Wal, come to find out, they was a-talkin' about Cap'n Kidd's treasures, and layin' out how they should get it, and a-settin' one another on with gret stories about it.

" 'I've heard that there was whole chists full o' gold guineas,' says one.

" 'And I've heard o' gold bracelets and ear-rings and finger-rings all sparklin' with diamonds,' says another.

" 'Maybe it's old silver plate from some o' them old West Indian grandees,' says another.

" 'Wal, whatever it is,' says Mother Hokum, 'I want to be into it,' says she.

" 'Wal, Sam, won't you jine?' says they.

" 'Wal, boys,' says I, 'I kind o' don't feel jest like j'inin'. I sort o' ain't clear about the rights on 't: seems to me it's mighty nigh like goin' to the Devil for money.'

" 'Wal,' says Mother Hokum, 'what if 't is? Money's money, get it how ye will; and the Devil's money'll buy as much meat as any. I'd go to the Devil if he gave good money.'

" 'Wal, I guess I wouldn't,' says I. 'Don't you 'member the sermon Parson Lothrop preached about hastin' to be rich, last sabba' day?'

" 'Parson Lothrop be hanged!' says she. 'Wal, now,' says she, 'I like to see a parson with his silk stockin's and great gold-headed cane, a-lollopin' on his carriage behind his fat, prancin' hosses, comin' to meetin' to preach to us poor folks not to want to be rich! How'd he like it to have forty-'leven children, and nothin' to put onto 'em or into 'em, I wonder? Guess if Lady Lothrop had to rub and scrub, and wear her fingers to the bone as I do, she'd want to be rich; and I guess the Parson, if he couldn't get a bellyful for a week, would be for diggin' up Kidd's money, or doing 'most anything else to make the pot bile.'

" 'Wal,' says I, 'I'll kind o' go with ye, boys, and sort o' see how things turn out; but I guess I won't take no shere in 't,' says I.

"Wal, they got it all planned out. They was to wait till the full moon, and then they was to get Primus King to go with 'em and help do the diggin'. Ye see, Hokum and Toddy Whitney and Wiggin are all putty softly fellers, and hate dreffully to work; and I tell you the Kidd money ain't to be got without a pretty tough piece o' diggin'. Why, it's jest like diggin' a well to get at it. Now, Primus King was the master hand for diggin' wells, and so they said they'd get him by givin' on him a shere.

"Harry Wiggin he didn't want no nigger a-sherin' in it, he said; but Toddy and Hokum they said that when there was such stiff diggin' to be done, they didn't care if they did go in with a nigger.

"Wal, Wiggin he said he hadn't no objection to havin' the nigger do the diggin', it was sherin' the profits he objected to.

" 'Wal,' said Hokum, 'you can't get him without,' says he. 'Primus knows too much,' says he: 'you can't fool him.' Finally they 'greed that they was to give Primus twenty dollars, and shere the treasure 'mong themselves.

"Come to talk to Primus, he wouldn't stick in a spade, unless they'd pay him aforehand. Ye see, Primus was up to 'em; he knowed about Gidger, and there wa'n't none on 'em that was particular good pay; and so they all jest hed to rake and scrape, and pay him down the twenty dollars among 'em; and they 'greed for the fust full moon, at twelve o'clock at night, the 9th of October.

"Wal, ye see, I had to tell Hepsy I was goin' out to watch. Wal, so I was; but not jest in the way she took it: but Lordy massy! a feller has to tell his wife suthin' to keep her quiet, ye know, 'specially Hepsy.

"Wal, wal, of all the moonlight nights that ever I did see, I never did see one equal to that. Why, you could see the color o' everything. I 'member I could see how the huckleberry-bushes on the rock was red as blood when the moonlight shone through 'em; 'cause the leaves, you see, had begun to turn.

"Goin' on our way we got to talkin' about the sperits.

" 'I ain't afraid on 'em,' says Hokum. 'What harm can a sperit do me?' says he. 'I don't care ef there's a dozen on 'em;' and he took a swig at his bottle.

(*230*)

" 'Oh! there ain't no sperits,' says Harry Wiggin. 'That 'ere talk's all nonsense;' and he took a swig at *his* bottle.

" 'Wal,' says Toddy, 'I don't know 'bout that 'ere. Me and Ike Sanders has seen the sperits in the Cap'n Brown house.⁹ We thought we'd jest have a peek into the window one night; and there was a whole flock o' black colts without no heads on come rushin' on us and knocked us flat.'

" 'I expect you'd been at the tahvern,' said Hokum.

" 'Wal, yes, we had; but them was sperits: we wa'n't drunk, now; we was jest as sober as ever we was.'

" 'Wal, they won't get away my money,' says Primus, 'for I put it safe away in Dinah's teapot afore I come out;' and then he showed all his ivories from ear to ear. 'I think all this 'ere's sort o' foolishness,' said Primus.

" 'Wal,' says I, 'boys, I ain't a-goin' to have no part or lot in this 'ere matter, but I'll jest lay it off to you how it's to be done. Ef Kidd's money is under this rock, there's sperits that watch it, and you mustn't give 'em no advantage. There mustn't be a word spoke from the time ye get sight o' the treasure till ye get it safe up on to firm ground,' says I. 'Ef ye do, it'll vanish right out o' sight. I've talked with them that has dug down to it and seen it; but they allers lost it, 'cause they'd call out and say suthin'; and the minute they spoke, away it went.'

"Wal, so they marked off the ground; and Primus he begun to dig, and the rest kind o' sot round. It was so still it was kind o' solemn. Ye see, it was past twelve o'clock, and every critter in Oldtown was asleep; and there was two whippoorwills on the great Cap'n Brown elm-trees, that kep' a-answerin' each other back and forward sort o' solitary like; and then every once in a while there'd come a sort o' strange whisper up among the elm-tree leaves, jest as if there was talkin' goin' on; and every time Primus struck his spade into the ground it sounded sort o' holler, jest as if he'd been a-diggin' a grave. 'It's kind o' melancholy,' says I, 'to think o' them poor critters that had to be killed and buried jest to keep this 'ere treasure. What awful things'll

be brought to light in the judgment day! Them poor critters they loved to live and hated to die as much as any on us;
but no, they hed to die jest to satisfy that critter's wicked
will. I've heard them as thought they could tell the Cap'n
Kidd places by layin' their ear to the ground at midnight,
and they'd hear groans and wailin's.' "

"Why, Sam! were there really people who could tell
where Kidd's money was?" I here interposed.

"Oh, sartin! why, yis. There was Shebna Bascom, he
was one. Shebna could always tell what was under the
earth. He'd cut a hazel-stick and hold it in his hand when
folks was wantin' to know where to dig wells; and that 'ere
stick would jest turn in his hand, and p'int down till it would
fairly grind the bark off; and ef you dug in that place you
was sure to find a spring. Oh yis! Shebna he's told many
where the Kidd money was, and been with 'em when they
dug for it; but the pester on 't was they allers lost it, 'cause
they would some on 'em speak afore they thought."

"But, Sam, what about this digging? Let's know what
came of it," said we, as Sam appeared to lose his way in his
story.

"Wal, ye see, they dug down about five feet, when
Primus he struck his spade smack on something that
chinked like iron.

"Wal, then Hokum and Toddy Whitney was into the
hole in a minute; they made Primus get out, and they took
the spade, 'cause they wanted to be sure to come on it
themselves.

"Wal, they begun, and they dug and he scraped, and
sure enough they come to a gret iron pot as big as your
granny's dinner-pot, with an iron bale to it.

"Wal, then they put down a rope, and he put the rope
through the handle; then Hokum and Toddy they clam-
bered upon the bank, and all on 'em began to draw up jest
as still and silent as could be. They drawed and they
drawed, till they jest got it even with the ground, when

(232)

Toddy spoke out all in a tremble, 'There,' says he, *'we've got it!'* And the minit he spoke they was both struck by *suthin'* that knocked 'em clean over; and the rope give a crack like a pistol-shot, and broke short off; and the pot went down, down, down, and they heard it goin', jink, jink, jink; and it went way down into the earth, and the ground closed over it; and then they heard the screechin'est laugh ye ever did hear."

"I want to know, Sam, did you see that pot?" I exclaimed at this part of the story.

"Wal, no, I didn't. Ye see, I jest happened to drop asleep while they was diggin', I was so kind o' tired, and I didn't wake up till it was all over.

"I was waked up, 'cause there was consid'able of a scuffle; for Hokum was so mad at Toddy for speakin', that he was a-fistin' on him; and old Primus he jest haw-hawed and laughed. 'Wal, I got *my* money safe, anyhow,' says he.

" 'Wal, come to,' says I. ''Tain't no use cryin' for spilt milk: you've jest got to turn in now and fill up this 'ere hole, else the selectmen'll be down on ye.'

" 'Wal,' says Primus, 'I didn't engage to fill up no holes;' and he put his spade on his shoulder and trudged off.

"Wal, it was putty hard work, fillin' in that hole; but Hokum and Toddy and Wiggin had to do it, 'cause they didn't want to have everybody a-laughin' at 'em; and I kind o' tried to set it home to 'em, showin' on 'em that 't was all for the best.

" 'Ef you'd 'a' been left to get that 'ere money, ther'd 'a' come a cuss with it,' says I. 'It shows the vanity o' hastin' to be rich.'

" 'Oh, you shet up!' says Hokum, says he. 'You never hasted to anything,' says he. Ye see, he was riled, that's why he spoke so."

"Sam," said we, after maturely reflecting over the story, "what do you suppose was in that pot?"

"Lordy massy, boys! ye never will be done askin' questions. Why, how should I know?"

Notes

1. William Kidd, c.1645–1701, in 1695 was commissioned by the colonial governor of Massachusetts Bay to suppress piracy. Soon after, however, Kidd himself became a pirate and, subsequently, was arrested, tried, convicted, and hanged in 1701. Folklore held that Kidd buried his treasure before his arrest, various accounts citing several locations along the Atlantic seaboard as his hiding place.

2. A shiftless Yankee, created by Harriet Beecher Stowe for her 1869 novel, *Oldtown Folks*, Sam Lawson, through his antics and patter, supplied comic relief. So popular was he among readers that Stowe used him in many succeeding stories.

3. "Like an unbodied joy whose race is just begun." From "To a Skylark" by Percy Bysshe Shelley, 1792–1822, English poet.

4. "Tell me not, in mournful numbers,/Life is but an empty dream!" From "A Psalm of Life" by Henry Wadsworth Longfellow, 1807–1822, American poet.

5. "The Ballad of Captain Kidd," a sea song.

6. Sam Lawson frequently garbled or misremembered facts, a literary device used for comic effect.

7. William Moore, a gunner on the *Adventure Galley*, Kidd's ship. Kidd was convicted of his murder.

8. Natick, Massachusetts, birthplace of Calvin Ellis Stowe, the author's husband.

9. See "The Ghost in the Cap'n Brown House."

THE GHOST IN THE CAP'N BROWN HOUSE

"The Ghost in the Cap'n Brown House" was another story in the Sam Lawson series that Harriet Beecher Stowe wrote for the *Atlantic Monthly* in 1870. In 1872 she issued these tales as *Oldtown Fireside Stories* (Boston: J.R. Osgood & Co.)

"Now, Sam, tell us certain true, are there any such things as ghosts?"

"Be there ghosts?" said Sam, immediately translating into his vernacular grammar. "Wal, now, that 'ere's jest the question, ye see."

"Well, grandma thinks there are, and Aunt Lois thinks it's all nonsense. Why, Aunt Lois don't even believe the stories in Cotton Mather's 'Magnalia.' "[1]

"Wanter know?" said Sam, with a tone of slow, languid meditation.

We were sitting on the bank of the Charles River, fishing. The soft melancholy red of evening was fading off in streaks on the glassy water, and the houses of Oldtown[2] were beginning to loom through the gloom, solemn and ghostly. There are times and tones and moods of nature that make all the vulgar, daily real seem shadowy, vague, and supernatural, as if the outlines of this hard material present were fading into the invisible and unknown. So Oldtown, with its elm-trees, its great square white houses, its meeting-house and tavern and blacksmith's shop and mill, which at high noon seem as real and as commonplace

(235)

as possible, at this hour of the evening were dreamy and solemn. They rose up blurred, indistinct, dark; here and there winking candles sent long lines of light through the shadows, and little drops of unforeseen rain rippled the sheeny darkness of the water.

"Wal, you see, boys, in them things it's jest as well to mind your granny. There's a consid'able sight o' gumption in grandmas. You look at the folks that's allus tellin' you what they don't believe,—they don't believe this, and they don't believe that,—and what sort o' folks is they? Why, like yer Aunt Lois, sort o' stringy and dry. There ain't no 'sorption got out o' not believin' nothin'.

"Lord a massy! we don't know nothin' 'bout them things. We hain't been there, and can't say that there ain't no ghosts and sich; can we, now?"

We agreed to that fact, and sat a little closer to Sam in the gathering gloom.

"Tell us about the Cap'n Brown house, Sam."

"Ye didn't never go over the Cap'n Brown house?"

No, we had not that advantage.

"Wal, yer see, Cap'n Brown he made all his money to sea, in furrin parts, and then come here to Oldtown to settle down.

"Now, there ain't no knowin' 'bout these 'ere old ship-masters, where they's ben, or what they's ben a-doin', or how they got their money. Ask me no questions, and I'll tell ye no lies, is 'bout the best philosophy for them. Wal, it didn't do no good to ask Cap'n Brown questions too close, 'cause you didn't git no satisfaction. Nobody rightly knew 'bout who his folks was, or where they come from, and, ef a body asked him, he used to say that the very fust he knowed 'bout himself he was a young man walkin' the streets in London.

"But, yer see, boys, he hed money, and that is about all folks wanter know when a man comes to settle down. And he bought that 'ere place, and built that 'ere house.

He built it all sea-cap'n fashion, so's to feel as much at home as he could. The parlor was like a ship's cabin. The table and chairs was fastened down to the floor, and the closets was made with holes to set the casters and the decanters and bottles in, jest's they be at sea; and there was stanchions to hold on by; and they say that blowy nights the cap'n used to fire up pretty well with his grog, till he hed about all he could carry, and then he'd set and hold on, and hear the wind blow, and kind o' feel out to sea right there to hum. There wasn't no Mis' Cap'n Brown, and there didn't seem likely to be none. And whether there ever hed been one, nobody knowed. He hed an old black Guinea[3] nigger-woman, named Quassia, that did his work. She was shaped pretty much like one o' these 'ere great crookneck squashes. She wa'n't no gret beauty, I can tell you; and she used to wear a gret red turban and a yaller short gown and red petticoat, and a gret string o' gold beads round her neck, and gret big gold hoops in her ears, made right in the middle o' Africa among the heathen there. For all she was black, she thought a heap o' herself, and was consid'able sort o' predominative over the cap'n. Lordy massy! boys, it's allus so. Get a man and a woman together,—any sort o' woman you're a mind to, don't care who 't is,—and one way or another she gets the rule over him, and he jest has to train to her fife. Some does it one way, and some does it another; some does it by jawin', and some does it by kissin', and some does it by faculty and contrivance; but one way or another they allers does it. Old Cap'n Brown was a good stout, stocky kind o' John Bull[4] sort o' fellow, and a good judge o' sperits, and allers kep' the best in them 'ere cupboards o' his'n; but, fust and last, things in his house went pretty much as old Quassia said.

"Folks got to kind o' respectin' Quassia. She come to meetin' Sunday regular, and sot all fixed up in red and yaller and green, with glass beads and what not, lookin' for all the world like one o' them ugly Indian idols; but she was well behaved as any Christian. She was a master hand at cookin'. Her bread and biscuits couldn't be beat, and no couldn't her pies, and there wa'n't no such poundcake as she made nowhere. Wal, this 'ere story I'm a-goin' to tell you was told me by Cinthy Pendleton. There ain't a more respectable gal, old or young, than Cinthy nowheres. She lives over to Sherburne now, and I hear tell she's sot up a manty-makin' business; but then she used to do tailorin' in Oldtown. She was a member o' the church, and a good Christian as ever was. Wal, ye see, Quassia she got Cinthy to come up and spend a week to the Cap'n Brown house, a-doin' tailorin' and a-fixin' over his close: 't was along toward the fust o' March. Cinthy she sot by the fire in the front parlor with her goose and her press-board and her work: for there wa'n't no company callin', and the snow was drifted four feet deep right across the front door: so there wa'n't much danger o' anybody comin' in. And the cap'n he was a perlite man to wimmen; and Cinthy she liked it jest as well not to have company, 'cause the cap'n he'd make himself entertainin' tellin' on her sea-stories, and all about his adventures among the Ammonites, and Perresites, and Jebusites,[5] and all sorts o' heathen people he'd been among.

"Wal, that 'ere week there come on the master snowstorm. Of all the snowstorms that hed ben, that 'ere was the beater; and I tell you the wind blew as if 't was the last chance it was ever goin' to hev. Wal, it's kind o' scary like to be shet up in a lone house with all natur' a kind o' breakin' out, and goin' on so, and the snow a-comin' down so thick ye can't see 'cross the street, and the wind a-pipin' and a-squealin' and a-rumblin' and a-tumblin' fust down this chimney and then down that. I tell you, it sort o' sets a feller thinkin' o' the three great things,—death, judgment, and etarnaty; and I don't care who the folks is, nor how good they be, there's times when they must be feelin' putty consid'able solemn.

"Wal, Cinthy she said she kind o' felt so along, and she hed a sort o' queer feelin' come over her as if there was somebody or somethin' round the house more'n appeared. She said she sort o' felt it in the air; but it seemed to her silly, and she tired to get over it. But two or three times, she said, when it got to be dusk, she felt somebody go by her up the stairs. The front entry wa'n't very light in the daytime, and in the storm, come five o'clock, it was so dark that all you could see was jest a gleam o' somethin', and two or three times when she started to go upstairs she see a soft white suthin' that seemed goin' up before her, and she stopped with her heart a-beatin' like a trip-hammer, and she sort o' saw it go up and along the entry to the cap'n's door, and then it seemed to go right through, 'cause the door didn't open.

"Wal, Cinthy says she to old Quassia, says she, 'Is there anybody lives in this house but us?'

" 'Anybody lives here?' says Quassia: 'what you mean?' says she.

"Says Cinthy, 'I thought somebody went past me on the stairs last night and to-night.'

"Lordy massy! how old Quassia did screech and laugh. 'Good Lord!' says she, 'how foolish white folks is! Somebody went past you? Was't the capt'in?'

" 'No, it wa'n't the cap'n,' says she: 'it was somethin' soft and white, and moved very still; it was like somethin' in the air,' says she.

"Then Quassia she haw-hawed louder. Says she, 'It's hy-sterikes, Miss Cinthy; that's all it is.'

"Wal, Cinthy she was kind o' 'shamed, but for all that she couldn't help herself. Sometimes evenin's she'd be a-settin' with the cap'n, and she'd think she'd hear somebody a-movin' in his room overhead; and she knowed it wa'n't Quassia, 'cause Quassia was ironin' in the kitchen. She took pains once or twice to find out that 'ere.

"Wal, ye see, the cap'n's room was the gret front upper

chamber over the parlor, and then right oppisite to it was the gret spare chamber where Cinthy slept. It was jest as grand as could be, with a gret four-post mahogany bedstead and damask curtains brought over from England; but it was cold enough to freeze a white bear solid,—the way spare chambers allers is. Then there was the entry between, run straight through the house: one side was old Quassia's room, and the other was a sort o' store-room, where the old cap'n kep' all sorts o' traps.

"Wal, Cinthy she kep' a-hevin' things happen and a-seein' things, till she didn't railly know what was in it. Once when she come into the parlor jest at sundown, she was sure she see a white figure a-vanishin' out o' the door that went towards the side entry. She said it was so dusk, that all she could see was jest this white figure, and it jest went out still as a cat as she come in.

"Wal, Cinthy didn't like to speak to the cap'n about it. She was a close woman, putty prudent, Cinthy was.

"But one night, 'bout the middle o' the week, this 'ere thing kind o' come to a crisis.

"Cinthy said she'd ben up putty late a-sewin' and a-finishin' off down in the parlor; and the cap'n he sot up with her, and was consid'able cheerful and entertainin', tellin' her all about things over in the Bermudys, and off to Chiny and Japan, and round the world ginerally. The storm that hed been a-blowin' all the week was about as furious as ever; and the cap'n he stirred up a mess o' flip, and hed it for her hot to go to bed on. He was a good-natured critter, and allers had feelin's for lone women: and I s'pose he knew 't was sort o' desolate for Cinthy.

"Wal, takin' the flip so right the last thing afore goin' to bed, she went right off to sleep as sound as a nut, and slep' on till somewhere about mornin', when she said somethin' waked her broad awake in a minute. Her eyes flew wide open like a spring, and the storm hed gone down and the moon come out; and there, standin' right in the moonlight by her bed, was a woman jest as white as a sheet, with black hair hangin' down to her waist, and the brightest, mournfullest black eyes you ever see. She stood there lookin' right at Cinthy; and Cinthy thinks that was what waked her up; 'cause, you know, ef anybody stands and looks steady at folks asleep it's apt to wake 'em.

"Any way, Cinthy said she felt jest as ef she was turnin' to stone. She couldn't move nor speak. She lay a minute, and then she shut her eyes, and begun to say her prayers; and a minute after she opened 'em, and it was gone.

"Cinthy was a sensible gal, and one that allers hed her thoughts about her; and she jest got up and put a shawl round her shoulders, and went first and looked at the doors, and they was both on 'em locked jest as she left 'em when she went to bed. Then she looked under the bed and in the closet, and felt all round the room: where she couldn't see she felt her way, and there wa'n't nothin' there.

"Wal, next mornin' Cinthy got up and went home, and she kep' it to herself a good while. Finally, one day when she was workin' to our house she told Hepsy about it, and Hepsy she told me."

"Well, Sam," we said, after a pause, in which we heard only the rustle of leaves and the ticking of branches against each other, "what do you suppose it was?"

"Wal, there 't is: you know jest as much about it as I do. Hepsy told Cinthy it might 'a' ben a dream; so it might, but Cinthy she was sure it wa'n't a dream, 'cause she remembers plain hearin' the old clock on the stairs strike four while she had her eyes open lookin' at the woman; and then she only shet 'em a minute, jest to say 'Now I lay me,' and opened 'em and she was gone.

"Wal, Cinthy told Hepsy, and Hepsy she kep' it putty close. She didn't tell it to nobody except Aunt Sally Dickerson and the Widder Bije Smith and your Grandma Badger and the minister's wife, and they every one o' 'em 'greed it ought to be kep' close, 'cause it would make talk. Wal, come spring somehow or other it seemed to 'a' got all over Old-town. I heard on 't to the store and up to the tavern; and Jake Marshall he says to me one day, 'What's this 'ere about the cap'n's house?' And the Widder Loker she says to me, 'There's ben a ghost seen in the cap'n's house;' and I heard on 't clear over to Needham and Sherburne.

"Some o' the women they drew themselves up putty stiff and proper. Your Aunt Lois was one on 'em.

" 'Ghost,' says she; 'don't tell me! Perhaps it would be best ef 'twas a ghost,' says she. She didn't think there ought to be no sich doin's in nobody's house; and your grandma she shet her up, and told her she didn't oughter talk so."

"Talk how?" said I, interrupting Sam with wonder. "What did Aunt Lois mean?"

"Why, you see," said Sam mysteriously, "there allers is folks in every town that's just like the Sadducees[6] in old times: they won't believe in angel nor sperit, no way you can fix it; and ef things is seen and done in a house, why, they say, it's 'cause there's somebody there; there's some sort o' deviltry or trick about it.

"So the story got round that there was a woman kep' private in Cap'n Brown's house, and that he brought her from furrin parts; and it growed and growed, till there was all sorts o' ways o' tellin' on 't.

"Some said they'd seen her a-settin' at an open winder. Some said that moonlight nights they'd seen her a-walkin' out in the back garden kind o' in and out 'mong the bean-poles and squash-vines.

"You see, it come on spring and summer; and the winders o' the Cap'n Brown house stood open, and folks was all a-watchin' on 'em day and night. Aunt Sally Dicker-son told the minister's wife that she'd seen in plain daylight a woman a-settin' at the chamber winder atween four and five o'clock in the mornin',—jist a-settin' a-lookin' out and a-doin' nothin', like anybody else. She was very white and pale, and had black eyes.

(242)

"Some said that it was a nun the cap'n had brought away from a Roman Catholic convent in Spain, and some said he'd got her out o' the Inquisition.[7]

"Aunt Sally said she thought the minister ought to call and inquire why she didn't come to meetin', and who she was, and all about her: 'cause, you see, she said it might be all right enough ef folks only knowed jest how things was; but ef they didn't, why, folks will talk."

"Well, did the minister do it?"

"What, Parson Lothrop? Wal, no, he didn't. He made a call on the cap'n in a regular way, and asked arter his health and all his family. But the cap'n he seemed jest as jolly and chipper as a spring robin, and he gin the minister some o' his old Jamaiky;[8] and the minister he come away and said he didn't see nothin'; and no he didn't. Folks never does see nothin' when they ain't lookin' where 't is. Fact is, Parson Lothrop wa'n't fond o' interferin'; he was a master hand to slick things over. Your grandma she used to mourn about it, 'cause she said he never gin no p'int to the doctrines; but 't was all of a piece, he kind o' took everything the smooth way.

"But your grandma she believed in the ghost, and so did Lady Lothrop. I was up to her house t'other day fixin' a door-knob, and says she, 'Sam your wife told me a strange story about the Cap'n Brown house.'

" 'Yes, ma'am, she did,' says I.

" 'Well, what do you think of it?' says she.

" 'Wal, sometimes I think, and then ag'in I don't know,' says I. 'There's Cinthy she's a member o' the church and a good pious gal,' says I.

" 'Yes, Sam,' says Lady Lothrop, says she; 'and Sam,' says she, 'it is jest like something that happened once to my grandmother when she was livin' in the old Province House in Bostin.' Says she, 'These 'ere things is the mysteries of Providence, and it's jest as well not to have 'em too much talked about.'

" 'Jest so,' says I,—'jest so. That 'ere's what every woman I've talked with says; and I guess, fust and last, I've talked with twenty,—good, safe church members,—and they's every one o' opinion that this 'ere ought n't to be talked about. Why, over to the deakin's t'other night we went it all over as much as two or three hours, and we concluded that the best way was to keep quite still about it; and that's jest what they say over to Needham and Sherburne. I've been all round a-hushin' this 'ere up, and I hain't found but a few people that hedn't the particulars one way or another.' This 'ere was what I says to Lady Lothrop. The fact was, I never did see no report spread so, nor make sich sort o' sarchin's o' heart, as this 'ere. It really did beat all; 'cause, ef 't was a ghost, why there was the p'int proved, ye see. Cinthy's a church member, and she see it, and got right up and sarched the room: but then ag'in, ef 't was a woman, why that 'ere was kind o' awful; it give cause, ye see, for thinkin' all sorts o' things. There was Cap'n Brown, to be sure, he wa'n't a church member; but yet he was as honest and regular a man as any goin', as fur as any on us could see. To be sure, nobody knowed where he come from, but that wa'n't no reason agin him: this 'ere might a ben a crazy sister, or some poor critter that he took out o' the best o' motives; and the Scriptur' says, 'Charity hopeth all things.'[9] But then, ye see, folks will talk,—that 'ere's the pester o' all these things,—and they did some on 'em talk consid'able strong about the cap'n; but somehow or other, there didn't nobody come to the p'int o' facin' on him down, and sayin' square out, 'Cap'n Brown, have you got a woman in your house, or hain't you? or is it a ghost, or what is it?' Folks somehow never does come to that. Ye see, there was the cap'n so respectable, a-settin' up every Sunday there in his pew, with his ruffles round his hands and his red broadcloth cloak and his cocked hat. Why, folks' hearts sort o' failed 'em when it come to sayin' anything

(244)

right to him. They thought and kind o' whispered round that the minister or the deakins oughter do it: but Lordy massy! ministers, I s'pose, has feelin's like the rest on us; they don't want to eat all the hard cheeses that nobody else won't eat. Anyhow, there wasn't nothin' said direct to the cap'n; and jest for want o' that all the folks in Oldtown kep' a-bilin' and a-bilin' like a kettle o' soap, till it seemed all the time as if they'd bile over.

"Some o' the wimmen tried to get somethin' out o' Quassy. Lordy massy! you might as well 'a' tried to get it out an old tom-turkey, that'll strut and gobble and quitter, and drag his wings on the ground, and fly at you, but won't say nothin'. Quassy she screeched her queer sort o' laugh; and she told 'em that they was a-makin' fools o' themselves, and that the cap'n's matters wa'n't none o' their bisness; and that was true enough. As to goin' into Quassia's room, or into any o' the store-rooms or closets she kep' the keys of, you might as well hev gone into a lion's den. She kep' all her places locked up tight; and there was no gettin' at nothin' in the Cap'n Brown house, else I believe some o' the wimmen would 'a' sent a sarch-warrant."

"Well," said I, "what came of it? Didn't anybody ever find out?"

"Wal," said Sam, "it come to an end sort o', and didn't come to an end. It was jest this 'ere way. You see, along in October, jest in the cider-makin' time, Abel Flint he was took down with dysentery and died. You 'member the Flint house: it stood on a little rise o' ground jest lookin' over towards the Brown house. Wal, there was Aunt Sally Dickerson and the Widder Bije Smith, they set up with the corpse. He was laid out in the back chamber, you see, over the milk-room and kitchen; but there was cold victuals and sich in the front chamber, where the watchers sot. Wal, now, Aunt Sally she told me that between three and four o'clock she heard wheels a-rumblin', and she went to the

(245)

winder, and it was clear starlight; and she see a coach come up to the Cap'n Brown house; and she see the cap'n come out bringin' a woman all wrapped in a cloak, and old Quassy came after with her arms full o' bundles; and he put her into the kerridge, and shet her in, and it driv off; and she see old Quassy stand lookin' over the fence arter it. She tried to wake up the widder, but 't was towards mornin', and the widder allers was a hard sleeper; so there wa'n't no witness but her."

"Well, then, it wasn't a ghost," said I, "after all, and it was a woman."

"Wal, there 't is, you see. Folks don't know that 'ere yit, 'cause there it's jest as broad as 't is long. Now, look at it. There's Cinthy, she's a good, pious gal: she locks her chamber-doors, both on 'em, and goes to bed, and wakes up in the night, and there's a woman there. She jest shets her eyes, and the woman's gone. She gits up and looks and both doors is locked jest as she left 'em. That 'ere woman wa'n't flesh and blood now, no way,—not such flesh and blood as we knows on; but then they say Cinthy might hev dreamed it!

"Wal, now, look at it t'other way. There's Aunt Sally Dickerson; she's a good woman and a church member: wal, she sees a woman in a cloak with all her bundles brought out o' Cap'n Brown's house, and put into a kerridge, and driv off, atween three and four o'clock in the mornin'. Wal, that 'ere shows there must 'a' ben a real live woman kep' there privately, and so what Cinthy saw wasn't a ghost.

"Wal, now, Cinthy says Aunt Sally might 'a' dreamed it,—that she got her head so full o' stories about the Cap'n Brown house, and watched it till she got asleep, and hed this 'ere dream; and, as there didn't nobody else see it, it might 'a' ben, you know. Aunt Sally's clear she didn't dream, and then ag'in Cinthy's clear she didn't dream; but which on 'em was awake, or which on 'em was asleep, is what ain't settled in Oldtown yet."

Notes

1. Cotton Mather, 1663–1728, American Congregational clergyman, in 1702 published *Magnalia Christi Americana*, a history of New England Puritanism.

2. Fictional name of Natick, Massachusetts.

3. Region of western Africa.

4. The personification of England; hence, a typical Englishman.

5. Peoples mentioned in the Old Testament. The Perresites, a sly pun, refers to the biblical Perizzites.

6. An ancient Jewish sect that denied the existence of spirits, ghosts, angels, demons—any supernatural beings.

7. A Roman Catholic church court assembled to discover, punish, and prevent heresy.

8. Rum from Jamaica, West Indies.

9. Charity . . . "Beareth all things, believeth all things, hopeth all things." *1 Corinthians*. XIII, 7.

OLDTOWN FIRESIDE TALKS
OF THE REVOLUTION

The eager reception of Sam Lawson tales prompted Stowe to continue writing about him, and in 1881 she enlarged *Oldtown Fireside Stories* (Boston: J. R. Osgood & Co., 1872) by adding five stories, including "Oldtown Fireside Talks of the Revolution," all previously published in the *Atlantic Monthly* or the *Christian Union*. She retitled the volume *Sam Lawson's Oldtown Stories* (Boston: Houghton, Mifflin & Co.).

The sacred work of preparation for Thanksgiving was at hand. Our kitchen was fragrant with the smell of cinnamon, cloves, and allspice, which we boys were daily set to pound in the great lignum-vitae mortar. Daily the great oven flamed without cessation; and the splitting of oven-wood kept us youngsters so busy, that we scarce had a moment to play: yet we did it with a cheerful mind, inspired by the general aroma of coming festivity abroad in the house.

Behold us this evening around the kitchen-fire, which crackled and roared up the wide chimney, brightening with its fluttering radiance the farthest corner of the ample room. A tub of rosy-cheeked apples, another of golden quinces, and a bushel-basket filled with ruby cranberries, stood in the midst of the circle. All hands were busy. Grandmother in one corner was superintending us boys as we peeled and quartered the fruit,—an operation in which grandfather took a helping hand; Aunt Lois was busily looking over and sorting cranberries, when a knock at the door announced a visitor.

"Well, now, I s'pose that's Sam Lawson, of course," snapped Aunt Lois.

Aunt Lois generally spoke with a snap; but about Thanksgiving time it had a cheery ring, like the snapping of our brisk kitchen-fire.

"Good evenin', Miss Badger and Miss Lois," said Sam. "I see yer winders so bright, I couldn't help wantin' to come in and help ye pare apples, or suthin'."

We boys made haste to give Sam the warmest welcome, and warmest place in the chimney-corner, and to accommodate him with a tin pan full of quinces, and a knife, when he was soon settled among us.

"Wal, this 'ere does look cheerful,—looks like Thanksgivin'," he began. "Wal, Lordy massy! we've got a great deal to be thankful for in this 'ere land o' privileges; hain't we, deacon? I was a-comin' 'round by Miss Lothrop's to-day; and her Dina, she told me the Doctor was gettin' a great sermon out on the hundred and twenty-fourth Psalm: 'If it had not been the Lord who was on our side when men rose up against us, then they had swallowed us up.'[1] He's a-goin' to show all our deliverances in the war. I expect it'll be a whale of a sermon, 'cause, when our minister sets out to do a thing, he mos' generally does it up to the handle. Tell ye what, boys, you must listen with all your ears: you'll never know what times them was if you don't—you don't know what liberty cost us all. There's your gran'ther, now, he could tell ye: he 'members when he went off to Lexington[2] with his gun on his shoulders."

"Why, grandfather! did you go?" we both exclaimed with wide eyes.

"Well, boys," said my grandfather, "'t ain't worth talkin' about what I did. I was in my mill that day minding my business, when brother Con, he burst in and says he,

'Look here, Bill, the regulars are goin' up to Concord³ to destroy our stores, and we must all go. Come, get your gun.' Well, I said I was a miller, and millers were exempt from duty; but Con wouldn't let me alone. 'Get down your gun,' says he. 'Suppose we're going to let them British fellers walk over us?' says he. Well, Con always had his way of me; and I got my gun, and we started out through the woods over to Concord. We lived at Weston then, ye see. Well, when we got on the brow of the hill, we looked over, and, sure enough, there on burying-ground hill was the British regulars. The hill was all alive with 'em, marching here and there in their scarlet coats like so many bees out of a hive.

" 'Con,' says I, 'jest look there. What are you going to do?'

" 'Shoot some of 'em, I know,' says Con.

"And so we ran along, hiding behind trees and bushes and stone walls, till we got near enough to get a shot at 'em. You see, they broke up into companies, and went here and there about town, looking for the stores; and then, as we got a chance here and there, we marked our men, and popped, and then we'd run, and take aim somewhere else."

"Wal, now, that 'are wa'n't the hull on 't," said Sam. "Why, there was hundreds of fellers doin' just the same all round: it was jest pop-pop-pop! from every barn, and every bush, and clump o' trees, all along the way. Men was picked off all the time; and they couldn't see who did it, and it made 'em mad as fury. Why, I 'member Mis' Tom Bigelow, she that was Sary Jones, told me how they sot her mother's house afire and burnt it down, 'cause their nigger man Caesar popped at 'em out o' the buttery window. They didn't tell him to; but Caesar, he was full of fight, like all the rest on 'em. Lordy massy! the niggers went for suthin' in them times! Their blood was up as quick as anybody's. Why, there was old Pompey Lovejoy lived over by Pomp's pond in Andover, he hitched up his wagon, and driv over

(*250*)

with two barrels o' cider and some tin dippers, and was round all day givin' drinks o' cider to our men when they got het and thirsty and tired. It was a pretty warm day for April, that was. Pomp has told me the story many a time. 'Twas all the cider he had; but cider goes for suthin', as well as gunpowder in its place, and Pomp's cider come jest right that day."

"But grandfather," said I, "what happened to you over there?"

"Well, you see," said grandfather placidly, "I wasn't killed; but I come pretty nigh it. You see, they sent into Boston for reënforcements; and by the time we got to Lexington, Earl Percy[4] was marching out with fresh troops and cannon. Con and I were standing on the meetin'-house steps, when there come a terrible bang, and something struck right over our heads, and went into the meetin'-house. 'Why, Bill!' says Con, 'what's that?'—'They've got cannon: that's what that is,' says I. 'Let's run 'round the other side.' So we did; but just as we got 'round there, there come another bang, and a ball crashed right through the meetin'-house, and come out of the pulpit window. Well, we saw there was no staying there: so we run then, and got into a little clump of trees behind a stone wall; and there we saw 'em go by,—Earl Percy on his horse, and all his troops, ever so grand. He went on up to Concord. Fact is, if it hadn't been for him and his men, those regulars would all have been cut off: they wouldn't one of 'em have got back, for the whole country was up and fighting. The militia came pouring in from Weston and Acton and Billriky,[5]— all the towns 'round. Then their Colonel Smith[6] was wounded and a good many others, and lots of 'em killed and our minute-men coming on 'em before and behind, and all around. But ye see, we couldn't stand regular troops and cannon; and so, when they come on, we had to give back. Earl Percy came up, and formed a hollow square, and they marched into it, and so gave 'em time to rest."

(*251*)

"Wal, there was need enough on 't," said Sam.

"The regulars had been hectored and picked, and driv 'round so from piller to post, that they was dog tired. Jimmy Irwin, he was a little chap then; but he telled me how he see the men jest throw 'emselves down on the ground, their tongues out o' their mouths like hunting-dogs. You see, they had about two hundred wounded, and twenty-eight or nine was taken prisoners, and sixty-four killed outright: so Lord Percy had his hands full o' takin care o' the mess they'd got up."

"Yes," said my grandfather, "there were dead men lying all around the road as we came back. There, boys!" he said, pointing to a gun and powder-horn over the chimney, "we picked up these when we were coming home. We found them on a poor fellow who lay there dead in the road: there's some blood of his on it to this day. We couldn't help feeling it was most too bad too."

"Poor fellow! he wa'n't to blame," said my grandmother. "Soldiers have to go as they're bid. War's an awful thing."

"Then they shouldn't have begun it," interposed Aunt Lois. " 'They that take the sword shall perish by the sword.' "[7]

"Well, grandpapa," said I, "what were the stores they went up to get?"

"They were stores laid up to enable us to go to war, and they were 'round in different places. There were two twenty-four-pounders that they spiked, and they threw about five hundred pounds of ball into the river or wells, and broke up sixty barrels of flour, and scattered it about."

"Wal," said Sam triumphantly, "there was one lot they didn't get. Cap'n Tim Wheeler had about the biggest lot o' wheat, and rye-flour, and corn-meal stored up in his barn, with some barrels of his own. So when this 'ere fine jaybird of an officer came to him all so grand, and told him to open his barn and let him look in, the cap'n, he took his key, and walked right out, and opened the barn-door; and the officer was tickled to pieces. He thought he'd got such a haul!

" 'If you please, sir,' says the cap'n, 'I'm a miller, and get my living by grinding grain. I'm a poor man. You can see my mill out there. I grind up a lot o' grain in the winter, and get it ready to sell in the spring. Some's wheat, and some's rye, and some's corn-meal; and this wheat is mine, and this rye is mine, and this corn-meal is mine;' and, when he spoke, he put his hand on his own barrels.

" 'Oh! if this is your private property,' says the officer, 'we sha'n't touch that: we don't meddle with private property.' And so he turned on his heel, and the cap'n, he locked up his barn."

"Was that telling the truth?" said I.

"Wal, you see it was true what he said," said Sam. "Them bar'ls he laid his hands on was his'n."

"But Aunt Lois told me yesterday it was as bad to act a lie as to speak one," said I.

"Well, so I did," said Aunt Lois. "The truth is the truth, and I'll stick to it."

"But, Aunt Lois, would you have told him, and let him break up all those barrels?"

"No, I shouldn't," said Aunt Lois. "I should have done just as Cap'n Tim did; but I should have done *wrong*. Right is right, and wrong is wrong, even if I can't come up to it always."

"What would you have done, grandfather?" said I.

My grandfather's mild face slowly irradiated, as when moonbeams pass over a rock.

"Well, boys," he said, "I don't think I should have let him break up those barrels. If it was wrong to do as Cap'n Wheeler did, I think most likely I should 'a' done it. I don't suppose I'm any better than he was."

"Well, at any rate," said Aunt Lois, "what folks do in war time is no rule for ordinary times: everything is upset then. There ain't any of the things they do in war time that are according to Gospel teaching; but, if you boys were to do just as Cap'n Wheeler did, I should say you lied by speaking the truth."

"Well, well," said my grandmother, "those were dreadful times. Thank the Lord that they are past and gone, and we don't have such awful cases of conscience as we did then. I never could quite see how we did right to resist the king at all."

"Why, the Bible says, 'Resist the devil,' "[8] said Aunt Lois.

A general laugh followed this sally.

"I always heard," said my grandfather, by way of changing the subject, "that they meant to have taken Mr. Adams and Mr. Hancock[9] and hung 'em."

"Wal, to be sure they did," said Sam Lawson. "I know all about that 'are. Sapphira Clark, up to Lexington, she told me all about that 'are, one day when I was to her house puttin' down her best parlor carpet. Sapphira wa'n't but ten or eleven years old when the war broke out; but she remembered all about it. Ye see, Mr. Hancock and Mr. Adams was a-staying hid up at their house. Her father, Mr. Jonas Clark, was minister of Lexington; and he kep' 'em quite private, and didn't let nobody know they was there. Wal, Sapphira said they was all a-settin' at supper, when her father, he heard a great rapping at the front-door; and her father got up and went and opened it; and she looked after him into the entry, and could see a man in a scarlet uniform standing at the door, and she heard him ask, 'Are Sam Adams and John Hancock here?' And her father answered, 'Oh, hush! Don't mention those names here.'— 'Then,' says the man, 'I come to tell you the British troops will be along by sunrise; and, if they are in your house, they'd better escape right away.' "

"That must have been Colonel Paul Revere,"[10] said Aunt Lois. "He went all through the country, from Boston to Concord, rousing up people, and telling 'em to be ready."

"Well, what did Mr. Adams and Hancock do?"

"Wal, they got ready right away, and slipped quietly out the back-door, and made their way over to Burlington, and staid in the minister's house over there out of the way of the battle."

"What would the British have done with 'em if they had caught them?" said I.

"Hung 'em—high as Haman,"[11] said my Aunt Lois sententiously. "That's what they'd have done. That's what they'd 'a' done to them, and to General Washington,[12] and lots more, if they'd had their way."

"Oh, yes!" said grandfather, "they were mighty high-stepping at first. They thought they had only to come over and show themselves, and they could walk through the land, and hang and burn and slay just whom they'd a mind to."

"Wal, they found 't was like jumping into a hornets' nest," said Sam Lawson. "They found that out at Lexington and Bunker Hill."[13]

"Brother Con was in those trenches at Bunker Hill," said grandfather. "There they dug away at the breast-works, with the bom'-shells firing 'round 'em. They didn't mind them more than if they'd been hickory-nuts. They kep' fellows ready to pour water on 'em as they fell."

"Well, I never want to feel again as I did that day," said grandmother. "I was in Boston, visiting cousin Jemima Russell, and we were all out on the roof of the house. The roofs everywhere were all alive with people looking through spy-glasses; and we could hear the firing, but couldn't tell how the day was going. And then they set Charlestown on fire; and the blaze and smoke and flame rose up, and there was such a snapping and crackling, and we could hear roofs and timbers falling, and see people running this way and that with their children—women scared half to death a-flying; and we knew all the time there was cousin Jane Wilkinson in that town sick in bed, with a baby only a few days old. It's a wonder how Jane ever lived

(255)

through it; but they did get her through alive, and her baby too. That burning Charlestown settled the point with a good many. They determined then to fight it through: it was so mean and cruel and needless."

"Yes," said my grandfather, "that day settled the question that we would be free and independent, or die; and though our men had to retreat, yet it was as good as a defeat to the British. They lost ten hundred and fifty-four in killed and wounded, and we only four hundred and fifty-three; and our men learned that they could fight as well as the British. Congress went right to work to raise an army, and appointed General Washington commander. Your gran'ther Stowe, boys, was orderly of the day when General Washington took the command at Cambridge."

"Wal," said Sam, "I was in Cambridge that day and saw it all. Ye see, the army was drawn up under the big elm there; and Ike Newel and I, we clim up into a tree, and got a place where we could look down and see. I wa'n't but ten year old then; but, if ever a mortal man looked like the angel of the Lord, the gineral looked like it that day."

"Some said that there was trouble about having General Ward[14] give up the command to a Southern man," said my grandfather. "General Ward was a brave man and very popular; but everybody was satisfied when they came to know General Washington."

"There couldn't no minister have seemed more godly than he did that day," said Sam. "He read out of the hymn-book the hundred and first Psalm."

"What is that psalm?" said I.

"Laws, boys! I know it by heart," said Sam, "I was so impressed hearin' on him read it. I can say it to you:—

    " 'Mercy and judgment are my song,
    And since they both to thee belong,
    My gracious God, my righteous King,
    To thee my songs and vows I bring.

If I am raised to bear the sword,
I'll take my counsels from thy word.
Thy justice and thy heavenly grace
Shall be the pattern of my ways.
I'll search the land, and raise the just
To posts of honor, wealth, and trust:
The men who work thy righteous will
Shall be my friends and favorites still.
The impious crew, the factious band,
Shall hold their peace, or quit the land;
And all who break the public rest,
Where I have power, shall be suppressed.' "

"And he did it too," remarked Aunt Lois.

"He trusted in the Lord, and the Lord brought him to honor," said my grandmother. "When he took the army, everything was agin' us: it didn't seem possible we should succeed."

"Wal, he was awful put to it sometimes," said Sam Lawson. "I 'member Uncle David Morse was a-tellin' me 'bout that 'are time down in New York when the Massachusetts and Connecticut boys all broke and run."

"Massachusetts boys run? How came that Sam?" said I.

"Wal, you see, sometimes fellows will get a-runnin'; and it jest goes from one to another like fire, and ye can't stop it. It was after the battle of Long Island,[15] when our men had been fighting day after day, and had to retreat. A good many were wounded, and a good many of 'em were sick and half-sick; and they'd got sort o' tired and discouraged.

"Well, Lord Howe[16] and the British came to make a landing at Kipp's Bay, round by New York; and the troops set to guard the landing began to run, and the Massachusetts and Connecticut men were sent to help 'em. Uncle David says that the fellows that run spread the panic among 'em; and they looked ahead, and saw an ox-drag on top of a

(257)

hill they was to pass, and they thought 't was a cannon pintin' right at 'em; and the boys they jest broke and run,— cut right across the road, and cleared over the fence, and streaked it off cross-lots and up hill like a flock o' sheep. Uncle David, he run too; but he'd been sick o' dysentary, and was so weak he couldn't climb the fence: so he stopped and looked back, and saw Gineral Washington cantering up behind 'em, shouting, and waving his sword, looking like a flamin' fire. Oh, he was thunderin' mad, the gineral was! And when he see the fellows skittering off cross-lots, he jest slammed his hat down on the ground, and give up. 'Great heavens!' says he, 'are these the men I've got to fight this battle with?'

"Wal, Uncle David, he picked up the gineral's hat, and come up and made his bow, and said, 'Gineral, here's your hat.'

" 'Thank you, sir!' said the gineral. 'I'm glad to see one brave fellow that can stand his ground. *You* didn't run.'

"Uncle David said he felt pretty cheap, 'cause he know'd in his own heart that he would 'a' run, only he was too weak to git over the fence; but he didn't tell the gineral that, I bet! He put the compliment in his pocket, and said nothing; for now the gineral's aides came riding up full drive, and told him they must be off out of the field in a minute, or the British would have 'em, and so one on 'em took Uncle David up behind him, and away they cantered. It was a pretty close shave too: the British was only a few rods behind 'em."

"Oh, dear, if they had caught him!" said I. "Only think!"

"Well, they would have hung him; but we should have had another in his place," said Aunt Lois. "The war wouldn't 'a' stopped."

"Well, 't was to be as 't was," said my grandmother. "The Lord had respect to the prayers of our fathers, and he'd decreed that America should be free."

(258)

"Yes," said Sam: "Parson Lothrop said in one of his sermons, that men always was safe when they was goin' in the line o' God's decrees: I guess that 'are was about it. But, massy! is that 'are the nine o'clock bell? I must make haste home, or I dun' know what Hetty'll say to me."

Notes

1. Verses 2–3.

2. Lexington, Massachusetts, the site of the start of the American Revolution, April 19, 1775.

3. Concord, Massachusetts, to which a detachment of British soldiers had been sent to seize the military stores that the American colonists had collected there.

4. Hugh Smithson, 1715–1786, made Earl Percy in 1766, commanded a force of 1,000 men and rescued the embattled British at Lexington.

5. Billerica, a town near Concord.

6. Francis Smith, a British lieutenant-colonel, led the forces sent to destroy the colonists's military supplies stored at Concord.

7. "All they that take the sword shall perish with the sword." *Matthew.* XXVI, 52.

8. "Resist the Devil, and he will flee from you." *James* IV, 7.

9. Samuel Adams, 1722–1803; John Hancock, 1737–1793, American Revolutionary leaders.

10. Paul Revere, 1735–1818, American patriot, remembered for his ride from Boston to Lexington, April 18–19, 1775, to warn the colonists that the British soldiers were on the march.

11. Haman, 5th-century Persian prince, hanged on the very gallows he ordered built to execute another.

12. George Washington, 1732–1799, commander-in-chief of the American Revolutionary forces and later first president of the United States.

13. Site in Charlestown (Boston), Massachusetts, of battle fought on June 17, 1775.

14. Artemas Ward, 1727–1800, commander of Massachusetts troops in 1775.

15. British forces, on August 27, 1776, defeated the American colonists.

16. William Howe, 1729–1814, British general, victor at the battles of Long Island and Bunker Hill.

LAUGHIN' IN MEETIN'

First published in the *Christian Union*, June 26, 1872, "Laughin' in Meetin'" was later collected in *Sam Lawson's Oldtown Fireside Stories* (Boston: Houghton, Mifflin & Co., 1881).

We were in disgrace, we boys; and the reason of it was this: we had laughed out in meeting-time! To be sure, the occasion was a trying one, even to more disciplined nerves. Parson Lothrop had exchanged pulpits with Parson Summeral, of North Wearem. Now, Parson Summeral was a man in the very outset likely to provoke the risibles of unspiritualized juveniles. He was a thin, wiry, frisky little man, in a powdered white wig, black tights, and silk stockings, with bright knee-buckles and shoe-buckles; with round, dark, snapping eyes; and a curious, high, cracked, squeaking voice, the very first tones of which made all the children stare and giggle. The news that Parson Summeral was going to preach in our village spread abroad among us as a prelude to something funny. It had a flavor like the charm of circus-acting; and, on the Sunday morning of our story, we went to the house of God in a very hilarious state, all ready to set off in a laugh on the slightest provocation.

The occasion was not long wanting. Parson Lothrop had a favorite dog yclept Trip, whose behavior in meeting was notoriously far from that edifying pattern which befits a minister's dog on Sundays. Trip was a nervous dog, and a

(*261*)

dog that never could be taught to conceal his emotions or to respect conventionalities. If anything about the performance in the singers' seat did not please him, he was apt to express himself in a lugubrious howl. If the sermon was longer than suited him, he would gape with such a loud creak of his jaws as would arouse everybody's attention. If the flies disturbed his afternoon's nap, he would give sudden snarls or snaps; or, if anything troubled his dreams, he would bark out in his sleep in a manner not only to dispel his own slumbers, but those of certain worthy deacons and old ladies whose sanctuary repose was thereby sorely broken and troubled. For all these reasons, Madam Lothrop had been forced, as a general thing, to deny Trip the usual sanctuary privileges of good family dogs in that age, and shut him up on Sundays to private meditation. Trip, of course, was only the more set on attendance, and would hide behind doors, jump out windows, sneak through byways and alleys, and lie hid till the second bell had done tolling, when suddenly he would appear in the broad aisle, innocent and happy, and take his seat as composedly as any member of the congregation.

Imagine us youngsters on the *qui vive* with excitement at seeing Parson Summeral frisk up into the pulpit with all the vivacity of a black grasshopper. We looked at each other, and giggled very cautiously, with due respect to Aunt Lois's sharp observation.

At first, there was only a mild, quiet simmering of giggle compressed decorously within the bounds of propriety; and we pursed our muscles up with stringent resolution whenever we caught the apprehensive eye of our elders.

But when, directly after the closing notes of the tolling second bell, Master Trip walked gravely up the front aisle, and, seating himself squarely in front of the pulpit, raised his nose with a critical air toward the scene of the forthcoming performance, it was too much for us: the repression was almost convulsive. Trip wore an alert, attentive air, befitting a sound, orthodox dog who smells a possible heresy, and deems it his duty to watch the performances narrowly. Evidently he felt called upon to see who and what were to occupy that pulpit in his master's absence.

Up rose Parson Summeral; and up went Trip's nose, vibrating with intense attention.

The Parson began in his high-cracked voice to intone the hymn,—

> "Sing to the Lord aloud,"

when Trip broke into a dismal howl.

The Parson went on to give directions to the deacon, in the same voice in which he had been reading, so that the whole effect of the performance was somewhat as follows:—

> " 'Sing to the Lord aloud.'

> "(Please to turn out that dog),—

> " 'And make a joyful noise.' "[1]

The dog was turned out, and the choir did their best to make a joyful noise; but we boys were upset for the day, delivered over to the temptations of Satan, and plunged in waves and billows of hysterical giggle, from which neither winks nor frowns from Aunt Lois, nor the awful fear of the tithing-man, nor the comforting bits of fennel and orange-peel passed us by grandmother, could recover us.

Everybody felt, to be sure, that here was a trial that called for some indulgence. Hard faces, even among the stoniest saints, betrayed a transient quiver of the risible muscles; old ladies put up their fans; youths and maidens in the singers' seat laughed outright; and, for the moment, a general snicker among the children was pardoned. But I was one of that luckless kind, whose nerves, once set in vibration, could not be composed. When the reign of gravity and decorum had returned, Harry and I sat by each other, shaking with suppressed laughter. Everything in the subsequent exercises took a funny turn, and in the long prayer, when everybody else was still and decorous, the whole scene came over me with such overpowering force, that I exploded with laughter, and had to be taken out of meeting and marched home by Aunt Lois, as a convicted criminal. What especially moved her indignation was, that, the more she rebuked and upbraided, the more I laughed, till the tears rolled down my cheeks; which Aunt Lois construed into willful disrespect to her authority, and resented accordingly.

By Sunday evening, as we gathered around the fire, the reaction from undue gayety to sobriety had taken place; and we were in a pensive and penitent state. Grandmother was gracious and forgiving; but Aunt Lois still preserved that frosty air of reprobation which she held to be a salutary means of quickening our consciences for the future. It was, therefore, with unusual delight that we saw our old friend Sam come in, and sit himself quietly down on the block in the chimney-corner. With Sam we felt assured of indulgence and patronage; for, though always rigidly moral and instructive in his turn of mind, he had that fellow-feeling for transgressors which is characteristic of the loose-jointed, easy-going style of his individuality.

"Lordy massy, boys—yis," said Sam virtuously, in view of some of Aunt Lois's thrusts, "ye ought never to laugh nor cut up in meetin'; that 'ere's so: but then there is times when the best on us gets took down. We gets took unawares, ye see,—even ministers does. Yis, natur' will git the upper hand afore they know it."

"Why, Sam, ministers don't ever laugh in meetin'! do they?"

We put the question with wide eyes. Such a supposition bordered on profanity, we thought: it was approaching the sin of Uzzah,[2] who unwarily touched the ark of the Lord.

"Laws, yes. Why, hevn't you never heard how there was a council held to try Parson Morrel for laughin' out in prayer-time?"

"Laughing in prayer-time!" we both repeated, with uplifted hands and eyes.

My grandfather's mild face became luminous with a suppressed smile, which brightened it as the moon does a cloud; but he said nothing.

"Yes, yes," said my grandmother, "that affair did make a dreadful scandal in the time on't! But Parson Morrel was a good man; and I'm glad the council wasn't hard on him."

"Wal," said Sam Lawson, "after all, it was more Ike Babbit's fault that 't was anybody's. Ye see, Ike he was allers for gettin' what he could out o' the town; and he would feed his sheep on the meetin'-house green. Somehow or other, Ike's fences allers contrived to give out, come Sunday, and up would come his sheep; and Ike was too pious to drive 'em back Sunday, and so there they was. He was talked to enough about it: 'cause, ye see, to hev sheep and lambs a-ba-a-in' and a-blatin' all prayer and sermon time wa'n't the thing. 'Member that 'ere old meetin'-house up to the North End, down under Blueberry Hill, the land sort o' sloped down, so as a body hed to come into the meetin'-house steppin' down instead o' up.

"Fact was, they said 't was put there 'cause the land wa'n't good for nothin' else; and the folks thought puttin' a meetin'-house on't would be a clear savin'. But Parson Morrel he didn't like it, and was free to tell 'em his mind on 't,— that 't was like bringin' the lame and the blind to the Lord's sarvice; but there 't was.

"There wa'n't a better minister, nor no one more set by in all the State, than Parson Morrel. His doctrines was right up and down, good and sharp; and he give saints and

(265)

sinners their meat in due season; and for consolin' and comfortin' widders and orphans, Parson Morrel hedn't his match. The women sot lots by him; and he was allus ready to take tea round, and make things pleasant and comfortable; and he hed a good story for every one, and a word for the children, and maybe an apple or a cooky in his pocket for 'em. Wal, you know there ain't no pleasin' everybody; and ef Gabriel[3] himself, right down out o' heaven, was to come and be a minister, I expect there'd be a pickin' at his wings, and sort o' fault-findin'. Now, Aunt Jerushy Scran and Aunt Polly Hokum they sed Parson Morrel wa'n't solemn enough. Ye see, there's them that thinks that a minister ought to be just like the town hearse, so that ye think of death, judgment, and eternity, and nothin' else, when ye see him round; and ef they see a man rosy and chipper, and hevin' a pretty nice, sociable sort of a time, why they say he ain't spiritooal minded. But, in my times, I've seen ministers the most awakenin' kind in the pulpit that was the liveliest when they was out on 't. There is a time to laugh,[4] Scriptur' says; though some folks never seem to remember that 'ere."

"But, Sam, how came you to say it was Ike Babbit's fault? What was it about the sheep?"

"Oh, wal, yis! I'm a-comin' to that 'ere. It was all about them sheep. I expect they was the instrument the Devel sot to work to tempt Parson Morrel to laugh in prayer-time.

"Ye see, there was old Dick, Ike's bell-wether, was the fightin'est old critter that ever yer see. Why, Dick would butt at his own shadder; and everybody said it was a shame the old critter should be left to run loose, 'cause he run at the children, and scared the women half out their wits. Wal, I used to live out in that parish in them days. And Lem Sudoc and I used to go out sparkin' Sunday nights, to see the Larkin gals; and we had to go right 'cross the lot where Dick was: so we used to go and stand at the fence, and call. And Dick would see us, and put down his head, and run at

us full chisel, and come bunt agin the fence; and then I'd
ketch him by the horns, and hold him while Lem run and
got over the fence t'other side the lot; and then I'd let go:
and Lem would holler, and shake a stick at him, and away
he'd go full butt at Lem; and Lem would ketch his horns,
and hold him till I came over,—that was the way we managed Dick; but, I tell you, ef he come sudden up behind a
fellow, he'd give him a butt in the small of his back that
would make him run on all fours one while. He was a great
rogue,—Dick was. Wal, that summer, I remember they hed
old Deacon Titkins for tithing-man; and I tell you he give it
to the boys lively. There wa'n't no sleepin' nor no playin';
for the deacon hed eyes like a gimblet, and he was quick as a
cat, and the youngsters hed to look out for themselves. It
did really seem as if the deacon was like them four beasts in
the Revelations[5] that was full o' eyes behind and before; for
which ever way he was standin', if you gave only a wink, he
was down on you, and hit you a tap with his stick. I know
once Lem Sudoc jist wrote two words in the psalm-book
and passed to Kesiah Larkin; and the deacon give him such
a tap that Lem grew red as a beet, and vowed he'd be up
with him some day for that.

"Well, Lordy massy, folks that is so chipper and high
steppin' has to hev their come-downs; and the deacon he
hed to hev his.

"That 'ere Sunday,—I 'member it now jest as well as if
't was yesterday,—the parson he give us his gret sermon,
reconcilin' decrees and free agency: everybody said that
'ere sermon was a masterpiece. He preached it up to Cambridge[6] at Commencement, that year. Wal, it so happened
it was one o' them bilin' hot days that come in August, when
you can fairly hear the huckleberries a-sizzlin' and cookin'
on the bushes, and the locust keeps a-gratin' like a red-hot
saw. Wal, such times, decrees or no decrees, the best on us
will get sleepy. The old meetin'-house stood right down at
the foot of a hill that kep' off all the wind; and the sun

blazed away at them gret west winders: and there was pretty sleepy times there. Wal, the deacon he flew round a spell, and woke up the children, and tapped the boys on the head, and kep' everything straight as he could, till the sermon was most through, when he railly got most tuckered out; and he took a chair, and he sot down in the door right opposite the minister, and fairly got asleep himself, jest as the minister got up to make the last prayer.

"Wal, Parson Morrel hed a way o' prayin' with his eyes open. Folks said it wa'n't the best way: but it was Parson Morrel's way, anyhow: and so, as he was prayin', he couldn't help seein' that Deacon Titkins was a-noddin' and a-bobbin' out toward the place where old Dick was feedin' with the sheep, front o' the meetin'-house door.

"Lem and me we was sittin' where we could look out; and we jest sees old Dick stop feedin' and look at the deacon. The deacon hed a little round head as smooth as an apple, with a nice powdered wig on it: and he sot there makin' bobs and bows; and Dick begun to think it was suthin sort o' pussonal. Lem and me was sittin' jest where we could look out and see the hull picter; and Lem was fit to split.

" 'Good, now,' says he: 'that critter'll pay the deacon off lively, pretty soon.'

"The deacon bobbed his head a spell; and old Dick he shook his horns, and stamped at him sort o' threat'nin'. Finally the deacon he give a great bow, and brought his head right down at him; and old Dick he sot out full tilt and come down on him ker chunk, and knocked him head over heels into the broad aisle: and his wig flew one way and he t' other; and Dick made a lunge at it, as it flew, and carried it off on his horns.

"Wal, you may believe, that broke up the meetin' for one while: for Parson Morrel laughed out; and all the gals and boys they stomped and roared. And the old deacon he got up and begun rubbin' his shins, 'cause he didn't see the joke on 't.

" 'You don't orter laugh,' says he: 'it's no laughin' matter; it's a solemn thing,' says he. 'I might hev been sent into 'tarnity by that darned critter,' says he. Then they all roared and haw-hawed the more, to see the deacon dancin' round with his little shiny head, so smooth a fly would trip up on 't. 'I believe, my soul, you'd laugh to see me in my grave,' says he.

"Wal, the truth on 't was, 't was jist one of them bustin' up times that natur has, when there ain't nothin' for it but to give in: 't was jest like the ice breakin' up in the Charles River,—it all come at once, and no whoa to 't. Sunday or no Sunday, sin or no sin, the most on 'em laughed till they cried, and couldn't help it.

"But the deacon, he went home feelin' pretty sore about it. Lem Sudoc, he picked up his wig, and handed it to him. Says he, 'Old Dick was playin' tithin'-man, wa'n't he, deacon? Teach you to make allowance for other folks that get sleepy.'

"Then Miss Titkins she went over to Aunt Jerushy Scran's and Aunt Polly Hokum's; and they hed a pot o' tea over it, and 'greed it was awful of Parson Morrel to set sich an example, and suthin' hed got to be done about it. Miss Hokum said she allers knew that Parson Morrel hedn't no spiritooality; and now it hed broke out into open sin, and led all the rest of 'em into it; and Miss Titkins, she said such a man wa'n't fit to preach; and Miss Hokum said she couldn't never hear him agin: and the next Sunday the deacon and his wife they hitched up and driv eight miles over to Parson Lothrop's and took Aunt Polly on the back seat.

"Wal, the thing growed and growed, till it seemed as if there wa'n't nothin' else talked about, 'cause Aunt Polly and Miss Titkins and Jerushy Scran they didn't do nothin' but talk about it; and that sot everybody else a-talkin'.

"Finally, it was 'greed they must hev a council to settle the hash. So all the wimmen they went to choppin' mince, and makin' up pumpkin pies and cranberry tarts, and b'ilin' doughnuts,—gettin' ready for the ministers and delegates; 'cause councils always eats powerful: and they hed quite a stir, like a gineral trainin'. The hosses they was hitched all up and down the stalls, a-stompin' and switchin' their tails; and all the wimmen was a-talkin'; and they hed up everybody round for witnesses. And finally Parson Morrel he says, 'Brethren,' says he, 'jest let me tell you the story jest as it happened; and, if you don't every one of you laugh as hard as I did, why, then, I'll give up.'

"The parson he was a master-hand at settin' off a story; and, afore he'd done, he got 'em all in sich a roar they didn't know where to leave off. Finally, they give sentence that there hedn't no temptation took him but such as is common to man; but they advised him afterwards allers to pray with his eyes shet; and the parson he confessed he orter 'a done it, and meant to do better in future: and so they settled it.

"So, boys," said Sam, who always drew a moral, "ye see, it larns you, you must take care what ye look at, ef ye want to keep from laughin' in meetin'."

Notes

1. "Make a joyful noise unto God, all ye lands." *Psalms*. LXVI, 1.

2. *II Samuel*. VI, 6–7.

3. An archangel appearing in both the Old and New Testaments.

4. "A time to weep, and a time to laugh; a time to mourn, and a time to dance." *Ecclesiastes*. III, 4.

5. *Revelation*. IV, 6.

6. Harvard University.

Juvenilia

GOVERNMENT

from *First Geography for Children*

In 1833, Corey & Fairbank of Cincinnati, Ohio, published *Primary Geography for Children*, Harriet Beecher Stowe's first book. This "poor little geography," as the young Miss Harriet referred to it, was credited to her and her sister, Catharine Beecher—"Principals of the Western Female Institute"—though Catharine did little more than edit and lend her then more illustrious name to the volume. To capitalize upon the immense popularity of *Uncle Tom's Cabin* in the early 1850s, Phillips, Sampson, and Company of Boston reissued the textbook in 1855 as the *First Geography for Children,* edited and revised by Catharine Beecher, from which this selection is taken.

There are many kinds of government in the world. I will tell you something about them. In those countries where the people are not educated they sometimes are divided into little tribes, and each one of these tribes is governed by a chief. There is often a council of old men in the tribe, who assist the chief by giving him advice. This is the kind of government that is common among the Indians in our country.

In some countries one man has all the power. If he wants the house, or the land, or any of the property of any person in the state, he can send and take it. There are no laws in these countries except those which this man chooses to make. He is commonly called a *king,* or an *emperor,* or a *czar,* or a *sultan.* This kind of government is called a *despotism.*

There is another kind of government, in which, although the king has much power, yet he governs according to laws and customs instead of doing as he pleases. This is called a *monarchy.*

There is another kind of government, which is partly carried on by the king and partly by the people. The people appoint the men who shall make their laws, and the king takes care that these laws are obeyed. The duties and rights of the people and king are all secured, sometimes by being written down, and sometimes they are understood without being written. This kind of government is called a *limited monarchy,* because the king's power is *limited* by the people. Sometimes it is called a *constitutional monarchy.*

The government of your own country is one in which all the power is in the hands of *the people.* The people appoint men to make laws for them, and other men to see that the laws are obeyed. This kind of government is called *republican,* or *democratic.* I will now give you some examples, that you may understand these kinds of government.

The United States of America have a republican government. The people of each state appoint one or two or more men who shall go to Congress and make laws for them. If these men do not make such laws as suit the people they can turn them out and appoint others. The people in the United States also choose a president; and it is the business of the president to see that these laws are kept. If they do not like their president they can choose another at the end of four years. On the opposite page is a picture of our Congress, which meets in Washington, the capital [not shown].

In Great Britain they have a constitutional monarchy. The people choose only a part of the men, who make their laws. The person who sees that the laws are kept is the king or queen of England. The people do not choose this ruler.

He must govern them as long as he lives; and when he dies his son or daughter becomes the sovereign, whether the people wish it or not.

But yet, in Great Britain, the king is obliged to govern his people by certain laws and rules, and the rights of the king and people are all agreed upon; so that this people have almost as much liberty as those in our country. In both of these countries no officer of government can take away the life or the property of any one in the land; but in Turkey, the sultan, if he wants money, can at any time send and kill some rich man and take his property.

In Great Britain and America no man can have his life taken away, or any punishment inflicted, until he has had a regular trial in a court of justice; but in Turkey, if a man is only suspected or accused of any thing wrong, the sultan can have him killed the first thing, without waiting to see whether it can be proved or not.

In some countries a man has a right to say any thing he chooses about the government, or the king, or president, or any of the officers; but in many countries, if a man should do this, he would be in danger of losing his life.

An American gentleman who was travelling in Italy said that he never dared to say one word about the government except sometimes when he was in a room with other American travellers. They would turn out all the servants and lock the doors, and then it would be safe for them to speak. Now, you know that in this country there is no place where a man cannot safely speak any thing he wishes.

It is just so about writing books and printing newspapers. People in this country can write any kind of a book that they please, and they can print any thing in a newspaper that they please. In some countries no man can write a book or print a paper without having it first looked over by the officers of government; and if there is any thing in it that the government does not like, he is obliged to leave it out.

You will hear the *freedom of the press* spoken of. This means the freedom to write or print any thing that a man pleases, without fear of the government.

Freedom of speech is the liberty of saying any thing a man pleases. I do not mean, however, that a man has a right to slander and abuse his neighbors. If a man writes any thing to injure the character of another man he can be tried for it in a court of justice, and, if it is proved, he can be punished. But this is a very different thing from being forbidden to publish any thing unless it is approved by the officers of government.

Liberty of conscience means that a man may be of any religion he thinks best. In some countries the people are all obliged to be, or to pretend to be, of one religion. If a man should profess to believe any other he would be in danger of losing his life. In other countries, though a man would not lose his life for not believing the established religion, yet he would not be allowed to hold any office under the government.

In our country a man may be a Catholic, or a Jew, or a Mahometan,[1] or of any other religion, just as he pleases. The countries where freedom of speech, and freedom of the press, and liberty of conscience are allowed generally have either constitutional monarchies or republican governments.

In those countries where the government is despotic these things are not allowed. If they were, the people would very soon find out their own rights, and endeavor to have more liberty.

I will now explain to you what noblemen are. In those countries where there are kings men have different titles. In Great Britain some are called dukes, some earls, and some barons. When people speak to these men they call them "your grace," or "my lord." If a man were asking any thing of a duke, he would say, "I would thank your grace to

(276)

do this or that for me." If a man were going to salute a nobleman, he would say, "How do you do, my lord?" instead of saying, "How do you do, sir?"

These noblemen have very large estates, many miles in extent. They divide these estates into parts; each part they hire out to some man. This man is called a tenant. So you would see on the estate of a nobleman a great number of small houses, in which the tenants live.

In many cases a nobleman has no power to sell his estate. It belongs to him only while he lives, and when he dies it belongs to his oldest son; so that the same estates remain in the same family for many hundreds of years. When a nobleman dies, his oldest son takes his title. If he had no children, then the brother or nearest relation takes it.

These noblemen form what are called the *court* of the king. They are generally considered very much superior to the common people. The noblemen are called the *aristocracy*. One great difference between the governments of America and those of Europe is, that in America they do not have any noblemen such as I have described to you. No man is distinguished or honored in this country unless he makes himself so by his own talents and industry. And do you not think it is a great deal better for men to be honored for what they do themselves than to be honored just because they had a title and estate left them by their parents?

I will now tell you what are the governments of all the countries in the world.

In North America, Russian America[2] is governed by the Czar of Russia, and British America by Great Britain.[3] The United States and the countries south of it are republics. The Indians are governed by chiefs.

In South America, Brazil is governed by an emperor, and the tribes of Patagonia[4] and a few of the native Indians in other parts of South America are governed by chiefs. All the other countries except these are republics. The West India islands, most of them, belong to England and Spain. St. Domingo is a despotism, with a black emperor.[5]

In Europe, Switzerland is the only country that is a republic. Russia, Austria, Turkey, and France are despotisms. The rest of the nations of Europe are limited monarchies—some like England, where the people have almost as much power as in the United States; and others where the king has most of the power, though he is so afraid of his people that he has to try to please them. Three countries have for several years been governed by queens—viz., England, Spain, and Portugal.

In Asia, Hindostan[6] belongs to Great Britain, and is governed by the queen's officers sent from that country. All the other countries are despotisms.

In Africa, there is one little republic of free Africans at Liberia. The colony of the Cape[7] and Sierra Leone belongs to Great Britain. All the other countries are despotisms.

In Oceanica, Australia is governed by Great Britain, and some of the other islands belong to European nations. All the rest are little despotisms, governed by savage kings or chiefs.

Questions.—What is the kind of government among the American Indians? What sort of government is a despotism? a monarchy? a limited or constitutional monarchy? a republican, or democratic? How is the government of our own country conducted? How are the people of Great Britain governed? What is said of Turkey, and how does their government differ from our country and Great Britain? What is said of some countries in regard to freedom of speech and freedom in printing books and papers? What is meant by freedom of the press? What is meant by freedom of speech? What is liberty of conscience? What is said about noblemen? What is the court of a king? What is the aristocracy of a nation? What great difference is there between the governments in Europe and those of our country? What are the governments in North America? South America? the West Indies? Europe? Asia? Africa? Oceanica?

Notes

1. A believer in Islam.

2. Alaska.

3. Canada.

4. The area in southern Argentina and Chile between the Andes and the Atlantic.

5. From 1849–1858 Faustin Elie Soulouque (1785–1867) ruled Haiti as Emperor Faustin.

6. India.

7. Republic of South Africa.

Nonfiction

THE EDMONDSONS

from *A Key to Uncle Tom's Cabin*

J.P. Jewett of Boston in 1853 published *A Key to Uncle Tom's Cabin: Presenting the Original Facts and Documents upon Which the Story Is Founded. Together with Corroborative Statements Verifying the Truth of the Work.* In its opening paragraph Harriet Beecher Stowe wrote:

> *At different times, doubt has been expressed whether the representations of "Uncle Tom's Cabin" are a fair representation of slavery as it at present exists. This work, more, perhaps, than any other work of fiction that ever was written, has been a collection and arrangement of real incidents, of actions really performed, of words and expressions really uttered,—grouped together with reference to a general result, in the same manner that the mosaic artist groups his fragments of various stones into one general picture. His is a mosaic of gems,—this is a mosaic of facts.*

From Part III of the work three selections are presented. "The Edmondsons" (Chapter VI) recounts the tribulations of one family, befriended by Stowe, her relatives, and friends, in purchasing its members from slavery. "The Case of Emily Russell" (Chapter VII) tells of a young girl's death en route to a slave auction in the south. "Kidnapping" (Chapter VIII) concerns three cases of capturing free slaves and selling them in the deep south, a lucrative practice for dishonest traders. The latter chapters are from *A Key to Uncle Tom's Cabin*, 1853.

Milly Edmondson is an aged woman, now upwards of seventy. She has received the slave's inheritance of entire ignorance. She cannot read a letter of a book, nor write her own name; but the writer must say that she was never so impressed with any presentation of the Christian religion as that which was made to her in the language and appearance of this woman during the few interviews that she had with her. The circumstances of the interviews will be detailed at length in the course of the story.

Milly is above the middle height, of a large, full figure. She dresses with the greatest attention to neatness. A plain Methodist cap shades her face, and the plain white Methodist handkerchief is folded across the bosom. A well-preserved stuff gown, and clean white apron, with a white pocket-handkerchief pinned to her side, completes the inventory of the costume in which the writer usually saw her. She is a mulatto, and must once have been a very handsome one. Her eyes and smile are still uncommonly beautiful, but there are deep-wrought lines of patient sorrow and weary endurance on her face, which tell that this lovely and noble-hearted woman has been all her life a slave.

Milly Edmondson was kept by her owners and allowed to live with her husband, with the express understanding and agreement that her service and value was to consist in breeding up her own children to be sold in the slave-market. Her legal owner was a maiden lady of feeble capacity, who was set aside by the decision of court as incompetent to manage her affairs.

The estate—that is to say, Milly Edmondson and her children—was placed in the care of a guardian. It appears that Milly's poor, infirm mistress was fond of her, and that Milly exercised over her much of that ascendancy which a strong mind holds over a weak one. Milly's husband, Paul Edmondson, was a free man. A little of her history, as she related it to the writer, will now be given in her own words:

"Her mistress," she said, "was always kind to her, 'poor thing!' but then she hadn't *sperit* ever to speak for herself, and her friends wouldn't let her have her own way. It always laid on my mind," she said, "that I was a slave. When

I wa'n't more than fourteen years old, Missis was doing some work one day that she thought she couldn't trust me with, and she says to me, 'Milly, now you see it's I that am the slave, and not you.' I says to her, 'Ah, Missis, I am a poor slave, for all that.' I's sorry afterwards I said it, for I thought it seemed to hurt her feelings.

"Well, after a while, when I got engaged to Paul, I loved Paul very much; but I thought it wa'n't right to bring children into the world to be slaves, and I told our folks that I was never going to marry, though I did love Paul. But that wa'n't to be allowed," she said, with a mysterious air.

"What do you mean?" said I.

"Well, they told me I must marry, or I should be turned out of the church—so it was," she added, with a significant nod. "Well, Paul and me, we was married, and we was happy enough, if it hadn't been for that; but when our first child was born I says to him, 'There 't is, now, Paul, our troubles is begun; this child is n't ours.' And every child I had, it grew worse and worse. 'Oh, Paul,' says I, 'what a thing it is to have children that is n't ours!' Paul he says to me, 'Milly, my dear, if they be God's children, it ain't so much matter whether they be ours or no; they may be heirs of the kingdom, Milly, for all that.' Well, when Paul's mistress died, she set him free, and he got him a little placc out about fourteen miles from Washington; and they let me live out there with him, and take home my tasks; for they had that confidence in me that they always know'd that what I said I'd do was as good done as if they'd seen it done. I had mostly sewing; sometimes a shirt to make in a day,—it was coarse like, you know,—or a pair of sheets, or some such; but, whatever 't was, I always got it done. Then I had all my housework and babies to take care of; and many's the time, after ten o'clock, I've took my children's clothes and washed 'em all out and ironed 'em late in the night, 'cause I couldn't never bear to see my children dirty,—always wanted to see 'em sweet and clean, and I brought 'em up and taught 'em the very best ways I was able. But nobody knows what I suffered; I never see a white man come on to the place that I didn't think, 'There, now, he's coming to look at my children;' and when I saw any white man going by, I've called in my children and hid 'em, for fear he'd see 'em and want to buy 'em. Oh, ma'am, mine's been a long sorrow, a long sorrow! I've borne this heavy cross a great many years."

"But," said I, "the Lord has been with you."

She answered, with very strong emphasis, "Ma'am, if the Lord hadn't held me up, I shouldn't have been alive this day. Oh, sometimes my heart's been so heavy, it seemed as if I *must* die; and then I've been to the throne of grace, and when I'd poured out all my sorrows there, I came away *light*, and felt that I could live a little longer."

This language is exactly her own. She had often a forcible and peculiarly beautiful manner of expressing herself, which impressed what she said strongly.

Paul and Milly Edmondson were both devout communicants in the Methodist Episcopal Church at Washington, and the testimony to their blamelessness of life and the consistence of their piety is unanimous from all who know them. In their simple cottage, made respectable by neatness and order, and hallowed by morning and evening prayer, they trained up their children, to the best of their poor ability, in the nurture and admonition of the Lord, to be sold in the slave-market. They thought themselves only too happy, as one after another arrived at the age when they were to be sold, that they were hired to families in their vicinity, and not thrown into the trader's pen to be drafted for the dreaded Southern market!

The mother, feeling, with a constant but repressed anguish, the weary burden of slavery which lay upon her, was accustomed, as she told the writer, thus to warn her daughters:—

"Now, girls, don't you never come to the sorrows that I have. Don't you never marry till you get your liberty. Don't you marry, to be mothers to *children that ain't your own*."

(286)

As a result of this education, some of her older daughters, in connection with the young men to whom they were engaged, raised the sum necessary to pay for their freedom before they were married. One of these young women, at the time that she paid for her freedom, was in such feeble health that the physician told her that she could not live many months, and advised her to keep the money, and apply it to making herself as comfortable as she could.

She answered, "If I had only two hours to live, I would pay down that money to die free."

If this was setting an extravagant value on liberty, it is not for an American to say so.

All the sons and daughters of this family were distinguished both for their physical and mental development, and therefore were priced exceedingly high in the market. The whole family, rated by the market prices which have been paid for certain members of it, might be estimated as an estate of fifteen thousand dollars. They were distinguished for intelligence, honesty, and faithfulness, but above all for the most devoted attachment to each other. These children, thus intelligent, were all held as slaves in the city of Washington, the very capital where our national government is conducted. Of course, the high estimate which their own mother taught them to place upon liberty was in the way of being constantly strengthened and reinforced by such addresses, celebrations, and speeches, on the subject of liberty, as every one knows are constantly being made, on one occasion or another, in our national capital.

On the 13th of April, the little schooner Pearl, commanded by Daniel Drayton, came to anchor in the Potomac River, at Washington.

The news had just arrived of a revolution in France,[1] and the establishment of a democratic government, and all Washington was turning out to celebrate the triumph of Liberty.

The trees in the avenue were fancifully hung with many-colored lanterns,—drums beat, bands of music played, the houses of the President and other high officials were illuminated, and men, women, and children were all turned out to see the procession, and to join in the shouts of liberty that rent the air. Of course, all the slaves of the city, lively, fanciful, and sympathetic, most excitable as they are by music and by dazzling spectacles, were everywhere listening, seeing, and rejoicing, in ignorant joy. All the heads of departments, senators, representatives, and dignitaries of all kinds, marched in procession to an open space on Pennsylvania Avenue, and there delivered congratulatory addresses on the progress of universal freedom. With unheard-of imprudence, the most earnest defenders of slaveholding institutions poured down on the listening crowd, both of black and white, bond and free, the most inflammatory and incendiary sentiments. Such, for example, as the following language of Hon. Frederick P. Stanton, of Tennessee:—

"We do not, indeed, propagate our principles with the sword of power; but there is one sense in which we are propagandists. We cannot help being so. Our example is contagious. In the section of this great country where I live, on the banks of the mighty Mississippi River, we have the true emblem of the tree of liberty. There you may see the giant cottonwood spreading his branches widely to the winds of heaven. Sometimes the current lays bare his roots, and you behold them extending far around, and penetrating to an immense depth in the soil. When the season of maturity comes, the air is filled with a cotton-like substance, which floats in every direction, bearing on its light wings the living seeds of the mighty tree. Thus the seeds of freedom have emanated from the tree of our liberties. They fill the air. They are wafted to every part of the habitable globe. And even in the barren sands of tyranny they are destined to take root. The tree of liberty will spring up everywhere, and nations shall recline in its shade."

(288)

Senator Foote, of Mississippi, also used this language:

"Such has been the extraordinary course of events in France, and in Europe, within the last two months, that the more deliberately we survey the scene which has been spread out before us, and the more rigidly we scrutinize the conduct of its actors, the more confident does our conviction become that the *glorious work* which has been so well begun cannot possibly fail of complete accomplishment; that the age of TYRANTS AND SLAVERY is rapidly drawing to a close; and that the happy period to be signalized by the *universal emancipation of man* from the *fetters of civil oppression,* and the recognition *in all countries* of the great principles of *popular sovereignty, equality, and* BROTHERHOOD, is, at this moment, visibly commencing."

Will any one be surprised, after this, that seventy-seven of the most intelligent young slaves, male and female, in Washington city, honestly taking Mr. Foote and his brother senators at their word, and believing that the age of tyrants and slavery was drawing to a close, banded together, and made an effort to obtain their part in this reign of universal brotherhood?

The schooner Pearl was lying in the harbor, and Captain Drayton was found to have the heart of a man. Perhaps he, too, had listened to the addresses on Pennsylvania Avenue,[2] and thought, in the innocence of his heart, that a man who really *did* something to promote universal emancipation was no worse than the men who only made speeches about it.

At any rate, Drayton was persuaded to allow these seventy-seven slaves to secrete themselves in the hold of his vessel, and among them were six children of Paul and Milly Edmondson. The incidents of the rest of the narrative will now be given as obtained from Mary and Emily Edmondson, by the lady in whose family they have been placed by the writer for an education.

(289)

Some few preliminaries may be necessary, in order to understand the account.

A respectable colored man, by the name of Daniel Bell, who had purchased his own freedom, resided in the city of Washington. His wife, with her eight children, were set free by her master, when on his death-bed. The heirs endeavored to break the will, on the ground that he was not of sound mind at the time of its preparation. The magistrate, however, before whom it was executed, by his own personal knowledge of the competence of the man at the time, was enabled to defeat their purpose; the family, therefore, lived as free for some years. On the death of this magistrate, the heirs again brought the case into court, and, as it seemed likely to be decided against the family, they resolved to secure their legal rights by flight, and engaged passage on board the vessel of Captain Drayton. Many of their associates and friends, stirred up, perhaps, by the recent demonstrations in favor of liberty, begged leave to accompany them in their flight. The seeds of the cottonwood were flying everywhere, and springing up in all hearts; so that, on the eventful evening of the 15th of April, 1848, not less than seventy-seven men, women, and children, with beating hearts, and anxious secrecy, stowed themselves away in the hold of the little schooner, and Captain Drayton was so wicked that he could not, for the life of him, say "Nay" to one of them.

Richard Edmondson had long sought to buy his liberty; had toiled for it early and late: but the price set upon him was so high that he despaired of ever earning it. On this evening, he and his three brothers thought, as the reign of universal brotherhood had begun, and the reign of tyrants and slavery come to an end, that they would take to themselves and their sisters that sacred gift of liberty, which all Washington had been informed, two evenings before, it was the peculiar province of America to give to all nations. Their two sisters, aged sixteen and fourteen, were hired out in families in the city. On this evening Samuel Edmondson called at the house where Emily lived, and told her of the projected plan.

"But what will mother think?" said Emily.

"Don't stop to think of her; she would rather we'd be free than to spend time to talk about her."

"Well, then, if Mary will go, I will."

The girls give as a reason for wishing to escape, that though they had never suffered hardships or been treated unkindly, yet they knew they were liable at any time to be sold into rigorous bondage, and separated far from all they loved.

They then all went on board the Pearl, which was lying a little way off from the place where vessels usually anchor. There they found a company of slaves, seventy-seven in number.

At twelve o'clock at night the silent wings of the little schooner were spread, and with her weight of fear and mystery she glided out into the stream. A fresh breeze sprang up, and by eleven o'clock next night they had sailed two hundred miles from Washington, and began to think that liberty was gained. They anchored in a place called Cornfield Harbor, intending to wait for daylight. All laid down to sleep in peaceful security, lulled by the gentle rock of the vessel and the rippling of the waters.

But at two o'clock at night they were roused by terrible noises on deck, scuffling, screaming, swearing, and groaning. A steamer had pursued and overtaken them, and the little schooner was boarded by an infuriated set of armed men. In a moment, the captain, mate, and all the crew were seized and bound, amid oaths and dreadful threats. As they, swearing and yelling, tore open the hatches on the defenseless prisoners below, Richard Edmondson stepped forward, and in a calm voice said to them, "Gentlemen, do yourselves no harm, for we are all here." With this exception, all was still among the slaves as despair could make it; not a word was spoken in the whole company. The men were all bound and placed on board the steamer; the women were left on board the schooner, to be towed after.

The explanation of their capture was this: In the morning after they had sailed, many families in Washington found their slaves missing, and the event created as great an excitement as the emancipation of France had, two days before. At that time they had listened in the most complacent manner to the announcement that the reign of slavery was near its close, because they had not the slightest idea that the language meant anything; and they were utterly confounded by this practical application of it. More than a hundred men, mounted upon horses, determined to push out into the country, in pursuit of these new disciples of the doctrine of universal emancipation. Here a colored man, by the name of Judson Diggs, betrayed the whole plot. He had been provoked, because, after having taken a poor woman, with her luggage, down to the boat, she was unable to pay the twenty-five cents that he demanded. So he told these admirers of universal brotherhood that they need not ride into the country, as their slaves had sailed down the river, and were far enough off by this time. A steamer was immediately manned by two hundred armed men, and away they went in pursuit.

When the cortége arrived with the captured slaves, there was a most furious excitement in the city. The men were driven through the streets bound with ropes, two and two. Showers of taunts and jeers rained upon them from all sides. One man asked one of the girls if she "didn't feel pretty to be caught running away," and another asked her, "if she wasn't sorry." She answered, "No, if it was to do again tomorrow, she would do the same." The man turned to a bystander and said, "Hain't she got good spunk?"

But the most vehement excitement was against Drayton and Sayres, the captain and mate of the vessel. Ruffians armed with dirk-knives and pistols crowded around them, with the most horrid threats. One of them struck so near Drayton as to cut his ear, which Emily noticed as bleeding. Meanwhile there mingled in the crowd multitudes of the relatives of the captives, who, looking on them as so many doomed victims, bewailed and lamented them. A brother-in-law of the Edmondsons was so overcome when he saw them that he fainted away and fell down in the street, and was carried home insensible. The sorrowful news spread to the cottage of Paul and Milly Edmondson; and, knowing that all their children were now probably doomed to the Southern market, they gave themselves up to sorrow. "Oh! what a day that was!" said the old mother when describing that scene to the writer. "Never a morsel of anything could I put into my mouth. Paul and me, we fasted and prayed before the Lord, night and day, for our poor children."

The whole public sentiment of the community was roused to the most intense indignation. It was repeated from mouth to mouth that they had been kindly treated and never abused; and what could have induced them to try to get their liberty? All that Mr. Stanton had said of the insensible influence of American institutions, and all his pretty similes about the cottonwood seeds, seemed entirely to have escaped the memory of the community, and they could see nothing but the most unheard-of depravity in the attempt of these people to secure freedom. It was strenuously advised by many that their owners should not forgive them,—that no mercy should be shown, but that they should be thrown into the hands of the traders, forthwith, for the Southern market,—that Siberia of the irresponsible despots of America.

When all the prisoners were lodged in jail, the owners came to make oath to their property, and the property also was required to make oath to their owners. Among them came the married sisters of Mary and Emily, but were not allowed to enter the prison. The girls looked through the iron grates of the third-story windows, and saw their sisters standing below in the yard weeping.

The guardian of the Edmondsons, who acted in the place of the real owner, apparently touched with their sorrow, promised their family and friends, who were anxious to purchase them, if possible, that they should have an opportunity the next morning. Perhaps he intended at the time to give them one; but as Bruin and Hill, the keepers of the large slave warehouse in Alexandria,[3] offered him four thousand five hundred dollars for the six children, they were irrevocably sold before the next morning. Bruin would listen to no terms which any of their friends could propose. The lady with whom Mary had lived offered a thousand dollars for her; but Bruin refused, saying he could get double that sum in the New Orleans market. He said he had had his eye upon the family for twelve years, and had the promise of them should they ever be sold.

While the girls remained in the prison they had no beds or chairs, and only one blanket each, though the nights were chilly; but, understanding that the rooms below, where their brothers were confined, were still colder, and that no blankets were given them, they sent their own down to them. In the morning they were allowed to go down into the yard for a few moments; and then they used to run to the window of their brothers' room, to bid them good-morning, and kiss them through the grate.

At ten o'clock, Thursday night, the brothers were handcuffed, and, with their sisters, taken into carriages by their new owners, driven to Alexandria, and put into a prison called a Georgia Pen. The girls were put into a large room alone, in total darkness, without bed or blanket, where they spent the night in sobs and tears, in utter ignorance of their brothers' fate. At eight o'clock in the morning they were called to breakfast, when, to their great comfort, they found their four brothers all in the same prison.

They remained here about four weeks, being usually permitted by day to stay below with their brothers, and at night to return to their own rooms. Their brothers had great anxieties about them, fearing they would be sold South. Samuel, in particular, felt very sadly, as he had been the principal actor in getting them away. He often said he would gladly *die* for them, if that would save them from the fate he feared. He used to weep a great deal, though he endeavored to restrain his tears in their presence.

While in the slave-prison they were required to wash for thirteen men, though their brothers performed a great share of the labor. Before they left, their size and height were measured by their owners. At length they were again taken out, the brothers handcuffed, and all put on board a steamboat, where were about forty slaves, mostly men, and taken to Baltimore. The voyage occupied one day and a night. When arrived in Baltimore, they were thrown into a slave-pen kept by a partner of Bruin and Hill. He was a man of coarse habits, constantly using the most profane language, and grossly obscene and insulting in his remarks to women. Here they were forbidden to pray together, as they had previously been accustomed to do; but by rising very early in the morning, they secured to themselves a little interval which they could employ, uninterrupted, in this manner. They, with four or five other women in the prison, used to meet together, before daybreak, to spread their sorrows before the Refuge of the afflicted; and in these prayers the hard-hearted slave-dealer was daily remembered. The brothers of Mary and Emily were very gentle and tender in their treatment of their sisters, which had an influence upon other men in their company.

At this place they became acquainted with Aunt Rachel, a most godly woman, about middle age, who had been sold into the prison away from her husband. The poor husband used often to come to the prison and beg the trader to sell her to *his* owners, who he thought were willing to purchase her, if the price was not too high. But he was driven off with brutal threats and curses. They remained in Baltimore about three weeks.

The friends in Washington, though hitherto unsuccessful in their efforts to redeem the family, were still exerting themselves in their behalf; and one evening a message was received from them by telegraph, stating that a person would arrive in the morning train of cars, prepared to bargain for the family, and that a part of the money was now ready. But the trader was inexorable, and in the morning, an hour before the cars were to arrive, they were all put on board the brig Union, ready to sail for New Orleans. The messenger came, and brought nine hundred dollars in money, the gift of a grandson of John Jacob Astor.[4] This was finally appropriated to the ransom of Richard Edmondson, as his wife and children were said to be suffering in Washington; and the trader would not sell the girls to them upon any consideration, nor would he even suffer Richard to be brought back from the brig, which had not yet sailed. The bargain was, however, made, and the money deposited in Baltimore.

On this brig the eleven women were put in one small apartment, and the thirty or forty men in an adjoining one. Emily was very seasick most of the time, and her brothers feared she would die. They used to come and carry her out on deck and back again, buy little comforts for their sisters, and take all possible care of them.

Frequently head winds blew them back so that they made very slow progress; and in their prayer-meetings, which they held every night, they used to pray that head winds might blow them to New York; and one of the sailors declared that if they could get within one hundred miles of

New York, and the slaves would stand by him, he would make way with the captain, and pilot them into New York himself.

When they arrived near Key West,[5] they hoisted a signal for a pilot, the captain being aware of the dangers of the place, and yet not knowing how to avoid them. As the pilot-boat approached, the slaves were all fastened below, and a heavy canvas thrown over the grated hatchway door, which entirely excluded all circulation of air, and almost produced suffocation. The captain and pilot had a long talk about the price, and some altercation ensued, the captain not being willing to give the price demanded by the pilot; during which time there was great suffering below. The women became so exhausted that they were mostly helpless; and the situation of the men was not much better, though they managed with a stick to break some holes through the canvas on their side, so as to let in a little air, but a few only of the strongest could get there to enjoy it. Some of them shouted for help as long as their strength would permit; and at length, after what seemed to them an almost interminable interview, the pilot left, refusing to assist them; the canvas was removed, and the brig obliged to turn tack, and take another course. Then, one after another, as they got air and strength, crawled out on deck. Mary and Emily were carried out by their brothers as soon as they were able to do it.

Soon after this the stock of provisions ran low, and the water failed, so that the slaves were restricted to a gill a day. The sailors were allowed a quart each, and often gave a pint of it to one of the Edmondsons for their sisters; and they divided it with the other women, as they always did every nice thing they got in such ways.

The day they arrived at the mouth of the Mississippi a terrible storm arose, and the waves rolled mountain high, so that, when the pilot-boat approached, it would some-

(297)

times seem to be entirely swallowed by the waves, and again it would emerge, and again appear wholly buried. At length they were towed into and up the river by a steamer, and there for the first time saw cotton plantations, and gangs of slaves at work on them.

They arrived at New Orleans in the night, and about ten the next day were landed and marched to what they called the show-rooms, and, going out into the yard, saw a great many men and women sitting around, with such sad faces that Emily soon began to cry, upon which an overseer stepped up and struck her on the chin, and bade her "stop crying, or he would give her something to cry about." Then pointing, he told her "there was the calaboose, where they whipped those who did not behave themselves!" As soon as he turned away, a slave-woman came and told her to look cheerful, if she possibly could, as it would be far better for her. One of her brothers soon came to inquire what the woman had been saying to her; and when informed, encouraged Emily to follow the advice, and endeavored to profit by it himself.

That night all four brothers had their hair cut close, their mustaches shaved off, and their usual clothing exchanged for a blue jacket and pants, all of which so altered their appearance that at first their sisters did not know them. Then, for three successive days, they were all obliged to stand in an open porch fronting the street, for passers-by to look at, except, when one was tired out, she might go in for a little time, and another take her place. Whenever buyers called, they were paraded in the auction-room in rows, exposed to coarse jokes and taunts. When any one took a liking to any girl in the company, he would call her to him, take hold of her, open her mouth, look at her teeth, and handle her person rudely, frequently making obscene remarks; and she must stand and bear it, without resistance. Mary and Emily complained to their brothers that they could not submit to such treatment. They conversed about it with Wilson, a partner of Bruin and Hill, who had the charge of the slaves at this prison. After this they were treated with more decency.

Another brother of the girls, named Hamilton, had been a slave in or near New Orleans for sixteen years, and had just purchased his own freedom for one thousand dollars; having once before earned that sum for himself, and then had it taken from him. Richard being now really free, as the money was deposited in Baltimore for his ransom, found him out the next day after their arrival at New Orleans, and brought him to the prison to see his brothers and sisters. The meeting was overpoweringly affecting.

He had never before seen his sister Emily, as he had been sold away from his parents before her birth.

The girls' lodging-room was occupied at night by about twenty or thirty women, who all slept on the bare floor, with only a blanket each. After a few days, word was received (which was *really incorrect*) that half the money had been raised for the redemption of Mary and Emily. After this they were allowed, upon their brother's earnest re-quest, to go to their free brother's house and spend their nights, and return in the mornings, as they had suffered greatly from the mosquitoes and other insects, and their feet were swollen and sore.

While at this prison, some horrible cases of cruelty came to their knowledge, and some of them under their own observation. Two persons, one woman and one boy, were whipped to death in the prison while they were there, though they were not in the same pen, or owned by the same trader, as themselves.

None of the slaves were allowed to sleep in the day-time, and sometimes little children sitting or standing idle all day would become so sleepy as not to be able to hold up their eyelids; but if they were caught thus by the overseer, they were cruelly beaten. Mary and Emily used to watch the little ones, and let them sleep until they heard the overseers coming, and then spring and rouse them in a moment.

One young woman, who had been sold by the traders for the worst of purposes, was returned, not being fortunate (?) enough to suit her purchaser; and, as is their custom in such cases, was most cruelly flogged,—so much so that some of her flesh mortified, and her life was despaired of. When Mary and Emily first arrived at New Orleans they saw and conversed with her. She was then just beginning to sit up; was quite small, and very fine-looking, with beautiful straight hair, which was formerly long, but had been cut off short by her brutal tormentors.

The overseer who flogged her said, in their hearing, that he would never flog another girl in that way—it was too much for any one to bear. They suggest that perhaps the reason why he promised this was because he was obliged to be her nurse, and of course saw her sufferings. She was from Alexandria, but they have forgotten her name.

One young man and woman of their company in the prison, who were engaged to be married, and were sold to different owners, felt so distressed at their separation that they could not do or did not labor well; and the young man was soon sent back, with the complaint that he would not answer the purpose. Of course, the money was to be refunded, and he flogged. He was condemned to be flogged each night for a week; and, after about two hundred lashes by the overseer, each one of the male slaves in the prison was required to come and lay on five lashes with all his strength, upon penalty of being flogged himself. The young woman, too, was soon sent there, with a note from her new mistress, requesting that she might be whipped a certain number of lashes, and enclosing the money to pay for it; which request was readily complied with.

While in New Orleans they saw gangs of women cleaning the streets, chained together, some with a heavy iron ball attached to the chain; a form of punishment frequently resorted to for household servants who had displeased their mistresses.

Hamilton Edmondson, the brother who had purchased his own freedom, made great efforts to get good homes for his brothers and sisters in New Orleans, so that they need not be far separated from each other. One day Mr. Wilson, the overseer, took Samuel away with him in a carriage, and returned without him. The brothers and sisters soon found that he was sold, and gone they knew not whither; but they were not allowed to weep, or even look sad, upon pain of severe punishment. The next day, however, to their great joy, he came to the prison himself, and told them he had a good home in the city with an Englishman, who had paid a thousand dollars for him.

After remaining about three weeks in this prison, the Edmondsons were told that in consquence of the prevalence of the yellow fever in the city, together with the fact of their not being acclimated, it was deemed dangerous for them to remain there longer; and besides this, purchasers were loth to give good prices under these circumstances. Some of the slaves in the pen were already sick; some of them old, poor, or dirty, and for these reasons greatly exposed to sickness. Richard Edmondson had already been ransomed, and must be sent back; and, upon the whole, it was thought best to fit out and send off a gang to Baltimore, without delay.

The Edmondsons received these tidings with joyful hearts, for they had not yet been undeceived with regard to the raising of the money for their ransom. Their brother who was free procured for them many comforts for the voyage, such as a mattress, blankets, sheets, and different kinds of food and drink; and, accompanied to the vessel by their friends there, they embarked on the brig Union just at night, and were towed out of the river. The brig had nearly a full cargo of cotton, molasses, sugar, etc.; and of course the space for the slaves was exceedingly limited. The space allotted the females was a little, close, filthy room, perhaps eight or ten feet square, filled with cotton within two or three feet of the top of the room, except the space directly under the hatchway door. Richard Edmondson kept his sisters upon deck with him, though without a shelter; prepared their food himself, made up their bed at night on the top of barrels, or wherever he could find a place, and then slept by their side. Sometimes a storm would arise in the middle of the night, when he would spring up and wake them, and, gathering up their bed and bedding, conduct them to a kind of a little pantry, where they could all three just stand, till the storm passed away. Sometimes he contrived to make a temporary shelter for them out of bits of boards, or something else on deck.

After a voyage of sixteen days, they arrived at Baltimore, fully expecting that their days of slavery were numbered. Here they were conducted back to the same old prison from which they had been taken a few weeks before, though they supposed it would be but for an hour or two. Presently Mr. Bigelow, of Washington, came for Richard. When the girls found that they were not to be set free too, their grief and disappointment were unspeakable. But they were *separated,*—Richard to go to his home, his wife, and children, and they to remain in the slave-prison. Wearisome days and nights again rolled on. In the mornings they were obliged to march round the yard to the music of fiddles, banjos, etc.; in the daytime they washed and ironed for the male slaves, slept some, and wept a great deal. After a few weeks their father came to visit them, accompanied by their sister.

His object was partly to ascertain what were the very lowest terms upon which their keeper would sell the girls, as he indulged a faint hope that in some way or other the money might be raised, if time enough were allowed. The trader declared he should soon send them to some other slave-market, but he would wait two weeks, and, if the friends could raise the money in that time, they might have them.

The night their father and sister spent in the prison with them, he lay in the room over their heads; and they could hear him groan all night, while their sister was weeping by their side. None of them closed their eyes in sleep.

In the morning came again the wearisome routine of the slave-prison. Old Paul walked quietly into the yard, and sat down to see the poor slaves marched around. He had never seen his daughters in such circumstances before, and his feelings quite overcame him. The yard was narrow, and the girls, as they walked by him, almost brushing him with their clothes, could just hear him groaning within himself, "Oh, my children, my children!"

After the breakfast, which none of them were able to eat, they parted with sad hearts, the father begging the keeper to send them to New Orleans, if the money could not be raised, as perhaps their brothers there might secure for them kind masters.

Two or three weeks afterwards Bruin and Hill visited the prison, dissolved partnership with the trader, settled accounts, and took the Edmondsons again in their own possession.

The girls were roused about eleven o'clock at night, after they had fallen asleep, and told to get up directly, and prepare for going home. They had learned that the word of a slave-holder is not to be trusted, and feared they were going to be sent to Richmond, Virginia, as there had been talk of it. They were soon on their way in the cars with Bruin, and arrived at Washington at a little past midnight.

Their hearts throbbed high when, after these long months of weary captivity, they found themselves once more in the city where were their brothers, sisters, and parents. But they were permitted to see none of them, and were put into a carriage and driven immediately to the slave-prison at Alexandria, where, about two o'clock at night, they found themselves in the same forlorn old room in which they had begun their term of captivity.

This was the latter part of August. Again they were employed in washing, ironing, and sewing by day, and always locked up by night. Sometimes they were allowed to sew in Bruin's house, and even to eat there. After they had been in Alexandria two or three weeks, their eldest married sister, not having heard from them for some time, came to see Bruin, to learn, if possible, something of their fate; and her surprise and joy were great to see them once more, even there. After a few weeks their old father came again to see them. Hopeless as the idea of their emancipation seemed, he still clung to it. He had had some encouragement of assistance in Washington, and he purposed to go North to see if anything could be done there; and he was anxious to obtain from Bruin what were the very lowest possible terms for which he would sell the girls. Bruin drew up his terms in the following document, which we subjoin:—

ALEXANDRIA, VA., Sept. 5, 1848.

The bearer, Paul Edmondson, is the father of two girls, Mary Jane and Emily Catharine Edmondson. These girls have been purchased by us, and once sent to the South; and, upon the positive assurance that the money for them would be raised if they were brought back, they were returned. Nothing, it appears, has as yet been done in this respect by those who promised, and we are on the very eve of sending them South the second time; and we are candid in saying that, if they go again, we will not regard any promises made in relation to them. The father wishes to raise money to pay for them, and intends to appeal to the liberality of the humane and the good to aid him, and has requested us to state in writing *the conditions upon which we will sell his daughters.*

We expect to start our servants to the South in a few days; if the sum of twelve hundred ($1200) dollars be raised and paid to us in fifteen days, or we be assured of that sum, then we will retain them for twenty-five days more, to give an opportunity for the raising of the other thousand and fifty ($1050) dollars; otherwise we shall be compelled to send them along with our other servants.

BRUIN & HILL.

Paul took his papers, and parted from his daughters sorrowfully. After this, the time to the girls dragged on in heavy suspense. Constantly they looked for letter, or message, and prayed to God to raise them up a deliverer from some quarter. But day after day and week after week passed, and the dreaded time drew near. The preliminaries for fitting up the gang for South Carolina commenced. Gay calico was bought for them to make up into "show dresses," in which they were to be exhibited on sale. They made them up with far sadder feelings than they would have sewed on their own shrouds. Hope had almost died out of their bosoms. A few days before the gang were to be sent off, their sister made them a sad farewell visit. They mingled their prayers and tears, and the girls made up little tokens of remembrance to send by her as parting gift to their brothers, and sisters, and aged father and mother, and with a farewell sadder than that of a death-bed the sisters parted.

The evening before the coffle was to start drew on. Mary and Emily went to the house to bid Bruin's family good-by. Bruin had a little daughter who had been a pet and favorite with the girls. She clung round them, cried, and begged them not to go. Emily told her that, if she wished to have them stay, she must go and ask her father. Away ran the little pleader, full of her errand; and was so very earnest in her importunities, that he, to pacify her, said he would consent to their remaining, if his partner, Captain Hill, would do so. At this time Bruin, hearing Mary crying aloud in the prison, went up to see her. With all the

(305)

earnestness of despair, she made her last appeal to his feelings. She begged him to make the case his own, to think of his own dear little daughter,—what if she were exposed to be torn away from every friend on earth, and cut off from all hope of redemption, at the very moment, too, when deliverance was expected! Bruin was not absolutely a man of stone, and this agonizing appeal brought tears to his eyes. He gave some encouragement that, if Hill would consent, they need not be sent off with the gang. A sleepless night followed, spent in weeping, groaning, and prayer. Morning at last dawned, and, according to orders received the day before, they prepared themselves to go, and even put on their bonnets and shawls, and stood ready for the word to be given. When the very last tear of hope was shed, and they were going out to join the gang, Bruin's heart relented. He called them to him, and told them they might remain! Oh, how glad were their hearts made by this, as they might *now* hope on a little longer! Either the entreaties of little Martha or Mary's plea with Bruin had prevailed.

Soon the gang was started on foot,—men, women, and children, two and two, the men all handcuffed together, the right wrist of one to the left wrist of the other, and a chain passing through the middle from the handcuffs of one couple to those of the next. The women and children walked in the same manner throughout, handcuffed or chained. Drivers went before and at the side, to take up those who were sick or lame. They were obliged to set off *singing!* accompanied with fiddles and banjos!—*"For they that carried us away captive required of us a song, and they that wasted us required of us mirth."*[6] And this is a scene of daily occurrence in a Christian country!—and Christian ministers say that the right to do these things is *given by God himself!!*

Meanwhile poor old Paul Edmondson went northward to supplicate aid. Any one who should have traveled in the cars at the time might have seen a venerable-looking black man, all whose air and attitude indicated a patient humility, and who seemed to carry a weight of overwhelming sorrow, like one who had long been acquainted with grief. That man was Paul Edmondson.

Alone, friendless, unknown, and, worst of all, black, he came into the great bustling city of New York, to see if they was any one there who could give him twenty-five hundred dollars to buy his daughters with. Can anybody realize what a poor man's feelings are, who visits a great, bustling, rich city, alone, and unknown, for such an object? The writer has now, in a letter from a slave father and husband who was visiting Portland[7] on a similar errand, a touching expression of it:—

"I walked all day, till I was tired and discouraged. Oh! Mrs. S——, when I see so many people who seem to have so many more things than they want or know what to do with, and then think that I have worked hard, till I am past forty, all my life, and don't own even my own wife and children, it makes me feel sick and discouraged!"

So, sick at heart and discouraged, felt Paul Edmondson. He went to the Anti-Slavery Office, and made his case known. The sum was such a large one, and seemed to many so exorbitant, that, though they pitied the poor father, they were disheartened about raising it. They wrote to Washington to authenticate the particulars of the story, and wrote to Bruin and Hill to see if there could be any reduction of price. Meanwhile, the poor old man looked sadly from one adviser to another. He was recommended to go to the Rev. H. W. Beecher,[8] and tell his story. He inquired his way to his door,—ascended the steps to ring the door-bell, but his heart failed him,—he sat down on the steps weeping!

There Mr. Beecher found him. He took him in, and inquired his story. There was to be a public meeting that night to raise money. The hapless father begged him to go and plead for his children. He did go, and spoke as if he were pleading for his own father and sisters. Other clergy-men followed in the same strain,—the meeting became enthusiastic, and money was raised on the spot, and poor old Paul laid his head that night on a grateful pillow,—not to sleep, but to give thanks!

Meanwhile the girls had been dragging on anxious days in the slave-prison. They were employed in sewing for Bruin's family, staying sometimes in the prison and some-times in the house.

It is to be stated here that Mr. Bruin is a man of very different character from many in his trade. He is such a man as never would have been found in the profession of a slave-trader, had not the most respectable and religious part of the community defended the right to buy and sell, as being conferred by God himself. It is a fact, with regard to this man, that he was one of the earliest subscribers to the "National Era,"9 in the District of Columbia; and when a certain individual there brought himself into great peril by assisting fugitive slaves, and there was no one found to go bail for him, Mr. Bruin came forward and performed this kindness.

While we abhor the horrible system and the horrible trade with our whole soul, there is no harm, we suppose, in wishing that such a man had a better occupation. Yet we cannot forbear reminding all such that, when we come to give our account at the judgment-seat of Christ, every man must speak *for himself alone;* and that Christ will not accept as an apology for sin the word of all the ministers and all the synods in the country. He has given fair warning, "Be-ware of false prophets;"10 and if people will not beware of them, their blood is upon their own heads.

The girls, while under Mr. Bruin's care, were treated with as much kindness and consideration as could possibly consist with the design of selling them. There is no doubt that Bruin was personally friendly to them, and really wished most earnestly that they might be ransomed; but then he did not see how he was to lose two thousand five hundred dollars. He had just the same difficulty on this subject that some New York members of churches have had, when they have had slaves brought into their hands as security for Southern debts. He was sorry for them, and wished them well, and hoped Providence would provide for them when they were sold, but still he could not afford to lose his money; and while such men remain elders and communicants in churches in New York, we must not be surprised that there remain slave-traders in Alexandria.

It is one great art of the enemy of souls to lead men to compound for their participation in one branch of sin by their righteous horror of another. The slave-trader has been the general scapegoat on whom all parties have vented their indignation, while buying of him and selling to him.

There is an awful warning given in the fiftieth Psalm to those who in word have professed religion, and in deed consented to iniquity, where from the judgment-seat Christ is represented as thus addressing them: "What hast *thou* to do to declare my statutes, or that thou shouldst take my covenant into thy mouth, seeing thou hatest instruction, and castest my words behind thee? When thou sawest a thief, then thou consentedst with him, and hast been partaker with adulterers."

One thing is certain, that all those who do these things, openly or secretly, must, at last, make up their account with a Judge who is no respecter of persons, and who will just as soon condemn an elder in the church for slave-trading as a professed trader; nay, He may make it more tolerable for the Sodom and Gomorrah[11] of the trade than for them,— for it may be, if the trader had the means of grace that they have had, that he would have repented long ago.

But to return to our history. The girls were sitting sewing near the open window of their cage, when Emily

(*309*)

said to Mary, "There, Mary, is that white man we have seen from the North." They both looked, and in a moment more saw their own dear father. They sprang and ran through the house and the office, and into the street, shouting as they ran, followed by Bruin, who said he thought the girls were crazy. In a moment they were in their father's arms, but observed that he trembled exceedingly, and that his voice was unsteady. They eagerly inquired if the money was raised for their ransom. Afraid of exciting their hopes too soon, before their free papers were signed, he said he would talk with them soon, and went into the office with Mr. Bruin and Mr. Chaplin. Mr. Bruin professed himself sincerely glad, as undoubtedly he was, that they had brought the money; but seemed much hurt by the manner in which he had been spoken of by the Rev. H. W. Beecher at the liberation meeting in New York, thinking it hard that no difference should be made between him and other traders, when he had shown himself so much more considerate and humane than the great body of them. He, however, counted over the money and signed the papers with great good will, taking out a five-dollar gold piece for each of the girls, as a parting present.

The affair took longer than they supposed, and the time seemed an age to the poor girls, who were anxiously walking up and down outside the room, in ignorance of their fate. Could their father have brought the money? Why did he tremble so? Could he have failed of the money, at last? Or could it be that their dear mother was dead, for they had heard that she was very ill!

At length a messenger came shouting to them, "You are free! You are free!" Emily thinks she sprang nearly to the ceiling overhead. They jumped, clapped their hands, laughed, and shouted aloud. Soon their father came to them, embraced them tenderly, and attempted to quiet them, and told them to prepare to go and see their mother. This they did, they know not how, but with considerable help from the family, who all seemed to rejoice in their joy. Their father procured a carriage to take them to the wharf, and, with joy overflowing all bounds, they bade a most affectionate farewell to each member of the family, not even omitting Bruin himself. The "good that there is in human nature"[12] for once had the upper hand, and all were moved to tears of sympathetic joy. Their father, with subdued tenderness, made great efforts to soothe their tumultuous feelings, and at length partially succeeded. When they arrived at Washington, a carriage was ready to take them to their sister's house. People of every rank and description came running together to get a sight of them. Their brothers caught them up in their arms, and ran about with them, almost frantic with joy. Their aged and venerated mother, raised up from a sick-bed by the stimulus of the glad news, was there, weeping and giving thanks to God. Refreshments were prepared in their sister's house for all who called, and, amid greetings and rejoicings, tears and gladness, prayers and thanksgivings, but without sleep, the night passed away, and the morning of November 4, 1848, dawned upon them free and happy.

This last spring, during the month of May, as the writer has already intimated, the aged mother of the Edmondson family came on to New York, and the reason of her coming may be thus briefly explained. She had still one other daughter, the guide and support of her feeble age, or as she calls her in her own expressive language, "the last drop of blood in her heart." She had also a son, twenty-one years of age, still a slave on a neighboring plantation. The infirm woman in whose name the estate was held was supposed to be drawing near to death, and the poor parents were distressed with the fear that, in case of this event, their two remaining children would be sold for the purpose of dividing the estate, and thus thrown into the dreaded Southern market. No one can realize what a constant horror the slave-prisons and the slave-traders are to all the unfortunate families in the vicinity. Everything for which other parents look on their children with pleasure and pride is to these poor souls a source of anxiety and dismay, because it renders the child so much more a merchantable article.

It is no wonder, therefore, that the light in Paul and Milly's cottage was overshadowed by this terrible idea.

The guardians of these children had given their father a written promise to sell them to him for a certain sum, and by hard begging he had acquired a hundred dollars towards the twelve hundred which were necessary. But he was now confined to his bed with sickness. After pouring out earnest prayers to the Helper of the helpless, Milly says, one day she said to Paul, "I tell ye, Paul, I'm going up to New York myself, to see if I can't get that money."

"Paul says to me, 'Why, Milly dear, how can you? Ye ain't fit to be off the bed, and ye's never in the cars in your life.'

" 'Never you fear, Paul,' says I; 'I shall go trusting in the Lord; and the Lord, He'll take me, and He'll bring me,—that I know.'

"So I went to the cars and got a white man to put me aboard; and, sure enough, there I found two Bethel[13] ministers; and one set one side o' me, and one set the other, all the way; and they got me my tickets, and looked after my things, and did everything for me. There didn't anything happen to me all the way. Sometimes, when I went to set down in the sitting-rooms, people looked at me and moved off so scornful! Well, I thought, I wish the Lord would give you a better mind."

Emily and Mary, who had been at school in New York State, came to the city to meet their mother, and they brought her directly to the Rev. Henry W. Beecher's house, where the writer then was.

The writer remembers now the scene when she first met this mother and daughters. It must be recollected that they had not seen each other before for four years. One was sitting each side the mother, holding her hand; and the air of pride and filial affection with which they presented her was touching to behold. After being presented to the writer, she again sat down between them, took a hand of each, and looked very earnestly first on one and then on the other; and then, looking up, said, with a smile, "Oh, these children,—how they do lie round our hearts!"

She then explained to the writer all her sorrows and anxieties for the younger children. "Now, madam," she says, "that man that keeps the great trading-house at Alexandria, *that man*," she said, with a strong, indigant expression, "has sent to know if there's any more of my children to be sold. That man said he wanted to see *me!* Yes, ma'am, he said he'd give twenty dollars to see me. I wouldn't see him, if he'd give me a hundred! He sent for me to come and see him, when he had my daughters in his prison. I wouldn't go to see him,—I didn't want to see them there!"

The two daughters, Emily and Mary, here became very much excited, and broke out in some very natural but bitter language against all slave-holders. "Hush, children! you must forgive your enemies,"[14] she said. "But they're so wicked!" said the girls. "Ah, children, you must hate the *sin,* but love the *sinner.*"[15] "Well," said one of the girls, "mother, if I was taken again and made a slave of, I'd kill myself." "I trust not, child,—that would be wicked." "But, mother, I *should;* I know I never could bear it." "Bear it, my child?" she answered, "it's they that bears the sorrow here is they that has the glories there."

There was a deep, indescribable pathos of voice and manner as she said these words,—a solemnity and force, and yet a sweetness, that can never be forgotten.

This poor slave-mother, whose whole life had been one long outrage on her holiest feelings,—who had been kept from the power to read God's Word, whose whole pilgrimage had been made one day of sorrow by the injustice of a Christian nation,—she had yet learned to solve the highest problem of Christian ethics, and to do what so few reformers can do,—hate the *sin,* but love the *sinner!*

A great deal of interest was excited among the ladies in Brooklyn[16] by this history. Several large meetings were held in different parlors, in which the old mother related her history with great simplicity and pathos, and a subscription for the redemption of the remaining two of her family was soon on foot. It may be interesting to know that the subscription list was headed by the lovely and benevolent Jenny Lind Goldschmidt.[17]

Some of the ladies who listened to this touching story were so much interested in Mrs. Edmondson personally, they wished to have her daguerreotype taken; both that they might be strengthened and refreshed by the sight of her placid countenance, and that they might see the beauty of true goodness beaming there.

She accordingly went to the rooms with them, with all the simplicity of a little child. "Oh," said she, to one of the ladies, "you can't think how happy it's made me to get here, where everybody is so *kind* to me! Why, last night, when I went home, I was so happy I couldn't sleep. I had to go and tell my Saviour, over and over again, how happy I was."

A lady spoke to her about reading something. "Law bless you, honey! I can't read a letter."

"Then," said another lady, "how have you learned so much of God, and heavenly things?"

"Well, 'pears like a *gift* from above."

"Can you have the Bible read to you?"

"Why, yes; Paul, he reads a little, but then he has so much work all day, and when he gets home at night he's so tired! and his eyes is bad. But then the *Sperit* teaches us."

"Do you go much to meeting?"

"Not much now, we live so far. In winter I can't never. But, oh! what meetings I have had, alone in the corner,—

my Saviour and only me!" The smile with which these words were spoken was a thing to be remembered. A little girl, daughter of one of the ladies, made some rather severe remarks about somebody in the daguerreotype rooms, and her mother checked her.

The old lady looked up, with her placid smile. "That puts me in mind," she said, "of what I heard a preacher say once. 'My friends,' says he, 'if you know of anything that will make a brother's heart glad, *run quick and tell it;* but if it is something that will only cause a sigh, bottle it up, bottle it up!' Oh, I often tell my children, 'Bottle it up, bottle it up!' "

When the writer came to part with the old lady, she said to her: "Well, good-by, my dear friend; remember and pray for me."

"Pray for *you!*" she said earnestly. "Indeed I shall,—I can't help it." She then, raising her finger, said, in an emphatic tone, peculiar to the old of her race, "Tell you what! we never gets no good bread ourselves till we begins *to ask for our brethren.*"

The writer takes this opportunity to inform all those friends, in different parts of the country, who generously contributed for the redemption of these children, that they are *at last free!*

The following extract from the letter of a lady in Washington may be interesting to them:—

"I have seen the Edmondson parents,—Paul and his wife Milly. I have seen the *free* Edmondsons,—mother, son, and daughter,—the very day after the great era of *free life* commenced, while yet the inspiration was on them, while the mother's face was all light and love, the father's eyes moistened and glistening with tears, the son calm in conscious manhood and responsibility, the daughter (not more than fifteen years old, I think) smiling a delightful appreciation of joy in the present and hope in the future, thus suddenly and completely unfolded."

Notes

1. The Revolution of February 24, 1848.

2. The Capitol is on Pennsylvania Avenue.

3. A port city in Virginia, seven miles south of Washington, D.C., on the Potomac River.

4. John Jacob Astor, 1763–1848, merchant and philanthropist.

5. An island off the coast of Florida.

6. *Psalms.* CXXXVII, 3.

7. A seaport in Maine, near Brunswick, where Harriet Beecher Stowe then lived.

8. Henry Ward Beecher, 1813–1886, clergyman and reformer; brother of Stowe.

9. The abolitionist newspaper in which *Uncle Tom's Cabin* was originally serialized.

10. *Matthew.* VII, 15.

11. Cities in the Old Testament whose residents were destroyed by God for their wickedness; hence, symbolically, doers of evil.

12. Source unknown.

13. A chapel for seamen.

14. Francis Bacon, 1561–1626, English philosopher, in *Apothegms*, Number 206.

15. Thomas Buchanan Read, 1822–1872, American poet, in *What a Word May Do.*

16. Brooklyn, New York, was the home of Henry Ward Beecher, with whom Stowe was then visiting.

17. Jenny Lind, 1820–1887, a Swedish singer.

THE CASE OF EMILY RUSSELL

from *A Key to Uncle Tom's Cabin*

Among those unfortunates guilty of loving freedom too well, was a beautiful young quadroon girl, named Emily Russell, whose mother is now living in New York. The writer has seen and conversed with her. She is a pious woman, highly esteemed and respected, a member of a Christian church.

By the avails of her own industry she purchased her freedom, and also redeemed from bondage some of her children. Emily was a resident of Washington, D. C., a place which belongs not to any state, but to the United States; and there, under the laws of the United States, she was held as a slave. She was of a gentle disposition and amiable manners; she had been early touched with a sense of religious things, and was on the very point of uniting herself with a Christian church; but her heart yearned after her widowed mother and after freedom, and so, on the fatal night when all the other poor victims sought the Pearl, the child Emily went also among them.

How they were taken has already been told.[1] The sin of the poor girl was inexpiable. Because she longed for her mother's arms and for liberty, she could not be forgiven. Nothing would do for such a sin, but to throw her into the hands of the trader. She also was thrown into Bruin & Hill's jail, in Alexandria. Her poor mother in New York received the following letter from her. Read it, Christian mother, and think what if your daughter had written it to you!

(318)

To Mrs. NANCY CARTWRIGHT, New York.

Alexandria, Jan. 22, 1850.

MY DEAR MOTHER: I take this opportunity of writing you a few lines, to inform you that I am in *Bruin's Jail,* and Aunt Sally and all of her children, and Aunt Hagar and all her children, and grandmother is almost crazy. My dear mother, will you please to come on as soon as you can? I expect to go away very shortly. O, mother! my dear mother! come now and see your distressed and heart-broken daughter once more. Mother! my dear mother! do not forsake me, for I feel desolate! Please to come now.

Your daughter,

EMILY RUSSELL.

P.S.—If you do not come as far as Alexandria, come to Washington, and do what you can.

That letter, blotted and tear-soiled, was brought by this poor washerwoman to some Christian friends in New York, and shown to them. "What do you suppose they will ask for her?" was her question. All that she had,—her little house, her little furniture, her small earnings,—all these poor Nancy was willing to throw in; but all these were but as a drop to the bucket.

The first thing to be done, then, was to ascertain what Emily could be redeemed for; and, as it may be an interesting item of American trade, we give the reply of the traders in full:

Alexandria, Jan. 31, 1850.

DEAR SIR: When I received your letter I had not bought the negroes you spoke of, but since that time I have bought them. All I have to say about the matter is, that we paid very high for the negroes, and cannot afford to sell the girl Emily for less than EIGHTEEN HUNDRED DOLLARS. This may seem a high price to you, but, cotton being very high, consequently slaves are high. We have two or three offers for Emily from *gentlemen* from the south. *She is said to be the finest-looking woman in this country.* As for Hagar and her seven children, we will take two thousand five hundred dollars for them. Sally and her four children, we will take for them two thousand eight hundred dollars. You may seem a little surprised at the difference in prices, but the difference in the negroes makes the difference in price. We expect to start south with the negroes on the 8th February, and if you intend to do anything, you had better do it soon.

Yours, respectfully,

BRUIN & HILL.

This letter came to New York before the case of the Edmondsons had called the attention of the community to this subject. The enormous price asked entirely discouraged effort, and before anything of importance was done they heard that the coffle had departed, with Emily in it.

Hear, O heavens! and give ear, O earth! Let it be known, in all the countries of the earth, that the market-price of a beautiful Christian girl in America is from EIGHTEEN HUNDRED to TWO THOUSAND DOLLARS; and yet, judicatories in the church of Christ have said, in solemn conclave, that AMERICAN SLAVERY AS IT IS IS NO EVIL!*

From the table of the sacrament and from the sanctuary of the church of Christ this girl was torn away, because her beauty was a salable article in the slave-market in New Orleans!

Perhaps some Northern apologist for slavery will say she was kindly treated here—not handcuffed by the wrist to a chain, and forced to walk, as articles less choice are; that a wagon was provided, and that she rode; and that food abundant was given her to eat, and that her clothing was warm and comfortable, and therefore no harm was done. We have heard it told us, again and again, that there is no harm in slavery, if one is only warm enough, and full-fed, and comfortable. It is true that the slave-woman has no protection from the foulest dishonor and the utmost insult

* The words of the Georgia Annual Conference: *Resolved.* "That slavery, *as it exists* in the United States, is not a moral evil."

(*320*)

that can be offered to womanhood,—none whatever in law or gospel; but, so long as she has enough to eat and wear, our Christian fathers and mothers tell us it is not so bad!

Poor Emily could not think so. There was no eye to pity, and none to help. The food of her accursed lot did not nourish her; the warmest clothing could not keep the chill of slavery from her heart. In the middle of the overland passage, sick, weary, heart-broken, the child laid her down and died. By that lonely pillow there was no mother. But there was one Friend, who loveth at all times, who is closer than a brother. Could our eyes be touched by the seal of faith, where others see only the lonely wilderness and the dying girl, we, perhaps, should see one clothed in celestial beauty, waiting for that short agony to be over, that He might redeem her from all iniquity, and present her fault-less before the presence of his Grace with exceeding joy!

Even the hard-hearted trader was touched with her sad fate, and we are credibly informed that he said he was sorry he had taken her.

Bruin & Hill wrote to New York that the girl Emily was dead. The Quaker, William Harned, went with the letter, to break the news to her mother. Since she had given up all hope of redeeming her daughter from the dreadful doom to which she had been sold the helpless mother had drooped like a stricken woman. She no longer lifted up her head, or seemed to take any interest in life.

When Mr. Harned called on her, she asked, eagerly, "Have you heard anything from my daughter?"

"Yes, I have," was the reply, "a letter from Bruin & Hill."

"And what is the news?"

He thought best to give a direct answer,—"*Emily is dead.*"

The poor mother clasped her hands, and, looking up-wards, said, "The Lord be thanked! He has heard my prayers at last!"

And, now, will it be said this is an exceptional case—it happens one time in a thousand? Though we know that this is the foulest of falsehoods, and that the case is only a specimen of what is acting every day in the American slave-trade, yet, for argument's sake, let us, for once, admit it to be true. If only once in this nation, under the protection of our law, a Christian girl had been torn from the altar and the communion-table, and sold to foulest shame and dishonor, would that have been a light sin? Does not Christ say, "Inasmuch as ye have done it unto *one of the least* of these, ye have done it unto me"?[2] O, words of woe for thee, America!—words of woe for thee, church of Christ! Hast thou trod them under foot and trampled them in the dust so long that Christ has forgotten them? In the day of judgment every one of these words shall rise up, living and burning, as accusing angels to witness against thee. Art thou, O church of Christ! praying daily, "Thy kingdom come"?[3] Darest thou pray, "Come, Lord Jesus, come quickly"? O, what if He should come? What if the Lord, whom ye seek, should *suddenly* come into his temple? If his soul was stirred within him when he found within his temple of old those that changed money, and sold sheep and oxen and doves, what will he say now, when he finds them selling body, blood and bones, of his own people? And is the Christian church, which justifies this enormous system,—which has used the awful name of her Redeemer to sanction the buying, selling and trading in the souls of men,—is this church the bride of Christ? Is she one with Christ, even as Christ is one with the Father? O, bitter mockery! Does this church believe that every Christian's body is a temple of the Holy Ghost? Or does she think those solemn words were idle breath, when, a thousand times, every day and week, in the midst of her, is this temple set up and sold at auction, to be bought by any godless, blasphemous man, who has money to pay for it!

As to poor Daniel Bell and his family, whose contested

claim to freedom was the beginning of the whole trouble, a few members of it were redeemed, and the rest were plunged into the abyss of slavery.[4] It would seem as if this event, like the sinking of a ship, drew into its maēlstrom the fate of every unfortunate being who was in its vicinity. A poor, honest, hard-working slaveman, of the name of Thomas Ducket, had a wife who was on board the *Pearl.* Tom was supposed to know the men who countenanced the enterprise, and his master, therefore, determined to sell him. He brought him to Washington for the purpose. Some in Washington doubted his legal right to bring a slave from Maryland for the purpose of selling him, and commenced legal proceedings to test the matter. While they were pending, the counsel for the master told the men who brought action against his client that Tom was anxious to be sold; that he preferred being sold to the man who had purchased his wife and children, rather than to have his liberty. It was well known that Tom did not wish to be separated from his family, and the friends here, confiding in the representations made to them, consented to withdraw the proceedings.

Some time after this, they received letters from poor Tom Ducket, dated ninety miles above New Orleans, complaining sadly of his condition, and making piteous appeals to hear from them respecting his wife and children. Upon inquiry, nothing could be learned respecting them. They had been sold and gone,—sold and gone,—no one knew whither; and as a punishment to Tom for his contumacy in refusing to give the name of the man who had projected the expedition of the *Pearl,* he was denied the privilege of going off the place, and was not allowed to talk with the other servants, his master fearing a conspiracy. In one of his letters he says, "I have seen more trouble here in one day than I have in all my life." In another, "I would be glad to hear from her [his wife], but I should be more glad to hear of her death than for her to come here."

In his distress, Tom wrote a letter to Mr. Bigelow, of Washington. People who are not in the habit of getting such documents have no idea of them. We give a *facsimile* of Tom's letter with all its poor spelling, all its ignorance, helplessness, and misery [not shown].

[*February* 18, 1852.
Mr. Bigelow. Dear Sir:—I write to let you know how I am getting along. Hard times here. I have not had one hour to go outside the place since I have been on it. I put my trust in the Lord to help me. I long to hear from you all. I written to hear from you all. Mr. Bigelow, I hope you will not forget me. You know it was not my fault that I am here. I hope you will name me to Mr. Geden, Mr. Chaplin, Mr. Bailey, to help me out of it. I believe that if they would make the least move to it that it could be done. I long to hear from my family how they are getting along. You will please to write to me just to let me know how they are getting along. You can write to me.

I remain your humble servant,
Thomas Ducket.

You can direct your letters to Thomas Ducket, in care of Mr. Samuel T. Harrison, Louisiana, near Bayou Goula. For God's sake let me hear from you all. My wife and children are not out of my mind day nor night.]

Notes

1. See the previous selection, "The Edmondsons."

2. *Matthew.* XXV, 40.

3. *Matthew.* V, 7.

4. See "The Edmondsons."

KIDNAPPING

from *A Key to Uncle Tom's Cabin*

The principle which declares that one human being may lawfully hold another as property leads directly to the trade in human beings; and that trade has, among its other horrible results, the temptation to the crime of kidnapping.

The trader is generally a man of coarse nature and low associations, hard-hearted, and reckless of right or honor. He who is not so is an exception, rather than a specimen. If he has anything good about him when he begins the business, it may well be seen that he is in a fair way to lose it.

Around the trader are continually passing and repassing men and women who would be worth to him thousands of dollars in the way of trade,—who belong to a class whose rights nobody respects, and who, if reduced to slavery, could not easily make their word good against him. The probability is that hundreds of free men and women and children are all the time being precipitated into slavery in this way.

The recent case of *Northrop*, tried in Washington, D. C., throws light on this fearful subject. The following account is abridged from the *New York Times:*

Solomon Northrop is a free colored citizen of the United States; he was born in Essex county, New York, about the year 1808; became early a resident of Washington county, and married there in 1829. His father and mother resided in the county of Washington about fifty years, till their decease, and were both free. With his wife and children he resided at Saratoga Springs in the winter of 1841, and while there was employed by two gentlemen to drive a team South, at the rate of a dollar a day. In fulfilment of his employment, he proceeded to New York, and, having taken out free papers, to show that he was a citizen, he went on to Washington city, where he arrived the second day of April, the same year, and put up at Gadsby's Hotel. Soon after he arrived he felt unwell, and went to bed.

While suffering with severe pain, some persons came in, and, seeing the condition he was in, proposed to give him some medicine, and did so. This is the last thing of which he had any recollection, until he found himself chained to the floor of Williams' slave-pen in this city, and handcuffed. In the course of a few hours, James H. Burch, a slave-dealer, came in, and the colored man asked him to take the irons off from him, and wanted to know why they were put on. Burch told him it was none of his business. The colored man said he was free, and told where he was born. Burch called in a man by the name of Ebenezer Rodbury, and they two stripped the man and laid him across a bench, Rodbury holding him down by his wrists. Burch whipped him with a paddle until he broke that, and then with a cat-o'-nine-tails, giving him a hundred lashes; and he swore he would kill him if he ever stated to any one that he was a free man. From that time forward the man says he did not communicate the fact from fear, either that he was a free man, or what his name was, until the last summer. He was kept in the slave-pen about ten days, when he, with others, was taken out of the pen in the night by Burch, handcuffed and shackled, and taken down the river by a steamboat, and then to Richmond, where he, with forty-eight others, was put on board the brig *Orleans*. There Burch left them. The brig sailed for New Orleans, and on arriving there, before she was fastened to the wharf, Theophilus Freeman, another slave-dealer, belonging in the city of New Orleans, and who in 1833 had been a partner with Burch in the slave-trade, came to the wharf, and received the slaves as they were landed, under his direction. This man was immediately taken by Freeman and shut up in his pen in that city. He was taken sick with the small-pox immediately after getting there, and was sent to a hospital, where he lay two or three weeks. When he had sufficiently recovered to leave the hospital, Freeman declined to sell him to any person in that vicinity, and sold him to a Mr. Ford, who resided in Rapides Parish, Louisiana, where he was taken and lived more than a year, and worked as a carpenter, working with Ford at that business.

Ford became involved, and had to sell him. A Mr. Tibaut became the purchaser. He, in a short time, sold him to Edwin Eppes, in Bayou Beouf, about one hundred and thirty miles from the mouth of Red river, where Eppes has retained him on a cotton plantation since the year 1843.

To go back a step in the narrative, the man wrote a letter, in June, 1841, to Henry B. Northrop, of the State of New York, dated and postmarked at New Orleans, stating that he had been kidnapped and was on board a vessel, but was unable to state what his destination was; but requesting Mr. N. to aid him in recovering his freedom, if possible. Mr. N. was unable to do anything in his behalf, in consequence of not knowing where he had gone, and not being able to find any trace of him. His place of residence remained unknown until the month of September last, when the following letter was received by his friends:

Bayou Beouf, August, 1852.
MR. WILLIAM PENY, or MR. LEWIS PARKER.

GENTLEMEN: It having been a long time since I have seen or heard from you, and not knowing that you are living, it is with uncertainty that I write to you; but the necessity of the case must be my excuse. Having been born free just across the river from you, I am certain you know me; and I am here now a slave. I wish you to obtain free papers for me, and forward them to me at Marksville, Louisiana, Parish of Avovelles, and oblige

Yours,
SOLOMON NORTHROP.

On receiving the above letter, Mr. N. applied to Governor Hunt, of New York, for such authority as was necessary for him to proceed to Louisiana as an agent to procure the liberation of Solomon. Proof of his freedom was furnished to Governor Hunt by affidavits of several gentlemen, General Clarke among others. Accordingly, in pursuance of the laws of New York, Henry B. Northrop was constituted an agent, to take such steps, by procur-

(*327*)

ing evidence, retaining counsel, &c., as were necessary to secure the freedom of Solomon, and to execute all the duties of his agency.

The result of Mr. Northrop's agency was the establishing of the claim of Solomon Northrop to freedom, and the restoring him to his native land.

It is a singular coincidence that this man was carried to a plantation in the Red river country, that same region where the scene of Tom's captivity was laid, and his account of this plantation, his mode of life there, and some incidents which he describes, form a striking parallel to that history. We extract them from the article of the *Times:*

The condition of this colored man during the nine years that he was in the hands of Eppes was of a character nearly approaching that described by Mrs. Stowe as the condition of "Uncle Tom" while in that region. During that whole period his hut contained neither a floor, nor a chair, nor a bed, nor a mattress, nor anything for him to lie upon, except a board about twelve inches wide, with a block of wood for his pillow, and with a single blanket to cover him, while the walls of his hut did not by any means protect him from the inclemency of the weather. He was sometimes compelled to perform acts revolting to humanity, and outrageous in the highest degree. On one occasion, a colored girl belonging to Eppes, about seventeen years of age, went one Sunday, without the permission of her master, to the nearest plantation, about half a mile distant, to visit another colored girl of her acquaintance. She returned in the course of two or three hours, and for that offence she was called up for punishment, which Solomon was required to inflict. Eppes compelled him to drive four stakes into the ground at such distances that the hands and ankles of the girl might be tied to them, as she lay with her face upon the ground; and, having thus fastened her down, he compelled him, while standing by himself, to inflict one hundred lashes upon her bare flesh, she being stripped naked. Having inflicted the hundred blows, Solomon refused to proceed any further. Eppes tried to compel him to go on, but he absolutely set him at defiance, and refused to murder the girl. Eppes then seized the whip, and applied it until he was too weary to continue it. Blood flowed from her neck to her feet, and in this condition she was compelled the next day to go into the field to work as a field-hand. She bears the marks still upon her body, although the punishment was inflicted four years ago.

When Solomon was about to leave, under the care of Mr. Northrop, this girl came from behind her hut, unseen by her master, and, throwing her arms around the neck of Solomon, congratulated him on his escape from slavery, and his return to his family; at the same time, in language of despair, exclaiming, "But, O God! what will become of me?"

These statements regarding the condition of Solomon while with Eppes, and the punishment and brutal treatment of the colored girls, are taken from Solomon himself. It has been stated that the nearest plantation was distant from that of Eppes a half-mile, and of course there could be no interference on the part of neighbors in any punishment, however cruel, or however well disposed to interfere they might be.

Had not Northrop been able to write, as few of the free blacks in the slave states are, his doom might have been sealed for life in this den of misery.

Two cases recently tried in Baltimore also unfold facts of a similar nature.

The following is from

THE CASE OF RACHEL PARKER AND HER SISTER.

It will be remembered that more than a year since a young colored woman, named Mary Elizabeth Parker, was abducted from Chester county and conveyed to Baltimore, where she was sold as a slave, and transported to New Orleans. A few days after, her sister, Rachel Parker, was also abducted in like manner, taken to Baltimore, and detained there in consequence of the interference of her Chester county friends. In the first case, Mary Elizabeth was, by an arrangement with the individual who had her in charge, brought back to Baltimore, to await her trial on a petition for freedom. So also with regard to Rachel. Both, after trial,—the proof in their favor being so overwhelming,—were discharged, and are now among their friends in Chester county. In this connection we give the narratives of both females, obtained since their release.

Rachel Parker's Narrative.

"I was taken from Joseph C. Miller's about twelve o'clock on Tuesday (Dec. 30th, 1851), by two men who came up to the house by the *back* door. One came in and asked Mrs. Miller where Jesse McCreary lived, and then seized me by the arm, and pulled me out of the house. Mrs. Miller called to her husband, who was in the *front* porch, and he ran out and seized the man by the collar, and tried to stop him. The other, with an oath, then told him to take his hands off, and if he touched me he would kill him. He then told Miller that I belonged to Mr. Schoolfield, in Baltimore. They then hurried me to a wagon, where there was another large man, put me in, and drove off.

"Mr. Miller ran across the field to head the wagon, and picked up a stake to run through the wheel, when one of the men pulled out a sword (I think it was a sword, I never saw one), and threatened to cut Miller's arm off. Pollock's wagon being in the way, and he refusing to get out of the road, we turned off to the left. After we rode away, one of the men tore a hole in the back of the carriage, to look out to see if they were coming after us, and they said they wished they had given Miller and Pollock a blow.

"We stopped at a tavern near the railroad, and I told the landlord (I think it was) that I was free. I also told several persons at the car-office; and a very nice-looking man at the car-office was talking at the door, and he said he thought that they had better take me back again. One of the men did not come further than the tavern. I was taken to Baltimore, where we arrived about seven o'clock the same evening, and I was taken to jail.

"The next morning, a man with large light-colored whiskers took me away by myself, and asked me if I was not Mr. Schoolfield's slave. I told him I was not; he said that I was, and that if I did not say I was he would 'cowhide me and salt me, and put me in a dungeon.' I told him I was free, and that I would say nothing but the truth."

Mary E. Parker's Narrative.

"I was taken from Matthew Donnelly's on Saturday night (Dec. 6th, or 13th, 1851); was caught whilst out of doors, soon

(330)

after I had cleared the supper-table, about seven o'clock, by two men, and put into a wagon. One of them got into the wagon with me, and rode to Elkton, Md., where I was kept until Sunday night at twelve o'clock, when I left there in the cars for Baltimore, and arrived there early on Monday morning.

"At Elkton a man was brought in to see me, by one of the men, who said that I was not his father's slave. Afterwards, when on the way to Baltimore in the cars, a man told me that I must say that I was Mr. Schoolfield's slave, or he would shoot me, and pulled a 'rifle' out of his pocket and showed it to me, and also threatened to whip me.

"On Monday morning, Mr. Schoolfield called at the jail in Baltimore to see me; and on Tuesday morning he brought his wife and several other ladies to see me. I told them I did not know them, and then Mr. C. took me out of the room, and told me who they were, and took me back again, so that I might appear to know them. On the next Monday I was shipped to New Orleans.

"It took about a month to get to New Orleans. After I had been there about a week, Mr. C. sold me to Madame C., who keeps a large flower-garden. She sends flowers to sell to the theatres, sells milk in market, &c. I went out to sell candy and flowers for her, when I lived with her. One evening, when I was coming home from the theatre, a watchman took me up, and I told him I was not a slave. He put me in the calaboose, and next morning took me before a magistrate, who sent for Madame C., who told him she bought me. He then sent for Mr. C., and told him he must account for how he got me. Mr. C. said that my mother and all the family were free, except me. The magistrate told me to go back to Madame C., and he told Madame C. that she must not let me go out at night; and he told Mr. C. that he must prove how he came by me. The magistrate afterwards called on Mrs. C., at her house, and had a long talk with her in the parlor. I do not know what he said, as they were by themselves. About a month afterwards, I was sent back to Baltimore. I lived with Madame C. about six months.

"There were six slaves came in the vessel with me to Baltimore, who belonged to Mr. D., and were returned because they were sickly.

"A man called to see me at the jail after I came back to Baltimore, and told me that I must say I was Mr. Schoolfield's slave, and that if I did not do it he would kill me the first time he got a chance. He said Rachel [her sister] said she came from Baltimore and was Mr. Schoolfield's slave. Afterwards some gentlemen called on me [Judge Campbell and Judge Bell, of Philadelphia, and William H. Norris, Esq., of Baltimore] and I told them I was Mr. Schoolfield's slave. They said they were my friends, and I must tell them the truth. I then told them who I was, and all about it.

"When I was in New Orleans Mr. C. whipped me because I said that I was free."

Elizabeth, by her own account above, was seized and taken from Pennsylvania, Dec. 6th or 13th, 1851, which is confirmed by other testimony.

It is conceded that such cases, when brought into Southern courts, are generally tried with great fairness and impartiality. The agent for Northrop's release testifies to this, and it has been generally admitted fact. But it is probably only one case in a hundred that can get into court;—of the multitudes who are drawn down in the ever-widening maëlstrom only now and then one ever comes back to tell the tale.

SOJOURNER TRUTH, THE LIBYAN SIBYL

from *Atlantic Monthly*

Transported from Africa as a child, Sojourner Truth, c.1797–1883, was enslaved to a succession of New York masters. Known simply as Isabella, she adopted in 1827 the name of the kind Quaker family who befriended her when she fled from a harsh master—Isabella Van Wagener. After her emancipation she preached on the streets of New York and was affiliated with various religious cults. In 1843 "voices" commanded Isabella to take the name of Sojourner Truth, a name symbolic of her mission in life—to wander the nation to spread the gospel. Later she would add her voice to the abolition and women's rights movements.

On one of her preaching tours in the east, Sojourner Truth called upon the author of *Uncle Tom's Cabin* to pay her respects to the lady who had done so much for her people. Harriet Beecher Stowe wrote this account of the 1855 visit in Andover, Massachusetts, and published it some eight years later in the *Atlantic Monthly,* April 1863.

M any years ago, the few readers of radical abolitionist papers must often have seen the singular name of Sojourner Truth announced as a frequent speaker at anti-slavery meetings, and as traveling on a sort of self-appointed agency through the country. I had myself often remarked the name, but never met the individual. On one occasion,[1] when our house was filled with company, several eminent clergymen being our guests, notice was brought up to me that Sojourner Truth was below and requested an interview. Knowing nothing of her but her singular name, I went down, prepared to make the interview short, as the pressure of many other engagements demanded.

When I went into the room, a tall, spare form arose to meet me. She was evidently a full-blooded African, and, though now aged and worn with many hardships, still gave the impression of a physical development which in early youth must have been as fine a specimen of the torrid zone as Cumberworth's celebrated statuette of the Negro Woman at the Fountain.[2] Indeed, she so strongly reminded me of that figure, that, when I recall the events of her life, as she narrated them to me, I imagine her as a living, breathing impersonation of that work of art.

I do not recollect ever to have been conversant with any one who had more of that silent and subtle power which we call personal presence than this woman. In the modern spiritualistic phraseology, she would be described as having a strong sphere. Her tall form, as she rose up before me, is still vivid to my mind. She was dressed in some stout, grayish stuff, neat and clean, though dusty from travel. On her head she wore a bright Madras handkerchief, arranged as a turban, after the manner of her race. She seemed perfectly self-possessed and at her ease,—in fact, there was almost an unconscious superiority, not unmixed with a solemn twinkle of humor, in the odd, composed manner in which she looked down on me. Her whole air had at times a gloomy sort of drollery which impressed one strangely.

"So this is *you?*" she said.

"Yes," I answered.

"Well, honey, de Lord bless ye! I jes' thought I'd like to come an' have a look at ye. You's heerd o' me, I reckon?" she added.

"Yes, I think I have. You go about lecturing, do you not?"

"Yes, honey, that's what I do. The Lord has made me a

sign unto this nation, an' I go round a-testifyin', an' showin' on 'em their sins agin my people."

So saying, she took a seat, and, stooping over and crossing her arms on her knees, she looked down on the floor, and appeared to fall into a sort of reverie. Her great gloomy eyes and her dark face seemed to work with some undercurrent of feeling; she sighed deeply, and occasionally broke out,—

"O Lord! O Lord! O the tears, an' the groans, an' the moans! O Lord!"

I should have said that she was accompanied by a little grandson of ten years,[3]—the fattest, jolliest woolly-headed little specimen of Africa that one can imagine. He was grinning and showing his glistening white teeth in a state of perpetual merriment, and at this moment broke out into an audible giggle, which disturbed the reverie into which his relative was falling.

She looked at him with an indulgent sadness, and then at me.

"Laws, ma'am, *he* don't know nothin' about it,—*he* don't. Why, I've seen them poor critturs, beat an' 'bused an' hunted, brought in all torn,—ears hangin' all in rags, where the dogs been a-bitin' of 'em!"

This set off our little African Puck[4] into another giggle, in which he seemed perfectly convulsed.

She surveyed him soberly, without the slightest irritation.

"Well, you may bless the Lord you *can* laugh; but I tell you, 't wa'n't no laughin' matter."

By this time I thought her manner so original that it might be worth while to call down my friends; and she seemed perfectly well pleased with the idea. An audience was what she wanted,—it mattered not whether high or low, learned or ignorant. She had things to say, and was ready to say them at all times, and to any one.

I called down Dr. Beecher, Professor Allen, and two or

(*335*)

three other clergymen, who, together with my husband and family, made a roomful.⁵ No princess could have received a drawing-room with more composed dignity than Sojourner her audience. She stood among them, calm and erect, as one of her own native palm-trees waving alone in the desert. I presented one after another to her, and at last said,—

"Sojourner, this is Dr. Beecher. He is a very celebrated preacher."

"*Is* he?" she said, offering her hand in a condescending manner, and looking down on his white head. "Ye dear lamb, I'm glad to see ye! De Lord bless ye! I loves preachers. I'm a kind o' preacher myself."

"You are?" said Dr. Beecher. "Do you preach from the Bible?"

"No, honey, can't preach from de Bible,—can't read a letter."

"Why, Sojourner, what do you preach from, then?"

Her answer was given with a solemn power of voice, peculiar to herself, that hushed every one in the room.

"When I preaches, I has just one text to preach from, an' I always preaches from this one. *My* text is, 'WHEN I FOUND JESUS.' "

"Well, you couldn't have a better one," said one of the ministers.

She paid no attention to him, but stood and seemed swelling with her own thoughts, and then began this narration:—

"Well, now, I'll jest have to go back, an' tell ye all about it. Ye see, we was all brought over from Africa, father an' mother an' I, an' a lot more of us; an' we was sold up an' down, an' hither an' yon; an' I can 'member when I was a little thing, not bigger than this 'ere," pointing to her grandson, "how my ole mammy would sit out o' doors in the evenin', an' look up at the stars an' groan. She'd groan an' groan, says I to her,—

(*336*)

" 'Mammy, what makes you groan so?'

"An' she'd say,—

" 'Matter enough, chile! I'm groanin' to think o' my poor children: they don't know where I be, an' I don't know where they be; they looks up at the stars, an' I looks up at the stars, but I can't tell where they be.

" 'Now,' she said, 'chile, when you're grown up, you may be sold away from your mother an' all your ole friends, an' have great troubles come on ye; an' when you has these troubles come on ye, ye jes' go to God, an' He'll help ye.'

"An' says I to her,—

" 'Who is God anyhow, mammy?'

"An' says she,—

" 'Why, chile, you jes' look up *dar!* It's Him that made all *dem!'*

"Well, I didn't mind much 'bout God in them days. I grew up pretty lively an' strong, an' could row a boat, or ride a horse, or work round, an' do 'most anything.

"At last I got sold away to a real hard massa an' missis.[6] Oh, I tell you, they *was* hard! 'Peared like I couldn't please 'em, nohow. An' then I thought o' what my old mammy told me about God; an' I thought I'd got into trouble, sure enough, an' I wanted to find God, an' I heerd some one tell a story about a man that met God on a threshin'-floor, an' I thought, 'Well an' good, I'll have a threshin'-floor, too.' So I went down in the lot, an' I threshed down a place real hard, an' I used to go down there every day an' pray an' cry with all my might, a-prayin' to the Lord to make my massa an' missis better, but it didn't seem to do no good; an' so says I, one day,—

" 'O God, I been a-askin' ye, an' askin' ye, for all this long time, to make my massa an' missis better, an' you don't do it, an' what *can* be the reason? Why, maybe you *can't.* Well, I shouldn't wonder ef you couldn't. Well, now, I tell you, I'll make a bargain with you. Ef you'll help me to git away from my massa an' missis, I'll agree to be good; but ef you don't help me, I really don't think I can be. Now,' says I, 'I want to git away; but the trouble's jest here: ef I try to git away in the night, I can't see; an' ef I try to git away in the daytime, they'll see me, an' be after me.'

"Then the Lord said to me, 'Git up two or three hours afore daylight, an' start off.'

"An' says I, 'Thank 'ee, Lord! that's a good thought.'

"So up I got, about three o'clock in the mornin', an' I started an' traveled pretty fast, till, when the sun rose, I was clear away from our place an' our folks, an' out o' sight. An' then I begun to think I did n't know nothin' where to go. So I kneeled down, and says I,—

" 'Well, Lord, you've started me out, an' now please to show me where to go.'

"Then the Lord made a house appear to me, an' He said to me that I was to walk on till I saw that house, an' then go in an' ask the people to take me. An' I traveled all day, an' did n't come to the house till late at night; but when I saw it, sure enough, I went in, an' I told the folks that the Lord sent me; an' they was Quakers, an' real kind they was to me.[7] They jes' took me in, an' did for me as kind as ef I'd been one of 'em; an' after they'd giv me supper, they took me into a room where there was a great, tall, white bed; an' they told me to sleep there. Well, honey, I was kind o' skeered when they left me alone with that great white bed; 'cause I never had been in a bed in my life. It never came into my mind they could mean me to sleep in it. An' so I jes' camped down under it on the floor, an' then I slep' pretty well. In the mornin', when they came in, they asked me ef I hadn't been asleep; an' I said, 'Yes, I never slep' better.' An' they said, 'Why, you haven't been in the bed!' An' says I, 'Laws, you didn't think o' sech a thing as my sleepin' in dat ar *bed*, did you? I never heerd o' sech a thing in my life.'

"Well, ye see, honey, I stayed an' lived with 'em. An' now jes' look here: instead o' keepin' my promise an' bein' good, as I told the Lord I would, jest as soon as everything got a-goin' easy, *I forgot all about God.*

(338)

"Pretty well don't need no help; an' I gin up prayin'. I lived there two or three years, an' then the slaves in New York were all set free,[8] an' ole massa came to our house to make a visit, an' he asked me ef I didn't want to go back an' see the folks on the ole place. An' I told him I did. So he said, ef I'd jes' git into the wagon with him, he'd carry me over. Well, jest as I was goin' out to git into the wagon, *I met God!* an' says I, 'O God, I did n't know as you was so great!' An' I turned right round an' come into the house an' set down in my room; for 't was God all around me. I could feel it burnin', burnin', burnin', all around me, an' goin' through me; an' I saw I was so wicked, it seemed as ef it would burn me up. An' I said, 'Oh, somebody, somebody, stand between God an' me, for it burns me!' Then, honey, when I said so, I felt as it were somethin' like an *amberill* [umbrella] that came between me an' the light, an' I felt it was *somebody*,—somebody that stood between me an' God; an' it felt cool, like a shade; an' says I, 'Who's this that stands between me an' God? Is it old Cato?' He was a pious old preacher; but then I seemed to see Cato in the light, an' he was all polluted an' vile, like me; an' I said, 'Is it old Sally?' an' then I saw her, an' she seemed jes' so. An' then says I, '*Who* is this?' An' then, honey, for a while it was like the sun shinin' in a pail o' water, when it moves up an' down; for I begun to feel 't was somebody that loved me; an' I tried to know him. An' I said, 'I know you! I know you! I know you!'—an' then I said, 'I don't know you! I don't know you! I don't know you!' An' when I said, 'I know you, I know you,' the light came; an' when I said, 'I don't know you, I don't know you,' it went, jes' like the sun in a pail o' water. An' finally somethin' spoke out in me an' said, '*This is Jesus!*' an' I spoke out with all my might, an' says I, '*This is Jesus!* Glory be to God!' An' then the whole world grew bright, an' the trees they waved an' waved in glory, an' every little bit o' stone on the ground shone like glass; an' I shouted an' said, 'Praise, praise, praise to the Lord!' An' I begun to feel sech a love in my soul as I never felt before,—love to all creatures. An' then, all of a sudden, it stopped, an' I said, 'Dar's de white folks, that have abused you an' beat you an' abused your people,—think o' them!' But then there came another rush of love through my soul, an' I cried out loud, 'Lord, Lord, I can love *even de white folks!*'

"Honey, I jes' walked round an' round in a dream. Jesus loved me! I knowed it,—I felt it. Jesus was my Jesus. Jesus would love me always. I did n't dare tell nobody; 't was a great secret. Everything had been got away from me that I ever had; an' I thought that ef I let white folks know about this, maybe they'd get *Him* away,—so I said, 'I'll keep this close. I won't let any one know.' "

"But, Sojourner, had you never been told about Jesus Christ?"

"No, honey. I had n't heerd no preachin',—been to no meetin'. Nobody had n't told me. I'd kind o' heerd of Jesus, but thought he was like Gineral Lafayette,[9] or some o' them. But one night there was a Methodist meetin' somewhere in our parts, an' I went; an' they got up an' begun for to tell der 'speriences; an' de fust one begun to speak. I started, 'cause he told about Jesus. 'Why,' says I to myself, 'dat man's found him, too!' An' another got up an' spoke, an' I said, 'He's found him, too!' An' finally I said, 'Why, they all know him!' I was so happy! An' then they sung this hymn" (here Sojourner sang, in a strange, cracked voice, but evidently with all her soul and might, mispronouncing the English, but seeming to derive as much elevation and comfort from bad English as from good):—

"There is a holy city,
    A world of light above,
Above the stairs and regions,*
    Built by the God of love.

* Starry Regions.

(340)

"An everlasting temple,
   And saints arrayed in white
There serve their great Redeemer
   And dwell with him in light.

"The meanest child of glory
   Outshines the radiant sun;
But who can speak the splendor
   Of Jesus on his throne?

"Is this the man of sorrows
   Who stood at Pilate's bar,
Condemned by haughty Herod
   And by his men of war?

"He seems a mighty conqueror,
   Who spoiled the powers below,
And ransomed many captives
   From everlasting woe.

"The hosts of saints around him
   Proclaim his work of grace,
The patriarchs and prophets,
   And all the godly race,

"Who speak of fiery trials
   And tortures on their way;
They came from tribulation
   To everlasting day.

"And what shall be my journey,
   How long I'll stay below,
Or what shall be my trials,
   Are not for me to know.

(341)

"In every day of trouble
I'll raise my thoughts on high,
I'll think of that bright temple
And crowns above the sky."

I put in this whole hymn,[10] because Sojourner, carried
away with her own feeling, sang it from beginning to end
with a triumphant energy that held the whole circle around
her intently listening. She sang with the strong barbaric
accent of the native African, and with those indescribable
upward turns and those deep gutturals which give such a
wild, peculiar power to the negro singing,—but, above all,
with such an overwhelming energy of personal appropria-
tion that the hymn seemed to be fused in the furnace of her
feelings and come out recrystallized as a production of her
own.

It is said that Rachel was wont to chant the Marseillaise
in a manner that made her seem, for the time, the very
spirit and impersonation of the gaunt, wild, hungry, aveng-
ing mob which rose against aristocratic oppression; and in
like manner Sojourner, singing this hymn, seemed to im-
personate the fervor of Ethiopia, savage, hunted of all
nations, but burning after God in her tropic heart, and
stretching her scarred hands towards the glory to be re-
vealed.[11]

"Well, den, ye see, after a while I thought I'd go back
an' see de folks on de ole place. Well, you know, de law had
passed dat de cullud folks was all free; an' my old missis, she
had a daughter married about dis time who went to live in
Alabama,—an' what did she do but give her my son, a boy
about de age of dis yer, for her to take down to Alabama?
When I got back to de ole place, they told me about it, an' I
went right up to see ole missis, an' says I,—

" 'Missis, have you been an' sent my son[12] away down
to Alabama?'

" 'Yes, I have,' says she; 'he's gone to live with your
young missis.'

(342)

" 'Oh, missis,' says I, 'how could you do it?'

" 'Poh!' says she 'what a fuss you make about a little nigger! Got more of 'em now than you know what to do with.'

"I tell you, I stretched up. I felt as tall as the world!

" 'Missis,' says I, *I'll have my son back agin!*'

"She laughed.

" *You* will, you nigger? How you goin' to do it? You ha'n't got no money.'

" 'No, missis, but *God* has, an' you'll see He'll help me!' An' I turned round, an' went out.

"Oh, but I *was* angry to have her speak to me so haughty an' so scornful, as ef my chile wasn't worth anything. I said to God, 'O Lord, render unto her double!' It was a dreadful prayer, an' I didn't know how true it would come.

"Well, I didn't rightly know which way to turn; but I went to the Lord, an' I said to Him, 'O Lord, ef I was as rich as you be, an' you was as poor as I be, I'd help you,—you *know* I would; and, oh, do help me!' An' I felt sure then that He would.

"Well, I talked with people, an' they said I must git the case before a grand jury. So I went into the town, when they was holdin' a court, to see ef I could find any grand jury. An' I stood round the court-house, an' when they was a-comin' out I walked right up to the grandest-lookin' one I could see, an' says I to him,—

" 'Sir, be you a grand jury?'

"An' then he wanted to know why I asked, an' I told him all about it; an' he asked me all sorts of questions, an' finally he says to me,—

" 'I think, ef you pay me ten dollars, that I'd agree to git your son for you.' An' says he, pointin' to a house over the way, 'You go long an' tell your story to the folks in that house, an' I guess they'll give you the money.'

"Well, I went, an' I told them, an' they gave me twenty dollars; an' then I thought to myself, 'Ef ten dollars will git him, twenty dollars will git him *sartin.*' So I carried it to the man all out, an' said,—

" 'Take it all,—only be sure an' git him.'

"Well, finally they got the boy brought back; an' then they tried to frighten him, an' to make him say that I wasn't his mammy, an' that he didn't know me; but they couldn't make it out. They gave him to me, an' I took him an' carried him home; an' when I came to take off his clothes, there was his poor little back all covered with scars an' hard lumps, where they'd flogged him.

"Well, you see, honey, I told you how I prayed the Lord to render unto her double. Well, it came true; for I was up at ole missis' house not long after, an' I heerd 'em readin' a letter to her how her daughter's husband had murdered her,—how he'd thrown her down an' stamped the life out of her when he was in liquor; an' my ole missis, she giv' a screech an' fell flat on the floor. Then says I, 'O Lord, I didn't mean all that! You took me up too quick.'

"Well, I went in an' tended that poor critter all night. She was out of her mind,—a-cryin,' an' callin' for her daughter; an' I held her poor ole head on my arm, an' watched for her as ef she'd been my babby. An' I watched by her, an' took care on her all through her sickness after that, an' she died in my arms, poor thing!"

"Well, Sojourner, did you always go by this name?"

"No, 'deed! My name was Isabella; but when I left the house of bondage, I left everything behind. I wa'n't goin' to keep nothin' of Egypt[13] on me, an' so I went to the Lord an' asked Him to give me a new name. And the Lord gave me Sojourner, because I was to travel up an' down the land, showin' the people their sins, an' bein' a sign unto them. Afterwards I told the Lord I wanted another name, 'cause everybody else had two names; and the Lord gave me Truth, because I was to declare the truth to the people.

"Ye see, some ladies have given me a white satin banner," she said, pulling out of her pocket and unfolding a white banner, printed with many texts, such as, "Proclaim liberty throughout all the land unto all the inhabitants thereof,"[14] and others of like nature. "Well," she said, "I journeys round to camp-meetin's, an' wherever folks is, an' I sets up my banner, an' then I sings, an' then folks always comes up round me, an' then I preaches to 'em. I tells 'em about Jesus, an' I tells 'em about the sins of this people. A great many always comes to hear me; an' they're right good to me, too, an' say they want to hear me agin."

We all thought it likely; and as the company left her, othey shook hands with her, and thanked her for her very original sermon; and one of the ministers was overheard to say to another, "There's more of the gospel in that story than in most sermons."

Sojourner stayed several days with us, a welcome guest. Her conversation was so strong, simple, shrewd, and with such a droll flavoring of humor, that the Professor was wont to say of an evening, "Come, I am dull, can't you get Sojourner up here to talk a little?" She would come up into the parlor, and sit among pictures and ornaments, in her simple stuff gown, with her heavy traveling-shoes, the central object of attention both to parents and children, always ready to talk or to sing, and putting into the common flow of conversation the keen edge of some shrewd remark.

"Sojourner, what do you think of Women's Rights?"

"Well, honey, I's ben to der meetings, an' harked a good deal. Dey wanted me fur to speak. So I got up. Says I, 'Sisters, I ain't clear what you'd be after. Ef women want any rights more'n dey's got, why don't dey jes' *take 'em,* an' not be talkin' about it?' Some on 'em came round me, an' asked why I didn't wear bloomers.[15] An' I told 'em I had bloomers enough when I was in bondage. You see," she said, "dey used to weave what dey called nigger-cloth, an' each one of us got jes' sech a strip, an' had to wear it width-wise. Them that was short got along pretty well, but as for me"—She gave an indescribably droll glance at her long limbs and then at us, and added, "Tell *you*, I had enough of bloomers in them days."

Sojourner then proceeded to give her views of the relative capacity of the sexes, in her own way.

"S'pose a man's mind holds a quart, an' a woman's don't hold but a pint; ef her pint is *full*, it's as good as his quart."

Sojourner was fond of singing an extraordinary lyric, commencing,—

> "I'm on my way to Canada,
>   That cold but happy land;
> The dire effects of slavery
>   I can no longer stand.
> O righteous Father,
>   Do look down on me,
> And help me on to Canada,
>   Where colored folks are free!"

The lyric ran on to state that, when the fugitive crosses the Canada line,

> "The Queen comes down unto the shore,
>   With arms extended wide,
> To welcome the poor fugitive
>   Safe on to Freedom's side."

In the truth thus set forth she seemed to have the most simple faith.

But her chief delight was to talk of "glory," and to sing hymns whose burden was,—

> "O glory, glory, glory,
>   Won't you come along with me?"[16]

and when left to herself she would often hum these with great delight, nodding her head.

On one occasion I remember her sitting at a window singing, and fervently keeping time with her head, the little black Puck of a grandson meanwhile amusing himself with ornamenting her red-and-yellow turban with green dandelion curls, which shook and trembled with her emotions, causing him perfect convulsions of delight.

"Sojourner," said the Professor to her one day when he heard her singing, "you seem to be very sure about heaven."

"Well, I be," she answered triumphantly.

"What makes you so sure there is any heaven?"

"Well, 'cause I got such a hankerin' arter it in here," she said, giving a thump on her breast with her usual energy.

There was at the time an invalid in the house, and Sojourner, on learning it, felt a mission to go and comfort her. It was curious to see the tall, gaunt, dusky figure stalk up to the bed, with such an air of conscious authority, and take on herself the office of consoler with such a mixture of authority and tenderness. She talked as from above, and at the same time if a pillow needed changing, or any office to be rendered, she did it with a strength and handiness that inspired trust. One felt as if the dark, strange woman were quite able to take up the invalid in her bosom and bear her as a lamb, both physically and spiritually. There was both power and sweetness in that great warm soul and that vigorous frame.

At length Sojourner, true to her name, departed. She had her mission elsewhere. Where now she is, I know not; but she left deep memories behind her.

To these recollections of my own, I will add one more anecdote, related by Wendell Phillips.[17] Speaking of the power of Rachel to move and bear down a whole audience by a few simple words, he said he never knew but one other human being that had that power, and that other was Sojourner Truth. He related a scene of which he was witness. It was at a crowded public meeting in Faneuil Hall, where

Frederick Douglass was one of the chief speakers.[18] Douglass had been describing the wrongs of the black race, and as he proceeded he grew more and more excited, and finally ended by saying that they had no hope of justice from the whites, no possible hope except in their own right arms. It must come to blood; they must fight for themselves, and redeem themselves, or it would never be done. Sojourner was sitting, tall and dark, on the very front seat, facing the platform; and in the hush of deep feeling, after Douglass sat down, she spoke out in her deep, peculiar voice, heard all over the house,—

"Frederick, *is God dead?*"

The effect was perfectly electrical, and thrilled through the whole house, changing as by a flash the whole feeling of the audience. Not another word she said or needed to say; it was enough.

It is with a sad feeling that one contemplates noble minds and bodies, nobly and grandly formed human beings, that have come to us cramped, scarred, maimed, out of the prison-house of bondage. One longs to know what such beings might have become if suffered to unfold and expand under the kindly developing influences of education.

It is the theory of some writers that to the African is reserved, in the later and palmier days of the earth, the full and harmonious development of the religious element in man. The African seems to seize on the tropical fervor and luxuriance of Scripture imagery as something native; he appears to feel himself to be of the same blood with those old burning, simple souls, the patriarchs, prophets, and seers, whose impassioned words seem only grafted as foreign plants on the cooler stock of the Occidental mind.

I cannot but think that Sojourner, with the same culture, might have spoken words as eloquent and undying as those of the African Saint Augustine or Tertullian.[19] How grand and queenly a woman she might have been, with her wonderful physical vigor, her great heaving sea of emotion, her power of spiritual conception, her quick penetration, and her boundless energy! We might conceive an African type of woman so largely made and moulded, so much fuller in all the elements of life, physical and spiritual, that the dark hue of the skin should seem only to add an appropriate charm, as Milton says of his Penseroso, whom he imagines

"Black, but such as in esteem
Prince Memnon's sister might beseem,
Or that starred Ethiop queen that strove
To set her beauty's praise above
The sea-nymph's."[20]

But though Sojourner Truth has passed away from among us as a wave of the sea, her memory still lives in one of the loftiest and most original works of modern art, the Libyan Sibyl, by Mr. Story, which attracted so much attention in the late World's Exhibition.[21] Some years ago, when visiting Rome, I related Sojourner's history to Mr. Story at a breakfast at his house. Already had his mind begun to turn to Egypt in search of a type of art which should represent a larger and more vigorous development of nature than the cold elegance of Greek lines. His glorious Cleopatra[22] was then in process of evolution, and his mind was working out the problem of her broadly developed nature, of all that slumbering weight and fullness of passion with which this statue seems charged, as a heavy thundercloud is charged with electricity.

The history of Sojourner Truth worked in his mind and led him into the deeper recesses of the African nature,—those unexplored depths of being and feeling, mighty and dark as the gigantic depths of tropical forests, mysterious as the hidden rivers and mines of that burning continent whose life-history is yet to be. A few days after, he told me that he had conceived the idea of a statue which he should call the Libyan Sibyl. Two years subsequently, I revisited Rome, and found the gorgeous Cleopatra finished, a thing to marvel at, as the creation of a new style of beauty, a new manner of art. Mr. Story requested me to come and repeat to him the history of Sojourner Truth, saying that the conception had never left him. I did so; and a day or two after, he showed me the clay model of the Libyan Sibyl. I have never seen the marble statue, but am told by those who have that it was by far the most impressive work of art at the Exhibition.

A notice of the two statues from the London "Athenæum"²³ must supply a description which I cannot give:—

The Cleopatra and the Sibyl are seated, partly draped with the characteristic Egyptian gown, that gathers about the torso and falls freely around the limbs; the first is covered to the bosom, the second bare to the hips. Queenly Cleopatra rests back against her chair in meditative ease, leaning her cheek against one hand, whose elbow the rail of the seat sustains; the other is outstretched upon her knee, nipping its forefinger upon the thumb thoughtfully, as though some firm, willful purpose filled her brain, as it seems to set those luxurious features to a smile as if the whole woman 'would.' Upon her head is the coif, bearing in front the mystic *uræus,* or twining basilisk of sovereignty, while from its sides depend the wide Egyptian lapels, or wings, that fall upon the shoulders. The *Sibilla Libica* has crossed her knees,—an action universally held amongst the ancients as indicative of reticence or secrecy, and of power to bind. A secret-keeping looking dame she is, in the full-bloom proportions of ripe womanhood, wherein choosing to place his figure the sculptor has deftly gone between the disputed point whether these women were blooming and wise in youth, or deeply furrowed with age and burdened with the knowledge of centuries, as Virgil, Livy, and Gellius²⁴ say. Good artistic example might be quoted on both sides. Her forward elbow is propped upon one knee; and to keep her secrets closer, for this Libyan woman is the closest of all the Sibyls, she rests her shut mouth upon one closed palm, as if holding the African mystery deep in the brooding brain that looks out through mournful, warning eyes, seen under the wide shade of the strange horned (ammonite) crest, that bears the mystery of the Tetragrammaton[25] upon its upturned front. Over her full bosom, mother of myriads as she was, hangs the same symbol. Her face has a Nubian cast, her hair wavy and plaited, as is meet.

We hope to see the day when copies both of the Cleopatra and the Libyan Sibyl shall adorn the Capitol at Washington.[26]

Notes

1. October 12, 1855, the 80th birthday of the Rev. Lyman Beecher, 1775–1863, Congregational clergyman, theologian, and father of Harriet Beecher Stowe.

2. Charles Cumberworth, 1811–1852, French sculptor. A copy of the statuette, Negro Woman at the Fountain, was owned by Stowe.

3. Sammy Banks, her constant traveling companion for more than 20 years.

4. In folklore and myth, a mischievous elf, a prankster.

5. Lyman Beecher; possibly, Darcia H. Allen, 1808–1870, onetime colleague of Beecher at Lane Theological Seminary, Cincinnati, Ohio; Calvin E. Stowe, 1802–1886, professor of sacred literature and husband of Harriet Beecher Stowe.

6. John J. Dumont of New Paltz, New York, in whose household she served from 1810–1827.

7. Isaac and Maria Van Wagener, whose family name she assumed.

8.   Mandatory emancipation of slaves in New York took effect in 1827, the law having first passed in 1817. Sojourner Truth's sense of time—when she fled from the Dumonts, how long she was with the Van Wageners, the date of liberation, etc.—is often hazy.

9.   Marie Jean Paul Roch Yves Gilbert Motier, the Marquis de Lafayette, 1757–1834, French general who served in the army of the American Revolution.

10.   "Holy City," anonymous.

11.   Elisa Rachel, 1821–1858, French actress. "*La Marseillaise*," patriotic French song by Claude Joseph Rouget de Lisle and closely identified with the French Revolution. Symbolically, Ethiopa refers to black Africa.

12.   Peter, for whose return she undertook successfully legal action.

13.   Symbolically, a condition of slavery, after the biblical nation of bondage.

14.   Inscription on the Liberty Bell in Independence Hall in Philadelphia.

15.   Long, loose, ankle-length trousers for women, introduced in the 1850s by Amelia Bloomer, 1818–1894, American social reformer.

16.   Sources unknown.

17.   American abolitionist and social reformer, 1811–1884.

18.   Faneuil Hall, a site in Boston, called "the cradle of American liberty," is associated with the patriotic oratory of the American Revolutionary period and, later, with the debates of various reform movements and discussions of public issues. Frederick Douglass, 1817–1895, was a former slave, journalist, abolitionist, and reformer.

19.   Aurelius Augustinus, 354–430, Roman Catholic bishop; Quintus Septimius Florens Tertullianus, c.150-c.230, ecclesiastical writer. Both men are regarded as fathers of the Catholic church.

20.   John Milton, 1608–1674, English poet, wrote *Il Penseroso*, c. 1632.

21. The statue of the Libyan Sibyl by William Wetmore Story, 1819–1895, American sculptor, was first exhibited at the International Exhibition in London in 1862.

22. A statue of the last queen of Egypt, Cleopatra, 69 B.C.–30 B.C.

23. A London club for eminent scientists, writers, and artists.

24. Publius Vergilius Maro, 70 B.C.–19 B.C., Roman epic poet; Titus Livius, 59 B.C.–17 A.D., Roman historian; Aulus Gellius, c.130–?, Roman writer of the second century.

25. The four-letter Hebrew word for God, not spoken aloud out of respect or fear.

26. A replica of the Cleopatra is in the Metropolitan Museum of Art in New York City, while the Libyan Sibyl is in the National Galley of Art in Washington, D.C.

LETTER II.

from *Sunny Memories of Foreign Lands.*

The popularity and impact of *Uncle Tom's Cabin* prompted the abolitionist leaders of Great Britain to invite Harriet Beecher Stowe to visit in 1853. Anticipating that such a tour would provide material for another book, she asked her younger brother, Charles Beecher, to accompany her on the trip to act as an assistant to her by keeping a daily journal, which served as the basis for *Sunny Memories of Foreign Lands,* first published in 1854 in two volumes by Phillips, Sampson and Company in Boston.

Stowe adopted in *Sunny Memories* the epistolary tradition common in the 17th and 18th centuries—the device of writing letters to family and friends. In this selection she writes to her father, Lyman Beecher, about her arrival in England and her first impressions of the land and its people.

D EAR FATHER:—

It was on Sunday[1] morning that we first came in sight of land. The day was one of a thousand—clear, calm, and bright. It is one of those strange, throbbing feelings, that come only once in a while in life; this waking up to find an ocean crossed and long-lost land restored again in another hemisphere; something like what we should suppose might be the thrill of awakening from life to immortality, and all the wonders of the world unknown. That low, green line of land in the horizon is Ireland; and we, with water smooth as a lake and sails furled, are running within a mile of the shore. Every body on deck, full of spirits and expectation, busy as can be looking through spyglasses, and exclaiming at every object on shore,—

"Look! there's Skibareen, where the worst of the famine was," says one.

"Look! that's a ruined Martello tower," says another.

We new voyagers, who had never seen any ruin more imposing than that of a cow house, and, of course, were ravenous for old towers, were now quite wide awake, but were disappointed to learn that these were only custom house rendezvous. Here is the county of Cork. Some one calls out,—

"There is O'Connell's[2] house;" and a warm dispute ensues whether a large mansion, with a stone chapel by it, answers to that name. At all events the region looks desolate enough, and they say the natives of it are almost savages. A passenger remarks, that "O'Connell never really did any thing for the Irish, but lived on his capacity for exciting their enthusiasm." Thereupon another expresses great contempt for the Irish who could be so taken in. Nevertheless, the capability of a disinterested enthusiasm is, on the whole, a nobler property of a human being than a shrewd self-interest. I like the Irish all the better for it.

Now we pass Kinsale lighthouse; there is the spot where the Albion[3] was wrecked. It is a bare, frowning cliff, with walls of rock rising perpendicularly out of the sea. Now, to be sure, the sea smiles and sparkles around the base of it, as gently as if it never could storm; yet under other skies, and with a fierce south-east wind, how the waves would pour in here! Woe then to the distressed and rudderless vessel that drifts towards those fatal rocks! This gives the outmost and boldest view of the point.

The Albion struck just round the left of the point, where the rock rises perpendicularly out of the sea. I well remember, when a child, of the newspapers being filled with the dreadful story of the wreck of the ship Albion—

(*355*)

how for hours, rudderless and helpless, they saw them-selves driving with inevitable certainty against these pitiless rocks; and how, in the last struggle, one human being after another was dashed against them in helpless agony.

What an infinite deal of misery results from man's helplessness and ignorance and nature's inflexibility in this one matter of crossing the ocean! What agonies of prayer there were during all the long hours that this ship was driving straight on to these fatal rocks, all to no purpose! It struck and crushed just the same. Surely, without the reve-lation of God in Jesus, who could believe in the divine goodness? I do not wonder the old Greeks so often spoke of their gods as cruel, and believed the universe was governed by a remorseless and inexorable fate. Who would come to any other conclusion, except from the pages of the Bible?

But we have sailed far past Kinsale point. Now blue and shadowy loom up the distant form of the Youghal Mountains, (pronounced *Yoole*.) The surface of the water is alive with fishing boats, spreading their white wings and skimming about like so many moth millers.

About nine o'clock we were crossing the sand bar, which lies at the mouth of the Mersey River, running up towards Liverpool. Our signal pennants are fluttering at the mast head, pilot full of energy on one wheel house, and a man casting the lead on the other.

"By the mark, five," says the man. The pilot, with all his energy, is telegraphing to the steersman. This is a very close and complicated piece of navigation, I should think, this running up the Mersey, for every moment we are passing some kind of a signal token, which warns off from some shoal. Here is a bell buoy, where the waves keep the bell always tolling; here, a buoyant lighthouse; and "See there, those shoals, how pokerish they look!" says one of the passengers, pointing to the foam on our starboard bow. All is bustle, animation, exultation. Now float out the American stars and stripes on our bow.

Before us lies the great city of Liverpool. No old cathedral, no castles, a real New Yorkish place.

"There, that's the fort," cries one. Bang, bang, go the two guns from our forward gangway.

"I wonder if they will fire from the fort," says another.

"How green that grass looks!" says a third; "and what pretty cottages!"

"All modern, though," says somebody, in tones of disappointment. Now we are passing the Victoria Dock. Bang, bang, again. We are in a forest of ships of all nations; their masts bristling like the tall pines in Maine; their many colored flags streaming like the forest leaves in autumn.

"Hark," says one; "there's a chime of bells from the city; how sweet! I had quite forgotten it was Sunday."

Here we cast anchor, and the small steam tender comes puffing alongside. Now for the custom house officers. State rooms, holds, and cabins must all give up their trunks; a general muster among the baggage, and passenger after passenger comes forward as their names are called, much as follows: "Snooks." "Here, sir." "Any thing contraband here, Mr. Snooks? Any cigars, tobacco, &c.?" "Nothing, sir."

A little unlocking, a little fumbling. "Shut up; all right; ticket here." And a little man pastes on each article a slip of paper, with the royal arms of England and the magical letters V. R.,[4] to remind all men that they have come into a country where a lady reigns, and of course must behave themselves as prettily as they can.

We were inquiring of some friends for the most convenient hotel, when we found the son of Mr. Cropper,[5] of Dingle Bank, waiting in the cabin, to take us with him to their hospitable abode. In a few moments after the baggage had been examined, we all bade adieu to the old ship, and went on board the little steam tender, which carries passengers up to the city.

This Mersey River would be a very beautiful one, if it

were not so dingy and muddy. As we are sailing up in the tender towards Liverpool, I deplore the circumstance feelingly. "What does make this river so muddy?"

"O," says a bystander, "don't you know that

'The quality of mercy is not strained'?"[6]

And now we are fairly alongside the shore, and we are soon going to set our foot on the land of Old England.

Say what we will, an American, particularly a New Englander, can never approach the old country without a kind of thrill and pulsation of kindred. Its history for two centuries was our history. Its literature, laws, and language are our literature, laws, and language. Spenser, Shakspeare, Bacon, Milton, were a glorious inheritance, which we share in common.[7] Our very life-blood is English life-blood. It is Anglo-Saxon vigor that is spreading our country from Atlantic to Pacific, and leading on a new era in the world's development. America is a tall, sightly young shoot, that has grown from the old royal oak of England; divided from its parent root, it has shot up in new, rich soil, and under genial, brilliant skies, and therefore takes on a new type of growth and foliage, but the sap in it is the same.

I had an early opportunity of making acquaintance with my English brethren; for, much to my astonishment, I found quite a crowd on the wharf, and we walked up to our carriage through a long lane of people, bowing, and looking very glad to see us. When I came to get into the hack it was surrounded by more faces than I could count. They stood very quietly, and looked very kindly, though evidently very much determined to look. Something prevented the hack from moving on; so the interview was prolonged for some time. I therefore took occasion to remark the very fair, pure complexions, the clear eyes, and the general air of health and vigor, which seem to characterize our brethren and sisters of the island. There seemed to be no occasion to ask them how they did, as they were evidently quite well. Indeed, this air of health is one of the most striking things when one lands in England.

They were not burly, red-faced, and stout, as I had sometimes conceived of the English people, but just full enough to suggest the idea of vigor and health. The presence of so many healthy, rosy people looking at me, all reduced as I was, first by land and then by sea sickness, made me feel myself more withered and forlorn than ever. But there was an earnestness and a depth of kind feeling in some of the faces, which I shall long remember. It seemed as if I had not only touched the English shore, but felt the English heart.

Our carriage at last drove on, taking us through Liverpool, and a mile or two out, and at length wound its way along the gravel paths of a beautiful little retreat, on the banks of the Mersey, called the "Dingle." It opened to my eyes like a paradise, all wearied as I was with the tossing of the sea. I have since become familiar with these beautiful little spots, which are so common in England; but now all was entirely new to me.

We rode by shining clumps of the Portugal laurel, a beautiful evergreen, much resembling our mountain rhododendron; then there was the prickly, polished, dark-green holly, which I had never seen before, but which is, certainly, one of the most perfect of shrubs. The turf was of that soft, dazzling green, and had that peculiar velvet-like smoothness, which seem characteristic of England. We stopped at last before the door of a cottage, whose porch was overgrown with ivy. From that moment I ceased to feel myself a stranger in England. I cannot tell you how delightful to me, dizzy and weary as I was, was the first sight of the chamber of reception which had been prepared for us. No item of cozy comfort that one could desire was omitted. The sofa and easy chair wheeled up before a cheerful coal fire, a bright little teakettle steaming in front of the grate, a table with a beautiful vase of flowers, books, and writing apparatus, and kind friends with words full of affectionate cheer,—all these made me feel at home in a moment.

The hospitality of England has become famous in the world, and, I think, with reason. I doubt not there is just as much hospitable feeling in other countries; but in England the matter of coziness and home comfort has been so studied, and matured, and reduced to system, that they really have it in their power to effect more, towards making their guests comfortable, than perhaps any other people.

After a short season allotted to changing our ship garments and for rest, we found ourselves seated at the dinner table. While dining, the sister-in-law of our friends came in from the next door, to exchange a word or two of welcome, and invite us to breakfast with them the following morning.

Between all the excitements of landing, and meeting so many new faces, and the remains of the dizzy motion of the ship, which still haunted me, I found it impossible to close my eyes to sleep that first night till the dim gray of dawn. I got up as soon as it was light, and looked out of the window; and as my eyes fell on the luxuriant, ivy-covered porch, the clumps of shining, dark-green holly bushes, I said to myself, "Ah, really, this is England!"

I never saw any plant that struck me as more beautiful than this holly. It is a dense shrub growing from six to eight feet high, with a thickly varnished leaf of green. The outline of the leaf is something like this. I do not believe it can ever come to a state of perfect development under the fierce alternations of heat and cold which obtain in our New England climate, though it grows in the Southern States. It is one of the symbolical shrubs of England, probably because its bright green in winter makes it so splendid a Christmas decoration. A little bird sat twittering on one of the sprays. He had a bright red breast, and seemed evidently to consider himself of good blood and family, with the best reason, as I afterwards learned, since he was no other than the identical robin redbreast renowned in song and story; undoubtedly a lineal descendant of that very cock robin whose death and burial form so vivid a portion of our childish literature.[8]

I must tell you, then, as one of the first remarks on matters and things here in England, that "robin redbreast" is not at all the fellow we in America take him to be. The character who flourishes under that name among us is quite a different bird; he is twice as large, and has altogether a different air, and as he sits up with military erectness on a rail fence or stump, shows not even a family likeness to his diminutive English namesake. Well, of course, robin over here will claim to have the real family estate and title, since he lives in a country where such matters are understood and looked into. Our robin is probably some fourth cousin, who, like others, has struck out a new course for himself in America, and thrives upon it.

We hurried to dress, remembering our engagements to breakfast this morning with a brother of our host, whose cottage stands on the same ground, within a few steps of our own. I had not the slightest idea of what the English mean by a breakfast, and therefore went in all innocence, supposing that I should see nobody but the family circle of my acquaintances. Quite to my astonishment, I found a party of between thirty and forty people. Ladies sitting with their bonnets on, as in a morning call. It was impossible, however, to feel more than a momentary embarrassment in the friendly warmth and cordiality of the circle by whom we were surrounded.

The English are called cold and stiff in their manners; I had always heard they were so, but I certainly saw nothing of it here. A circle of family relatives could not have received us with more warmth and kindness. The remark which I made mentally, as my eye passed around the circle, was—Why, these people are just like home; they look like us, and the tone of sentiment and feeling is precisely such

(361)

as I have been accustomed to; I mean with the exception of the antislavery question.

That question has, from the very first, been, in England, a deeply religious movement. It was conceived and carried on by men of devotional habits, in the same spirit in which the work of foreign missions was undertaken in our own country; by just such earnest, self-denying, devout men as Samuel J. Mills and Jeremiah Evarts.[9]

It was encountered by the same contempt and opposition, in the outset, from men of merely worldly habits and principles; and to this day it retains that hold on the devotional mind of the English nation that the foreign mission cause[10] does in America.

Liverpool was at first to the antislavery cause nearly what New York has been with us. Its commercial interests were largely implicated in the slave trade, and the virulence of opposition towards the first movers of the antislavery reform in Liverpool was about as great as it is now against abolitionists in Charleston.[11]

When Clarkson[12] first came here to prosecute his inquiries into the subject, a mob collected around him, and endeavored to throw him off the dock into the water; he was rescued by a gentleman, some of whose descendants I met on this occasion.

The father of our host, Mr. Cropper, was one of the first and most efficient supporters of the cause in Liverpool; and the whole circle was composed of those who had taken a deep interest in that struggle. The wife of our host was the daughter of the celebrated Lord Chief Justice Denman,[13] a man who, for many years, stood unrivalled, at the head of the legal mind in England, and who, with a generous ardor seldom equalled, devoted all his energies to this sacred cause.

When the publication of Uncle Tom's Cabin turned the attention of the British public to the existing horrors of slavery in America, some palliations of the system appeared in English papers. Lord Denman, though then in delicate health and advanced years, wrote a series of letters upon the subject—an exertion which entirely prostrated his before feeble health. In one of the addresses made at table, a very feeling allusion was made to Lord Denman's labors, and also to those of the honored father of the two Messrs. Cropper.

As breakfast parties are things which we do not have in America, perhaps mother[14] would like to know just how they are managed. The hour is generally somewhere between nine and twelve, and the whole idea and spirit of the thing is that of an informal and social gathering. Ladies keep their bonnets on, and are not dressed in full toilet. On this occasion we sat and chatted together socially till the whole party was assembled in the drawing room, and then breakfast was announced. Each gentleman had a lady assigned him, and we walked into the dining room, where stood the tables tastefully adorned with flowers, and spread with an abundant cold collation, while tea and coffee were passed round by servants. In each plate was a card, containing the name of the person for whom it was designed. I took my place by the side of the Rev. Dr. McNiel,[15] one of the most celebrated clergymen of the established church in Liverpool.

The conversation was flowing, free, and friendly. The old reminiscences of the antislavery conflict in England were touchingly recalled, and the warmest sympathy was expressed for those in America who are carrying on the same cause.

In one thing I was most agreeably disappointed. I had been told that the Christians of England were intolerant and unreasonable in their opinions on this subject; that they could not be made to understand the peculiar difficulties which beset it in America, and that they therefore made no distinction and no allowance in their censures. All this I found, so far as this circle were concerned, to be strikingly untrue. They appeared to be peculiarly affectionate in their feelings as regarded our country; to have the highest appreciation of, and the deepest sympathy with, our religious community, and to be extremely desirous to assist us in our difficulties. I also found them remarkably well informed upon the subject. They keep their eyes upon our papers, our public documents and speeches in Congress, and are as well advised in regard to the progress of the moral conflict as our Foreign Missionary Society is with the state of affairs in Hindostan and Burmah.

Several present spoke of the part which England originally had in planting slavery in America, as placing English Christians under a solemn responsibility to bring every possible moral influence to bear for its extinction. Nevertheless, they seem to be the farthest possible from an unkind or denunciatory spirit, even towards those most deeply implicated. The remarks made by Dr. McNiel to me were a fair sample of the spirit and attitude of all present.

"I have been trying, Mrs. S.," he said, "to bring my mind into the attitude of those Christians at the south who defend the institution of slavery. There are *real* Christians there who do this—are there not?"

I replied, that undoubtedly there were some most amiable and Christian people who defend slavery on principle, just as there had been some to defend every form of despotism.

"Do give me some idea of the views they take; it is something to me so inconceivable. I am utterly at a loss how it can be made in any way plausible."

I then stated that the most plausible view, and that which seemed to have the most force with good men, was one which represented the institution of slavery as a sort of wardship or guardian relation, by which an inferior race were brought under the watch and care of a superior race to be instructed in Christianity.

He then inquired if there was any system of religious instruction actually pursued.

In reply to this, I gave him some sketch of the operations for the religious instruction of the negroes, which had been carried on by the Presbyterian and other denominations. I remarked that many good people who do not take very extended views, fixing their attention chiefly on the efforts which they are making for the religious instruction of slaves, are blind to the sin and injustice of allowing their legal position to remain what it is.

"But how do they shut their eyes to the various cruelties of the system,—the separation of families—the domestic slave trade?"

I replied, "In part, by not inquiring into them. The best kind of people are, in general, those who *know* least of the cruelties of the system; they never witness them. As in the city of London or Liverpool there may be an amount of crime and suffering which many residents may live years without seeing or knowing, so it is in the slave states."

Every person present appeared to be in that softened and charitable frame of mind which disposed them to make every allowance for the situation of Christians so peculiarly tempted, while, at the same time, there was the most earnest concern, in view of the dishonor brought upon Christianity by the defence of such a system.

One other thing I noticed, which was an agreeable disappointment to me. I had been told that there was no social intercourse between the established church and dissenters. In this party, however, were people of many different denominations. Our host belongs to the established church; his brother, with whom we are visiting, is a Baptist, and their father was a Friend; and there appeared to be the utmost social cordiality.[16] Whether I shall find this uniformly the case will appear in time.

After the breakfast party was over, I found at the door an array of children of the poor, belonging to a school kept under the superintendence of Mrs. E. Cropper, and called, as is customary here, a ragged school.[17] The children, however, were any thing but ragged, being tidily dressed, remarkably clean, with glowing cheeks and bright eyes. I must say, so far as I have seen them, English children have a much healthier appearance than those of America. By the side of their bright bloom ours look pale and faded.

Another school of the same kind is kept in this neighborhood, under the auspices of Sir George Stephen,[18] a conspicuous advocate of the antislavery cause.

I thought the fair patroness of this school seemed not a little delighted with the appearance of her protégés, as they sung, with great enthusiasm, Jane Taylor's hymn, commencing,—

> 'I thank the goodness and the grace
> That on my birth have smiled,
> And made me in these Christian days
> A happy English child."[19]

All the little rogues were quite familiar with Topsy and Eva, and *au fait* in the fortunes of Uncle Tom;[20] so that, being introduced as the maternal relative of these characters, I seemed to find favor in their eyes. And when one of the speakers congratulated them that they were born in a land where no child could be bought or sold, they responded with enthusiastic cheers—cheers which made me feel rather sad; but still I could not quarrel with English people for taking all the pride and all the comfort which this inspiriting truth can convey.

They had a hard enough struggle in rooting up the old weed of slavery, to justify them in rejoicing in their freedom. Well, the day will come in America, as I trust, when as much can be said for us.

After the children were gone came a succession of calls; some from very aged people, the veterans of the old antislavery cause. I was astonished and overwhelmed by the fervor of feeling some of them manifested; there seemed to be something almost prophetic in the enthusiasm with which they expressed their hope of our final success in America. This excitement, though very pleasant, was wearisome, and I was glad of an opportunity after dinner to rest myself, by rambling uninterrupted, with my friends, through the beautiful grounds of the Dingle.

Two nice little boys were my squires on this occasion, one of whom, a sturdy little fellow, on being asked his name, gave it to me in full as Joseph Babington Macaulay, and I learned that his mother, by a former marriage, had been the wife of Macaulay's brother. Uncle Tom Macaulay,[21] I found, was a favorite character with the young people. Master Harry conducted me through the walks to the conservatories, all brilliant with azaleas and all sorts of flowers, and then through a long walk on the banks of the Mersey.

Here the wild flowers attracted my attention, as being so different from those of our own country. Their daisy is not our flower, with its wide, plaited ruff and yellow centre. The English daisy is

"The wee modest crimson-tipped flower,"

which Burns celebrates.[22] It is what we raise in greenhouses, and call the mountain daisy. Its effect, growing profusely about fields and grass plats, is very beautiful.

We read much, among the poets, of the primrose,

"Earliest daughter of the Spring.[23]

This flower is one, also, which we cultivate in gardens to some extent. The outline of it is as follows: The hue a delicate straw color; it grows in tufts in shady places, and has a pure, serious look, which reminds one of the line of Shakespeare—

"Pale primroses, which die unmarried."[24]

It has also the faintest and most ethereal perfume,—a perfume that seems to come and go in the air like music; and you perceive it at a little distance from a tuft of them, when you would not if you gathered and smelled them. On the whole, the primrose is a poet's and a painter's flower. An artist's eye would notice an exquisite harmony between the yellow-green hue of its leaves and the tint of its blossoms. I do not wonder that it has been so great a favorite among the poets. It is just such a flower as Mozart and Raphael would have loved.[25]

Then there is the bluebell, a bulb, which also grows in deep shades. It is a little purple bell, with a narrow green leaf, like a ribbon. We often read in English stories, of the gorse and furze; these are two names for the same plant, a low bush, with strong, prickly leaves, growing much like a juniper. The contrast of its very brilliant yellow, pea-shaped blossoms, with the dark green of its leaves, is very beautiful. It grows here in hedges and on commons, and is thought rather a plebeian affair. I think it would make quite an addition to our garden shrubbery. Possibly it might make as much sensation with us as our mullein does in foreign greenhouses.

After rambling a while, we came to a beautiful summer house, placed in a retired spot, so as to command a view of the Mersey River. I think they told me that it was Lord Denman's favorite seat. There we sat down, and in common with the young gentlemen and ladies of the family, had quite a pleasant talk together. Among other things we talked about the question which is now agitating the public mind a good deal,—Whether it is expedient to open the Crystal Palace[26] to the people on Sunday. They said that this course was much urged by some philanthropists, on the ground that it was the only day when the working classes could find any leisure to visit it, and that it seemed hard to shut them out entirely from all the opportunities and advantages which they might thus derive; that to exclude the laborer from recreation on the Sabbath, was the same as saying that he should never have any recreation. I asked, why the philanthropists could not urge employers to give their workmen a part of Saturday for this purpose; as it seemed to me unchristian to drive trade so that the laboring man had no time but Sunday for intellectual and social recreation. We rather came to the conclusion that this was the right course; whether the people of England will, is quite another matter.

The grounds of the Dingle embrace three cottages; those of the two Messrs. Cropper, and that of a son, who is married to a daughter of Dr. Arnold.[27] I rather think this way of relatives living together is more common here in England than it is in America; and there is more idea of home permanence connected with the family dwelling-place than with us, where the country is so wide, and causes of change and removal so frequent. A man builds a house in England with the expectation of living in it and leaving it to his children; while we shed our houses in America as easily as a snail does his shell. We live a while in Boston, and then a while in New York, and then, perhaps, turn up at Cincinnati. Scarcely any body with us is living where they expect to live and die. The man that dies in the house he was born in is a wonder. There is something pleasant in the permanence and repose of the English family estate, which we, in America, know very little of. All which is apropos to our having finished our walk, and got back to the ivy-covered porch again.

The next day at breakfast, it was arranged that we should take a drive out to Speke Hall, an old mansion, which is considered a fine specimen of ancient house architecture. So the carriage was at the door. It was a cool, breezy, April morning, but there was an abundance of wrappers and carriage blankets provided to keep us comfortable. I must say, by the by, that English housekeepers are bountiful in their provision for carriage comfort. Every household has a store of warm, loose over garments, which are offered, if needed, to the guests; and each carriage is provided with one or two blankets, manufactured and sold expressly for this use, to envelope one's feet and limbs; besides all which, should the weather be cold, comes out a long stone reservoir, made flat on both sides, and filled with hot water, for foot stools. This is an improvement on the primitive simplicity of hot bricks, and even on the tin foot stove, which has flourished in New England.

Being thus provided with all things necessary for comfort, we rattled merrily away, and I, remembering that I was in England, kept my eyes wide open to see what I could see. The hedges of the fields were just budding, and the green showed itself on them, like a thin gauze veil. These hedges are not all so well kept and trimmed as I expected to find them. Some, it is true, are cut very carefully; these are generally hedges to ornamental grounds; but many of those which separate the fields straggle and sprawl, and have some high bushes and some low ones, and, in short, are no more like a hedge than many rows of bushes that we have at home. But such as they are, they are the only dividing lines of the fields, and it is certainly a more picturesque mode of division than our stone or worm fences. Outside of every hedge, towards the street, there is generally a ditch, and at the bottom of the hedge is the favorite nestling-place for all sorts of wild flowers. I remember reading in stories about children trying to crawl through a gap in the hedge to get at flowers, and tumbling into a ditch on the other side, and I now saw exactly how they could do it.

As we drive we pass by many beautiful establishments, about of the quality of our handsomest country houses, but whose grounds are kept with a precision and exactness rarely to be seen among us. We cannot get the gardeners who are qualified to do it; and if we could, the painstaking, slow way of proceeding, and the habit of creeping thoroughness, which are necessary to accomplish such results, die out in America. Nevertheless, such grounds are exceedingly beautiful to look upon, and I was much obliged to the owners of these places for keeping their gates hospitably open, as seems to be the custom here.

After a drive of seven or eight miles, we alighted in front of Speke Hall. This house is a specimen of the old fortified houses of England, and was once fitted up with a moat and drawbridge, all in approved feudal style. It was built somewhere about the year 1500. The sometime moat was now full of smooth, green grass, and the drawbridge no longer remains.

This was the first really old thing that we had seen since our arrival in England. We came up first to a low, arched, stone door, and knocked with a great old-fashioned knocker; this brought no answer but a treble and bass duet from a couple of dogs inside; so we opened the door, and saw a square court, paved with round stones, and a dark, solitary yew tree in the centre. Here in England, I think, they have vegetable creations made on purpose to go with old, dusky buildings; and this yew tree is one of them. It has altogether a most goblin-like, bewitched air, with its dusky black leaves and ragged branches, throwing themselves straight out with odd twists and angular lines, and might put one in mind of an old raven with some of his feathers pulled out, or a black cat with her hair stroked the wrong way, or any other strange, uncanny thing. Besides this they live almost forever; for when they have grown so old that any respectable tree ought to be thinking of dying, they only take another twist, and so live on another hundred years. I saw some in England seven hundred years old, and they had grown queerer every century. It is a species of evergreen, and its leaf resembles our hemlock, only it is longer. This sprig gives you some idea of its general form. It is always planted about churches and graveyards; a kind of dismal emblem of immortality. This sepulchral old tree and the bass and treble dogs were the only occupants of the court. One of these, a great surly mastiff, barked out of his kennel on one side, and the other, a little wiry terrier, out of his on the opposite side, and both strained on their chains, as if they would enjoy making even more decided demonstrations if they could.

There was an aged, mossy fountain for holy water by the side of the wall, in which some weeds were growing. A door in the house was soon opened by a decent-looking serving woman, to whom we communicated our desire to see the hall.

We were shown into a large dining hall with a stone floor, wainscoted with carved oak, almost as black as ebony. There were some pious sentences and moral reflections inscribed in old English text, carved over the doors, and like a cornice round the ceiling, which was also of carved oak. Their general drift was, to say that life is short, and to call for watchfulness and prayer. The fireplace of the hall yawned like a great cavern, and nothing else, one would think, than a cart load of western sycamores could have supplied an appropriate fire. A great two-handed sword of some ancestor hung over the fireplace. On taking it down it reached to C——'s[28] shoulder, who, you know, is six feet high.

We went into a sort of sitting room, and looked out through a window, latticed with little diamond panes, upon a garden wildly beautiful. The lattice was all wreathed round with jessamines. The furniture of this room was modern, and it seemed the more unique from its contrast with the old architecture.

We went up stairs to see the chambers, and passed through a long, narrow, black oak corridor, whose slippery boards had the authentic ghostly squeak to them. There was a chamber, hung with old, faded tapestry of Scripture subjects. In this chamber there was behind the tapestry a door, which, being opened, displayed a staircase, that led delightfully off to nobody knows where. The furniture was black oak, carved, in the most elaborate manner, with cherubs' heads and other good and solemn subjects, calculated to produce a ghostly state of mind. And, to crown all, we heard that there was a haunted chamber, which was not to be opened, where a white lady appeared and walked at all approved hours.

Now, only think what a foundation for a story is here. If our Hawthorne could conjure up such a thing as the Seven Gables[29] in one of our prosaic country towns, what would he have done if he had lived here? Now he is obliged to get his ghostly images by looking through smoked glass at our square, cold realities; but one such old place as this is a standing romance. Perhaps it may add to the effect to say, that the owner of the house is a bachelor, who lives there very retired, and employs himself much in reading.

The housekeeper, who showed us about, indulged us with a view of the kitchen, whose snowy, sanded floor and resplendent polished copper and tin, were sights for a housekeeper to take away in her heart of hearts. The good woman produced her copy of Uncle Tom, and begged the favor of my autograph, which I gave, thinking it quite a happy thing to be able to do a favor at so cheap a rate.

After going over the house we wandered through the grounds, which are laid out with the same picturesque mixture of the past and present. There was a fine grove, under whose shadows we walked, picking primroses, and otherwise enacting the poetic, till it was time to go. As we passed out, we were again saluted with a *feu de joie* by the two fidelities at the door, which we took in very good part, since it is always respectable to be thorough in whatever you are set to do.

Coming home we met with an accident to the carriage which obliged us to get out and walk some distance. I was glad enough of it, because it gave me a better opportunity for seeing the country. We stopped at a cottage to get some rope, and a young woman came out with that beautiful, clear complexion which I so much admire here in England; literally her cheeks were like damask roses.

I told Isa I wanted to see as much of the interior of the cottages as I could; and so, as we were walking onward toward home, we managed to call once or twice, on the excuse of asking the way and distance. The exterior was very neat, being built of brick or stone, and each had attached to it a little flower garden. Isa said that the cottagers often offered them a slice of bread or tumbler of milk.

They have a way here of building the cottages two or three in a block together, which struck me as different from our New England manner, where, in the country, every house stands detached.

In the evening I went into Liverpool, to attend a party of friends of the antislavery cause. In the course of the evening, Mr. Stowe[30] was requested to make some remarks. Among other things he spoke upon the support the free part of the world give to slavery, by the purchase of the produce of slave labor; and, in particular, on the great quantity of slave-grown cotton purchased by England; suggesting it as a subject for inquiry, whether this cannot be avoided.

One or two gentlemen, who are largely concerned in the manufacture and importation of cotton, spoke to him on the subject afterwards, and said it was a thing which ought to be very seriously considered. It is probable that the cotton trade of Great Britain is the great essential item which supports slavery, and such considerations ought not, therefore, to be without their results.

When I was going away, the lady of the house said that the servants were anxious to see me; so I came into the dressing room to give them an opportunity.

While at Mr. C.'s,[31] also, I had once or twice been called out to see servants, who had come in to visit those of the family. All of them had read Uncle Tom's Cabin, and were full of sympathy. Generally speaking, the servants seem to me quite a superior class to what are employed in that capacity with us. They look very intelligent, are dressed with great neatness, and though their manners are very much more deferential than those of servants in our country, it appears to be a difference arising quite as much from self-respect and a sense of propriety as from servility. Every body's manners are more deferential in England than in America.

The next day was appointed to leave Liverpool. It had been arranged that, before leaving, we should meet the ladies of the Negroes' Friend Society, an association formed at the time of the original antislavery agitation in England. We went in the carriage with our friends Mr. and Mrs. E. Cropper. On the way they were conversing upon the labors of Mrs. Chisholm,[32] the celebrated female philanthropist, whose efforts for the benefit of emigrants are awakening a very general interest among all classes in England. They said there had been hesitation on the part of some good people, in regard to coöperating with her, because she is a Roman Catholic.

It was agreed among us, that the great humanities of the present day are a proper ground on which all sects can unite, and that if any feared the extension of wrong sentiments, they had only to supply emigrant ships more abundantly with the Bible. Mr. C. said that this is a movement exciting very extensive interest, and that they hoped Mrs. Chisholm would visit Liverpool before long.

The meeting was a very interesting one. The style of feeling expressed in all the remarks was tempered by a deep and earnest remembrance of the share which England originally had in planting the evil of slavery in the civilized world, and her consequent obligation, as a Christian nation, now not to cease her efforts until the evil is extirpated, not merely from her own soil, but from all lands.

The feeling towards America was respectful and friendly, and the utmost sympathy was expressed with her in the difficulties with which she is environed by this evil. The tone of the meeting was deeply earnest and religious. They presented us with a sum to be appropriated for the benefit of the slave, in any way we might think proper.

A great number of friends accompanied us to the cars, and a beautiful bouquet of flowers was sent, with a very affecting message from a sick gentleman, who, from the retirement of his chamber, felt a desire to testify his sympathy.

Now, if all this enthusiasm for freedom and humanity, in the person of the American slave, is to be set down as good for nothing in England, because there are evils there in society which require redress, what then shall we say of ourselves? Have we not been enthusiastic for freedom in the person of the Greek, the Hungarian, and the Pole, while protecting a much worse despotism than any from which they suffer? Do we not consider it our duty to print and distribute the Bible in all foreign lands, when there are three millions of people among whom we dare not distribute it at home, and whom it is a penal offence even to teach to read it? Do we not send remonstrances to Tuscany, about the Madiai, when women are imprisoned in Virginia for teaching slaves to read?[33] Is all this hypocritical, insincere, and impertinent in us? Are we never to send another missionary, or make another appeal for foreign lands, till we have abolished slavery at home? For my part, I think that imperfect and inconsistent outbursts of generosity and feeling are a great deal better than none. No nation, no individual is wholly consistent and Christian; but let us not in ourselves or in other nations repudiate the truest and most beautiful developments of humanity, because we have not yet attained perfection.

All experience has proved that the sublime spirit of foreign missions always is suggestive of home philanthropies, and that those whose heart has been enlarged by the love of all mankind are always those who are most efficient in their own particular sphere.

Notes

1. Actually, Saturday, April 9, 1853, according to Charles Beecher, 1815–1900, minister-brother of Stowe, who accompanied her on this trip and at her request kept a diary, upon which *Sunny Memories of Foreign Lands* is based. Stowe merged the entries for Saturday and Sunday for her letter.

2. Daniel O'Connell, 1775–1847, Irish statesman, called "the Liberator" of his country.

3. On April 22, 1822, the *Albion* was shipwrecked off the coast of Ireland. drowning Alexander Metcalf Fisher, a Yale professor of mathematics and natural philosophy and the fiancé of Catharine Esther Beecher, oldest sister of Stowe.

4. V.R., *Victoria Regina*, Alexandrina Victoria, 1819–1901, queen of Great Britain and Ireland, 1837–1901.

5. In Liverpool Stowe was the houseguest of John Cropper and his wife.

6. From *The Merchant of Venice* by William Shakespeare, 1564–1616, English dramatist.

7. Edmund Spenser, c.1552–1599, poet; William Shakespeare; Francis Bacon, 1561–1626, philosopher; John Milton, 1608–1674, poet.

8. "Who Killed Cock Robin?" Anonymous, nursery rhyme.

9. Samuel John Mills, 1783–1818, American clergyman; Jeremiah Evarts, 1781–1831, American lawyer, editor, and philanthropist.

10. A religious movement to Christianize peoples in lands other than America.

11. In South Carolina, one of the chief commercial seaports in the south and a center of antiabolitionist sentiment.

12. Thomas Clarkson, 1760–1846, English abolitionist.

13. Thomas Denman, 1779–1854, English jurist and, from 1832–1850, lord chief-justice, defended the publication of *Uncle Tom's Cabin* in England.

14. Lydia Beals Jackson Beecher, 1789–1869, third wife of Lyman Beecher and stepmother of Stowe.

15. Actually, Hugh McNeile, 1795–1879, Anglican clergyman.

16. The established (official and state-supported) church is the Church of England (Anglican). Dissenting churches are those Protestant churches not conforming to the principles of the Anglican Church. A Friend is more commonly known as a Quaker.

17. Mrs. Edward Cropper, sister-in-law of Stowe's host in Liverpool and herself hostess of the breakfast party, sponsored a free school for poor children of the city.

18. George Stephen, 1794–1879, lawyer, author, and reformer.

19. Jane Taylor, 1783–1824, English poet and author.

20. Characters in *Uncle Tom's Cabin*.

21. Thomas Babington Macaulay, 1800–1859, English historian.

22. From "To a Mountain Daisy" by Robert Burns, 1759–1796, Scottish poet.

23. Source unknown.

24. "Pale primroses, that die unmarried." From *The Winter's Tale*.

25. Wolfgang Amadeus Mozart, 1756–1791, Austrian composer; Raphael Sanzio, 1483–1520, Italian painter.

26. An exhibition hall originally built in London in 1851 and in 1852–1853 reerected in Sydenham, near London.

27. Not further identified.

28. Charles Beecher, Stowe's brother.

29. Nathaniel Hawthorne, 1804–1864, American author, wrote *The House of the Seven Gables* in 1851.

30. Calvin Ellis Stowe, 1802–1886, professor, minister, and husband of Stowe.

31. John Cropper, Stowe's host in Liverpool.

32. Caroline Jones Chisholm, 1808–1877, British reformer for the emigrant movement.

33. Tuscany, a region in the west center of Italy, was the site of numerous civil disturbances in the 1800s.

WHAT WILL YOU DO WITH HER?
OR, THE WOMAN QUESTION
from *The Chimney-Corner*

For a number of years Harriet Beecher Stowe wrote a column for the *Atlantic Monthly*. Under the pseudonym of
Christopher Crowfield she discussed a wide range of topics,
among them woman's place in society, the occupations
suited to womanhood, and the various aspects of woman
suffrage. The two essays here were first published in the
concluding months of 1865—"What Will You Do with Her?
Or, the Woman Question" and "Woman's Sphere." In 1868
several of her magazine columns were issued in book for-
mat under the title of *The Chimney-Corner,* the same name
she used for her column.

"Well, what will you do with her?" said I to my wife.

My wife had just come down from an interview with a
pale, faded-looking young woman in rusty black attire, who
had called upon me on the very common supposition that I
was an editor of the "Atlantic Monthly."[1]

By the by, this is a mistake that brings me, Christopher
Crowfield, many letters that do not belong to me, and
which might with equal pertinency be addressed, "To the
Man in the Moon." Yet these letters often make my heart
ache,—they speak so of people who strive and sorrow and
want help; and it is hard to be called on in plaintive tones
for help which you know it is perfectly impossible for you to
give.

(*380*)

For instance, you get a letter in a delicate hand, setting forth the old distress,—she is poor, and she has looking to her for support those that are poorer and more helpless than herself: she has tried sewing, but can make little at it; tried teaching, but cannot now get a school,—all places being filled, and more than filled; at last has tried literature, and written some little things, of which she sends you a modest specimen, and wants your opinion whether she can gain her living by writing. You run over the articles, and perceive at a glance that there is no kind of hope or use in her trying to do anything at literature; and then you ask yourself mentally, "What is to be done with her? What can she do?"

Such was the application that had come to me this morning,—only, instead of by note, it came, as I have said, in the person of the applicant, a thin, delicate, consumptive-looking being, wearing that rusty mourning which speaks sadly at once of heart bereavement and material poverty.

My usual course is to turn such cases over to Mrs. Crowfield; and it is to be confessed that this worthy woman spends a large portion of her time, and wears out an extraordinary amount of shoe-leather, in performing the duties of a self-constituted intelligence office.[2] Talk of giving money to the poor! what is that, compared to giving sympathy, thought, time, taking their burdens upon you, sharing their perplexities? They who are able to buy off every application at the door of their heart with a five or ten dollar bill are those who free themselves at least expense.

My wife had communicated to our friend, in the gentlest tones and in the blandest manner, that her poor little pieces, however interesting to her own household circle, had nothing in them wherewith to enable her to make her way in the thronged and crowded thoroughfare of letters,—that they had no more strength or adaptation to win bread for her than a broken-winged butterfly to draw a plough; and it took some resolution in the background of her tenderness to make the poor applicant entirely certain of this. In cases like this, absolute certainty is the very greatest, the only true kindness.

It was grievous, my wife said, to see the discouraged shade which passed over her thin, tremulous features when this certainty forced itself upon her. It is hard, when sinking in the waves, to see the frail bush at which the hand clutches uprooted; hard, when alone in the crowded thoroughfare of travel, to have one's last bank-note declared a counterfeit. I knew I should not be able to see her face, under the shade of this disappointment; and so, coward that I was, I turned this trouble, where I have turned so many others, upon my wife.

"Well, what shall we do with her?" said I.

"I really don't know," said my wife musingly.

"Do you think we could get that school in Taunton[3] for her?"

"Impossible; Mr. Herbert told me he had already twelve applicants for it."

"Couldn't you get her plain sewing? Is she handy with her needle?"

"She has tried that, but it brings on a pain in her side, and cough; and the doctor has told her it will not do for her to confine herself."

"How is her handwriting? Does she write a good hand?"

"Only passable."

"Because," said I, "I was thinking if I could get Steele and Simpson to give her law papers to copy."

"They have more copyists than they need now; and, in fact, this woman does not write the sort of hand at all that would enable her to get on as a copyist."

"Well," said I, turning uneasily in my chair, and at last hitting on a bright masculine expedient, "I'll tell you what must be done. She must get married."

"My dear," said my wife, "marrying for a living is the very hardest way a woman can take to get it. Even marrying for love often turns out badly enough. Witness poor Jane."

Jane was one of the large number of people whom it seemed my wife's fortune to carry through life on her back. She was a pretty, smiling, pleasing daughter of Erin, who had been in our family originally as nursery-maid. I had been greatly pleased in watching a little idyllic affair growing up between her and a joyous, good-natured young Irishman, to whom at last we married her. Mike soon after, however, took to drinking and unsteady courses; and the result has been to Jane only a yearly baby, with poor health and no money.

"In fact," said my wife, "if Jane had only kept single, she could have made her own way well enough, and might have now been in good health and had a pretty sum in the savings bank. As it is, I must carry not only her, but her three children, on my back."

"You ought to drop her, my dear. You really ought not to burden yourself with other people's affairs as you do," said I inconsistently.

"How can I drop her? Can I help knowing that she is poor and suffering? And if I drop her, who will take her up?"

Now there is a way of getting rid of cases of this kind, spoken of in a quaint old book, which occurred strongly to me at this moment:—

"If a brother or sister be naked, and destitute of daily food, and one of you say unto them, 'Depart in peace, be ye warmed and filled,' notwithstanding ye give them not those things which are needful to the body, what doth it profit?"[4]

I must confess, notwithstanding the strong point of the closing question, I looked with an evil eye of longing on this very easy way of disposing of such cases. A few sympathizing words, a few expressions of hope that I did not feel, a line written to turn the case into somebody else's hands,—

any expedient, in fact, to hide the longing eyes and imploring hands from my sight,—was what my carnal nature at this moment greatly craved.

"Besides," said my wife, resuming the thread of her thoughts in regard to the subject just now before us, "as to marriage, it's out of the question at present for this poor child; for the man she loved and would have married lies low in one of the graves before Richmond. It's a sad story,—one of a thousand like it. She brightened for a few moments, and looked almost handsome, when she spoke of his bravery and goodness. Her father and lover have both died in this war.[5] Her only brother has returned from it a broken-down cripple, and she has him and her poor old mother to care for, and so she seeks work. I told her to come again to-morrow, and I would look about for her a little to-day."

"Let me see, how many are now down on your list to be looked about for, Mrs. Crowfield?—some twelve or thirteen, are there not? You've got Tom's sister disposed of finally, I hope,—that's a comfort!"

"Well, I'm sorry to say she came back on my hands yesterday," said my wife patiently. "She is a foolish young thing, and said she didn't like living out in the country. I'm sorry, because the Morrises are an excellent family, and she might have had a life home there, if she had only been steady, and chosen to behave herself properly. But yesterday I found her back on her mother's hands again; and the poor woman told me that the dear child never could bear to be separated from her, and that she hadn't the heart to send her back."

"And in short," said I, "she gave you notice that you must provide for Miss O'Connor in some more agreeable way. Cross that name off your list, at any rate. That woman and girl need a few hard raps in the school of experience before you can do anything for them."

"I think I shall," said my long-suffering wife; "but it's a

pity to see a young thing put in the direct road to ruin."

"It is one of the inevitables," said I, "and we must save our strength for those that are willing to help themselves."

"What's all this talk about?" said Bob, coming in upon us rather brusquely.

"Oh, as usual, the old question," said I,—" 'What's to be done with her?' "

"Well," said Bob, "it's exactly what I've come to talk with mother about. Since she keeps a distressed women's agency office, I've come to consult her about Marianne. That woman will die before six months are out, a victim to high civilization and the Paddies.[6] There we are, twelve miles out from Boston, in a country villa so convenient that every part of it might almost do its own work,—everything arranged in the most convenient, contiguous, self-adjusting, self-acting, patent-right, perfective manner,—and yet I tell you Marianne will die of that house. It will yet be recorded on her tombstone, 'Died of conveniences.' For myself, what I languish for is a log-cabin, with a bed in one corner, a trundle-bed underneath for the children, a fireplace only six feet off, a table, four chairs, one kettle, a coffee-pot, and a tin baker,—that's all. I lived deliciously in an establishment of this kind last summer, when I was up at Lake Superior; and I am convinced, if I could move Marianne into it at once, that she would become a healthy and a happy woman. Her life is smothered out of her with comforts; we have too many rooms, too many carpets, too many vases and knickknacks, too much china and silver; she has too many laces and dresses and bonnets; the children all have too many clothes: in fact, to put it scripturally, our riches are corrupted, our garments are moth-eaten, our gold and our silver is cankered,[7] and, in short, Marianne is sick in bed, and I have come to the agency office for distressed women to take you out to attend to her.

"The fact is," continued Bob, "that since our cook married, and Alice went to California, there seems to be no possibility of putting our domestic cabinet upon any permanent basis. The number of female persons that have been through our house, and the ravages they have wrought on it for the last six months, pass belief. I had yesterday a bill of sixty dollars' plumbing to pay for damages of various kinds which had had to be repaired in our very convenient water-works; and the blame of each particular one had been bandied like a shuttlecock among our three household divinities. Biddy privately assured my wife that Kate was in the habit of emptying dustpans of rubbish into the main drain from the chambers, and washing any little extra bits down through the bowls; and, in fact, when one of the bathing-room bowls had overflowed so as to damage the frescoes below, my wife, with great delicacy and precaution, interrogated Kate as to whether she had followed her instructions in the care of the water-pipes. Of course she protested the most immaculate care and circumspection. 'Sure, and she knew how careful one ought to be, and wasn't of the likes of thim as wouldn't mind what throuble they made,—like Biddy, who would throw trash and hair in the pipes, and niver listen to her tellin'; sure, and hadn't she broken the pipes in the kitchen, and lost the stoppers, as it was a shame to see in a Christian house?' Ann, the third girl, being privately questioned, blamed Biddy on Monday, and Kate on Tuesday; on Wednesday, however, she exonerated both; but on Thursday, being in a high quarrel with both, she departed, accusing them severally, not only of all the evil practices aforesaid, but of lying and stealing, and all other miscellaneous wickednesses that came to hand. Whereat the two thus accused rushed in, bewailing themselves and cursing Ann in alternate strophes, averring that she had given the baby laudanum, and, taking it out riding, had stopped for hours with it in a filthy lane where the scarlet fever was said to be rife,—in short, made so fearful a picture that Marianne gave up the

child's life at once, and has taken to her bed. I have endeavored all I could to quiet her, by telling her that the scarlet
fever story was probably an extemporaneous work of fiction, got up to gratify the Hibernian anger at Ann; and that
it wasn't in the least worth while to believe one thing more
than another from the fact that any of the tribe said it. But
she refuses to be comforted, and is so Utopian as to lie there
crying, 'Oh, if I only could get one that I could trust,—one
that would really speak the truth to me,—one that I might
know really went where she said she went, and really did as
she said she did!' To have to live so, she says, and bring up
little children with those she can't trust out of her sight,
whose word is good for nothing,—to feel that her beautiful
house and her lovely things are all going to rack and ruin,
and she can't take care of them, and can't see where or
when or how the mischief is done,—in short, the poor child
talks as women do who are violently attacked with housekeeping fever tending to congestion of the brain. She actually yesterday told me that she wished, on the whole, she
never had got married, which I take to be the most positive
indication of mental alienation."

"Here," said I, "we behold at this moment two women
dying for the want of what they can mutually give one
another,—each having a supply of what the other needs,
but held back by certain invisible cobwebs, slight but strong,
from coming to each other's assistance. Marianne has
money enough, but she wants a helper in her family, such
as all her money has been hitherto unable to buy; and here,
close at hand, is a woman who wants home shelter, healthy,
varied, active, cheerful labor, with nourishing food, kind
care, and good wages. What hinders these women from
rushing to the help of one another, just as two drops of
water on a leaf rush together and make one? Nothing but
a miserable prejudice,—but a prejudice so strong that
women will starve in any other mode of life rather than

accept competency and comfort in this."

"You don't mean," said my wife, "to propose that our protégée should go to Marianne as a servant?"

"I do say it would be the best thing for her to do,—the only opening that I see, and a very good one, too, it is. Just look at it. Her bare living at this moment cannot cost her less than five or six dollars a week,—everything at the present time is so very dear in the city. Now by what possible calling open to her capacity can she pay her board and washing, fuel and lights, and clear a hundred and some odd dollars a year? She could not do it as a district school teacher; she certainly cannot, with her feeble health, do it by plain sewing; she could not do it as a copyist. A robust woman might go into a factory and earn more; but factory work is unintermitted, twelve hours daily, week in and out, in the same movement, in close air, amid the clatter of machinery; and a person delicately organized soon sinks under it. It takes a stolid, enduring temperament to bear factory labor. Now look at Marianne's house and family, and see what is insured to your protégée there.

"In the first place, a home,—a neat, quiet chamber, quite as good as she has probably been accustomed to,—the very best of food, served in a pleasant, light, airy kitchen, which is one of the most agreeable rooms in the house, and the table and table service quite equal to those of most farmers and mechanics. Then her daily tasks would be light and varied,—some sweeping, some dusting, the washing and dressing of children, the care of their rooms and the nursery,—all of it the most healthful, the most natural work of a woman,—work alternating with rest, and diverting thought from painful subjects by its variety, and, what is more, a kind of work in which a good Christian woman might have satisfaction, as feeling herself useful in the highest and best way; for the child's nurse, if she be a pious, well-educated woman, may make the whole course of nursery life an education in goodness. Then, what is far different from any other modes of gaining a livelihood, a woman in this capacity can make and feel herself really and truly beloved. The hearts of little children are easily gained, and their love is real and warm, and no true woman can become the object of it without feeling her own life made brighter. Again, she would have in Marianne a sincere, warm-hearted friend, who would care for her tenderly, respect her sorrows, shelter her feelings, be considerate of her wants, and in every way aid her in the cause she has most at heart,—the succor of her family. There are many ways besides her wages in which she would infallibly be assisted by Marianne, so that the probability would be that she could send her little salary almost untouched to those for whose support she was toiling,—all this on her part."

"But," added my wife, "on the other hand, she would be obliged to associate and be ranked with common Irish servants."

"Well," I answered, "is there any occupation, by which any of us gain our living, which has not its disagreeable side? Does not the lawyer spend all his days either in a dusty office or in the foul air of a court-room? Is he not brought into much disagreeable contact with the lowest class of society? Are not his labors dry and hard and exhausting? Does not the blacksmith spend half his life in soot and grime, that he may gain a competence for the other half? If this woman were to work in a factory, would she not often be brought into associations distasteful to her? Might it not be the same in any of the arts and trades in which a living is to be got? There must be unpleasant circumstances about earning a living in any way, only I maintain that those which a woman would be likely to meet with as a servant in a refined, well-bred Christian family would be less than in almost any other calling. Are there no trials to a woman, I beg to know, in teaching a district school, where all the boys, big and little, of a neighborhood congregate? For my part, were it my daughter or sister who was in necessitous

(389)

circumstances, I would choose for her a position such as I name, in a kind, intelligent, Christian family, before many of those to which women do devote themselves."

"Well," said Bob, "all this has a good sound enough, but it's quite impossible. It's true, I verily believe, that such a kind of servant in our family would really prolong Marianne's life years,—that it would improve her health, and be an unspeakable blessing to her, to me, and the children,—and I would almost go down on my knees to a really well-educated, good American woman who would come into our family and take that place; but I know it's perfectly vain and useless to expect it. You know we have tried the experiment two or three times of having a person in our family who should be on the footing of a friend, yet do the duties of a servant, and that we never could make it work well. These half-and-half people are so sensitive, so exacting in their demands, so hard to please, that we have come to the firm determination that we will have no sliding-scale in our family, and that whoever we are to depend on must come with bona fide willingness to take the position of a servant, such as that position is in our house; and that, I suppose, your protégée would never do, even if she could thereby live easier, have less hard work, better health, and quite as much money as she could earn in any other way."

"She would consider it a personal degradation, I suppose," said my wife.

"And yet, if she only knew it," said Bob, "I should respect her far more profoundly for her willingness to take that position, when adverse fortune has shut other doors."

"Well, now," said I, "this woman is, as I understand, the daughter of a respectable stone-mason, and the domestic habits of her early life have probably been economical and simple. Like most of our mechanics' daughters, she has received in one of our high schools an education which has cultivated and developed her mind far beyond those of her parents and the associates of her childhood. This is a common fact in our American life. By our high schools the daughters of plain workingmen are raised to a state of intellectual culture which seems to make the disposition of them in any kind of industrial calling a difficult one. They all want to teach school,—and schoolteaching, consequently, is an overcrowded profession,—and, failing that, there is only millinery and dressmaking. Of late, it is true, efforts have been made in various directions to widen their sphere. Typesetting and bookkeeping are in some instances beginning to be open to them.

"All this time there is lying, neglected and despised, a calling to which womanly talents and instincts are peculiarly fitted,—a calling full of opportunities of the most lasting usefulness; a calling which insures a settled home, respectable protection, healthful exercise, good air, good food, and good wages; a calling in which a woman may make real friends, and secure to herself warm affection: and yet this calling is the one always refused, shunned, contemned, left to the alien and the stranger, and that simply and solely because it bears the name of *servant.* A Christian woman, who holds the name of Christ in her heart in true devotion, would think it the greatest possible misfortune and degradation to become like him in taking upon her 'the form of a servant.'[8] The founder of Christianity says: 'Whether is greater, he that sitteth at meat or he that serveth? But I am among you as he that serveth.'[9] But notwithstanding these so plain declarations of Jesus, we find that scarce any one in a Christian land will accept real advantages of position and employment that come with that name and condition."

"I suppose," said my wife, "I could prevail upon this woman to do all the duties of the situation, if she could be, as they phrase it, 'treated as one of the family.' "

"That is to say," said Bob, "if she could sit with us at the same table, be introduced to our friends, and be in all respects as one of us. Now, as to this, I am free to say that I have no false aristocratic scruples. I consider every well-educated woman as fully my equal, not to say my superior; but it does not follow from this that she would be one whom I should wish to make a third party with me and my wife at meal-times. Our meals are often our seasons of privacy,— the times when we wish in perfect unreserve to speak of matters that concern ourselves and our family alone. Even invited guests and family friends would not be always welcome, however agreeable at times. Now a woman may be perfectly worthy of respect, and we may be perfectly respectful to her, whom nevertheless we do not wish to take into the circle of intimate friendship. I regard the position of a woman who comes to perform domestic service as I do any other business relation. We have a very respectable young lady in our employ who does legal copying for us, and all is perfectly pleasant and agreeable in our mutual relations; but the case would be far otherwise were she to take it into her head that we treated her with contempt, because my wife did not call on her, and because she was not occasionally invited to tea. Besides, I apprehend that a woman of quick sensibilities, employed in domestic service, and who was so far treated as a member of the family as to share our table, would find her position even more painful and embarrassing than if she took once for all the position of a servant. We could not control the feelings of our friends; we could not always insure that they would be free from aristocratic prejudice, even were we so ourselves. We could not force her upon their acquaintance, and she might feel far more slighted than she would in a position where no attentions of any kind were to be expected. Besides which, I have always noticed that persons standing in this uncertain position are objects of peculiar antipathy to the servants in full; that they are the cause of constant and secret cabals and discontents; and that a family where the two orders exist has always raked up in it the smouldering embers of a quarrel ready at any time to burst out into open feud."

"Well," said I, "here lies the problem of American life. Half our women, like Marianne, are being faded and made old before their time by exhausting endeavors to lead a life of high civilization and refinement with only such untrained help as is washed up on our shores by the tide of emigration. Our houses are built upon a plan that precludes the necessity of much hard labor, but requires rather careful and nice handling. A well-trained, intelligent woman, who had vitalized her finger-ends by means of a well-developed brain, could do all the work of such a house with comparatively little physical fatigue. So stands the case as regards our houses. Now, over against the women that are perishing in them from too much care, there is another class of American women that are wandering up and down, perishing for lack of some remunerating employment. That class of women, whose developed brains and less developed muscles mark them as peculiarly fitted for the performance of the labors of a high civilization, stand utterly aloof from paid domestic service. Sooner beg, sooner starve, sooner marry for money, sooner hang on as dependents in families where they know they are not wanted, than accept of a quite home, easy, healthful work, and certain wages, in these refined and pleasant modern dwellings of ours."

"What is the reason of this?" said Bob.

"The reason is, that we have not yet come to the full development of Christian democracy. The taint of old aristocracies is yet pervading all parts of our society. We have not yet realized fully the true dignity of labor, and the surpassing dignity of domestic labor. And I must say that the valuable and courageous women who have agitated the doctrines of Woman's Rights among us have not in all things seen their way clear in this matter."

"Don't talk to me of those creatures," said Bob, "those men-women, those anomalies, neither flesh nor fish, with their conventions, and their cracked woman-voices strained in what they call public speaking, but which I call public squeaking! No man reverences true women more than I do. I hold a real, true, thoroughly good *woman,* whether in my parlor or my kitchen, as my superior. She can always teach me something that I need to know. She has always in her somewhat of the divine gift of prophecy; but in order to keep it, she must remain a woman. When she crops her hair, puts on pantaloons, and strides about in conventions, she is an abortion, and not a woman."

"Come! come!" said I, "after all, speak with deference. We that choose to wear soft clothing and dwell in kings' houses must respect the Baptists, who wear leathern girdles, and eat locusts and wild honey. They are the voices crying in the wilderness, preparing the way for a coming good.¹⁰ They go down on their knees in the mire of life to lift up and brighten and restore a neglected truth; and we that have not the energy to share their struggle should at least refrain from criticising their soiled garments and ungraceful action. There have been excrescences, eccentricities, peculiarities, about the camp of these reformers; but the body of them have been true and noble women, and worthy of all the reverence due to such. They have already in many of our States reformed the laws relating to woman's position, and placed her on a more just and Christian basis. It is through their movements that in many of our States a woman can hold the fruits of her own earnings, if it be her ill luck to have a worthless, drunken spendthrift for a husband. It is owing to their exertions that new trades and professions are opening to woman; and all that I have to say to them is, that in the suddenness of their zeal for opening new paths for her feet, they have not sufficiently considered the propriety of straightening, widening, and mending the one broad, good old path of domestic labor, established by God himself. It does appear to me, that, if at least a portion of their zeal could be spent in removing the stones out of this highway of domestic life, and making it pleasant and honorable, they would effect even more. I would not have them leave undone what they are doing; but I would, were I worthy to be considered, humbly suggest to their prophetic wisdom and enthusiasm, whether, in this new future of women which they wish to introduce, women's natural, God-given employment of *domestic service* is not to receive a new character, and rise in a new form.

" 'To love and serve' is a motto worn with pride on some aristocratic family shields in England. It ought to be graven on the Christian shield. *Servant* is the name which Christ gives to the *Christian;* and in speaking of his kingdom as distinguished from earthly kingdoms, he distinctly said, that rank there should be conditioned, not upon desire to command, but on willingness to serve.

" 'Ye know that the princes of the Gentiles exercise dominion over them, and they that are great exercise authority upon them. But it shall not be so among you: but whosoever will be great among you, let him be your minister; and whosoever will be chief among you, let him be your *servant.*'[11]

"Why is it, that this name of servant, which Christ says is the highest in the kingdom of heaven, is so dishonored among us professing Christians, that good women will beg or starve, will suffer almost any extreme of poverty and privation, rather than accept home, competence, security, with this honored name?"

"The fault with many of our friends of the Woman's Rights order," said my wife, "is the depreciatory tone in which they have spoken of the domestic labors of a family as being altogether below the scope of the faculties of woman. *'Domestic drudgery'* they call it,—an expression that has done more harm than any two words that ever were put together.

"Think of a woman's calling clear-starching and ironing domestic drudgery, and to better the matter turning to typesetting in a grimy printing office! Call the care of china and silver, the sweeping of carpets, the arrangement of parlors and sitting-rooms, drudgery; and go into a factory and spend the day amid the whir and clatter and thunder of machinery, inhaling an atmosphere loaded with wool and machine grease, and keeping on the feet for twelve hours, nearly continously! Think of its being called drudgery to take care of a clean, light, airy nursery, to wash and dress and care for two or three children, to mend their clothes, tell them stories, make them playthings, take them out walking or driving; and rather than this, to wear out the whole livelong day, extending often deep into the night, in endless sewing, in a close room of a dressmaking establishment! Is it any less drudgery to stand all day behind a counter, serving customers, than to tend a door-bell and wait on a table? For my part," said my wife, "I have often thought the matter over, and concluded, that, if I were left in straitened circumstances, as many are in a great city, I would seek a position as a servant in one of our good families."

"I envy the family that you even think of in that connection," said I. "I fancy the amazement which would take possession of them as you began to develop among them."

"I have always held," said my wife, "that family work, in many of its branches, can be better performed by an educated woman than an uneducated one. Just as an army where even the bayonets think is superior to one of mere brute force and mechanical training, so, I have heard it said, some of our distinguished modern female reformers show an equal superiority in the domestic sphere,—and I do not doubt it. Family work was never meant to be the special province of untaught brains. I have sometimes thought I should like to show what I could do as a servant."

"Well," said Bob, "to return from all this to the question, What's to be done with her? Are you going to *my* distressed woman? If you are, suppose you take *your* distressed woman along, and ask her to try it. I can promise her a pleasant house, a quiet room by herself, healthful and not too hard work, a kind friend, and some leisure for reading, writing, or whatever other pursuit of her own she may choose for her recreation. We are always quite willing to lend books to any who appreciate them. Our house is surrounded by pleasant grounds, which are open to our servants as to ourselves. So let her come and try us. I am quite sure that country air, quiet security, and moderate exercise in a good home, will bring up her health; and if she is willing to take the one or two disagreeables which may come with all this, let her try us."

"Well," said I, "so be it; and would that all the women seeking homes and employment could thus fall in with women who have homes and are perishing in them for want of educated helpers!"

On this question of woman's work I have yet more to say, but must defer it till another time.

Notes

1. A periodical established in Boston in 1857.

2. An employment agency for domestic help (servants, maids, cooks, etc.).

3. City in southeastern Massachusetts.

4. *James.* II, 15–16.

5. American Civil War, 1861–1865.

6. Irishmen, slang.

7. "Lay not up for yourselves treasures upon earth, where moth and rust doth corrupt, and where thieves break through and steal." *Matthew.* VI, 19.

8. *Philippians.* II, 7.

9. *Luke.* XXII, 27.

10. See *Matthew.* III, 3–4.

11. *Matthew.* XX, 25–27.

WOMAN'S SPHERE

from *The Chimney-Corner*

"**W**hat do you think of this Woman's Rights question?" said Bob Stephens. "From some of your remarks, I apprehend that you think there is something in it. I may be wrong, but I must confess that I have looked with disgust on the whole movement. No man reverences women as I do; but I reverence them *as* women. I reverence them for those very things in which their sex differs from ours; but when they come upon our ground, and begin to work and fight after our manner and with our weapons, I regard them as fearful anomalies, neither men nor women. These Woman's Rights Conventions appear to me to have ventilated crudities, absurdities, and blasphemies. To hear them talk about men, one would suppose that the two sexes were natural-born enemies, and wonder whether they ever had fathers and brothers. One would think, upon their showing, that all men were a set of ruffians, in league against women,—they seeming, at the same time, to forget how on their very platforms the most constant and gallant defenders of their rights are men. Wendell Phillips and Wentworth Higginson[1] have put at the service of the cause masculine training and manly vehemence, and complacently accepted the wholesale abuse of their own sex at the hands of their warrior sisters. One would think, were all they say of female powers true, that our Joan-of-Arcs[2] ought to have disdained to fight under male captains."

(*399*)

"I think," said my wife, "that, in all this talk about the rights of men, and the rights of women, and the rights of children, the world seems to be forgetting what is quite as important, the *duties* of men and women and children. We all hear of our *rights* till we forget our *duties;* and even theology is beginning to concern itself more with what man has a right to expect of his Creator than what the Creator has a right to expect of man."

"You say the truth," said I; "there is danger of just this overaction; and yet rights must be discussed; because, in order to understand the duties we owe to any class, we must understand their rights. To know our duties to men, women, and children, we must know what the rights of men, women, and children justly are. As to the 'Woman's Rights movement,' it is not peculiar to America, it is part of a great wave in the incoming tide of modern civilization; the swell is felt no less in Europe, but it comes over and breaks on our American shore, because our great wide beach affords the best play for its waters; and as the ocean waves bring with them kelp, seaweed, mud, sand, gravel, and even putrefying débris, which lie unsightly on the shore, and yet, on the whole, are healthful and refreshing,—so the Woman's Rights movement, with its conventions, its speech-makings, it crudities, and eccentricities, is nevertheless a part of a healthful and necessary movement of the human race towards progress. This question of Woman and her Sphere is now, perhaps, the greatest of the age. We have put Slavery under foot, and with the downfall of Slavery the only obstacle to the success of our great democratic experiment is overthrown, and there seems no limit to the splendid possibilities which it may open before the human race.

"In the reconstruction that is now coming there lies more than the reconstruction of States[3] and the arrangement of the machinery of government. We need to know and feel, all of us, that, from the moment of the death of

Slavery, we parted finally from the régime and control of all the old ideas formed under old oppressive systems of society, and came upon a new plane of life.

"In this new life we must never forget that we are a peculiar people, that we have to walk in paths unknown to the Old World,[4]—paths where its wisdom cannot guide us, where its precedents can be of little use to us, and its criticisms, in most cases, must be wholly irrelevant. The history of our war has shown us of how little service to us in any important crisis the opinions and advice of the Old World can be. We have been hurt at what seemed to us the want of sympathy, the direct antagonism, of England. We might have been less hurt if we had properly understood that Providence had placed us in a position so far ahead of her ideas or power of comprehension that just judgment or sympathy was not to be expected from her.

"As we went through our great war with no help but that of God, obliged to disregard the misconceptions and impertinences which the foreign press rained down upon us, so, if we are wise, we shall continue to do. Our object must now be to make the principles on which our government is founded permeate consistently the mass of society, and to purge out the leaven of aristocratic and Old World ideas. So long as there is an illogical working in our actual life, so long as there is any class denied equal rights with other classes, so long will there be agitation and trouble."

"Then," said my wife, "you believe that women ought to vote?"

"If the principle on which we founded our government is true, that taxation must not exist without representation, and if women hold property and are taxed, it follows that women should be represented in the State by their votes, or there is an illogical working of our government."

"But, my dear, don't you think that this will have a bad effect on the female character?"

"Yes," said Bob, "it will make women caucus holders, political candidates."

"It may make this of some women, just as of some men," said I. "But all men do not take any great interest in politics; it is very difficult to get some of the best of them to do their duty in voting, and the same will be found true among women."

"But, after all," said Bob, "what do you gain? What will a woman's vote be but a duplicate of that of her husband or father, or whatever man happens to be her adviser?"

"That may be true on a variety of questions; but there are subjects on which the vote of women would, I think, be essentially different from that of men. On the subjects of temperance, public morals, and education, I have no doubt that the introduction of the female vote into legislation, in States, counties, and cities, would produce results very different from that of men alone. There are thousands of women who would close grogshops, and stop the traffic in spirits, if they had the legislative power; and it would be well for society if they had. In fact, I think that a State can no more afford to dispense with the vote of women in its affairs than a family. Imagine a family where the female has no voice in the housekeeping! A State is but a larger family, and there are many of its concerns which, equally with those of a private household, would be bettered by female supervision."

"But fancy women going to those horrible voting-places! It is more than I can do myself," said Bob.

"But you forget," said I, "that they are horrible and disgusting principally because women never go to them. All places where women are excluded tend downward to barbarism; but the moment she is introduced, there come in with her courtesy, cleanliness, sobriety, and order. When a man can walk up to the ballot-box with his wife or his sister on his arm, voting-places will be far more agreeable than now, and the polls will not be such bear-gardens that refined men will be constantly tempted to omit their political duties there.

"If for nothing else, I would have women vote, that the business of voting may not be so disagreeable and intolerable to men of refinement as it now is; and I sincerely believe that the cause of good morals, good order, cleanliness, and public health would be a gainer not merely by the added feminine vote, but by the added vote of a great many excellent but too fastidious men, who are now kept from the polls by the disagreeables they meet there.

"Do you suppose that, if women had equal representation with men in the municipal laws of New York, its reputation for filth during the last year would have gone so far beyond that of Cologne,[5] or any other city renowned for bad smells? I trow not. I believe a lady mayoress would have brought in a dispensation of brooms and whitewash, and made a terrible searching into dark holes and vile corners, before now. Female New York, I have faith to believe, has yet left in her enough of the primary instincts of womanhood to give us a clean, healthy city, if female votes had any power to do it."

"But," said Bob, "you forget that voting would bring together all the women of the lower classes."

"Yes; but, thanks to the instincts of their sex, they would come in their Sunday clothes; for where is the woman that has n't her finery, and will not embrace every chance to show it? Biddy's parasol, and hat with pink ribbons, would necessitate a clean shirt in Pat as much as on Sunday. Voting would become a fête, and we should have a population at the polls as well dressed as at church. Such is my belief."

"I do not see," said Bob, "but you go to the full extent with our modern female reformers."

"There are certain neglected truths, which have been held up by these reformers, that are gradually being accepted and infused into the life of modern society; and their recognition will help to solidify and purify democratic institutions. They are:—

"1. The right of every woman to hold independent property.

"2. The right of every woman to receive equal pay with man for work which she does equally well.

"3. The right of any woman to do any work for which, by her natural organization and talent, she is peculiarly adapted.

"Under the first head, our energetic sisters have already, by the help of their gallant male adjutants, reformed the laws of several of our States, so that a married woman is no longer left the unprotected legal slave of any unprincipled, drunken spendthrift who may be her husband,— but, in case of the imbecility or improvidence of the natural head of the family, the wife, if she have the ability, can conduct business, make contracts, earn and retain money for the good of the household; and I am sure no one can say that immense injustice and cruelty are not thereby prevented.

"It is quite easy for women who have the good fortune to have just and magnanimous husbands to say that they feel no interest in such reforms, and that they would willingly trust their property to the man to whom they give themselves; but they should remember that laws are not made for the restraint of the generous and just, but of the dishonest and base. The law which enables a married woman to hold her own property does not forbid her to give it to the man of her heart, if she so pleases; and it does protect many women who otherwise would be reduced to the extremest misery. I once knew an energetic milliner who had her shop attached four times, and a flourishing business broken up in four different cities, because she was tracked from city to city by a worthless spendthrift, who only waited till she had amassed a little property in a new place to swoop down upon and carry it off. It is to be hoped that the time is not distant when every State will give to woman a fair chance to the ownership and use of her own earnings and her own property.

"Under the head of the right of every woman to do any work for which by natural organization and talent she is especially adapted, there is a word or two to be said.

"The talents and tastes of the majority of women are naturally domestic. The family is evidently their sphere, because in all ways their organization fits them for that more than for anything else.

"But there are occasionally women who are exceptions to the common law, gifted with peculiar genius and adaptations. With regard to such women, there has never seemed to be any doubt in the verdict of mankind that they ought to follow their nature, and that their particular sphere was the one to which they are called. Did anybody ever think that Mrs. Siddons and Mrs. Kemble and Ristori had better have applied themselves sedulously to keeping house, because they were women, and 'woman's noblest station is retreat'?[6]

"The world has always shown a fair average of good sense in this matter, from the days of the fair Hypatia in Alexandria, who, we are told, gave lectures on philosophy behind a curtain, lest her charms should distract the attention of too impressible young men, down to those of Anna Dickinson.[7] Mankind are not, after all, quite fools, and seem in these cases to have a reasonable idea that exceptional talents have exceptional laws, and make their own code of proprieties.

"Now there is no doubt that Miss Dickinson, though as relating to her femininity she is quite as pretty and modest a young woman as any to be found in the most sheltered circle, has yet a most exceptional talent for public speaking, which draws crowds to hear her, and makes lecturing for her a lucrative profession, as well as a means of advocating just and generous sentiments, and of stimulating her own sex to nobler purposes; and the same law which relates to

Siddons and Kemble and Ristori relates also to her.

"The doctrine of *vocations* is a good one and a safe one. If a woman mistakes her vocation, so much the worse for her; the world does not suffer, but she does, and the suffering speedily puts her where she belongs. There is not near so much danger from attempts to imitate Anna Dickinson as there is from the more common feminine attempts to rival the *demi-monde* of Paris in fantastic extravagance and luxury.

"As to how a woman may determine whether she has any such vocation, there is a story quite in point. A good Methodist elder was listening to an ardent young mechanic who thought he had a call to throw up his shop and go to preaching.

" 'I feel,' said the young ardent, 'that I have a call to preach.'

" 'Hast thou noticed whether people seem to have a call to hear thee?' said the shrewd old man. 'I have always noticed that a true call of the Lord may be known by this, 'that people have a *call* to hear.' "

"Well," said Bob, "the most interesting question still remains: What are to be the employments of woman? What ways are there for her to use her talents, to earn her livelihood and support those who are dear to her, when Providence throws that necessity upon her? This is becoming more than ever one of the pressing questions of our age. The war has deprived so many thousands of women of their natural protectors, that everything must be thought of that may possibly open a way for their self-support."

"Well, let us look over the field," said my wife. "What is there for woman?"

"In the first place," said I, "come the professions requiring natural genius,—authorship, painting, sculpture, with the subordinate arts of photographing, coloring, and finishing; but when all is told, these furnish employment to a very limited number,—almost as nothing to the whole.

Then there is teaching, which is profitable in its higher branches, and perhaps the very pleasantest of all the callings open to woman; but teaching is at present an overcrowded profession, the applicants everywhere outnumbering the places. Architecture and landscape gardening are arts every way suited to the genius of woman, and there are enough who have the requisite mechanical skill and mathematical education; and, though never yet thought of for the sex, that I know of, I do not despair of seeing those who shall find in this field a profession at once useful and elegant. When women plan dwelling-houses, the vast body of tenements to be let in our cities will wear a more domestic and comfortable air, and will be built more with reference to the real wants of their inmates."

"I have thought," said Bob, "that agencies of various sorts, as canvassing the country for the sale of books, maps and engravings, might properly employ a great many women. There is a large class whose health suffers from confinement and sedentary occupations, who might, I think, be both usefully and agreeably employed in business of this sort, and be recruiting their health at the same time."

"Then," said my wife, "there is the medical profession."

"Yes," said I. "The world is greatly obliged to Miss Blackwell[8] and other noble pioneers who faced and overcame the obstacles to the attainment of a thorough medical education by females. Thanks to them, a new and lucrative profession is now open to educated women in relieving the distresses of their own sex; and we may hope that in time, through their intervention, the care of the sick may also become the vocation of cultivated, refined, intelligent women, instead of being left, as heretofore, to the ignorant and vulgar. The experience of our late war has shown us what women of a high class morally and intellectually can do in this capacity. Why should not this experience inaugurate a new and sacred calling for refined and educated women? Why should not NURSING become a vocation equal in dignity and in general esteem to the medical profession, of which it is the right hand? Why should our dearest hopes, in the hour of their greatest peril, be committed into the hands of Sairey Gamps, when the world has seen Florence Nightingales?"⁹

"Yes, indeed," said my wife; "I can testify, from my own experience, that the sufferings and dangers of the sick-bed, for the want of intelligent, educated nursing, have been dreadful. A prejudiced, pig-headed, snuff-taking old woman, narrow-minded and vulgar, and more confident in her own way than seven men that can render a reason, enters your house at just the hour and moment when all your dearest earthly hopes are brought to a crisis. She becomes absolute dictator over your delicate, helpless wife and your frail babe,—the absolute dictator of all in the house. If it be her sovereign will and pleasure to enact all sorts of physiological absurdities in the premises, who shall say her nay? 'She knows her business, she hopes!' And if it be her edict, as it was of one of her class whom I knew, that each of her babies shall eat four baked beans the day it is four days old, eat them it must; and if the baby die in convulsions four days after, it is set down as the mysterious will of an overruling Providence.

"I know and have seen women lying upon laced pillows, under silken curtains, who have been bullied and dominated over in the hour of their greatest helplessness by ignorant and vulgar tyrants, in a way that would scarce be thought possible in civilized society, and children that have been injured or done to death by the same means. A celebrated physician told me of a babe whose eyesight was nearly ruined by its nurse taking a fancy to wash its eyes with camphor,—'to keep it from catching cold,' she said. I knew another infant that was poisoned by the nurse giving it laudanum in some of those patent nostrums which these ignorant creatures carry secretly in their pockets, to secure quiet in their little charges. I knew one delicate woman who never recovered from the effects of being left at her first confinement in the hands of an ill-tempered, drinking nurse, and whose feeble infant was neglected and abused by this woman in a way to cause lasting injury. In the first four weeks of infancy the constitution is peculiarly impressible; and infants of a delicate organization may, if frightened and ill-treated, be the subjects of just such a shock to the nervous system as in mature age comes from the sudden stroke of a great affliction or terror. A bad nurse may affect nerves predisposed to weakness in a manner they never will recover from. I solemnly believe that the constitutions of more women are broken up by bad nursing in their first confinement than by any other cause whatever. And yet there are at the same time hundreds and thousands of women, wanting the means of support, whose presence in a sick-room would be a benediction. I do trust that Miss Blackwell's band of educated nurses will not be long in coming, and that the number of such may increase till they effect a complete revolution in this vocation. A class of cultivated, well-trained, intelligent nurses would soon elevate the employment of attending on the sick into the noble calling it ought to be, and secure for it its appropriate rewards."

"There is another opening for woman," said I,—"in the world of business. The system of commercial colleges now spreading over our land is a new and most important development of our times. There that large class of young men who have either no time or no inclination for an extended classical education can learn what will fit them for that active material life which in our broad country needs so many workers. But the most pleasing feature of these institutions is, that the complete course is open to women no less than to men, and women there may acquire that knowledge of bookkeeping and accounts, and of the forms and principles of business transactions, which will qualify them for some of the lucrative situations hitherto monopolized by the other sex. And the expenses of the course of instruction are so arranged as to come within the scope of very moderate means. A fee of fifty dollars entitles a woman to the benefit of the whole course, and she has the privilege of attending at any hours that may suit her own engagements and convenience."

"Then, again," said my wife, "there are the departments of millinery and dressmaking, and the various branches of needlework, which afford employment to thousands of women; there is typesetting, by which many are beginning to get a living; there are the manufactures of cotton, woolen, silk, and the numberless useful articles which employ female hands in their fabrication,—all of them opening avenues by which, with more or less success, a subsistence can be gained."

"Well, really," said Bob, "it would appear, after all, that there are abundance of openings for women. What is the cause of the outcry and distress? How is it that we hear of women starving, driven to vice and crime by want, when so many doors of useful and profitable employment stand open to them?"

"The question would easily be solved," said my wife, "if you could once see the kind and class of women who thus suffer and starve. There may be exceptions, but too large a portion of them are girls and women who can or will do no earthly thing well,—and, what is worse, are not willing to take the pains to be taught to do anything well. I will describe to you one girl, and you will find in every intelligence-office a hundred of her kind to five thoroughly trained ones.

"Imprimis: she is rather delicate and genteel-looking, and you may know from the arrangement of her hair just what the last mode is of disposing of rats or waterfalls. She has a lace bonnet with roses, a silk mantilla, a silk dress trimmed with velvet, a white skirt with sixteen tucks and an embroidered edge, a pair of cloth gaiters, underneath which are a pair of stockings without feet, the only pair in her possession. She has no under-linen, and sleeps at night in the working-clothes she wears in the day. She never seems to have in her outfit either comb, brush, or tooth-brush of her own,—neither needles, thread, scissors, nor pins; her money, when she has any, being spent on more important articles, such as the lace bonnet or silk mantilla, or the rats and waterfalls that glorify her head. When she wishes to sew, she borrows what is needful of a convenient next neighbor; and if she gets a place in a family as second girl, she expects to subsist in these respects by borrowing of the better-appointed servants, or helping herself from the family stores.

"She expects, of course, the very highest wages, if she condescends to live out; and by help of a trim outside appearance, and the many vacancies that are continually occurring in households, she gets places, where her object is to do just as little of any duty assigned to her as possible, to hurry through her performances, put on her fine clothes, and go a-gadding. She is on free-and-easy terms with all the men she meets, and ready at jests and repartee, sometimes far from seemly. Her time of service in any one place lasts indifferently from a fortnight to two or three months, when she takes her wages, buys her a new parasol in the latest style, and goes back to the intelligence-office. In the different families where she has lived she has been told a hundred times the proprieties of household life, how to make beds, arrange rooms, wash china, glass, and silver, and set tables; but her habitual rule is to try in each place how small and how poor services will be accepted. When she finds less will not do, she gives more. When the mistress follows her constantly, and shows an energetic determination to be well served, she shows that she can serve well; but the moment such attention relaxes, she slides back again. She is as destructive to a house as a fire; the very spirit of wastefulness is in her; she cracks the china, dents the silver, stops the water-pipes with rubbish, and, after she is gone, there is generally a sum equal to half her wages to be expended in repairing the effects of her carelessness. And yet there is one thing to be said for her: she is quite as careful of her employer's things as of her own. The full amount of her mischiefs often does not appear at once, as she is glib of tongue, adroit in apologies, and lies with as much alertness and as little thought of conscience as a blackbird chatters. It is difficult for people who have been trained from childhood in the school of verities,—who have been lectured for even the shadow of a prevarication, and shut up in disgrace for a lie, till truth becomes a habit of their souls,—it is very difficult for people so educated to understand how to get on with those who never speak the truth except by mere accident, who assert any and every thing that comes into their heads with all the assurance and all the energy of perfect verity.

"What becomes of this girl? She finds means, by begging, borrowing, living out, to keep herself extremely trim and airy for a certain length of time, till the rats and water-falls, the lace hat and parasol, and the glib tongue, have done their work in making a fool of some honest young mechanic who earns three dollars a day. She marries him with no higher object than to have somebody to earn money for her to spend. And what comes of such marriages?

"That is one ending of her career; the other is on the street, in haunts of vice, in prison, in drunkenness, and death.

"Whence come these girls? They are as numerous as yellow butterflies in autumn; they flutter up to cities from the country; they grow up from mothers who ran the same sort of career before them; and the reason why in the end they fall out of all reputable employment and starve on poor wages is, that they become physically, mentally, and morally incapable of rendering any service which society will think worth paying for."

"I remember," said I, "that the head of the most celebrated dressmaking establishment in New York, in reply to the appeals of the needlewomen of the city for sympathy and wages, came out with published statements to this effect: that the difficulty lay, not in unwillingness of employers to pay what work was worth, but in finding any work worth paying for; that she had many applicants, but among them few who could be of real use to her; that she, in common with everybody in this country who has any kind of serious responsibilities to carry, was continually embarrassed for want of skilled workpeople who could take and go on with the labor of her various departments without her constant supervision; that, out of a hundred girls, there would not be more than five to whom she could give a dress to be made and dismiss it from her mind as something certain to be properly done.

"Let people individually look around their own little sphere, and ask themselves if they know any woman really excelling in any valuable calling or accomplishment who is suffering for want of work. All of us know seamstresses, dressmakers, nurses, and laundresses who have made themselves such a reputation, and are so beset and overcrowded with work, that the whole neighborhood is constantly on its knees to them with uplifted hands. The fine seamstress, who can cut and make trousseaus and layettes in elegant perfection, is always engaged six months in advance; the pet dressmaker of a neighborhood must be engaged in May for September, and in September for May; a laundress who sends your clothes home in nice order always has all the work that she can do. Good work in any department is the rarest possible thing in our American life; and it is a fact that the great majority of workers, both in the family and out, do only tolerably well,—not so badly that it actually cannot be borne, yet not so well as to be a source of real, thorough satisfaction. The exceptional worker in every neighborhood, who does things really *well*, can always set her own price, and is always having more offering than she can possibly do.

"The trouble, then, in finding employment for women lies deeper than the purses or consciences of the employers: it lies in the want of education in women; the want of *education,* I say,—meaning by education that which fits a woman for practical and profitable employment in life, and not mere common-school learning."

"Yes," said my wife; "for it is a fact that the most troublesome and helpless persons to provide for are often those who have a good medium education, but no feminine habits, no industry, no practical calculation, no muscular strength, and no knowledge of any one of woman's peculiar duties. In the earlier days of New England, women, as a class, had far fewer opportunities for acquiring learning, yet were far better educated, physically and morally, than now. The high school did not exist; at the common school they learned reading, writing, and arithmetic, and practiced spelling; while at home they did the work of the household. They were cheerful, bright, and active, ever on the alert, able to do anything, from the harnessing and driving of a horse to the finest embroidery. The daughters of New England in those days looked the world in the face without a fear. They shunned no labor; they were afraid of none; and they could always find their way to a living."

"But although less instructed in school learning," said I, "they showed no deficiency in intellectual acumen. I see no such women, nowadays, as some I remember of that olden time,—women whose strong minds and ever-active industry carried on reading and study side by side with household toils.

"I remember a young lady friend of mine, attending a celebrated boarding-school, boarded in the family of a woman who had never been to school longer than was necessary to learn to read and write, yet who was a perfect cyclopedia of general information. The young scholar used to take her Chemistry and Natural Philosophy into the kitchen, where her friend was busy with her household work, and read her lessons to her, that she might have the benefit of her explanations; and so, while the good lady scoured her andirons or kneaded her bread, she lectured to her protégée on mysteries of science far beyond the limits of the textbook. Many of the graduates of our modern high schools would find it hard to shine in conversation on the subjects they had studied, in the searching presence of some of these vigorous matrons of the olden time, whose only school had been the leisure hours gained by energy and method from their family cares."

"And in those days," said my wife, "there lived in our families a class of American domestics, women of good sense and good powers of reflection, who applied this sense and power of reflection to household matters. In the early part of my married life, I myself had American 'help'; and they were not only excellent servants, but trusty and invaluable friends. But now, all this class of applicants for domestic service have disappeared, I scarce know why or how. All I know is, there is no more a Betsey or a Lois, such as used to take domestic cares off my shoulders so completely."

"Good heavens! where are they?" cried Bob. "Where do they hide? I would search through the world after such a prodigy!"

"The fact is," said I, "there has been a slow and gradual reaction against household labor in America. Mothers began to feel that it was a sort of *curse*, to be spared, if possible, to their daughters; women began to feel that they were fortunate in proportion as they were able to be entirely clear of family responsibilities. Then Irish labor began to come in, simultaneously with a great advance in female education.

"For a long while nothing was talked of, written of, thought of, in teachers' meetings, conventions, and assemblies, but the neglected state of female education; and the whole circle of the arts and sciences was suddenly introduced into our free-school system, from which needlework as gradually and quietly was suffered to drop out. The girl who attended the primary and high school had so much study imposed on her that she had no time for sewing or housework; and the delighted mother was only too happy to darn her stockings and do the housework alone, that her daughter might rise to a higher plane than she herself had attained to. The daughter, thus educated, had, on coming to womanhood, no solidity of muscle, no manual dexterity, no practice or experience in domestic life; and if she were to seek a livelihood, there remained only teaching, or some feminine trade, or the factory."

"These factories," said my wife, "have been the ruin of hundreds and hundreds of our once healthy farmers' daughters and others from the country. They go there young and unprotected; they live there in great boarding-houses, and associate with a promiscuous crowd, without even such restraints of maternal supervision as they would have in great boarding-schools; their bodies are enfeebled by labor often necessarily carried on in a foul and heated atmosphere; and at the hours when off duty, they are exposed to all the dangers of unwatched intimacy with the other sex.

"Moreover, the factory girl learns and practices but one thing,—some one mechanical movement, which gives no scope for invention, ingenuity, or any other of the powers called into play by domestic labor; so that she is in reality unfitted in every way for family duties.

"Many times it has been my lot to try, in my family service, girls who have left factories; and I have found them wholly useless for any of the things which a woman ought to be good for. They knew nothing of a house, or what ought to be done in it; they had imbibed a thorough contempt of household labor, and looked upon it but as a *dernier ressort;* and it was only the very lightest of its tasks that they could even begin to think of. I remember I tried to persuade one of these girls, the pretty daughter of a fisherman, to take some lessons in washing and ironing. She was at that time engaged to be married to a young mechanic, who earned something like two or three dollars a day.

" 'My child,' said I, 'you will need to understand all kinds of housework if you are going to be married.'

"She tossed her little head,—

" 'Indeed, she wasn't going to trouble herself about that.'

" 'But who will get up your husband's shirts?'

" 'Oh, he must put them out. I'm not going to be married to make a slave of myself!'

"Another young factory girl, who came for table and parlor work, was so full of airs and fine notions that it seemed as difficult to treat with her as with a princess. She could not sweep, because it blistered her hands, which, in fact, were long and delicate; she could not think of putting them into hot dish-water, and for that reason preferred washing the dishes in cold water; she required a full hour in the morning to make her toilet; she was laced so tightly that she could not stoop without vertigo; and her hoops were of dimensions which seemed to render it impossible for her to wait upon table; she was quite exhausted with the effort of ironing the table-napkins and chamber-towels: yet she could not think of 'living out' under two dollars a week.

"Both these girls had had a good free-school education, and could read any amount of novels, write a tolerable letter, but had not learned anything with sufficient accuracy to fit them for teachers. They were pretty, and their destiny was to marry and lie a deadweight on the hands of some honest man, and to increase, in their children, the number of incapables."

"Well," said Bob, "what would you have? What is to be done?"

"In the first place," said I, "I would have it felt, by those who are seeking to elevate woman, that the work is to be done, not so much by creating for her new spheres of action as by elevating her conceptions of that domestic vocation to which God and Nature have assigned her. It is all very well to open to her avenues of profit and advancement in the great outer world; but, after all, *to make and keep a home* is, and ever must be, a woman's first glory, her highest aim. No work of art can compare with a perfect home; the training and guiding of a family must be recognized as the highest work a woman can perform; and female education ought to be conducted with special reference to this.

"Men are trained to be lawyers, to be physicians, to be mechanics, by long and self-denying study and practice. A man cannot even make shoes merely by going to the high school and learning reading, writing, and mathematics; he cannot be a bookkeeper or a printer simply from general education.

"Now women have a sphere and profession of their own,—a profession for which they are fitted by physical organization, by their own instincts, and to which they are directed by the pointing and manifest finger of God,—and that sphere is *family life*. Duties to the state and to public life they may have; but the public duties of women must bear to their family ones the same relation that the family duties of men bear to their public ones. The defect in the late efforts to push on female education is, that it has been for her merely general, and that it has left out and excluded all that is professional; and she undertakes the essential duties of womanhood, when they do devolve on her, without any adequate preparation."

"But is it possible for a girl to learn at school the things which fit for her family life?" said Bob.

"Why not?" I replied. "Once it was thought impossible in school to teach girls geometry or algebra, or the higher mathematics; it was thought impossible to put them

(418)

through collegiate courses; but it has been done, and we see it. Women study treatises on political economy in schools, and why should not the study of domestic economy form a part of every school course? A young girl will stand up at the blackboard, and draw and explain the compound blow-pipe, and describe all the processes of making oxygen and hydrogen. Why should she not draw and explain a refrigerator as well as an air-pump? Both are to be explained on philosophical principles. When a schoolgirl, in her chemistry, studies the reciprocal action of acids and alkalies, what is there to hinder the teaching her its application to the various processes of cooking where acids and alkalies are employed? Why should she not be led to see how effervescence and fermentation can be made to perform their office in the preparation of light and digestible bread? Why should she not be taught the chemical substances by which food is often adulterated, and the test by which such adulterations are detected? Why should she not understand the processes of confectionery, and know how to guard against the deleterious or poisonous elements that are introduced into children's sugar-plums and candies? Why, when she learns the doctrine of mordants, the substances by which different colors are set, should she not learn it with some practical view to future life, so that she may know how to set the color of a fading calico or restore the color of a spotted one? Why, in short, when a girl has labored through a profound chemical work, and listened to courses of chemical lectures, should she come to domestic life, which presents a constant series of chemical experiments and changes, and go blindly along as without chart or compass, unable to tell what will take out a stain, or what will brighten a metal, what are common poisons and what their antidotes, and not knowing enough of the laws of caloric to understand how to warm a house, or of the laws of atmosphere to know how to ventilate one? Why should the preparation of food, that subtile art on which life, health, cheerfulness, good temper, and good looks so largely depend, forever be left in the hands of the illiterate and vulgar?

"A benevolent gentleman has lately left a large fortune for the founding of a university for women; and the object is stated to be to give to women who have already acquired a general education the means of acquiring a professional one, to fit themselves for some employment by which they may gain a livelihood.

"In this institution the women are to be instructed in bookkeeping, stenography, telegraphing, photographing, drawing, modeling, and various other arts; but, so far as I remember, there is no proposal to teach domestic economy as at least *one* of woman's professions.

"Why should there not be a professor of domestic economy in every large female school? Why should not this professor give lectures, first on house planning and building, illustrated by appropriate apparatus? Why should not the pupils have presented to their inspection models of houses planned with reference to economy, to ease of domestic service, to warmth, to ventilation, and to architectural appearance? Why should not the professor go on to lecture further on house-fixtures, with models of the best mangles, washing-machines, clothes-wringers, ranges, furnaces, and cooking-stoves, together with drawings and apparatus illustrative of domestic hydraulics, showing the best contrivances for bathing-rooms and the obvious principles of plumbing, so that the pupils may have some idea how to work the machinery of a convenient house when they have it, and to have such conveniences introduced when wanting? If it is thought worth while to provide at great expense apparatus for teaching the revolutions of Saturn's moons and the precession of the equinoxes, why should there not be some also to teach what it may greatly concern a woman's earthly happiness to know?

"Why should not the professor lecture on home chemistry, devoting his first lecture to bread-making? and why might not a batch of bread be made and baked and exhibited to the class, together with specimens of morbid anatomy in the bread line,—the sour cotton bread of the baker; the rough, big-holed bread; the heavy, fossil bread; the bitter bread of too much yeast,—and the causes of their defects pointed out? And so with regard to the various articles of food,—why might not chemical lectures be given on all of them, one after another? In short, it would be easy to trace out a course of lectures on common things to occupy a whole year, and for which the pupils, whenever they come to have homes of their own, will thank the lecturer to the last day of their life.

"Then there is no impossibility in teaching needle-work, the cutting and fitting of dresses, in female schools. The thing is done very perfectly in English schools for the working classes. A girl trained at one of these schools came into a family I once knew. She brought with her a sewing-book, in which the process of making various articles was exhibited in miniature. The several parts of a shirt were first shown, each perfectly made, and fastened to a leaf of the book by itself, and then the successive steps of uniting the parts, till finally appeared a miniature model of the whole. The sewing was done with red thread, so that every stitch might show, and any imperfections be at once remedied. The same process was pursued with regard to other garments, and a good general idea of cutting and fitting them was thus given to an entire class of girls.

"In the same manner the care and nursing of young children and the tending of the sick might be made the subject of lectures. Every woman ought to have some general principles to guide her with regard to what is to be done in case of the various accidents that may befall either children or grown people, and of their lesser illnesses, and ought to know how to prepare comforts and nourishment for the sick. Hawthorne's satirical remarks upon the contrast between the elegant Zenobia's conversation, and the smoky porridge she made for him when he was an invalid, might apply to the volunteer cookery of many charming women."[10]

"I think," said Bob, "that your Professor of Domestic Economy would find enough to occupy his pupils."

"In fact," said I, "were domestic economy properly honored and properly taught, in the manner described, it would open a sphere of employment to so many women in the home life, that we should not be obliged to send our women out to California or the Pacific to put an end to an anxious and aimless life.

"When domestic work is sufficiently honored to be taught as an art and science in our boarding-schools and high-schools, then possibly it may acquire also dignity in the eyes of our working classes, and young girls who have to earn their own living may no longer feel degraded in engaging in domestic service. The place of a domestic in a family may become as respectable in their eyes as a place in a factory, in a printing-office, in a dressmaking or millinery establishment, or behind the counter of a shop.

"In America there is no class which will confess itself the lower class, and a thing recommended solely for the benefit of any such class finds no one to receive it.

"If the intelligent and cultivated look down on household work with disdain; if they consider it as degrading, a thing to be shunned by every possible device,—they may depend upon it that the influence of such contempt of woman's noble duties will flow downward, producing a like contempt in every class in life.

"Our sovereign princesses learn the doctrine of equality very quickly, and are not going to sacrifice themselves to what is not considered *de bon ton* by the upper classes; and the girl with the laced hat and parasol, without underclothes, who does her best to 'shirk' her duties as housemaid, and is looking for marriage as an escape from work, is a fair copy of her mistress, who married for much the same reason, who hates housekeeping, and would rather board or do anything else than have the care of a family. The one is about as respectable as the other.

"When housekeeping becomes an enthusiasm, and its study and practice a fashion, then we shall have in America that class of persons to rely on for help in household labors who are now going to factories, to printing-offices, to every kind of toil, forgetful of the best life and sphere of woman."

Notes

1. Wendell Phillips, 1811–1884, American advocate of woman suffrage, abolition, and penal and labor reform; Thomas Wentworth Higginson, 1823–1911, American author.

2. Joan of Arc, 1412–1431, national heroine of France who commanded her countrymen in their fight against England.

3. The period, 1867–1877, following the American Civil War during which the seceded states were reorganized and reestablished into the United States.

4. Europe.

5. City on the Rhine River in Germany.

6. Sarah Kemble Siddons, 1775–1831, English actress; Frances (Fanny) Anne Kemble, 1809–1893, English-American actress; Adelaide Ristori, 1822–1906, Italian actress. Quotation from *Advice to a Lady* by George Lyttelton, 1709–1773, English author.

7. Hypatia, d. 415, philosopher and teacher in ancient Egypt; Anna Elizabeth Dickinson, 1842–1932, American advocate of women's rights.

8. Elizabeth Blackwell, 1821–1910, first American female physician.

9. Sairey Gamp, a drunken, old woman who works as a nurse in *Martin Chuzzlewit,* a novel by Charles Dickens, 1812–1870, English author; Florence Nightingale, 1820–1910, English founder of nursing as a profession.

10. Nathaniel Hawthorne, 1804–1864, American novelist. Zenobia is a character in *The Blithedale Romance,* 1852.

Thomas K.
Mrs. Hooker
James   William
Katherine   Lyman   Edward   Mrs. Perkins   Charles   Mrs. Stowe   Henry Ward

THE BEECHER FAMILY

The Beecher Family, c. 1859. *Left to right:* Isabella, Thomas K., Catharine E., William, Lyman, Edward, Mary, Charles, Harriet, Henry Ward. Insets: James (l.) and George, both deceased at time of photograph.

Harriet Beecher Stowe, c. 1852–1853

Calvin Ellis Stowe, c. 1830s

Twin daughters, Harriet and Eliza, with mother

Georgiana, c. 1865

Henry Ellis, c. 1860s

Frederick William, c. 1861

Charles Edward, c. 1875–1880

Harriet Beecher Stowe in parlor of Forest Street home in
Hartford, August 18, 1886

Letters

TO CALVIN ELLIS STOWE, JANUARY 1, 1847

On the occasion of their 11th wedding anniversary, Stowe wrote to her husband a letter that gives insight into their marital relationship. Stowe was then in Brattleboro, Vermont, undergoing a nine-month treatment at a water cure establishment. Calvin Ellis Stowe, 1802–1886, minister and professor of theology, was home in Cincinnati, Ohio, taking care of their five children.

Credit: *Schlesinger Library, Radcliffe College, Beecher-Stowe Collection*

My Dearest Husband,

It has occurred to me during the visions of my head on my bed that this seventh of January now coming is the anniversary[1] of our wedding some eleven years ago and thereupon I have been back and thought matters all over and all the way in which the Lord hath led us to humble us and prove us and show us what was in our hearts. Now I am not precisely sure that I have got the date of the thing exactly right but that is no particular matter as you know that my forte is not in remembering dates—even those most fully engraven on my heart. I was at that date a very different being from what I am now and stood in relation to my Heavenly Father in a very different attitude. My whole desire was to live in love, absorbing passionate devotion to one person. Our separation was my first trial, but then came a world of comfort in the hope of being a mother.² No creature ever so longed to see the face of a little one or had such a heart full of love to bestow. Here came in trial again sickness, pain, perplexity, constant discouragement—bearing wasting days and nights—a cross, deceitful, unprincipled nurse—a husband gone—no friend but Anna.³ When you came back, you came only to increasing perplexities. Ah, how little comfort had I in being a mother—how was all that I proposed met and crossed and my way ever hedged up! In short, God would teach me that I should make no family be my chief good and portion, and bitter as the lesson has been I thank Him for it from my very soul.

For a few days past I have thought of you almost constantly night and day and with the deepest affection and solicitude. There is a tone about your letters which occasions me much solicitude. I am quite sure that were I only with you, heart to heart, that the dark and *morbid* thoughts which seem to be so often rising in your mind would be dissipated. Why dwell so much on past errors and mistakes, either yours or mine. Let us think of them only to correct them not to lacerate our own hearts or each other. One might naturally [have] inferred that from the union of two persons, both morbidly sensitive and acute, yet in many respects opposite—one hasty and impulsive—the other sensitive and brooding—one the very personification of exactness and routine and the other to whom everything of the kind was an irksome effort—from all this what should one infer but some painful friction. But all this would not after all have done so very much had not Providence, as if intent to try us, thrown upon us the heaviest external pressure, just the very things calculated to irritate and try and drive even wise men mad. I think that I have erred *perhaps* in too stringently pressing on you the retention of a situation which brought this pressure upon you, but it was because I verily thought that Jesus so required and that to shrink would be treachery to Him. This you will understand and appreciate. But still when you have failed, your faults have been to me those of one beloved—of the man who after all would be the choice of my heart still were I to choose—for were I now free I should again love just as I did and again feel that I could give up all to and for you— and if I do not love and never can love again with the blind and unwise love with which I married I love quite as truly though I am *sure* that we shall find no trouble in anything else.

For, notwithstanding the excessive sensitiveness which you speak of, I think I can ask you, Did you ever speak to me in a considerate, careful, affectionate manner of my faults [and] find me unwilling to listen? I want you to think over our intercourse on this point. As to confession of faults under hasty and irritated censure, I know I never made any. But is not such hasty censure *always* in a measure unjust—and often entirely so? And being unjust has it any tendency to lead either to confession or repentance? For example, when a wife is daily and hourly tried by a careless servant who leaves undone half she tells her and spoils her best plans and arrangements, yet in spite of all this difficulty has by great effort been punctual in her hours for four or five days of the week. At last comes a day when she fails—if then her husband tells her that it's always just so— things *never* are regular—is it likely to make her confess her faults. What he accuses her of is not true—though it *is* true that she has failed that time. This fault, my dear, is not peculiar to you but is, I believe, very general among your sex in their efforts for domestic reform.

Now when a woman is faithfully and with much painful effort trying to discharge her duties in points where it is very difficult and where she is conscious of a perpetual liability, when she knows how strenuous an effort she is making and how much she really does accomplish, is it not very discouraging the very moment she fails to be addressed as if she had made no effort and taken no pains and never done anything?

One thing would make a great difference with me. If when you have said things hastily and unjustly you would only be willing to *retract* them in calmer moments. This is what you almost never do in any particular case. Like what you complain of in me you are willing [in] general to admit that you are often hasty and unjust but very seldom— almost never—to admit in any particular case. You leave the poisoned arrow in the wound. Now my nature is such that I *cannot* forget such words,—if they are only taken back I get over them directly but if not they remain for months—it is a peculiar tenacity of mine that I would but cannot escape from. Now I will promise and try and be very good about owning *my* sins if you will only do so too and this one thing will make a vast difference in my happiness and in yours. It does seem to me that with such a foundation for mutual respect and affection as there is in us—with such true and real and deep love that we might exercise a correcting power over each other—that I might help you to be kind and considerate—you me to be systematic and regular. I am sure [I] want all the help you can give me and "if there be [therefore] any consolation in Christ, *if any comfort of love*,"[4] we *must* do it. I have strong hopes that we shall be happier when we come together after this year of trial than even in the first months of our love. If you knew how much I long to see you, how glad I should be to put my arms around you and comfort you in all your trials. Sometimes it seems to me that I cannot stay longer, that I *must* come home. But I have at heart a strong presentiment that God who has so long tried us will soon bring us together in peace. *Hope then in God* far more wisely. You, my dear, are a far better man now than then—far more worthy my love and it only remains that a few more traces of the earthly be burned away in the fires of affliction to make you the

Christian that I know you have longed to be. People of your hypochondriac turn are apt to fall into the sin of unthankfulness and discontent. Being constitutionally liable to fasten on what is unpleasant rather than what is pleasant you are prone to forget mercies and to dwell only on discouragements.

I therefore hold an omen of good that your letters during the severe trials of this last year have shown so many recognitions of the mercy of God and evidences of a thankful spirit. I trust you will still cultivate the grace of thankfulness by a daily recounting of the mercies of God—for it is only when we show such a spirit that He can safely and without injury to our spiritual welfare free us from sorrows and grant us blessings.

For me my usual feeling is this. "I am God's child. Let Him do what He will with me." Whether He restore me to full health or whether I must always remain a shattered, broken invalid just able to creep along by great care, it is alike well. Cannot you bring yourself to feel the same? It was my strongest objection when I weighed the question of remaining here this winter that I feared it might prove a too protracted and severe trial for you and it was only at your solicitations and representations that I remained. For though my own judgment was consumed in taking this course I consulted for *your* best interests and that of the family *eventually* yet I felt so weak in resolution that a few such letters, thin as you have lately written, would have brought me home with a right good will—glad of an excuse. But you decided otherwise and in your decision I supposed I had all the light which God [deigned?] under the circumstances to afford me. Cannot you now since my return is impossible till the opening of spring traveling compose yourself and hold out in patience a little longer— a little—only a little while and we shall meet again. Write me, however, just as you feel. You ought to have the relief of expressing yourself freely in some direction.

I wonder what old Lady [Overacre's?]⁵ opinion of the married state is and why wives can be better dispensed with in summer than in winter. It is a curious question to my mind. Her remarks are quite vexatious to me—as if I were staying away for my own pleasure and amusement and were not as much a sufferer by it. The bells are ringing for church and I must stop for the present.

In reflecting on our future reunion, our marriage, the past obstacles to our happiness, it seems to be that they are of two or three kinds—first, those from physical causes both in you and in me—such on your part as hypochondriacal, morbid instability for which the only remedy is in physical care [and] attention to the laws of health—and on my part from the same cause, an excess of sensitiveness and of confusion and want of control of mind and memory. This always increases on my part in proportion as I am blamed or found fault with. I hope [that] will decrease with returning health. I hope that we shall both be impressed with a most solemn sense of the importance of a wise and constant attention to the laws of *health*.

Then in the second place is (has been) the want of any definite plan of mutual watchfulness with regard to each other's improvement, of a definite time and place for doing it with a firm determination to improve and be improved by each other—to confess our faults one to another that we may be healed. If we are only faithful and constant in this.

It has been evident to my mind that you have been these two years gaining on your constitutional defects, as the influence of Christ over you becomes more decided, and from Anna's account and your own I trust that you have now almost entirely obtained the mastery of yourself in the most difficult point of all. May God bless and comfort you.

As to the dates of your letters I will try.

The first is postmarked November 7. The second was part of a letter on [illegible]. The next is November 22. The next November 25. The next December 8. The next December 15-December 21. December 31 the last with an order on Wilbur.⁶ I am glad you got my bookmark before New Year's. It was a happy thought but I sent two days before it in a letter some cards for the children and a week before that a neck ribbon for Anna, of which I do not hear. I must put in here a word for Anna, which you cut off and give her. Of course this letter is for yourself alone.

Yours with much love,

Dear Anna,

I got your very welcome Christmas letter and it was truly refreshing to me. Thank mother for her kindness to you and the children and give my love to her and father.⁷

Notes

1. Actually, January 6, 1836.

2. During the first year of their marriage Calvin went to Europe on a double mission: to purchase books for Lane Theological Seminary, at which he was a faculty member, and at the request of the state legislature to collect information on education to aid in establishing a public school system in Ohio. In September, while he was still abroad, twin daughters, Harriet Beecher, 1836–1907, and Eliza Tyler, 1836–1906, were born to the Stowes.

3. Anna Smith, English nurse for the Stowe children.

4. *Philippians*. II, 1.

5. Reference unknown.

6. Wilbur may have been one of a number of donors who financed Stowe's treatment at the water cure.

7. Lydia Beals Jackson Beecher, 1789–1869, Stowe's stepmother and third wife of Lyman Beecher, 1775–1863, clergyman.

TO FREDERICK DOUGLASS, JULY 9, 1851

Seeking background material for *Uncle Tom's Cabin*, then being serialized in the *National Era*, an abolitionist newspaper, Stowe wrote to Frederick Douglass, 1817–1895, ex-slave, prominent antislavery leader, and journalist of the *North Star*, a paper he founded in Rochester, New York. In her letter she tells of her position on the relationship of church and slavery.

Frederick Douglass, Esq., Sir,

You may perhaps have noticed in your editorial readings a series of articles that I am furnishing for the *Era* under the title of *Uncle Tom's Cabin, or, Life among the Lowly*. In the course of my story, the scene will fall upon a cotton plantation. I am very desirous here to gain information from one who has been an actual laborer on one and it occurred to me that in the circle of your acquaintance there might be one who would be able to communicate to me some such information as I desire. I have before me an able paper written by a southern planter in which the details and modus operandi are given from *his* point of sight.

I am anxious to have some more from another standpoint. I wish to be able to make a picture that shall be graphic and true to nature in its details. Such a person as Henry Bibb,[1] if in this country, might give me just the kind of information I desire. You may possibly know of some other person. I will subjoin to this letter a list of questions

(435)

which, in that case, you will do me a favor by enclosing to the individual with a request that he will at earliest convenience answer them.

For some few weeks past, I have received your paper through the mail and have read it with great interest and desire to return my acknowledgements for it. It will be a pleasure to me at some time, when less occupied, to contribute something to its columns.

I have noticed with regret your sentiments on two subjects,—the church—and African colonization—and with the more regret, because I think you have a considerable share of reason for your feelings on both these subjects, *but* I would willingly, if I could, modify your views on both points.

In the first place you say the church is "for slavery." There is a sense in which this may be true. The American church of all denominations, *taken* as a body, comprises the best and most conscientious people in the country. I do *not* say it comprises *none but these*—or that none such are found out of it—but only that if a census were taken of the purest and most high-principled men and women of our country the *majority* of them would be found to be professors of religion in some of the various Christian denominations.

This fact has given to the church great weight in this country. The general and predominant spirit of intelligence and probity and piety of its majority has given it that degree of weight—that it has the *power* to decide the great moral questions of the day.

Whatever it unitedly and decidedly sets itself against as a moral evil it *can* put down.

In this sense the church is responsible for the sin of slavery. Dr. Barnes has beautifully and briefly expressed this on the last page of his work on slavery when he says, "Not all the force *out* of the church could sustain slavery an hour, if it were not sustained *in* it."[2]

It then appears that the church has the *power* to put an

(436)

end to this evil and does not do it. In this sense she may be said to be *pro slavery*. But the church has the same power over intemperance and Sabbath breaking—and sin of all kind. No doubt if the moral power of the church were brought up to the N[ew] Testament point it is sufficient to put an end to all these too.

But I would ask you would you consider it a fair representation of the Christian church in this country to say it is pro intemperance, pro Sabbath breaking and pro everything which it might put down if it was in a higher state of moral feeling?

If you should make a list of all the abolitionists of the country I think you would find a majority of them in the church—certainly some of the most influential and efficient ones are ministers.

I am a minister's daughter, a minister's wife and I have had six brothers in the ministry—(one is in Heaven)[3]—and I certainly ought to know something of the feelings of ministers. I was a child in 1821 when the Missouri question was agitated and one of the strongest and deepest impressions on my mind were my father's sermons and prayers, and the anguish of his soul for the poor slave at that time.[4] I remember his preaching drawing tears down the hardest faces of the old farmers. I remember his prayers night and morning in the family for "poor oppressed bleeding Africa," that the time of her deliverance might come, prayers offered with strong cryings and tears, and which indelibly impressed my heart and made me what I am from my soul, the enemy of all slavery. Every brother I have has been in his sphere a leading antislavery man—one of them was to the last hour of his life the bosom friend and counselor of Lovejoy[5] and all have been known and read of all men. As for myself and husband we have lived on the border of a slave state,[6]—and we have never for years shrunk from the fugitive. We have helped them with all we had to give. I have received the children of liberated slaves into a family

(437)

school and taught them with my own children—and it has been the influence that we found *in the church* and by the altar that has made us all do this. Gather up all the sermons that have been published on this offensive and unchristian Law[7] and you will find that those against it are numerically more than those in its favor—and yet some of the strongest opponents have not published their sermons—out of thirteen ministers who meet with my husband weekly for discussion of moral subjects only three are found who will acknowledge or obey this law in any shape.

After all, my brother, the strength and hope of your oppressed race does lie in the *church*. In hearts united to Him of Whom it is said He shall spare the souls of the needy—and precious shall their blood be in His sight.[8] Everything is against you—but *Jesus Christ* is for you—and He has not forgotten His church, misguided and erring though it be. I have looked all the field over with despairing eyes.

I see no hope except in Him. This movement must and will become a purely religious one—the light will spread in churches—the tone of feeling will rise—Christians north and south will give up all connection with and take up their testimony against it—and thus the work will be done.

Notes

1. Born in 1815, Bibb, a fugitive slave, established an antislavery newspaper in Canada, became a prominent lecturer, and wrote a widely read slave narrative, *Narrative of the Life and Adventures of Henry Bibb, an American Slave, Written by Himself,* 1849.

2. Albert Barnes, 1798–1870. American clergyman and author, wrote in 1846 "There is no power *out* of the church that could sustain slavery

an hour if it were not sustained *in* it" in *An Inquiry into the Scriptual Views of Slavery.*

3. George Beecher, 1807–1843.

4. The Missouri Compromise of 1820 admitted Missouri into the Union as a slave state in 1821 and prohibited slavery in the rest of the territory acquired earlier in the Louisiana Purchase. Lyman Beecher, 1775–1863.

5. Edward Beecher, 1803–1895, was with Elijah Parish Lovejoy, 1802–1837, clergyman, journalist, and abolitionist, when he was attacked and killed by a proslavery mob at Alton, Illinois.

6. The Stowes for many years lived in Cincinnati, Ohio, across the river from Kentucky.

7. The Fugitive Slave Law of 1850 demanded that all citizens aid in the return of runaway slaves.

8. *Psalms.* LXXII, 13 and 14. "He shall spare the poor and needy, and shall save the souls of the needy. He shall redeem their soul from deceit and violence: and precious shall their blood be in his sight."

TO THOMAS DENMAN, JANUARY 20, 1853

Thomas Denman, 1779–1854, the first Baron Denman and from 1832–1850 lord-chief justice of England, upon the publication of *Uncle Tom's Cabin* wrote a series of letters depicting the horrors of slavery in support of the novel. In a deferential tone Stowe requests the continued help of the distinguished jurist and that of his colleagues as well.

Credit: *The Huntington Library, San Marino, California, HM 24162*

My Lord,

Could anything flatter me into an unwarrantable estimate of myself, it would be commendation from such sources as your Lordship.

But I am utterly incredulous of all that is said; it passes by me like a dream. I can only see that when a Higher Being has proposed to be accomplished, He can make even "a grain of mustard seed"[1] the means.

I wrote what I did because as a woman, as a mother, I was oppressed and broken-hearted with the sorrows and injustice I saw, because as a Christian I felt the dishonor to Christianity—because as a lover of my country, I trembled at the coming day of wrath. It is no merit in the sorrowful that they weep, or to the oppressed and smothering that they gasp and struggle, nor to me, that I must speak for the oppressed—who cannot speak for themselves. My Lord, such men as your Lordship have great power. You can do

(*440*)

much. The expression of your opinion is of great weight. So does this horrible evil paralyze public sentiment here, that we who stand for liberty must look for aid from the public sentiment of nations, and in that sentiment none are so powerful as the great minds of England. The hope therefore which I conceive from seeing such men in England as Bishop Whately, the earls of Carlisle and Shaftsbury, Arthur Helps, Kingsley[2] and your Lordship interested in our movements is great. Each man of any distinction in England has weight with a certain circle of minds here; by their distance from the coil, and entire disconnection, can present it, in a light very different from which any native born American can. Anyone here can be hushed down—for all the capital—all the political power—and much of the ecclesiastical—is against the agitation of this subject, but you can force them to agitate. In your reviews in your literature, you can notice and hold up before the world, those awful facts which but for you, they would scornfully go on denying as they have done.

Furthermore, there are men in slave states repressed and kept under who are more glad than they dare say at what you do. They hope that you will keep on such opinions of things as they can take advantage of to bring in emancipation.

I [am] now nearly through with the prep[aration] of a vol[ume] entitled *Key to Uncle Tom's Cabin*. It contains documentary and attested evidence, to show that if my representation have erred anywhere it is by being under rather than overcolored. Oh, my Lord, never was such an awful story told under the sun. I have written it in perfect horror; one third of the book is taken up with legal documents, statute laws, decisions of courts, report of trials. It is worse than I supposed or dreamed. My Lord, I am conscious that this is not my work, for mine is another field, but I was forced to do it by the unblushing denials and the most impudent representations with regard to what I said in my

(*441*)

book on slave law. It seems to me that this tremendous story cannot be told in the civilized world without forcing attention. On the whole, there is hope—there is movement, there is evidently "a stirring of bones in this valley of vision."[3] Standing as I do, between the living and the dead, feeble in health, and often very sorrowful, I have little realization of anything personal in this matter further than the consciousness of struggle and labor. I thank your Lordship therefore more for the noble and hearty interest which you feel in this sacred and suffering cause than for the very kind opinion which you [have] been kind enough to express of me. It has done much good. All that the book has done might have been crushed in this country, but for the sympathy and support of your country. May God bless it and you is the prayer of yours very gratefully.

Notes

1. A frequent allusion in the New Testament.

2. Richard Whately, 1787–1863, English prelate and theologian; George William Frederick Howard, 1802–1864, 7th earl of Carlisle, English statesman; Anthony Ashley Cooper, 1801–1885, 7th earl of Shaftsbury, English philanthropist; Arthur Helps, 1813–1875, English author; Charles Kingsley, 1819–1875, English clergyman and author.

3. A garbled allusion to *Isaiah*. XXII, 1 and 5.

TO HENRY WADSWORTH LONGFELLOW,
JANUARY 27, 1853

Caught in a difficult position, the possible evasion of copyright law, Stowe wrote to the American poet, Henry Wadsworth Longfellow, 1807–1882, seeking permission to quote two of his poems in *A Key to Uncle Tom's Cabin.*

Credit: *Harriet Beecher Stowe Collection (#6318-c),*
Clifton Waller Barrett Library, University of
Virginia Library

Dear Sir,

In the work which I am now preparing, *A Key to Uncle Tom's Cabin,* I am very desirous of being allowed to quote two of your poems on slavery—for I cannot repress the desire to solace myself and my readers with now and then a pearl which has been cast on shore by the wide waves of this most angry and stormy subject. In fact, in my innocence I had already quoted them, never thinking but that poet's songs were as universal property as bird's songs or wildflowers but have been recalled to earthly considerations by suggestions of the sacredness of copyright, etc. I therefore write to ask your sanction to my publishing the "Quadroon Girl" and the "Slave in the Dismal Swamp" in parts of my book where poetry can speak better than prose.[1]

Yours very truly.

(443)

1. Quoted respectively in "Part II: Chapter IV" and "Part III: Chapter IV," *A Key to Uncle Tom's Cabin.*

TO FREDERICK LAW OLMSTED, 1856

Frederick Law Olmsted, 1822–1903, best known as a land-scape architect and designer of many of America's city parks, was in his youth a journalist. *The New York Times* sent him south to report on the effects of slavery on the economy. His communications appeared weekly in the newspaper and were collected in 1856 in *A Journey in the Seaboard Slave States*, a copy of which Stowe apparently "found lying on my table."

Stowe, in the middle of writing her second slave novel, *Dred: A Tale of the Great Dismal Swamp*, set in North Carolina, asked Olmsted for a few botanical details, just as she earlier had written Frederick Douglass for aid in setting her plantation scenes in *Uncle Tom's Cabin*. In praising Olmsted's book, she, perhaps experiencing again the anger *Uncle Tom's Cabin* incurred, sounds sad when she tells him that his work is "exceedingly calculated to do more good with less friction."

Credit: *By permission of the Houghton Library, Harvard University*

Mr. Olmsted, Dear Friend,

On Saturday last I found lying on my table your book, for which I am truly grateful. I have plunged into it with the deepest interest so much that as [I am] in the midst of the novel, the scene of which is laid in North Carolina, and therefore anxious for details I was. Excuse me if I ask a few questions.

Of what species is the pine of which you make so great mention and of which the greater part of the pine forests are composed? Are the mosses and flowers which grow under them of the same species that grow in the pine forests in the northern states? Did you notice that white, crispy, frosty looking moss which grows on pinelands with us? Also the feathery green ground pine? Pray, what is the catbrier of which you make such frequent mention? Is holly like the English? Have you ever seen it employed for hedges? I wish very much if you are in our vicinity you would make me a call, for I should like very much to read you some parts and get a little help from you about laying out the topographical details. It is necessary for me to get a perfect, definite idea of the country where I suppose the scene will be laid, and in conversing with you I could do it.

I am charmed with your book. It is extremely graphic and readable and exceedingly calculated to do more good with less friction. Pray, excuse my troubling you to answer so many questions. My own experience sensibly convinces me how much it is in these times to ask for a letter from any in our busy world.

Very sincerely, your friend.

TO ELIZABETH CLEGHORN GASKELL,
JULY 10, 1860

Mrs. Elizabeth Gaskell, 1810–1865, English novelist and contemporary of Harriet Beecher Stowe, was equally committed to revealing social inequities. The women had met in the company of the English writer, William Makepeace Thackery, 1811–1863, in 1860. In this letter Stowe proposes a joint book about Italy, a proposal that reveals not only her entrepreneurship but also her ties to an international community of literary women. The project, however, was never carried out.

My Dear Mrs. Gaskell,

M r. Lowe[1] has written me that you seemed favorably inclined to entertain a project for a sort of partnership with me in a work on Italy.

It had been my intention to get such a work out before leaving England, but I found the state of my family to be such that I could not leave them any longer. Home became in my eyes worth a thousand books and to get there a month sooner worth any sacrifice. Also, I wanted to prepare my materials a little more at my leisure. I was ready to give up my chance of an English copyright but my publishers were disappointed at this and wished to cast about for some means to secure it. The idea of joint authorship had been proposed to me and it then occurred to me that you had been to Italy-had had like me a lovely time there

[and] *must* have thought—even probably written a great deal about it and had never published. Could we not in some way unite our forces without interfering with each other's individuality [and] secure copyright mutually in our respective countries and divide the profits. I have always sympathized so heartily with your views and opinions on all subjects as to feel that there would be enough accord in the work. In cases where we may have taken views slightly different, let *both* be presented. There *are* two views often— both true, both important. By arrangement under topics this result might be secured.

As the work must *appear* first in England, and the copyright *here* can be secured without any other formality than merely the recording of a printed title page. The editorial or arranging duties will devolve on you. It will have to be arranged somewhat in this way. I shall send you all I have to say and you will then take it and arrange it with yours. Wherever in treating a topic you shall perceive that you have had more information or better you will without scruple remodel it by your better light and if you differ in opinion you can freely express your difference. *Truth* is struck out in this way.

The idea I have of the book is that of paragraphs on topics with each a heading. This gives scope for the greatest freedom and variety. I shall be busying myself with it immediately and meanwhile hope to hear from you more particularly as to how the proposition strikes [you] and your views concerning it.

I have been reading *The Mill on the Floss*. How strong and striking! Can you tell me what is the *true* history of Miss Evans.[2] We all want to know what to think of her.

With best love to your girls I am very affectionately yours.

Notes

1. Sampson Low, 1797–1886, English publisher.

2. Mary Ann Evans, 1819–1880, English novelist, wrote *The Mill on the Floss* in 1860 under the pseudonym of George Eliot.

TO HENRY WARD BEECHER,
NOVEMBER 2, 1862

In this letter to her brother, the prominent clergyman, reformer, and editor, Stowe demonstrates her concern for the management of the Civil War by remonstrating with him for his views on the leadership of Abraham Lincoln, 1809–1865, the martyred 16th president of the United States, 1861–1865. Henry Ward Beecher, 1813–1887, had written in his newspaper, the *Independent,* that Lincoln was "destitute of a single capacity for leadership," a criticism that she assailed as *"hopeless"* and demoralizing.

Dear Henry,

I have watched your leaders for some time and heard the remarks upon them, debating with myself what plan of compaign you have in view. That the administration ought to have its measures criticized I freely grant, but I am not able to see of what practical use will be some things that you say, for example, that the president is a man destitute of a single capacity for leadership, that he has no steady plan but does from time to time what this or that person advises him to.

That kind of criticism is *hopeless* so far as its effects go. It is merely proving to a crew in a storm that the only man who can hold the helm is drunk or imbecile.

If he is all this, a man without capacity, without plan or the power of forming one, what shall *we* do about it? As you

(450)

say in your last letter, he is to be our president for these two years, and had he better have a nation and army who trust him or a nation and army who think him a well-meaning imbecile? The general tone of your articles is deeply discouraging to that very class whose demoralization and division would be [a] most hopeless defeat for us.

Again, I am not at all sure that McClellan[1] has not been more sinned against than sinning. Col. Green, Fred's colonel[2] [who has] just resigned, having worn out his strength in the struggle, says McClellan is a soldierly man and has the capacity to go through with things but that whenever he seems on the eve of accomplishing anything he is pulled back by a string from Washington. Siegel's opinion expressed to Agnes Beecher's husband[3] I got her to write—to send to you. The well-known enthusiastic confidence of the army is another thing in his favor.

Your evident championship of Fremont[4] (you know that we all are his friends) has been spoken of by some as injuring the effect of some of the best things you have said. People lay down the paper and say, "Oh, well, he's a Fremont man. That's what's the matter with him."

I think Fremont has been abused and McClellan I *know* has been too, but I do believe in both as patriots and unselfish seekers of the country's good and I have some reason, for I have heard some things in very straight course from both.

These things suggested [are] by way of inquiry. Your argument of this week on voting for the administration and including all other kinds of support is yet broader. Go to Washington yourself, see with your own eyes, talk with Chase and Seward[5] and Lincoln and see if you can't throw out a few notes of encouragement. Every man's heart sinks like a stone that reads your leaders and many think if this be so, [he] may as well try another party.

Will you go to Washington with me in a week or two? I will go if you will.

(*451*)

This merely as suggestion but it embodies the opinion of everybody I know and I know people whose opinions are worth consideration.

Ever your loving sister.

Notes

1. George Brinton McClelland, 1826–1885, Union general.

2. William B. Greene, First Regiment Massachusetts Volunteers Heavy Artillery; Frederick William Stowe, 1840–1870?, Stowe's son.

3. Franz Siegal, 1824–1902, Civil War general; Mrs. Edward H. (Agnes Beecher) Allen, 1831–1923, whose husband served under Siegal.

4. John Charles Fremont, 1813–1890, American explorer, general, and politician who once ran for the presidency.

5. Salmon Portland Chase, 1808–1873, secretary of the treasury; William Henry Seward, 1801–1872, secretary of state.

TO FREDERICK WILLIAM GUNN,
MAY 17, 1864

Frederick William Gunn, 1816–1881, founded and directed for 40 years the Gunnery School in Washington, Connecticut. Charles Edward Stowe, 1850–1934, attended this private boys' academy and ultimately from it ran away to sea. These two letters illustrate Stowe's strong mothering instincts and give insight into her philosophy of child rearing.

Credit: *Beecher Family Papers, Manuscripts and Archives, Yale University Library*

My Dear Friend (Mr. Gunn),

We have been moving—moving into an unfinished house—which is still under hammer and saw and everything only partially recovered from the great confusion—and we only half settled.[1] As Charley's father was summoned to Cincinnati and Charley has been our sole male, we have kept him some days beyond time.

I have great hopes of the boy. He is still chaotic, unformed, but there are times when he talks with me with heart openess of his sins, faults, prospects, telling me alike the good and the bad. In these good hours he sees and admits that the disciplining of your school has been exactly what he needed and that you had been a true friend. He says that Mr. Gunn enchants all the boys so that no matter what he does to them they can't help loving him. In other moods he sometimes quarrels with restraint—feels wild impulses to fly and wander.

I have explained to him the philosophy of the change of life in boys, its cravings, morbid longings and dangers and warned him against fatal habits resulting from these physical cravings. He talks and resolves sensibly in these hours and I have good hope that he will keep his resolutions.

The only point where I would make a suggestion is this. Where a boy who is intensely approbative as Charley [and] had a habit like that of untruth to combat, it is desirable as much as possible to save his character with other boys. If he feels that he have lost the esteem of his community it presses him downward, and approbativeness seeks its aliment by going after low associates. Charley does mean to be truthful, but many time by a sort of natural indirectness he exposes himself to suspicion. I hope you will as much as possible guard his return [and] let him feel that he may win confidence and standing—that is all. Much in Charley that seems like insincerity may be accounted for if we consider that two opposite natures, an Esau and a Jacob,[2] are struggling in him and now one and now the other gains the ascendency. In one nature he loves and appreciates your work and manly resolves for the future. In the other he is cross-grained and contrary and suspicious—and tempted to evade what he knows is right. I have seen this crossing of two contending natures in more than one young person who as either nature prevails say they love or hate the same thing.

Please give my love to Mrs. Gunn and say that my head is so upset with moving that I really can't tell whether Charley brought back his sheets or not. I think they are left with you, but if anything is missing he ought to bring, if she will advise me, I will send it. I want before long to come and see you.

I am your sincere friend.

Notes

1. The Stowes were settling into *Oakholm*, their first home in Hartford, Connecticut.

2. Twin brothers in the Bible.

TO FREDERICK WILLIAM GUNN,
JUNE 6, 1864

My Dear Mr. Gunn,

My boy came home to me after four days' experience of sailor life, heartbroken at leaving the ship, pining for the sea like a schoolgirl for her home.

He had been so happy. He had got his outfit all prepared—his plans of life. Said he had eighteen dollars a month and no expenses. He would save his money and then at the end of six months if he could get his father's consent he would go on board a square-rigger and make thirty-two dollars a month. And he wasn't sick, and had done man's work for five days, shoveling and cleaning, etc. and liked it.

When I told him of the grief he had caused his father, he seemed taken aback and said, "I wrote to him and I thought that though he might not be willing to *send* me, yet when he knew that I really could earn eighteen dollars a month he would be glad—and I could save money; for I should have no expenses, and instead of being a drag and expense I could be sending home money. I was willing to work and work hard. The captain told me that he was short of hands and that I must do man's work and I did it and liked it. The other sailors grumbled about the provision and work but I like everything. I never ate with such appetite or felt so well"—and then came a whole list of instances of men in New York, shipowners, dockmasters, etc. who had risen from before the mast and he was going to do

(456)

it. I let him tell all through and then I took up my line of reply.

I told him that there was a mixture of what was truly respectable with what was very wrong in what he had been doing. That it was *wrong* for him with so little consideration for his father to take his case into his own hands and dilated in all the consequences that might have ensued. On the other hand, it was respectable to be willing to go to work immediately—and to work hard—that he had not run away for a spree or for amusement but with a definite and well-considered plan of earning his own living.

The fault of his plan I told him was this—that it was premature—that he was not yet sufficiently educated to *rise* at sea—that he wrote a miserable hand and was a poor speller and did not understand bookkeeping or accounts and that if he went to sea in this state he would be and remain a mere low ignorant common sailor all his life. If he really wished to go to sea, I wished him to go prepared to rise to be something more than that. That if he would go to work now [and] energetically acquire a handsome hand, reform his spelling, learn bookkeeping and accounts, we would use our influence to get him a good ship and let him try the sea.

There is a commercial school here in Hartford where commercial arithmetic, writing, spelling, bookkeeping are the special branches and in that we have placed him. He begins today and seems to like the school. I have fitted up his room and we have him now between us once more.

Charley is in the midst of the general breakup that precedes manhood, and in this stage of things such passions are often kindled. Charley's passion is for the sea—it is a *passion*. There is no more use opposing a boy who is in love with the sea than one who is in love with a woman. The course we pursue is exactly what my father took with Henry Ward at the same age under the same circumstances. It gains time for us. He looks forward now to a year of preparation as Henry did when he went to Mount Pleasant.[1]

One thing one sees—Charley has inherited from his father a physical, constitutional love of the sea. He has been every vacation to the seaside or coasting with his father. He has read a library of sea stories. And so when he was put to Latin and felt that he was constantly behindhand, constantly at the tail and appearing to disadvantage, approbativeness, which is very strong in him, was exacerbated and kept constantly saying in his ear—there is something you can do, a line where you can do well and be praised; you can be first-rate in something—and so he fled to it.

Last night I saw your letter on Charley's table and asked to read it. He made no objections and when I spoke with him as I often do, saying that you were a true friend and really loved him, he smiled and made no reply. When I asked him if he would not after all like to go back he answered firmly *no*—that he preferred to be where he was. I am perfectly sure he could not be persuaded to go back— and if forced back he could be kept only by force.

He is very much altered in some respects. No longer gay, chatty, talkative, he is silent, inclining to be alone, reticent—and brooding. He is no longer to be won by a kiss and a hug. He is not a little Charley any longer. He is looking into life—longing for the things of manhood— and I speak more to his reason than to his sentiment. And since he *will* walk the precipice I try to steady his hand. He is thrown on his responsibility. He understands that he is now trying *his* plan and that we in good faith are giving him the means to do it. There must be men of the sea. If he is called for that, I will not dispute his vocation.

You could hardly advise us to force him back to you— and you will perceive at once why we keep him here and that it is from no lack of confidence in you. The object at this time of life for parents and teachers is not to have their own way—but to make a good man—not to preserve their authority but to preserve the boy. And if we should force Charley back, he would again go to sea, and *this time* would not be so artless as to send us the name of his vessel.

His father is happy once more, happier in having Charley's study opening from his own than if he were in the best school away. I wanted to put this responsibility onto your broader shoulders, my good friend, but God has suffered it to come back on us. We cannot shirk "Our Charley."[2]

Notes

1. Lyman Beecher, 1775–1863, clergyman, enrolled Henry Ward Beecher, 1813–1895, minister and younger brother of Stowe, in Mount Pleasant Institution in Amherst, Massachusetts, in 1827 ostensibly to prepare him for a career in the navy.

2. A reference to a character modeled after her son in stories she wrote.

TO SARA PAYSON WILLIS PARTON, FEBRUARY 15, 1868

Writing to Sara Parton, 1811–1872, a childhood friend, Stowe reminisces about their schoolgirl days, touches upon her position on woman's rights, chides Parton's husband, a well-known biographer, about his choice of subjects, and deplores the prevalence of smoking. In short, a chatty, rambling, friendly letter. Parton was herself a very popular writer under the name of Fanny Fern.

Credit: *The Sophia Smith Collection (Women's History Archive), Smith College*

My Dear Sara Willis,

I hold to woman's rights to the extent that a woman's own native name never ought to die out and be merged in the name of any man whatever. In Geneva they have a custom—puzzling enough at first sight—by which the man adopts his wife's name in addition to his own. Thus the Mr. Fazi,[1] with whom I boarded, becomes Mr. Fazi *Meyer* by his wife, etc., etc. Mr. Stowe by this usage becomes Mr. Stowe Beecher and so on.

But "Sara Willis" brings back a world of thoughts and remembrances.[2] Do you ever meet Urania Battell? About three or four years ago I saw and had a talk with her about you and the old days. I do not often meet her—only once in many years—but found her much such a woman as one might have predicted from her good, wholesome, steady

(460)

youth. I have the greatest faculty of remembering people's looks and I think that I could draw a picture of many of my girls—Urania, with her long, curling auburn hair, her fresh, clean, ruddy complexion and her dovelike hazel eyes. Her mouth alone prevented her being as striking a beauty as her sister Irene but there was something wholesome and noble about her air.[3] You also I remember, with your head of light, crepe curls, with your bonnet always tipped on one side, and you, with a most insidious leaning towards that broad sound of laughing and conjuration which is the horror of well-regulated schoolma'ams and the many scrapes which occasioned for you secret confabulations with sister Katy[4] up in her room. She had always a warm side towards you. Do you remember the vacation at Guilford[5]—and your irrepressibility? The idea that *you* have daughters—can I believe it a granddaughter? So I have been informed, but shan't believe it till I hear it.

Next summer you and Mr. Parton[6] must come and see us in Hartford and I will put you through the old paces and you shall perform a penance for some of your old sins. Poor, old Dr. Strong![7] Let us hope he will not appear to you. And poor, brave, sad hearted *Miss* Strong,[8] who fought her life battle so keenly and hardly—peace to her. You wouldn't trouble her now for the world, for now you know what a life battle is.

As to husbands, I am sorry to hear that yours shares the common, modest imbecility of authorhood, but, Sara, *I* am not a bit better, not so good. I can scold my husband bravely when I have him all alone, and can advise him to speak up but a snuffling Yankee businessman takes me in hook and line and does pretty much as he pleases with me. I have concluded that there is no way but to let a lawyer (my brother-in-law,[9] say) do the talking for and make my contracts. I tell him what I want and he does the talking and they don't get *him* to unsay and tread back as they would be sure to do me. If all who have to do with authors were like

(461)

Bonner,[10] our way would be a straight one. But don't for the world think this talk has any reference to "my friend and pitcher," J. T. Fields, who has always done well by me and is an agreeable man to boot, and his wife still more so.[11]

What can your husband be wanting to write a life of Voltaire[12] for? Is he going to try to make us *like* him as he did Aaron Burr?[13] But I shan't like him and I can't. I hate him. I have an *antipathy* to him like that of Margaret for Mephistophiles.[14] You see, he has no interest in anything— 'tis written on his brow. He feels no love for any living soul. I took it into my head not long ago to read his romances. They are keen and witty as the Devil himself and as utterly unloving and unbelieving. Such *utter* depths of faithlessness in God and man and woman and things present and things to come and life and death—all tossed and whirled hither and thither gave me exactly the feeling about him that poor Margaret had for Mephistophiles.

I confess I did have a kind feeling towards him in reading Taine.[15] Very early in life he had something good in him, but the tares choked the good seed and he became utterly faithless. To bury oneself in such an author is like going into a cavern of mephitic gas, isn't it? You see, Mr. Parton, I am talking to you over Sara's shoulder.

What earthly good is it to learn that man is a poor, miserable, trashy, dirty, utterly contemptible humbug— beginning in darkness and ending in nowhere—which seems to be about what Voltair makes of him. I know you are going to reconstruct him and turn him out a tip-top saint and so I will have my time of railing in advance.

By the by, both of you, have you read Gail Hamilton's *Woman's Wrongs*?[16] If you haven't, *read it*, before you are a day older. It's decidedly the brightest, cleanest, healthiest, noblest kind of a book. Do you know her? She is a trump— a real original—healthy—largehearted and simple-minded—and good as she can be.

I am quite jubilant over Mr. Parton's article on smoking.[17] It's true—every word—and I am not without hope that it may do some good. I am in all the agony of exhortation and warning and argument with my Charley,[18] aged 17, who has tasted the evil tree and vowed to abstain. 'Tis incredible in how many ways a boy who is trying to clear himself of this habit is everywhere tempted by those who *should* be examples. The clergy in our Episcopal church are dreadful. The apostolic succession must be all smoke, judging by them. Then, doctors, lawyers, governors, judges— all smokers! But for that good word I thank your husband. Every *little* helps. Now, Sara, sometime next summer you will come this way, won't you?

Your handwriting hasn't changed a bit since you were a girl.

Yours affectionately.

Notes

1. James Fazy, 1796–1878, Swiss statesman and journalist with whom Stowe stayed while on vacation in Switzerland in June 1853.

2. Parton and Stowe attended Hartford Female Seminary in Connecticut.

3. Urania Battell also was a pupil at Hartford Female Seminary as was her sister, Irene. Stowe began her teaching career here while still a student herself.

4. Catharine Esther Beecher, 1800–1878, pioneer in higher education for women, founder of Hartford Female Seminary, and oldest sister of Stowe.

5. Nutplains in Guilford, Connecticut, was the childhood home of Stowe's mother.

6. James Parton, 1822–1891, American biographer and third husband of Sara Willis.

7. Possibly, a Congregational minister who served as a spiritual adviser to the students at Hartford Female Seminary.

8. Frances A. Strong, 1814–1853, American educator, was successively a pupil, student teacher, and principal of Hartford Female Seminary.

9. Thomas Clap Perkins, 1798–1870.

10. Robert Bonner, 1824–1899, American publisher and founder of the *New York Ledger*. Under the pseudonym of Fanny Fern, Parton, from 1855 until her death, wrote a weekly column in the *Ledger*.

11. James Thomas Fields, 1817–1881, American publisher and editor; Annie Adams Fields, 1834–1915, American author who after Stowe's death wrote *Life and Letters of Harriet Beecher Stowe*, 1897.

12. Pseudonym for Francois Marie Arouet, 1694–1778, French writer. Parton published his *Life of Voltaire* in 1881.

13. Aaron Burr, 1756–1836, American politician and vice president, 1801–1805, was tried for treason. In 1857 Parton wrote *The Life and Times of Aaron Burr*.

14. Characters in *Faust* by Johann Wolfgang Goethe, 1749–1832, German poet.

15. Hippolyte Adolphe Taine, 1828–1893, French historian.

16. Pseudonym for Mary Abigail Dodge, 1830–1896, American writer. *Woman's Wrongs* appeared in 1868.

17. *Smoking and Drinking*, 1868.

18. Charles Edward Stowe, 1850–1934, clergyman and last of Stowe's seven children.

TO WILLIAM LLOYD GARRISON,
NOVEMBER 9, 1868

William Lloyd Garrison, 1805–1879, abolitionist, founder
and president of the American Antislavery Society, 1843–
1865, and editor of the *Liberator*, followed up his work to
free slaves with efforts after the Civil War to educate blacks.
Stowe asked his help in funding schools near her winter
home in Florida.

Dear Mr. Garrison,

When you were here, you promised to make some
inquiries, relative to the support of a teacher for the colored people in my school district at Mandarin, Florida.

General Howard[1] has promised me to erect school
buildings if I will agree to keep up a school. There is a well-
educated young northern lady now on the grounds. If the
society[2] will allow me three hundred dollars ($300.) a year,
I think that with it I can not only keep up a school in my
own district, where there are now forty colored children
without any means of instruction, but can also keep up a
school in a Negro settlement four miles off, where there
are thirty families settled on government land. With three
hundred dollars, I think I could take care of both these
places, for the Negroes themselves will do everything they
are able.

General Howard told me that this year they had contributed two hundred thousand dollars for the support of

their own schools! which, I think, is more than all the whites of the south, put together, have done.

Will you be kind enough to make the application for me, as I do not know really to whom to write.

Truly yours.

Notes

1.   Oliver Otis Howard, 1839–1909, served as a Union general during the Civil War. From 1865–1874 he was chief of the Freedmen's Bureau, an agency that supervised the affairs of the emancipated slaves and provided education for them.

2.   The American Antislavery Society was disbanded on April 9, 1870. After the freeing of the slaves its funds were disbursed in providing education for blacks.

TO SARA PAYSON WILLIS PARTON, JULY 25, 1869

To her former classmate at Hartford Female Seminary in Connecticut, Stowe wrote her view of woman suffrage. Sara Parton, 1811–1872, under the pseudonym of Fanny Fern, was a well-known writer and columnist.

Credit: *The Sophia Smith Collection (Women's History Archive), Smith College*

My Dearly Beloved Sara,

You are a good girl to stick to your old grandma so well and like all I do. It shows what a nice child you are.

I am just as scared as I can be, for I have done just as your Jim[1] told me to—*and it's all in print* in the September *Atlantic*[2] and now I feel really frightened at what I have done; and ready to run behind a door.

But it is *right* and *just*. I am sure it would be a shame to let that dear angel bear the whole fault and shame of that guilty life *after* her death as well as all her life. So I spoke— and *quod scripsit scripst*.[3] I believe my Latin is deserting me with the rest of my senses today. There never was and never will be another woman like Lady Byron. If Jim had seen *her* he never could have had another doubt of the immortality of the soul and the final triumph of good. It was as good as seeing an angel right from the other side.

I have been salting daily in water.[4] By the by, now I

think of it, Bushnell has been shown up in the neatest way in the last *Hearth and Home* by a lady—No. 32. Don't fail to read it. It is, as you say, a nice ladylike "toasting fork"— and, you see, as I am on friendly terms with the family *I* couldn't have done it and so I am immensely tickled that it's done and done well.[5]

Yes, I do believe in Female Suffrage. The more I think of it the more absurd this whole government of men over women looks. A friend of mine put it rather nicely the other night. "I don't much care about voting," she said the other day, "but I feel as the girl did who was offended when the cake plate was not passed her.

'Why, I thought you did not love cake.'

'But I'd like to have the chance of refusing it,' says she."

This agreement of Tom, Dick and Harry not to pass the cake plate lest we make ourselves sick with cake seems absurd.

Dare not trust us with suffrage lest we become unwomanly. Let them try it unsexed. I should like to see what could make women other than women and men than men. The colors we are dyed in are warranted to wash, and now I lay my commands on you. You and Mr. Parton *both* must without delay get and read John Stuart Mill's book just published by the Appletons.[6] It has wholly converted me. I was only right in spots before; now I am all clear.

Good-bye. Write me some more.

Still direct to 1217 Hartford.

Notes

1. James Parton, 1822–1891, American biographer and third husband of Sara Willis.

2. For the *Atlantic Monthly* (September 1869) Stowe wrote "The True Story of Lady Byron's Life," an article that fomented an international controversy. She charged that Lady Byron, Anne Isabella Milbanks Byron, 1792–1860, left her husband, Lord Byron, George Noel Gordon Byron, 1788–1824, one of England's most celebrated poets, in 1816 because she discovered his incestuous relationship with his half sister.

3. Usually, *quod scripsi scripsi*—what I have written I have written.

4. Stowe was then vacationing at West Port Point, Bristol County, Massachusetts.

5. Horace Bushnell, 1802–1876, American Congregational clergyman and theologian, in 1869 published *Woman's Suffrage: The Reform against Nature*. In the July 31, 1869, issue (Number 32) of *Hearth and Home*, a weekly household periodical coedited by Stowe, Lucia Gilbert Calhoun wrote an unfavorable review, "A Woman's View of Dr. Bushnell's Book."

6. John Stuart Mill, 1806–1873, English philosophical writer, in 1869 published *On the Subjection of Women*. D. Appleton & Co. issued the work in America.

TO RALPH WALDO EMERSON,
[NOT EARLIER THAN] JULY 29, 1869

In a letter than shows her connectedness to a literary contemporary, Stowe asked the help of the eminent American
philosopher, essayist, and poet, Ralph Waldo Emerson,
1803–1882. Her letter, somewhat mutilated, solicits an article on woman suffrage.

Credit: *By permission of the Houghton Library,
Harvard University*

Dear Mr. Emerson,

The proprietors of the *Hearth and Home*[1] are desirous
of having in their paper a discussion by the very best minds
of our country of the Woman Question of our present
day—or to put it more specifically the Question of Female
Suffrage. I am requested by them to secure articles to this
intent. Reading your letter to the Suffrage Convention in Boston,[2] I was struck with some of the sentiments of it. . . . [We?] desire that you . . . [write for?] our
paper . . . starting in . . . [date? and give your?]impressions
of the present position of the subject as it stands in our
country. You might with perhaps *less* offense and with
more profit than anyone give a little *well-timed advice* to the
zealous, earnest leaders of this movement to avoid shocking the *public taste* by a too prominent urging of extreme
views, which are not essential to the main point—and by an

(*470*)

ungraceful and ungracious manner of presenting the truth—and at the same time give to the cause the support of a respectful and delicate consideration.

In regard to the financial part, the proprietors of *Hearth and Home* offer $50 for a short article of about two columns of that paper. They always remit cheque immediately on receipt of articles.

. . . [We hope that you will?] speak a word both of encouragement and advice and also that your name should set many in more fastidious circles to giving serious thought to a subject which as yet has only struck them as matter for jest and ridicule. To take it out of the sphere of ridicule into that of rational consideration is the peculiar province of the true Philosopher and I for one woman should regard such words spoken just now as . . . [conclusion missing].

Notes

1. Donald Grant Mitchell ("Ik Marvel"), 1822–1908, American essayist and novelist, and Mary Mapes Dodge, 1831–1905, American author and editor, founded the *Hearth and Home*, a weekly household periodical for which Stowe served as coeditor for a short time.
2. Emerson's letter to the Essex County Woman Suffrage Association was printed in the *Boston Daily Advertiser* on July 29, 1869, and in the *New York Times* on July 30, 1869.

TO LADY AMBERLEY, JUNE 23, 1870

In a letter of appreciation Stowe wrote Lady Amberley, wife of John Russell (Viscount Amberley), 1842–1876, sometime Liberal Member of Parliament, she thanks the couple for their efforts in support of woman suffrage. Though she predicts the extension of the vote to Englishwomen before their American counterparts, full suffrage was not granted until 1928, eight years after the enfranchisement of women in the United States.

Credit: *The Library of Congress*

Dear Lady Amberley,

I must seize a moment to thank you for sending me your admirable address before the Strand Institute.[1] It is one of the best and most complete presentations of the whole subject I ever saw and we in America must thank you for it. It is a noble *deed* for you to speak because *you* are in no sense in need of the rights or a sufferer from the wrongs you speak of.

I have just made an abstract of it for the *Christian Union*, my brother's paper and mine,[2] and shall send you the paper when it appears. I am delighted to hear you so gallantly resolving to push the question and make a hustings affair of it. Go on, my dear, you are sure to conquer and you fight charmingly and your victory must precede ours. You preceded us in Negro emancipation and you will in this. You handle your weapons beautifully. There is some sense in rank and all that sort of thing, sometimes, when the right sort of person makes it a fort for fighting the battle of humanity and there are weak fashionables here in America who will hear a viscountess or duchess when they would scoff at Mrs. Stanton and Susan Anthony.[3] *That*, you see, amuses me, for *I* don't like you one whit the more for your rank and station, though I do like you more for the *use* you are making of it.

I like you for being a wholehearted, large-souled, generous woman—brave and courageous—gallant and chivalrous—and bless God that you *happen* in this day of ours to be in the *nobility*. Lord Amberley's articles please me no less. His statement on the importance of suffrage to the *weak* hits the nail straight on the head. That was why we gave it to the Negro and the Chinese man—and why we *ought* still more to give it to the women of the same. To be sure, universal suffrage is a terrible thing, *but* there is no help for it—it has *got* to come and we may as well let it come under guidance as without.

"The Kingdom" is coming and the world is frightened with the answer to its prayers. A colored stewardess on the steamer said to me the other day, "We keep a praying everyday, Thy will be done, but when it is done what a fuss we make about it!"[4]

We have all been spending the winter at our place in Florida among our orange trees.[5] It is a wild, uncultured country forest all around. The sea on one side and the broad St. Johns five miles wide on the other. From September to May our trees have been burdened with fruit. Now we are back in our Hartford house, where we had so pleasant a visit from you.

My daughters send you their love and my husband[6] desires his regards to yourself and Lord Amberley. We hope to see him one day premier of England.

Ever Truly Yours.

Notes

1. Strand Institute, a cultural and intellectual society.

2. In 1870 a syndicate, including Stowe and her brother, Henry Ward Beecher, 1813–1887, clergyman, bought a moribund religious newspaper, renamed it the *Christian Union*, and appointed Beecher its editor. For several years Stowe contributed to it articles, sketches, and serializations of novels.

3. Elizabeth Cady Stanton, 1815–1902, and Susan Brownell Anthony, 1820–1906, American suffragists.

4. See *Matthew*. V, 9–13.

5. Mandarin.

6. Twin daughters, Harriet Beecher, 1836–1907, and Eliza Tyler, 1836–1912, and Calvin Ellis Stowe, 1802–1886, minister and professor of theology.

TO SAMUEL L. CLEMENS, 1876

In Hartford, Connecticut, Stowe and Samuel L. Clemens ("Mark Twain"), 1835–1910, were across-the-lawn neighbors. One day the noted American humorist paid an impromptu visit to his fellow writer. Upon his return home his wife chided him for his informality in dress, inspiring Clemens to amend his lapse by sending his tie to Mrs. Stowe via his butler. Stowe's witty note is her reply to his playful action.

Credit: *The Bancroft Library, University of California, Berkeley*

Dear Mr. Clemens,

You have discovered a *principle*. You probably don't know it—as didn't Sir Isaac Newton[1] when the apple fell—but you have. You have discovered that a man can call by instalments. It is a discovery! and may be applied to many uses. Allow me to thank you for the prolonged pleasure.

Yours truly.
    May not a man in extremis send his hat and boots to call? I suggest the question.

Notes

1. English mathematician, 1642–1727, who formulated the universal law of gravitation.

TO OLIVER WENDELL HOLMES,
SEPTEMBER 8, 1892

In a poignant letter to Oliver Wendell Holmes, 1809–1894,
American writer, Stowe discusses candidly her mental and
physical condition in her "declining years."

Credit: *The Library of Congress*

My Dear Friend, Dr. Holmes,

Your more than kind, your most charming, really
lovely letter of January 31 was to me the profoundest surprise and the greatest pleasure I have had in many a day—I
might say year. That you should remember and think of
me and write me so at length, with your own hand, too, is a
kind courtesy and an honor that I sincerely appreciate.

I must tell you, my dear friend, if you do not know it
yourself—and I say it not to flatter but because it is true—
your lamp burns as brightly as ever. The oil in it has not
run low, leaving but a feeble gleam, as mine has done. Your
noble and beautiful lines to our friend Whittier[1] show no
diminution of mental power, but only the sweetness and
richness of many summers.

I am glad to know how you pass your time, and that
you have such a peaceful, cheerful, happy life. That you
make others happy I know, for your presence always was
like sunshine.

As to myself, there is not so much to tell as of you. I am

passing the last days of my life in the city where I passed my schoolgirl life.[2] My physical health, since I recovered from the alarming illness[3] I had four years ago, has been excellent, and I am almost always cheerful and happy. My mental condition might be called nomadic. I have no fixed thoughts or objects. I wander at will from one subject to another. In pleasant summer weather I am out of doors most of the time, rambling about the neighborhood and calling upon my friends. I do not read much. Now and then I dip into a book much as a hummingbird, poised in air on whirring wings, darts into the heart of a flower, now here, now there, and away. Pictures delight me and afford me infinite diversion and interest. I pass many pleasant hours looking over books of pictures.

Of music I am also very fond. I could not have too much of it, and I never do have as much as I should like. The street bands, even organs, give me great pleasure, but especially the singing and playing of my kind friends, who are willing to gratify me in this respect.

I make no mental effort of any sort; my brain is tired out. It was a woman's brain and not a man's, and finally from sheer fatigue and exhaustion in the march and strife of life it gave out before the end was reached. And now I rest me, like a moored boat, rising and falling on the water, with loosened cordage and flapping sail.

I thank you very much for your kind words regarding myself. Blessed I have been in many ways, in seeing many of the desires of my heart fulfilled, and in having the love of many people, as has been made manifest to me in these declining years. Sorrows also I have had, which have left their mark on my heart and brain.

But they are all passed on. I have come to the land of Beulah, which is heaven's borderland, from whence we can see into the gates of the Celestial City; and even now all tears wiped from our eyes.[4]

Thanking you again and again for your great kindness

(477)

in writing and letting me know of your friendship and regard for me.

I am most sincerely your friend.

Notes

1. John Greenleaf Whittier, 1807–1892, American poet.

2. In her youth Stowe attended, and later taught at, the Hartford Female Seminary, founded by her elder sister, Catharine E. Beecher, 1800–1878, in Hartford, Connecticut.

3. Stowe apparently suffered a stroke then, from which she recovered, though in a diminished capacity.

4. In *The Pilgrim's Progress* (1678) by John Bunyan, 1628–1688, English writer, Beulah is the land of rest, "where the sun shineth night and day." The pilgrims remain here until it is time to cross over the river of Death and enter into the Celestial City.

The Lyman Beecher House, Litchfield, Connecticut, the birthplace of Harriet Beecher Stowe. The portion of the house that remains today is incorporated into the dormitory of a private school.

The Lyman Beecher House in the Walnut Hills section of Cincinnati, Ohio. This 22-room brick house, restored and renamed the Harriet Beecher Stowe House in the 1980s, serves as both an historical shrine and a cultural center.

The Harriet Beecher Stowe House, Brunswick, Maine, the residence most associated with the writing of *Uncle Tom's Cabin*. The house is now one component in a restaurant-motel complex.

"The Stone Cabin," Andover, Massachusetts. In 1852 the Stowe family moved here when Calvin E. Stowe accepted a professorship in theology at the divinity school.

Oakholm, the dream house in Hartford of Harriet Beecher Stowe. Stowe actively assisted in the planning and building of "my house with *eight* gables."

The 19th-century "cottage" on Forest Street in Hartford, Connecticut. Calvin E. Stowe, in retirement, sits on the front porch of the house in which Harriet Beecher Stowe lived from 1873 until her death in 1896.

The winter home of the Stowes in Mandarin, Florida, on the Saint Johns River.

Poetry

CONSOLATION
Written after the Second Battle of Bull Run

Harriet Beecher Stowe first wrote poetry in the form of a dramatic verse play—*Cleon*—when she was 14 years old. Though never completed, it was remarkable for its setting in the time of Nero and its use of an advanced vocabulary. During her lifetime Stowe wrote and published much poetry, little of which remains popular today.

"Consolation" was first printed in the *Independent* on September 18, 1862. The subtitle was added for subsequent reprintings: Bull Run, a small river in Eastern Virginia, was the site of two Union Army defeats during the American Civil War, the first in July of 1861 and again on August 29–30, 1862.

"And I saw a new heaven and a new earth: for the first heaven and the first earth were passed away; and there was no more sea."[1]

Ah, many-voiced and angry! how the waves
    Beat turbulent with terrible uproar!
Is there no rest from tossing,—no repose?
    Where shall we find a haven and a shore?

What is secure from the land-dashing wave?
    There go our riches, and our hopes fly there;
There go the faces of our best beloved,
    Whelmed in the vortex of its wild despair.

Whose son is safe? whose brother, and whose home?
  The dashing spray beats out the household fire;
By blackened ashes weep our widowed souls
  Over the embers of our lost desire.

By pauses, in the fitful moaning storm,
  We hear triumphant notes of battle roll.
Too soon the triumph sinks in funeral wail;
  The muffled drum, the death march, shakes the soul!

Rocks on all sides, and breakers! at the helm
  Weak human hand and weary human eyes.
The shout and clamor of our dreary strife
  Goes up conflicting to the angry skies.

But for all this, O timid hearts, be strong;
  Be of good cheer, for, though the storm must be,
It hath its Master: from the depths shall rise
  New heavens, new earth, where shall be no more sea.

No sea, no tossing, no unrestful storm!
  Forever past the anguish and the strife;
The poor old weary earth shall bloom again,
  With the bright foliage of that better life.

And war, and strife, and hatred, shall be past,
  And misery be a forgotten dream.
The Shepherd God shall lead his peaceful fold
  By the calm meadows and the quiet stream.

Be still, be still, and know that he is God;
  Be calm, be trustful; work, and watch, and pray,
Till from the throes of this last anguish rise
  The light and gladness of that better day.

Notes

1. *Revelation*. XXI, 1.

WHEN I AWAKE I AM STILL WITH THEE

More familiarly known as "Still, Still with Thee," this religious poem first appeared in the *Independent* on September 9, 1852. Set to music by several composers, it is anthologized in dozens of hymnals of all denominations and remains a popular hymn in Protestant churches. Written by Harriet Beecher Stowe in Brunswick, Maine, on August 30, 1852, this poem appears as verse VII in the poetry sequence called "Hours of the Night; or Watches of Sorrow."

Still, still with Thee, when purple morning breaketh,
When the bird waketh and the shadows flee;
Fairer than morning, lovelier than the daylight,
Dawns the sweet consciousness, *I am with Thee!*

Alone with Thee, amid the mystic shadows,
The solemn hush of nature newly born;
Alone with Thee in breathless adoration,
In the calm dew and freshness of the morn.

As in the dawning o'er the waveless ocean
The image of the morning star doth rest,
So in this stillness Thou beholdest only
Thine image in the waters of my breast.

Still, still with Thee! as to each new-born morning
A fresh and solemn splendor still is given,
So doth the blessed consciousness, awaking,
Breathe, each day, nearness unto Thee and heaven.

When sinks the soul, subdued by toil, to slumber,
Its closing eye looks up to Thee in prayer;
Sweet the repose beneath the wings o'ershading,
But sweeter still to wake and find Thee there.

So shall it be at last, in that bright morning
When the soul waketh and life's shadows flee;
O in that hour, fairer than daylight dawning,
Shall rise the glorious thought, *I am with Thee!*